ECONOMIC DOCTRINE AND METHOD

ECONOMISTS OF THE TWENTIETH CENTURY

General Editors: Mark Perlman, *University Professor of Economics, Emeritus, University of Pittsburgh* and Mark Blaug, *Professor Emeritus, University of London; Professor Emeritus, University of Buckingham and Visiting Professor, University of Exeter*

This innovative series comprises specially invited collections of articles and papers by economists whose work has made an important contribution to economics in the late twentieth century.

The proliferation of new journals and the ever-increasing number of new articles make it difficult for even the most assiduous economist to keep track of all the important recent advances. By focusing on those economists whose work is generally recognized to be at the forefront of the discipline, the series will be an essential reference point for the different specialisms included.

A list of published and future titles in this series is printed at the end of this volume.

Economic Doctrine and Method

Selected Papers of R.W. Clower

Robert W. Clower

Hugh C. Lane Professor of Economic Theory
University of South Carolina
Honorary Fellow
Brasenose College, Oxford
Professor Emeritus
University of California, Los Angeles

ECONOMISTS OF THE TWENTIETH CENTURY

Edward Elgar

Published by
Edward Elgar Publishing Limited
Gower House
Croft Road
Aldershot
Hants GU11 3HR
England

Edward Elgar Publishing Company
Old Post Road
Brookfield
Vermont 05036
USA

HB
119
.C56
A25
1995

British Library Cataloguing in Publication Data
Clower, Robert W.
  Economic Doctrine and Method: Selected
  Papers of R.W. Clower. – (Economists of
  the Twentieth Century Series)
  I. Title II. Series
  330

Library of Congress Cataloguing in Publication Data
Clower, Robert W.
  Economic doctrine and method : selected papers of R.W. Clower /
Robert W. Clower.
    p. cm. — (Economists of the twentieth century)
  Includes index.
  1. Clower, Robert W. 2. Economists—United States. 3. Economics.
I. Title. II. Series.
HB119.C56A25 1995
330.1—dc20

94–45015
CIP

ISBN 1 85898 004 6

Printed and Bound in Great Britain by
Hartnolls Limited, Bodmin, Cornwall.

Contents

PART V APPENDIX

Introduction

I was unable at first to greet with any enthusiasm Edward Elgar's suggestion that I assemble a collection of papers not included in *Money and Markets: Selected Essays of R.W. Clower* (Cambridge University Press, 1984), first because I am inept at routine editorial work, second because it would disturb the tranquility of my 'golden' (i.e. physically decaying) years. All the same I wavered towards undertaking the task because the collection would contain papers that I am still glad I published, most of which I feel other economists might enjoy reading (many for the first time). The collection would also include recent material on economic method and theoretical foundations that might add 'boost' to an engine of inquiry that seems recently to have lost much of its forward thrust.

I still had reservations, but after re-reading material that might be included in the volume, I concluded that the work of selection and commentary would be intellectually satisfying and that the resulting volume would offer modern students a potentially instructive 'live history' of one person's attempt to enhance scientific understanding of observed economic phenomena during the last half of the twentieth century. Not altogether incidentally, the volume would also help clear the way for a new book on monetary microeconomics that I am currently writing jointly with a long-time friend and professional colleague, Peter Howitt, of the University of Western Ontario.

The papers in this volume, taken together with those included in *Money and Markets*, provide fairly complete coverage of my writings over the four decades 1953–1993. The Appendix (Part V) provides a complete list (up to June 1994) of my publications.

With the exception of the papers in Part I, all selections appear in chronological order. This arrangement accurately reflects the development of my thinking (I seldom agonize over imperfections in earlier work, or ruminate over other bygones). It is also as logical as any other basis for ordering selections within each topical area.

Of course, no collection of writings can constitute more than an imperfect attempt to 'codify' economic method or to 'explain' observed economic phenomena. When writing a paper, one naturally presumes that one has something useful to say; but presumption and reality do not always correspond. In empirical science, every question that one 'answers' evokes new questions that remain to be addressed; so every science is a never-ending story of unfinished inquiry.

As for 'progress' in one's thought over time, I have long been a believer in what Edward Leamer, in his provocative study of econometric *Specification Searches* (John Wiley, 1978), called 'Sherlock Holmes inference': one should not attempt to theorize without factual evidence, and since new evidence is always coming to light, one's inferences from past evidence are always subject to revision (and, if one is honest, being revised). I shall say no more about subject matter. My papers already say all I want at the present time; but I have added a few short additional 'notes' at the start of some of the chapters.

I am grateful to the following for permission to reproduce in facsimile various specified essays (as noted by chapter numbers in brackets):

American Economic Association
'An Investigation into the Dynamics of Investment', *American Economic Review*, **LXIV**(1), March 1954, pp. 64–81. (9)
'The Present State of International Liquidity Theory' with Richard Lipsey, *American Economic Review*, **LVIII**(2), (May 1968), pp. 586–95. (24)
Review of 'Keynesian Economics: The Search for First Principles' by Alan Coddington, *Journal of Economic Literature*, **XXII**, September 1984, pp. 1115–16. (30)
Review of 'The Origins of the Keynesian Revolution: The Development of Keynes' Theory of Employment and Output' by Robert W. Dimand, *Journal of Economic Literature*, **XXVII**, December 1989, pp. 1679–81. (32)

Cambridge University Press
'Monetary History and Positive Economics', *Journal of Economic History*, **XXIV**(3), September 1964, pp. 364–80. (3)
'Ohlin and the *General Theory*' in Lars Jonung (ed.), *The Stockholm School of Economics Revisited*, 1991, Cambridge University Press, pp. 245–62. (22)
'Money and Markets', Afterword in D.A. Walker (ed.), *Money and Markets*, 1984, Cambridge University Press, pp. 259–72. (26)

Eastern Economic Association
'The Obscurantist Approach to Economics: Shackle on Keynes', *Eastern Economic Journal*, **2**(1), January 1975, pp. 99–101. (29)

Econometric Society
'Price Determination in a Stock-Flow Economy', with D.W. Bushaw, *Econometrica*, **22**(3), July 1954, pp. 328–43. (11)

Edinburgh University Press
'Income, Wealth, and the Theory of Consumption', with M. Bruce Johnson, *Essays in Honour of Sir John Hicks*, 1968, Edinburgh University Press, pp. 45–96. (7)
'Mainsprings of African Economic Progress', *Fifth Melville J. Herskovitz Memorial Lecture*, University of Edinburgh Centre of African Studies, pp. 1–14. (23)

Elsevier Science Publishers
'Trade Specialists and Money in an Ongoing Exchange Economy' with Daniel Friedman in Richard H. Day and Gunnar Eliasson (eds), *The Dynamics of Market Economies*, 1986, Elsevier Science Publishers B.V., pp. 115–29. (16)
'Comment: "On the Behavioral and Rational Foundations of Economic Dynamics"' by Herbert A. Simon in Richard H. Day and Gunnar Eliasson (eds), *The Dynamics of Market Economies*, 1986, Elsevier Science Publishers B.V., pp. 42–4. (27)

Review of 'Disequilibrium Foundations of Equilibrium Economics' by Franklin M. Fisher, *Journal of Economic and Business Organization*, **7**(2), June 1986, pp. 222–3. (31)

Greek Economic Review
'Keynes's General Theory: A Contemporary Perspective', *Greek Economic Review*, **12**, Supplement, Autumn 1990, pp. 73–84. (21)

Kent State University Press
'Snarks, Quarks, and Other Fictions' in L.P. Cain and P.J. Uselding (eds), *Business Enterprise and Economic Change*, 1973, Kent State University Press, pp. 3–14. (4)

McGraw-Hill
'Are Administered Prices Socially Undesirable?' in M.B. Johnson (ed.), *The Attack on Corporate America*, 1978, McGraw-Hill, pp. 174–7. (25)

Oxford University Press
'Permanent Income and Transitory Balances: Hahn's Paradox', *Oxford Economic Papers*, **15**(2), July 1963, pp. 177–90. (6)

Pakistan Economic Journal
'Competition, Monopoly, and the Theory of Price', *Pakistan Economic Journal*, September 1955, pp. 219–26. (12)

The Quarterly Review of Economics and Business
'Mathematics and Economics: The Contemporary Prospect', *The Quarterly Review of Economics and Business*, **1**(2), May 1961, pp. 37–45. (5)

Richard D Irwin Inc
'Toward a Generalized Theory of Price Determination' with D.W. Bushaw, in *Introduction to Mathematical Economics*, 1957, Richard D. Irwin Inc., pp. 176–93. (13)

Royal Economic Society and Basil Blackwell Ltd
'Productivity, Thrift and the Rate of Interest', *Economic Journal*, **LXIV**(253), March 1954, pp. 107–15. (10)
'Some Theory of an Ignorant Monopolist', *Economic Journal*, **LXIX**, December 1959, pp. 705–16. (14)

Siena University Economic Review
'New Directions for Keynesian Economics', *Siena University Economic Review*, Spring 1987, pp. 1–17. (18)

Southern Economic Journal
'Economics as an Inductive Science', *Southern Economic Journal*, **60**(4), April 1994, pp. 805–14. (1)

Review of 'Value and Capital: Fifty Years Later', Lionel W. McKenzie and Stefano Zamagni (eds), *Southern Economic Journal*, **58**(4), April 1992, pp. 1127–8. (33)
Review of 'The Joan Robinson Legacy' Ingred H. Rima (ed.), *Southern Economic Journal*, **60**(2), October 1993, 508–9. (34)

Springer-Verlag
'Reflections on the Keynesian Perplex', *Zeitschrift für Nationalökonomie*, **35**, 1975, pp. 1–24. (17)

University of South Carolina Business and Economic Review
'How Economists Think', *Business and Economic Review*, University of South Carolina Division of Research, **36**(1), Oct.–Dec. 1989, pp. 9–17. (2)

WEA International
'Business Investment and the Theory of Price', *Proceedings of the Twenty-Eighth Annual Conference of the Western Economic Association*, 1953, pp. 22–4. (8)
'Oligopoly Theory: A Dynamical Approach', *Proceedings of the Thiry-Fourth Annual Conference of the Western Economic Association*, 1959, pp. 16–19. (15)

PART I

DOCTRINE AND METHOD

Part I: Doctrine and method

Part I starts with my most recent (1994) thoughts on economic doctrine and method, then backtracks to 1972 (reprinted 1989 without significant change), and then backtracks further to 1964 and my first written reflections on Milton Friedman's work. This early review article is followed by a mildly whimsical (but deadly serious) 1973 paper on the role of economic theory in economic history, and then the argument moves back to my first published paper on method (1961). The two final selections reflect my dawning awareness (to which allusion is made in the 1994 paper [Chapter 1]) of the use of axiomatic methods in economics (methods that were just then starting to permeate economic theorizing, mainly through the influence of Gerard Debreu's *Theory of Value* (1959); both selections also reflect my suspicion that such an approach has serious limitations as a road to useful knowledge in the empirical (inductive) sciences. The final selection merits special mention because it reflects so clearly both the (false) allure of the Neowalrasian code (specifically, the meretriciousness of the optimizing behaviour paradigm), and its dangers: appearances to the contrary notwithstanding, no part of the paper depends on, or derives persuasive value from either 'the code' or 'the paradigm'. My present belief, indeed, is that economics has little prospect of ever becoming a respectable and respected inductive science unless in the very near future its leading practitioners explicitly disown and discard the Neowalrasian code and all its trappings.

[1]

Economics as an Inductive Science*

ROBERT W. CLOWER
University of South Carolina
Columbia, South Carolina

Logic is the art of going wrong with confidence.

Anonymous [30, 197]

It seems appropriate to begin by recalling something from our founder, so I start with a passage from the *Wealth of Nations* where Smith writes about "Institutions for the Education of Youth" [48, 763]:

> If the teacher happens to be a man of sense, it must be an unpleasant thing to him to be conscious, while he is lecturing his students, that he is either speaking or reading nonsense, or what is very little better than nonsense.

All who have taught macroeconomics at any time during the past forty years will know this feeling well; for macroeconomic theory has been riddled with Kuhnian anomalies [32, 202 ff.] since its inception. Strangely, few teachers of *micro*economics seem embarrassed by the purely theoretical material they teach and which their students are required to read and regurgitate, although microtheory is at least as objectionable as macroeconomic theory. That we who teach any kind of "pure" theory ought to be as embarrassed with microeconomics[1] as with macroeconomics is the position I propose to argue here.

Before I proceed, let me emphasize that by "pure theory" I do not mean what most working economists, including, I imagine, our most recent Nobel Laureates, Douglas North and Robert Fogel, mean when they use the word "theory" without further qualification. Generally speaking, we mean by "theory" the fact-oriented creative mixture of intuition, casual empirical knowledge, and seat-of-the pants logic that is found in virtually all "applied economic analysis" and, indeed, in virtually everything called "economics" before 1950 [20, 284]. By pure theory I mean the axiomatically-based *neowalrasian* analysis of Arrow-Debreu [3], Debreu [15], Arrow and Hahn [4] and closely related offshoots that serve as a standard of "economic correctness" in all modern

---

*Presidential Address delivered at the sixty-third annual meeting of the Southern Economic Association, New Orleans, Louisiana, November 22, 1993. For comments on an earlier draft, I wish to thank—but not incriminate—Meyer Burstein, Paul Davidson, Mohammed Dore, Robert Eisner, Milton Friedman, Martin Hellwig, Peter Howitt, Bruce Johnson, Richard Lipsey, Thomas Rhymes, Robert Solow, Vela Velupillai, and Donald Walker.

1. I have in mind particularly such self styled "New Keynesians" as Mankiw and Stiglitz. The former claims a link with Keynes because involuntary unemployment, monetary noneutrality, and sticky wages and prices are acknowledged to exist [33, 565]. And, judging from his 1993 principles text [51, 682–83], Stiglitz would agree that by introducing ad hoc theoretical gimmicks into standard textbook theory Mankiw and other New Keynesians have "reincarnated" Keynesian Economics ". . . into a body with firm microeconomic muscle" [33, 560].

teaching not only in microeconomics but in macroeconomics, money and banking, finance, and econometrics.

The phrase "economic correctness" corresponds to what Peter Howitt, in a recent paper [26], calls "The Neowalrasian Code":

> Adherence to an increasingly complex code of formal ideas has become the overriding criterion of success, rather than fruitful modelling of observed phenomena. The code of modern economics has become for the most part that of neowalrasian analysis, with its rules for modelling all behaviour as the outcome of rational choice. [. . .] But accounting for some phenomenon in a discipline dominated by an elaborate code consists not of telling stories designed to convince others that this is why the phenomenon exists, or why it appears the way it does, but of telling stories, no matter how ad hoc, that incorporate some aspect of the phenomenon, no matter how trivial, without violating the code. [. . .] Economists building "rational models" to account for things not found in conventional theory think of themselves as seeking explanations in the usual sense, whereas in fact they are addressing purely semantic questions that don't even arise once one ventures out of the neowalrasian cloister. Only by the rarest fluke could someone working under such a delusion come up with a convincing scientific explanation of anything.

I have titled my paper "Economics as an Inductive Science" in recognition of the contrast between inductive (fact-oriented) science and the kind of microeconomic theory—really "verbal mathematics" [20, 278]—our contemporary textbooks contain, which Whewell [56, 14] aptly characterized as a philosophy (some might say *catechism*)

> . . . constructed on notions obscure, vague, and unsubstantial, and held in spite of the want of correspondence between its doctrines and the actual train of physical events [. . .] . . . the object is not to interpret nature, but man's mind.

Joan Robinson [42, 122] long ago described the central problem of economics as being to understand how the economic system works, or as Keynes once expressed the issue [28, 35], "Is the economic system self-adjusting?" More generally, as the astronomer Simon Newcomb [35, 9] observed:

> There is nothing in the wonders of the heavens or the mysteries of chemical combination better fitted to kindle our curiosity, and to gratify our desire to understand what is going on around us, than the study of the social organism.

To date, however, we economists have failed to seriously address much less resolve these issues.

How are the myriad economic activities of the millions of independent transactors in private ownership economies coordinated? It is correct, of course, to assert that the coordination of economic activities is performed by an "invisible hand," or "the price system," [2] through variations in prices and quantities in response to changing "market conditions": correct, to be sure, but just as surely inane, because such a response is no more informative than an appeal to Jupiter or Providence [1, 144]. An intellectually respectable answer should consist of something more than tired clichés; observable economic events derive ultimately not from unspecified coordinating mechanisms, whether invisible hands, price systems or neowalrasian "auctioneers" but, as James Tobin has indicated, from definable actions of real people [54, 796]. What we economists have yet to explain is the working of the *fingers* of the invisible hand [9].

A partial explanation for our failure heretofore to explain the modus operandi of "the market" may lie in our infatuation with technique. It is widely believed that a great achievement of

---

2. Cf. Coase [14, 387–9]; for a critique of Coase, see Clower [12].

postmarshallian (neowalrasian) economics was the "discovery" of exact conditions under which perfect coordination of individual economic activities will be achieved automatically [44, 469–70; 30, 41–53]. The truth is quite otherwise. The neowalrasian version of general equilibrium theory provides a mathematically rigorous statement of conditions under which a competitive equilibrium "exists," but the statement is interpretable only for a hypothetical world where coordination uses no resources, where no agent ever imagines that a failure of coordination might prevent trading plans from being completed, and where institutions such as business firms and markets through which agents routinely interact in real-world economies are not just absent but otiose. In truth, neowalrasian theory makes no mention of any mechanism or agent that undertakes the task of coordination.[3] The closest it comes is in the theory of "tâtonnement," where it is postulated that prices adjust to eliminate discrepancies between demand and supply. But if we ask, Who changes prices?, Who pays whom, and with what?, Who matches buyers with sellers?, Who pays the costs of arranging and executing transactions?, Who goes long or short when demands don't match supplies?, and What incentives motivate any agent to perform coordinating tasks?, then the theory is silent.

How might we resolve these and similar questions? Einstein wrote [18, 98]:

> Science is the attempt to make the chaotic diversity of our sense-experience correspond to a logically uniform system of thought. [. . .] The sense experiences are the given subject matter, but the theory that shall interpret them is man-made. It is the result of an extremely laborious process of adaptation: hypothetical, never completely final, always subject to question and doubt.

Of course, Einstein's reference is to Physics and Astronomy; but from a non-normative point of view, economics is just Social Astronomy. Its purported aim is to enhance understanding of the working of the economic universe. If we are ever to be taken seriously as scientists we would be well advised to proceed with this task as most practitioners of other inductive sciences have proceeded—by taking a hard look at the world around us in a serious effort to lend intellectual order to the "chaos" that strikes our eyes at first sight.

What conceptual framework is appropriate as empirical background for economic theory, supposing we wish to portray salient aspects of real-world economic behavior during, say, the past three centuries? More shortly, what are we to regard as relevant stylized facts? I propose the following (cf. Clower [8, 206–7]:

1) Trading occurs in decentralized, geographically disconnected, privately owned and operated retail, wholesale, and auction markets. Centralized direction or attempted improvement of coordination occurs only as an incidental aspect of law enforcement.
2) In all exchanges, sellers routinely insist on receiving cash or its equivalent for every sale. All advanced economies are "monetary."
3) No transactor has direct knowledge about the state of the economy at any point in time, about the supposed laws that govern its behavior, or about the trading plans of any other transactor. What is known must first be learned.
4) All exchange economies (historically) have been self-organized: markets are created and operated as income-earning institutions by self-interested individuals who, in exchange for implicit or explicit fees, provide physical facilities (location, office equipment, trans-

---

3. For an extensive critical discussion of this and related issues, by a doctoral student working under the supervision of Kenneth Arrow in the late 1960s, see Starr [49].

port, telephone and other communication devices, etc.) to "give wing" to what Adam Smith called "the propensity" to truck and barter.

5) Prices "asked," "bid," and "realized" are "made" by agents, not by ineffable "market forces" [36, vol. 1, 76–83].

6) Transactors are able routinely to execute pairwise (commodity for "money") trades at such times, and in such size lots, as they desire, generally without previous communication with any market maker. Because the probability is zero that sales of any commodity will equal purchases over any specified time interval, actual markets almost never "clear."

How does this conception of economic "reality" compare with the conception logically implied by neowalrasian theory? To save time, let me state the main points baldly, leaving any needed elaboration for later. In neowalrasian theory:

(i) Although there are demands and supplies, *there are no markets.*

(ii) *There is no communication between prospective trading agents;* prospective trades are signalled only to a central "demon."

(iii) *Agents generate no observable data;* "trading plans" are stored, as it were, in the random access memory of the mediating "demon."

(v) *There are no endogenous institutions:* all behavioral logistics are imposed from outside the theory (contrived ad hoc by theorists).

(vi) *No agent announces bid or asked prices;* rates of exchange are proposed and changed only by a demon mediator.

(vii) *There is no competition among agents,* because agents never interact directly.

(viii) *No agent voluntarily holds inventories or buffer stocks.*

(ix) *There is no money or other medium of exchange* [14, 28].

(x) *There is no trading;* the theory does not define, much less deal with, commodity transfers from one agent to another [49]. Appropriate "logistical" embellishments can and have been invented and added to the neowalrasian model [2; 10; 13; 15; 28; 37; 38], but always on an ad hoc basis.

Has a more counterfactual collection of ideas ever before been assembled? My answer is affirmative. Keynes argued that ideas rather than vested interests prevail in the long run. However that might be, we know that through much of history (specifically from 400 B.C. until 1500 A.D.) theories that were arguably useless, mindless or vacuous have never been discarded without a struggle. And, indeed, after Newton, at least one empirically vacuous "hard science" enjoyed not just popularity but positive acclaim for more than two centuries; so neowalrasian analysis, having existed little more than half a century, is not unique in its apparent disregard of common sense.

The "hard science" I have in mind is the mathematical theory of ideal fluids, known more familiarly as classical or "rational" hydrodynamics, which ruled the roost in the study of fluid motion from the middle of the Seventeenth until the beginning of the Twentieth Century [17, 303–394]. Early in its history, as a result of brilliant work with Newton's pure theory of fluid motion in so-called "ideal" fluids (which are unknown in real life), the mathematicians Daniel Bernoulli, D'Alembert, Euler, and Lagrange developed hydrodynamics into an academic study so abstract as almost to count as pure mathematics. Indeed, one scholar described its status at the turn of the twentieth century as one in which ". . . fluid dynamicists were divided into hydraulic engineers who observed what could not be explained, and mathematicians who explained things that could not be observed" [6, 4]. For want of alternative teaching materials, students interested in applied hydrodynamics were taught the classical theory of nonexistent fluids, augmented by a pseudoscience called "the science of coefficients" that bore a striking resemblance to contemporary econometrics. Then during the last half of the nineteenth century [40, 23], the inductively motivated work of Helmholtz, Lamb, Kelvin, Rayleigh, Lanchester and others transformed hydrodynamics into a discipline that could help working engineers design real airplanes [17, 337, ff]. The story is summarized in a paragraph of Prandtl and Tietjen's classic memoir [40, 3]:

> . . . the great growth in technical achievement which began in the nineteenth century left scientific knowledge far behind. The multitudenous problems of practice could not be answered by the hydrodynamics of Euler; they could not even be discussed. This was chiefly because, starting from Euler's equations of motion, the science had become more and more a purely academic analysis of the hypothetical frictionless "ideal fluid."

I won't waste time drawing obvious parallels between "rational" hydrodynamics and most of what passes for "serious" theory in contemporary economics. Suffice it to say that, in my opinion, what we presently possess by way of so-called pure economic theory is objectively indistinguishable from what the physicist Richard Feynman, in an unflattering sketch of nonsense "science," called "cargo cult science" [19, 308].

Unlike neowalrasian theory, rational hydrodynamics dealt with real-time rather than virtual processes; its "agents" [ideal fluids] no doubt were fantasies, but its "operations" [activities] had real world counterparts[4] hence its theoretical implications could be compared with analogous factual findings about real fluids. These comparisons bred numerous scientific paradoxes—evident inconsistencies that could not be resolved without significant extensions of conventional theory [7, 3–4]. Neowalrasian analysis is an entirely different animal. It does not deal with calendar time or with real-time processes; it is concerned exclusively with hypothetical mental states (Walras called them "trading dispositions") of "agents" whose "actions" are described in terms of concepts (e.g., production, consumption, choice) that strongly, but misleadingly suggest observability. Because "actions" in neowalrasian theory refer to "plans" [15, 37–8, 43] that are purely mental if not positively metaphysical, the implications of so-called actions could be confronted "empirically" only by a demonic being (e.g., the neowalrasian "auctioneer") capable of collecting data by reading minds and performing other feats that would make an episode of TV's *Star Trek* series seem like live news from CNN!

The scientific vacuousness of neowalrasian theory appears not to be recognized by some of its leading practitioners. How else can we account for Frank Hahn's assertion, in connection with the postulated "existence" of a large number of "contingent futures markets," that we have here ". . . an empirical confrontation since we know that these markets are in fact very scarce" [22, 15]. Arrow-Debreu theory deals with an indefinitely great number of "commodities" and excess demand functions, but it does not define much less deal with anything that remotely resembles a market in the ordinary sense of that word (but compare [15, 76, 80]); how, then, can fewness of actual spot or future markets be brought into empirical confrontation with neowalrasian theory? A more remarkable example of similar confusion is Koopman's discussion [31, 62–3] of "Survival of Consumers in a Competitive Equilibrium"! Finally, in the same vein, a distinguished colleague, referring obliquely to the "stylized facts" 1–6, above, wrote in a recent letter:

---

4. To appreciate the critical importance, for purposes of empirical confrontation, of theories that refer in their logical foundations to real-time processes, see Schwinger's account [46, 81–5] of the conjectured properties of the graviton, a theoretical entity that is as yet unknown to experimental science.

> . . . you know as well as I do that all the Walrasians are perfectly aware of the basic facts about organized markets. [. . .] I presume that they must be taking it for granted that, with enough competition, the general-equilibrium model will give broad steady-state results that approximate [the basic facts]. They have not proved that, but neither have you disproved it."

This passage reflects not only an apparent unawareness of the vacuousness of neowalrasian analysis, but an unawareness also of the impossibility of proof or disproof of any assertion about real-time processes [23, 270]. Inductive sciences deal with plausible inference, not with demonstrative reasoning [39, v].

It will be obvious from what has gone before that I see no way to make progress in economic science except by first discarding neowalrasian analysis. As indicated by the cases just discussed, the neowalrasian code exerts an insidious influence even on those who, like myself, have long harbored doubts about conventional formalist economics. For reasons that even in retrospect are inexplicable to me, my every attempt to break out of the neowalrasian mold seemed to end in a toy model that has a fundamentally neowalrasian cast;[5] in effect, the neowalrasian code acts like a black hole, consuming everything it touches and cloning even residual orts into an Arrow-Debreu monster. I speak with some passion on this point because I, like many of my friends and colleagues, have felt "the power of the Neowalrasian Code"[6] and can only now recognize (in the clear light of hindsight) how the code corrupts and weakens the scientific force of one's theoretical work.

In calling for radical reconstruction of economic theory, I am sounding a tocsin that James Tobin rang more than twenty years ago, echoing earlier warnings by Oskar Morganstern [36; 54, 293–7] and Milton Friedman [20, 291–300]. And Herbert Simon's entire professional career has been dominated by the same concern to inject *process* into formal models so that economic theory can be confronted with empirical evidence [47, vol. 1, xix–xx]. I am well aware of the difficulty of reconstructing doctrine in which ". . . there is no agreed procedure for knocking out error" [41, 75]. In that connection, let me emphasize that my discontents with neowalrasian analysis concern not its lack of "realism" but its scientific vacuousness; it deserves to be discarded not for lack of realism, whatever that term might mean, but for the reasons that Galileo and Newton discarded Aristotelian physics—because it inhibits coherent intellectual analysis, that is to say *serious theorizing,* about observable events.[7]

In an unguarded address to The Econometric Society in 1968, Frank Hahn remarked [21, 2]:

> . . . there is something scandalous in the spectacle of so many people refining the analysis of economic states which they have no reason to suppose will ever . . . come about. . . . It is an unsatisfactory and slightly dishonest state of affairs."

Hahn's phrase "slightly dishonest" understates the case. In the first chapter of *Value and Capital* [24, 7], Hicks asserts "This is a work on Theoretical Economics, considered as the logical

---

5. Classic examples of what I mean by "toy model" are the search-theoretic "Rube Goldberg" monetary machines constructed by Kiotaki and Wright [29] and by Aiyagari and Wallace [2]. For details, see Clower [12]. For further examples, see Diamond [16] and Howitt [25, 176 ff.]. To my chagrin, I find that I have unintentionally constructed some toy models of my own; but to spare myself further embarrassment, I leave the identification of particular instances "as an exercise for the interested reader."

6. The quoted phrase is my recollection of a sentiment voiced by Peter Howitt in the course of oral discussion at the Montevideo conference (above, reference [26]).

7. The difficulty, as described by Born in his explanation of Einstein's theory of relativity, is that when one becomes habituated to conventional habits of thought (e.g., to the idea that the earth is the center of the physical universe, to the idea that absolute space and time are inherent features of "reality"), supposedly "true" theoretical results become problematic ". . . due to a confusion of habits of thought with logical consistency, a tendency we all recognize to be an obstacle to progress." [7, 226]

analysis of an economic system of private enterprise, without any inclusion of reference to institutional controls." Similarly Debreu, in the preface to his book [15, x] says: ". . . the theory . . . is logically entirely disconnected from its interpretations." In the event, however, neither Hicks in his purportedly "pure logical analysis" [24, 7] nor Debreu in his more conspicuously formal *Theory of Value* [15, viii] hesitate to write freely about "markets" when in strict logic they must be referring instead to demand and supply functions. Thus their supposed reliance on formalism is a sham. What they seem actually to discuss is the real world as they conceive it intuitively— or more probably the world as they imagine it was conceived by Hicks as reflected in the text of *Value and Capital* (the influence of Hicks's work on all later neowalrasian writings is vastly more powerful than is commonly recognized). The actual subject matter of so called formal theory these days is *sui generis;* in no way is it the abstract world of sets, elements, axioms, and mathematical operations that most theorists pretend to take as their formal, technical universe of discourse.

All things considered, therefore, Hahn's phrase "slightly dishonest" should probably be replaced by the more concise term "fraudulent." The apochryphal Judge Howlson of "Truth in Teaching" fame [50] would have a field day in court if one of our leading graduate schools in economics were ever charged with false advertising; for perhaps Howlson's most trenchant remark in the "truth" case was: "It seems paradoxical beyond endurance to rule that a manufacturer of shampoos may not endanger a student's scalp but a premier education institution is free to stuff his skull with nonsense" [50, 191].

I have much to say about the direction reconstruction of economic theory should take, but that is another article, or more accurately a book called *Monetary Economies* on which Peter Howitt and I are presently working. One broad comment is in order here, however: an *inductive* science of economics must start from explicit recognition that every observable action of real-life transactors entails finite set-up costs—real or subjective costs that are largely independent of the level of activity to which the observable action is related. In short, economies of scale are ubiquitous, and must be accommodated in any real-time description of economic processes. Neowalrasian analysis is limited strictly to convex economies [15, x; 30, 35–7; 11, 449–50]; so any reconstructed theory must deal with systems that involve nonconvexities in essential ways. This means, among other things, that the whole of modern welfare economics must be consigned to metaphysical oblivion. And that is just a minor casualty, because only slightly less draconian changes are needed to lend honesty to other constrained-optimization branches of economic theory such as the theory of "demand," the theory of "cost and production," and on and on. But instead of indicating what must go, let me sketch briefly some of the things that Howitt and I expect to restate or create and keep.

Specifically, we propose to contribute through our book to the development of a discipline that deals in an intellectually coherent manner with:

(i) Self-organizing firms, markets, and related institutions, including such things as Merchant Courts (see [5]), that make and enforce laws respecting property rights and contracts;

(ii) Business operations, costs, revenues, and survival strategies, replacing Vinerian and related fables of production and cost theory with ideas that are consistent with fact-based research;

(iii) Household behavior: choosing income and determining budgeted expenditure, choosing the timing, frequency (lot size) and composition of actual purchases;

(iv) Determining (time-averaged) holdings of money and other trade inventories;

(iv) Competition as a struggle for economic viability;

(v) The *modus operandi* of the invisible hand (an aspect of business behavior and the operations of market-making firms);

(v) The reasons why, in economic affairs as in freeway traffic flows and field theories of light and gravity, all action and reaction involve only "neighborhood" effects, never "action at a distance" or by metaphysical entities such as "the invisible hand."

In reconstructing our discipline, and throughout the inductive science of economics, I would urge that our motto be: *If it isn't common sense, it's probably wrong*.

Let me end by drawing attention to the 1983 introduction to the enlarged edition of *The Foundations of Economic Analysis* [45] where Paul Samuelson refers nostalgically to the joy of having been born an economist in 1932—because then there was so much still to be "discovered" that economics seemed like a well-stocked but seldom-fished pond: one could hook something juicy with every cast of the line. It occurs to me to wonder what has changed since 1932 in the way of improved understanding of how actual economic systems work? Isn't 1993 just as good a time to be "born" an economist? We may or may not make significant progress during the next century towards reconstructing economics as an inductive science—progress in converting the present subject from a quasi-religious academic catechism into a respectable and respected intellectual pursuit. Whether, if and when such a time comes, we economists will deserve to be thought of as "humble, competent people, on a level with dentists" [26, 373], is an open question; but if such a time should ever come, we'll surely have no reason to feel humble.

Postscript

At a luncheon address to the Canadian Economic Association in Ottawa on June 5, 1993, I displayed a picture of the 1638 goose-powered space vehicle of *The Man in the Moone* [53, 16] as a mechanical analog of economic theory circa 1995. With the thought that it may furnish intellectual fun as well as profit, I reproduce the figure here.

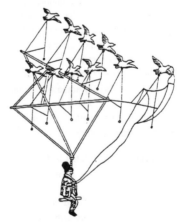

𝕬𝕹𝕬𝕷𝕺𝕲 𝕸𝕺𝕯𝕰𝕷
𝕺𝖋
𝕰𝕮𝕺𝕹𝕺𝕸𝕴𝕮 𝕿𝕳𝕰𝕺𝕽𝖄
{𝕮𝕴𝕽𝕮𝕬. 1995}

Reproduced from: Taylor, J.W.R. *The Lore of Flight*. Göthenberg: Tre Tryckare Cagner & Co., 1970.

References

1. Ahmed, Syed. "Adam Smith's Four Invisible Hands," *History of Political Economy*, Spring 1990, 137–44.

2. Aiyagari, Rao and Neil Wallace, "Existence of Steady States with Positive Consumption in the Kiyotaki-Wright Model." *Review of Economic Studies*, October 1991, 901–16.

3. Arrow, Kenneth J. and Gerard Debreu, "Existence of an Equilibrium for a Competitive Economy." *Econometrica* July 1954, 265–90.

4. ——— and Frank H. Hahn. *General Competitive Analysis*. San Francisco: Holden-Day, 1971.

5. Benson, Bruce L., "The Spontaneous Evolution of Commercial Law." *Southern Economic Journal*, January 1989, 644–61.

6. Birkhoff, Garret M. *Hydrodynamics*. Princeton, N.J.: Princeton University Press, 1960.

7. Born, Max. *Einstein's Theory of Relativity*, revised edition. New York: Dover, 1962.

8. Clower Robert. W., "The Anatomy of Monetary Theory." *American Economic Review*, February 1977, 206–12.

9. ———. "The Fingers of the Invisible Hand," forthcoming in *Brock Review*. St. Catherines: Brock University Press, 1994.

10. ——— and Daniel Friedman. "Trade Specialists and Money in an Ongoing Exchange Economy," in *The Dynamics of Market Economies*, edited by Richard Day and Gunnar Eliasson. Amsterdam: North-Holland, 1986, pp. 115–29.

11. ——— and P. W. Howitt. "The Transactions Theory of the Demand for Money: A Reconsideration." *Journal of Political Economy*, June 1978, 449–66.

12. ——— and ———. "Money, Markets and Coase," forthcoming in volume to be published by organizers of conference on "Is Economics Becoming a Hard Science?" Paris: October, 1992.

13. ——— and ———. "Foundations of Economics," forthcoming in volume to be published by organizers of conference on "Is Economics Becoming a Hard Science?" Paris: October, 1992.

14. Coase, Ronald H., "The Nature of the Firm." *Economica*, November, 1937, 386–405.

15. Debreu, Gerard. *Theory of Value: An Axiomatic Analysis of Economic Equilibrium*. New Haven: Yale University Press, 1959.

16. Diamond, Peter A., "Aggregate Demand Measurement in Search Equilibrium." *Journal of Political Economy*, October 1982, 881–94.

17. Durand, William F. *Aerodynamic Theory, Vol. 1*. New York: Dover, 1963.

18. Einstein, A. *Out of My Later Years*. New York: Philosophical Library, Inc., 1950.

19. Feynman, Richard P., *"Surely You're Joking, Mr. Feynman"*. New York: Bantam Books, 1986.

20. Friedman, Milton. *The Methodology of Positive Economics*. Chicago: University of Chicago Press, 1953.

21. Hahn, Frank H., "Some Adjustment Problems." *Econometrica*, January 1970, 1–17.

22. ———. "On The Notion of Equilibrium in Economics." An Inaugural Lecture. Cambridge: Cambridge University Press, 1973.

23. Hanson, Norwood R. *Perception and Discovery*. San Francisco: Freeman, Cooper & Company, 1969.

24. Hicks, J. R. *Value and Capital*. Oxford: Clarendon Press. 1939.

25. Howitt, Peter W. *The Keynesian Recovery*. Ann Arbor: University of Michigan Press, 1990.

26. ———, "Cash in Advance: Foundations in Retreat." Paper presented at conference in honor of 60th birthday of Axel Leijonhufvud, Montevideo, Uruguay, September 6, 1993.

27. Keynes, John M. *Essays in Persuasion*. London: Macmillan & Co., 1933.

28. ———, "A Self-Adjusting Economic System?" *The New Republic*, February 20, 1935, 35–37.

29. Kiyotaki, N. and R. Wright, "On Money as a Medium of Exchange." *Journal of Political Economy*, August, 1989, 927–54.

30. Kline, Morris. *Mathematics: The Loss of Certainty*. New York: Oxford University Press, 1980.

31. Koopmans, Tjalling C. *Three Essays on the State of Economic Science*. New York: McGraw-Hill, 1957.

32. Kuhn, Thomas S. *The Essential Tension*. Chicago: University of Chicago Press, 1977.

33. Mankiw, N. Gregory, "The Reincarnation of Keynesian Economics." *European Economic Review* 36, 1992, 559–65.

34. Morganstern, Oskar, "Professor Hicks on Value and Capital." *Journal of Political Economy*, June 1941, 361–93.

35. Newcomb, Simon. *Principles of Political Economy*. New York: Harper & Brothers, 1886.

36. Osborne, M. F. M. *The Stock Market From a Physicist's Viewpoint*. Temple Hills, Maryland: Published by the author, 1970.

37. Ostroy, Joseph M., "The Informational Efficiency of Monetary Exchange." *American Economic Review*, September 1973, 597–610.

38. ——— and Ross M. Starr, "Money and the Decentralization of Exchange." *Econometrica*, October 1974, 1093–113.

39. Polya, Georg. *Induction and Analogy in Mathematics*, 2 vols. Princeton: Princeton University Press, 1954.

40. Prandtl, L., and Tietjens, O. G. *Fundamentals of Hydro-and Aeromechanics*. New York: Dover, 1957.

41. Robinson, Joan. *Economic Philosophy*. London: C. A. Watts, 1962.

42. ———. "Economics Today." Basel Lecture, 1969, reprinted in *Collected Work Vol. 4*. Oxford: Blackwell, 1973, 122–6.

43. Samuelson, Paul A. *Foundations of Economic Analysis*. Cambridge, Mass.: Harvard University Press, 1947.

44. ———. *Collected Scientific Papers, Vol. III*. Cambridge, Mass.: MIT Press, 1972.

45. ———. *Foundations of Economic Analysis*, Enlarged Edition. Cambridge: Harvard University Press, 1983.

46. Schwinger, Julian. *Sources, Particles, and Fields*. Reading, Mass.: Addison-Wesley, 1970.

47. Simon, Herbert S. *Models of Bounded Rationality*, 2 vols. Cambridge, Mass.: MIT Press, 1982.

48. Smith, Adam. *An Inquiry into the Nature and Causes of The Wealth of Nations*, Campbell & Skinner, general editors. Oxford: Clarendon Press, 1976.

49. Starr, R. "Notes on Microeconomic Monetary Theory." Chapter 1 of *Ph.D. Dissertation*. Stanford University, 1971.

50. Stigler, George J. "A Sketch of the History of Truth in Teaching," in *The Citizen and the State*, George J. Stigler. Chicago: University of Chicago Press, 1975, pp. 189–93. (Originally published in the *Journal of Political Economy*, March/April, 1973, 491–95.)

51. Stiglitz, Joseph E. *Economics*. New York: Norton, 1993.

52. Sutton, Oswald G. *The Science of Flight*. Harmondsworth: Penguin Books, 1955.

53. Taylor, Jonathan W. R. *The Lore of Flight*. Göthenberg: Tre Tryckare Cagner & Co., 1970.

54. Tobin, James, "Are New Classical Models Plausible Enough to Guide Policy?" *Journal of Money, Credit and Banking*, November 1980, Part 2, 788–99.

55. ———, "The Future of Keynesian Economics." *Eastern Economic Journal*, October–December 1988, 347–58.

56. Whewell, William. *History of the Inductive Sciences*. London: Parker and Son, reprinted in *Selected Writings on the History of Science*, edited by Y. Elkana. Chicago: University of Chicago Press, 1960.

57. Young, Warren, "The early reactions to *Value and Capital*." *Review of Political Economy*, 3.3, 1991, 289–308.

2

How Economists Think

Robert W. Clower

Or, why economists shouldn't use contemporary economic theory to justify programs of social reform and economic control.

Nearly 70 years ago, the noted British economist and statesman J. M. Keynes remarked rather wistfully how splendid it would be if economists could someday manage to get themselves thought of as "humble, competent people, on a level with dentists." So it would be — if the reputation were deserved. Unfortunately, there is a kernel of truth in the popular view that economics is "the science whose practitioners, even if laid end to end, still would not reach agreement."

This article is a lightly edited version of a lecture originally presented at Monash University in September 1972 and later published by Monash as the Sixth Monash Economics Lecture.

Personally, I doubt if economics has more than its fair share of arrogant quacks; it must be admitted, however, that contemporary economics is more accurately regarded as a way of thinking about certain kinds of problems than as a settled body of knowledge. In these circumstances, ideological and methodological biases occasionally have as much influence as factual evidence in determining what some economists think and say — so much so that economists themselves are generally loath to lend credence to any but narrowly technical pronouncements by fellow economists. We can hardly be surprised, therefore, if the public at large is disposed to view economists and their work with a certain amount of suspicion.

Granted that the ideas of economists are not generally held in high esteem, wherein lies the fault? Is economics, by its nature, essentially different from other sciences in outlook, method, and logical structure — or is the problem simply that economists have somehow failed to convey to the general public an accurate impression of the nature of their discipline and the reliability of the conclusions to which it leads?

In my opinion, the explanation lies in the second of these alternatives. In everyday discussion of economic problems — and even in academic instruction — economists tend to proceed on the supposition that those they presume to instruct have a good general background knowledge about economic phenomena, as well as a clear appreciation of the nature of scientific inquiry. This procedure is natural. After all, economics is concerned for the most part with thoroughly commonplace phenomena: consumption, production, and related activities with which everyone may be presumed to be more or less directly familiar; and we live in a society where Science (definitely with a capital S) is almost a part of the air we breathe.

In these circumstances, most people would think it perverse if economists insisted on treating their discipline as anything more than systematized common sense.

But would it really be so perverse? Let us examine the issue more closely.

We all have some notion of the nature of the economic system, just as we all have some notion of the nature of the solar system. In the latter case, we realize that our personal knowledge is not sufficiently connected or reliable for us to explain why, for example, ocean tides occur twice each day when the earth revolves just once about its axis, or what the precise nature is of the forces that generate observed patterns of planetary motion. In matters of this kind, most of us are willing to admit that common sense is no substitute for the accumulated wisdom of generations of professional astronomers. In the former case, however, many of us take it for granted that things are just as they appear to us — that what we know from our personal experience is as good a guide to correct understanding of economic events as the "fanciful speculations" of professional economists. The presumption is natural — as natural, in fact, as it once was to suppose that the stars revolve every 24 hours around an earth that stands still at the center of the universe.

All the same, we should not really be surprised to discover that in order to make sense even of the most elementary "facts" of economic experience, we may have to begin by acknowledging that things are not exactly as they appear to us, which would require (among other things) that we start by discarding intuitive preconceptions about the nature of economic phenomena in favor of an abstract framework of ideas that might initially seem unnatural, artificial, and offensive to common sense.

Science: Fact or Fiction?

Contrary to popular opinion and the pretensions of some scientists, the bulk of all knowledge commonly regarded as "scientific" is expressed in terms of stories that differ little from stories told by writers of serious novels. The resemblance is not accidental. The aim of the novelist is to persuade us that his story might almost be true, while that of the scientist is to persuade us that outwardly chaotic sense data fall into meaningful patterns. We might argue that the two situations differ in that the scientist doesn't invent his facts (at least, he is not supposed to), whereas the novelist is not so constrained. On further reflection, however, the two cases seem to be indistinguishable. *Although the scientist does not invent his facts, he does choose them.*

More precisely, he selects from an infinity of possible facts collections in which (for reasons best known to him) he is able to "recognize" interesting patterns. In exactly the same manner, the novelist chooses from an infinity of possible characters and situations just that combination about which he thinks a good story can be told. In both cases, therefore, it is strictly true to say that the artist "invents" his story. We need not be surprised, therefore, to find "order" in economic or social phenomena any more than we are surprised to find "order" in natural phenomena — or in any good novel. Scientists would not bother to write about "nature" or "society" any more than novelists would bother to write about "life" unless they were first convinced that what they had to say made a story worth telling.

How do scientists go about the business of selecting facts in order to "discover" or "invent" intellectually satisfying stories about "designs in nature?" Procedures vary greatly from one discipline to another and also from one area of inquiry to another within any given discipline. The construction of scientific stories is a creative art rather than a technical skill. Little of a specific nature can be said about such matters, therefore, except in relation to the practice of particular investigators working with particular problems. We may clarify our general understanding of the creative process, however, by considering an example from the dawn of modern science.

"Science," as we now understand the term, is generally acknowledged to begin with Galileo's studies of the motion of free-falling bodies. Before Galileo, science (known then as "natural philosophy") was just a minor part of an all-embracing conceptual scheme Aristotle and the Scholastic philosophers had erected to give unity to all fields of human thought and knowledge: politics, poetry, ethics, theology, public administration, domestic housekeeping, and natural philosophy. Underlying this scheme was a quasi-religious presupposition that the meaning of things is to be found in the purpose they serve in the affairs of God and Man. As F. S. Taylor observed in *Science Past and Present:*

> It was transparently clear... that the world and all that's in it [had been] created for the service of man, and that man had been created for the service of God. That was a perfectly intelligible scheme of the world. The sun was there to give us light and to tell the time and mark out the calen-

dar by his motions. The stars and planets were a means of distributing beneficent and maleficent influences to the things on earth to which they were sympathetically linked; plants and animals were there to give us food and pleasure, and we were there to please God by doing his will.[1]

Students of nature before Galileo's time would have found it not only unreasonable but nearly inconceivable that anyone should be

---

". . . the proper business of economists is to advance their own understanding of how the economic system works."

---

so lacking in good sense as to be concerned *only* with the kind of phenomena that obsess modern scientists.

Galileo did not attempt to challenge or refute the Aristotelian scheme (he hardly could, for its essentially religious nature insulated it from serious criticism by any kind of argument or evidence); instead, he turned his back on the "large issues" of his time and wrote a series of stories about narrowly, circumscribed aspects of experience. The key to his achievement, and also to all later progress in science, lies not so much in what he took into account as in what he chose to ignore.

The kernel of Galileo's method is contained in a short passage of his *Discourses* in which the motion of free-falling bodies is discussed by three men: Simplicio, representing an Aristotelian; Salviati, representing Galileo; and Sagredo, representing a disinterested but helpful friend.

Salviati: I greatly doubt that Aristotle ever tested by experiment whether it be true that two stones, one weighing 10 times as much as the other, if allowed to fall, at the same instant, from a height of, say, 100 cubits (150 feet), would so differ in speed that when the heavier had reached the ground, the other would not have fallen more than 10 cubits . . .

Sagredo: . . . I, who have made the test, can assure you that a cannon ball weighing 100 or 200 pounds, or even more, will not reach the ground by as much as a span ahead of a musket ball weighing only half a pound . . .

Simplicio: Your discussion is really admirable; yet I do not find it easy to believe that a bird shot falls as swiftly as a cannon ball.

Salviati: Why not say a grain of sand as rapidly as a grindstone? But, Simplicio, I trust you will not follow the example of many others who divert the discussion from its main intent and fasten upon some statement of mine which lacks a hairbreadth of the truth and, under this hair, hides the fault of another which is as big as a ship's cable. Aristotle says . . . an iron ball of 100 pounds falling from a height of 100 cubits reaches the ground before a 1 pound ball has fallen a single cubit. I say . . . they arrive at the same time. You find, on making the experiment, that the larger outstrips the smaller by two finger breadths . . .; now you would not hide behind these two fingers the 99 cubits of Aristotle, nor would you mention my small error and at the same time pass over in silence his very large one.[2]

We could hardly have a clearer example than this of the confusion that can result from supposing that a naive first glance at "the facts" is a sufficient basis for understanding observed phenomena. Bodies of different weight falling freely in air indeed do not travel precisely the same distance in a given interval of time, but this is much less significant than the fact that they do travel nearly the same distance.

Galileo's work leads us to what is perhaps the most fundamental principle underlying the modern scientist's search for "order in nature." In choosing a set of facts and weaving them into a story, the scientist views observed phenomena not as they *actually appear* but rather as he thinks they *would appear* if Nature were gracious enough to spare him the trouble of "thinking away" extraneous complications by omitting them in the first place.

Unfortunately, Nature is seldom so gracious. To see patterns in phenomena, the scientist usually must remove himself at least one step from reality. He must use his imagination to invent artful caricatures of experience he knows to be literally false in the hope that he may thereby see designs that might otherwise be overlooked because they lack "a hairbreadth of the truth." This is seldom as easy as it sounds. In most cases, the task of recognizing patterns entails much more than an act of creative imagination. Galileo had to "think away" not only air resistance but also an entire philosophical tradition. Copernicus had to "think away" God's concern with Man before he could simplify the description of astronomical events by putting the sun at the center of the solar system. Darwin had to "think away" the Creation to make sense of evolution. And Einstein had to "think away" the very existence of matter in order to fit electromagnetic energy into a story that would simultaneously accommodate Newton's laws of motion.

Scientific Explanation

I have been concerned more, so far, with artistic than routine aspects of scientific inquiry, my aim being to emphasize the essentially fictional nature of the stories scientists tell. Unlike the "characters" found in works of fiction, however, the "characters" appearing in scientific stories (phenomena associated with observable objects and events) appear again and again with essentially unchanged identities in the writings of successive generations of scholars. Scientific stories thus exhibit a cumulative character lacking in ordinary works of fiction. Stories told by one scientist are seized upon by others, reworked, expanded, and passed on to other scientists with similar subject matter interests.

Obviously, this kind of community enterprise could not long be sustained unless all scholars engaged in it subscribed to certain ground rules governing the arrangement, analysis, and communication of ideas among themselves. In fact, we find that just such rules do prevail in every established science. Since no two sciences deal with exactly the same phenomena or problems, each has certain procedures peculiar to it. (The "experimental method," for example, has little place in astronomy or economics, but plays a crucial role in physics and chemistry.) By and large, however, different sciences are more like different breeds of cat or dog than members of different species, for though they differ in details of scope and content, they all conform to a common pattern in fundamentals of logical structure and conceptual orientation.

The nature of this common pattern of scientific explanation may be clarified by considering a second important milestone in the development of modern science: Isaac Newton's "discovery" of the theory of universal gravitation. According to tradition, Newton stumbled upon the basic ideas of his theory late one autumn evening as he was preparing to take a nap under an apple tree in the garden attached to his family home in Woolsthorpe, England. By some strange coincidence, a full moon was rising just as an overripe apple fell to the ground, narrowly missing Newton's head. Tradition deserts us here, the story scarce begun, but from evidence contained in the *Principia* and some of Newton's other writings, we may imagine that Newton's subsequent chain of thought must have gone something as follows ...

How odd ... the moon going up and the apple down! Why don't the moon and the apple obey the same natural laws ... or do they? Hmmmm .... Now, let me see ... Yes! I believe they do! (At this point Newton takes a twig and sketches a diagram on the ground, of which a facsimile is shown in the Figure.) Suppose I threw the apple toward my aunt's house. Galileo's studies and the feebleness of my arm convince me the apple would follow a parabolic path (N in the figure), and fall to Earth long before it broke any windows. But suppose I had the strength of Atlas; then the apple would describe a similar path, but it might not fall to Earth until it had reached the shores of France ... or Greece ... or even the outer reaches of the Antipodes (paths F, G, and S). Indeed, if Atlas were as mighty as some legends suggest, then even though the apple fell constantly toward the center of the earth — attracted there like all natural bodies — it might at the same time

FIGURE.

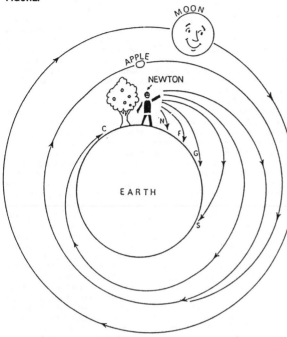

transverse such a vast lateral distance as to circle the globe before coming to ground (path C). Hah! Yes! So if I were Atlas (and if I'd had a little more sugar and milk with my afternoon tea), I could impart such force to the apple that it would circle the earth endlessly, its path paralleling that of the moon. So the moon *does* obey the same laws as the apple . . . but who in the world could have thrown it up there . . .? You don't suppose those old legends . . . No! *Hypotheses non fingo!* It's time I had my snooze.[3]

Our reconstruction of Newton's story accurately expresses the main outlines of a train of thought Newton himself presented in the *Principia*. The story is of general interest for historical reasons as well, as for its own sake. For our purposes, however, it is significant mainly as a classic example of a category of scientific stories called "conceptual experiments" (also "thought experiments" and "gedankenexperimenten") that exhibit in miniature the logical structure and conceptual orientation of scientific stories generally.

Though Newton's conceptual experiment consists of nothing more than an intuitively persuasive story and a related diagram (both of which grossly distort "the facts"), the experiment neatly captures the essential features of an extremely complex problem. The theory of universal gravitation, an elaborately technical and intuitively incomprehensible system of ideas, is at bottom merely a complicated variation on the simpler theme discussed in the conceptual experiment. Given the conceptual experiment, one can "understand" the theory of universal gravitation; without the conceptual experiment, the general theory is just analytical gibberish.

A similar observation applies quite generally to all scientific stories. Certain portions of every science are expressed in formal mathematical language. Specialists may become so bemused with the precision and logical elegance of these creations that they come to think of themselves not as empirical scientists who make use of mathematical ideas but rather as mathematicians who employ a peculiar terminology. This results not in science but in nonsense.

A scientific story cannot be considered acceptable unless it provides the reader with enough information to figure out not only what the teller of the story is saying but also what he is talking about. An important virtue of conceptual experiments is that they serve both purposes simultaneously.

Although the results of Newton's experiment may seem "obvious" to modern minds, they could not have been achieved in his day by anyone but a genius. They were *not* reached, for example, by Galileo or Kepler, both of whom had at their disposal all the "facts" available to Newton. As in our earlier discussion of Galileo's work, so also here we are reminded in the strongest possible manner that *what we are able to see by looking at "the facts" depends in an essential way on what we expect to see before we look at them.*

The key to Newton's achievement lies in the kind of questions his conceptual experiment prompted him to pose. He did not ask, "Why does the apple fall?" or, "Why does the moon circle the earth?" Instead, he asked questions of the form, "If we suppose . . . then what may we conclude?" The difference in language may be slight, but the difference in perspective is monumental. An acceptable scientific story should be so phrased as to force us to ask "if-then" rather than "why" questions. Another important virtue of conceptual experiments is that they force us to do just this.

There are two additional aspects of Newton's work that merit special comment. First, although our version of Newton's story does not suggest this, the logical structure of his conceptual experiment is the same as the description of a parlor game like Parcheesi or chess. The description of such a game consists in every case of a set of rules (assumptions) that prescribe the manner in which specified pieces (apple, moon) may be played or moved (acted upon) by the various players (Newton, gravity). Of course, it is one thing to know the rules of a game and be able to play it, quite another to figure out the rules by observing it's being played.

The purpose of a conceptual experiment — like that of any good scientific story — is to provide a provisional solution to the second of these problems. The person conducting the experiment starts with factual data, which may be regarded as various moves in a game directed by Nature. Unfortunately, the experimenter has no way of knowing in advance if the "moves" as he sees them are truly associated with any set of "rules." Neither has he any way of knowing the object of the game. (How could one discover that the object of chess was to checkmate the king if one never observed the game's being played out?) Moreover, he cannot be sure that the "moves" he sees come from just *one* game. (Consider the predicament of a per-

son who tries to make sense of the actions of a group of bridge players who are simultaneously playing chess to keep their minds occupied between hands!)

To add to his difficulties, he cannot tell if he has identified either all relevant "pieces" (phenomena) or all of the "players" (natural and human forces) Nature sends into the game. Considering just these difficulties (there are many others), we must surely count it remarkable that anyone has ever managed to arrive at even a partial set of rules by the route Newton pioneered. But the fact is that they have and, indeed never by any essentially different route.

My second comment is closely related to the first. It has been said that half the battle in solving any problem consists in formulating it so that one can recognize its solution if one is fortunate enough to find it. Explicit recognition of the analogy between parlor games and conceptual experiments (more generally, between parlor games and scientific stories) effectively provides the basis for just such a formulation. Equally important, the game formulation permits one to communicate accurately to other scientists, not only one's conception of a problem, but also the precise rules one has managed to infer from the facts at his or her disposal or has imposed on the basis of other considerations.

Without such communication among scholars, the scientific enterprise could hardly be purposeful, much less cumulative and fruitful. A scientific story that cannot be expressed explicitly as a "game" must, therefore, be counted a dubious contribution to scientific knowledge.

Economics: The Vision of Adam Smith

I have emphasized four main themes in the preceding remarks:

the deceptiveness of appearances as a guide to rational understanding of observed events; the fictitious nature of the stories scientists tell; the dependence of scientific inquiry upon agreed upon ground rules for analyzing and communicating ideas about experience; and the crucial role that informal conceptual experiments (scientific parables) play in scientific explanation. It remains for me to relate these themes to the ideas of contemporary economists.

Let us begin by looking once more to the past, this time to the history of economics. The origins of economics, like those of every other intellectual discipline, may be traced back to early Greece and Rome, but economics was regarded then as a branch of domestic science, dealing with such matters as the management of slaves and the allocation of manure among alternative agricultural uses. In the revival of learning that followed the Middle Ages, economics emerged in a new guise as a branch of "moral philosophy" concerned with such issues as the ethics of loan interest and the justness of market determined wages and prices. By the beginning of the eighteenth century, the subject had lost most of its theological overtones and had started to take definite shape as a science — but largely as a branch of political theory dealing with questions of government intervention in economic affairs. Then, in 1776, the Scottish moral philosopher Adam Smith published the first edition of his monumental *Inquiry into the Nature and Causes of the Wealth of Nations*, and economics began to assume its modern form as an essentially independent science.

Smith lived in an age when the traditional right of rulers to impose arbitrary and oppressive restrictions on the political and economic liberties of their subjects was coming under increasingly strong attack in all parts of the civilized world. As other men of that time were arguing that democracy could and should replace autocracy in the sphere of politics, so Adam Smith argued that laissez faire could and should replace government direction and regulation of economics.

The "should" is so mixed with the "could" portion of Smith's analysis as to make his book seem almost as much a political tract as an economic treatise. What has given the book lasting significance, however, is the cogent case Smith made for believing the economic

remarked in the *General Competitive Analysis,* "The immediate 'common sense' answer to the question, 'What will an economy motivated by greed and controlled by a large number of different agents look like?' is probably, 'There will be chaos.'"[5] That is certainly the answer that would have been given by most of Smith's contemporaries — at least before they read his book. The greatness of Smith's accomplishment lies precisely in the fact that he, unlike his predecessors, was able to "think away" extraneous complications and perceive an order in economic

he can obtain. As a consequence, "natural forces" of market competition — the result of each individual attempting to "buy cheap and sell dear" — come into action to establish equality between demand and supply for each commodity at rates of exchange (prices) that reflect supplies forthcoming from relatively efficient producers and demands forthcoming from relatively eager consumers. Common sense to the contrary notwithstanding, therefore, the economic system is an essentially self-regulating mechanism that, like the human physiological system, tends naturally toward a state of "equilibrium" (homeostasis) if simply left to itself. Such, in essence, is the message of Adam Smith.

"In no sense . . . is contemporary economic theory a suitable instrument for elaborating positive programs of social reform and economic control."

---

activities of individuals could be coordinated more effectively through the indirect and impersonal action of "natural forces" of competition and self-interest than the direct and often ill-conceived action of government authorities. In effect, Smith opened the eyes of humankind to the existence of a "grand design" in economic affairs similar to that Newton had shown to exist in the realm of physical phenomena. The impact of Smith's ideas upon his contemporaries was quick and widespread; as Alexander Gray observed in his *Development of Economic Doctrine:* "Before Adam Smith there had been much economic discussion; with him we reach the stage of discussing economics."[4]

That Smith's vision of the economic system should ever have been considered "original" may well seem strange to modern minds, but that is only because we now "see" economic phenomena in the light of his conception. As Arrow and Hahn

affairs that common sense could never reveal.

It is one thing, of course, to say that Smith's conception of economic phenomena is original, another to suggest that it corresponds to contemporary facts of experience. According to Smith, society in its economic aspect is a vast concourse of people held together by the desire of each to exchange goods and services with others. Each individual is only concerned directly with furthering his own self-interest, but in pursuing this aim each is led as if by "an invisible hand" to promote the interests of others.

Forbidden by law and social custom to acquire the property of other people by force, fraud, or stealth, each individual attempts to maximize his own gains from trade by specializing in the production of goods and services for which he has a comparative advantage, trading his surplus produce for the produce of others on the best terms

The Contemporary Scene

Nearly 200 years have elapsed since Adam Smith's death. In the course of those two centuries, the superstructure of economic science has grown apace. To say that Smith would hardly recognize the science he is credited with fathering would hardly do justice to the changes that have occurred.

If we look behind outward appearances and focus attention on Smith's initial vision, however, we can hardly help feeling that things have not, after all, changed that much. The foundations of contemporary economic analysis are, in truth, remarkably similar to those laid down originally by Adam Smith. Specifically, it must be recognized that at the present time, just as in Adam Smith's day, what we have by way of theoretical understanding of the working of a market economy is strictly in the nature of a magic castle: satisfying to the imagination but not of much use for solving a housing shortage.

Let me be more explicit. A convincing demonstration of the logical consistency of Smith's conception of the economic system even under highly idealized conditions was not forthcoming until the 1950's. As a result of more recent work, it is now recognized that even this weak result (i.e., logical consistency) cannot be established for an economy in which trade takes place in decentralized markets and involves the use of money and other financial instruments as exchange intermediaries. Thus, our most powerful contemporary tools of theoretical analysis appear to be applicable only to economic systems devoid of just those institutional features that seem to lie at the heart of our most pressing practical problems.

Now I should not like to assert that this body of knowledge is worthless. Among other things, it has a certain value as an instrument for analyzing weaknesses in piecemeal programs of economic intervention: pointing out the dangers of minimum wage laws as devices for improving the economic well-being of lower-income groups, tracing out the probable consequences of fixed exchange rates and inflationary government financial policies, suggesting possible adverse effects on per capita national income of tax policies that aim at a more equal distribution of income and wealth, and so forth.

In no sense, however, is contemporary economic theory a suitable instrument for elaborating positive programs of social reform and economic control. For that purpose, we need a body of knowledge that has far more empirical content than the theory we presently possess — a body of knowledge that permits us to predict major features of the economic future, say, six months or a year ahead, with at least as much accuracy as meteorologists are currently able to predict the general character of next month's weather.

To some extent, our problem is one of inadequate factual knowledge. For reasons I need not go into here, economists have always

had to rely for the most part on data collected by governments and business firms for their own purposes. The kind of data that is urgently needed to improve our present understanding of economic events — mainly, information about holdings of money and other financial assets by individual households and business firms and related information about stocks of goods in process, trade credit, and overdraft facilities — currently is not available in sufficient detail to

---

"Granted that the ideas of economists are not generally held in high esteem, wherein lies the fault?"

---

be of any use, or is simply not collected at all. But it really is no good to fulminate at the powers that be for failing to meet this need. The sad fact is that the relevance of this kind of information cannot be documented by reference to established theory.

Let me conclude by recalling another remark by J. M. Keynes, this one from the concluding chapter of his *General Theory*. "The ideas of economists," said Keynes, "are more powerful than is commonly understood. Practical men, who believe themselves to be quite exempt from any intellectual influences, are usually the slaves of some defunct economist. Madmen in authority, who hear voices in the air, are distilling their frenzy from some academic scribbler of a few years back."[5] Personally, I doubt if there was much truth in Keynes's remark at the time he made it — 50 years ago. In recent years, however, economists have come to play an increasingly prominent role as advisors to governments. Whether this

indicates that "madmen in authority" or the public at large are beginning to take the ideas of economists more seriously is an open question; the record in most countries indicates that after economists give their advice, the local "madmen" go ahead and do what they intended to do, regardless. There can be no doubt, however, that economists are beginning to take *themselves* more seriously, and to my mind *this* is dangerous.

I should not like to be accused of fouling my own nest or even of the less heinous crime of obscurantism. As a specialist in economic theory who has dealt from time to time with practical problems of economic policy, however, I am tempted to say of my advice-giving colleagues what Wellington is reputed to have said of his foot soldiers: "I don't know how they strike you, but by God, sir, they surely frighten me."

The basis of my fear is not personal and professional knowledge of instances in which policy action recommended by economists has turned out to be misguided. I should no more think of burdening the economics profession with the sins of its practitioners than of burdening the medical profession with the sins of its quacks. No, my misgivings derive from a deeper source: professional awareness of the unsettled and uncertain state of contemporary intellectual understanding of forces governing the coordination of economic activities in the world in which we actually live. To put the matter bluntly, we do not know enough to distinguish cases of economic toothache from cases of social lockjaw. In economics, as in dentistry, intelligent diagnosis is a prerequisite for effective treatment. Lacking a secure basis for such diagnosis, we are about as likely to maim as cure the patient. So economists who are anxious to offer policy advice, and people — madmen in authority or otherwise — who are quick to seek and follow such advice, fill me with uneasiness, if not terror.

Economics has, I think, a great future as a science that produces results. Like Keynes, therefore, I look forward to a time when economists will be known as "humble, competent people, on a level with dentists." For the immediate future, however, it seems to me that the proper business of economists is to advance their own understanding of how the economic system works. It will be time enough for economists to bring light to the world when they are able to convince themselves that they are no longer groping in the dark. □

[1] F. S. Taylor, *A Short History of Science and Scientific Thought* (New York: Norton, 1949), p. 131.

[2] Galileo Galilei, *Dialogues Concerning Two New Sciences*, trans. H. Crew and A. DeSalvio (New York: Dover, 1952), pp. 105-112.

[3] Sir Isaac Newton, *Principia*, vol. 2: *The System of the World*, trans. Andrew Motte, revised Florian Cajori (Berkeley and Los Angeles: University of California Press, 1962).

[4] Alexander Gray, *Development of Economic Doctrine* (London: Longmans Green & Co., 1931), p.123.

[5] K. J. Arrow and F. H. Hahn, *General Competetive Analysis* (San Francisco: Holden-Day, Inc., 1971), p. vii.

[6] John Maynard Keynes, *The General Theory of Employment, Interest and Money* (New York: Harcourt Brace & Co., 1936), p. 383.

3

Reprinted from THE JOURNAL OF ECONOMIC HISTORY
Volume XXIV, September 1964, Number 3

Monetary History and Positive Economics*

We economists are essentially only dilettanti in the field of historical research, with the usual faults of all dilettantism: over-hasty conclusions, insufficient criticism of sources, tendentious colouring of facts, and even, on occasion, unconscious fabrication of them.

KNUT WICKSELL

I

If successful prediction were the sole criterion of the merit of a science, economics should long since have ceased to exist as a serious intellectual pursuit. Accurate prognosis is not its forte. The real strength of the discipline lies in another direction—namely, in its apparently limitless capacity to rationalize events after they happen. This helps explain the indifference of most economic theorists to "the lessons of history"; men to whom all things are possible have little to learn from experiments conducted in the laboratory of time. It also helps explain the indifference of most economic historians to abstract theory; what have they to learn from a subject that "yields no predictions, summarizes no empirical generalizations, provides no useful framework of analysis"?[1]

Recent years have, of course, witnessed some changes in the attitude of theorists toward economic history and in the attitude of economic historians toward theory. Rummaging in attics and excavating ancient files have not yet become popular sports, but the production of historical statistics is very nearly one already. The problem is to put the data now becoming available to good use. This is hardly a novel problem; men have been debating the merits of alternative epistemologies since the dawn of time. But economic history is currently in a state of flux, forced by external pressures to become less humane, torn by internal discord as to how this should be done.[2] Thus the future direction of the subject may well depend as much on the methodological views of econ-

---

* A review of *A Monetary History of the United States, 1867-1960*, by Milton Friedman and Anna Jacobson Schwartz. Princeton: published for the NBER by Princeton University Press, 1963. Pp. xxiv, 860. $15.00.

[1] Milton Friedman, "The Marshallian Demand Curve," in *Essays in Positive Economics* (Chicago: University of Chicago Press, 1953), p. 92.

[2] See papers by Rostow, Meyer and Conrad, and Kuznets on "The Integration of Economic Theory and Economic History," JOURNAL OF ECONOMIC HISTORY, XVII (Dec. 1957), 509-53 (Kuznets' "Summary of Discussion and Postscript" is especially relevant); also Lance E. Davis, Jonathan R. T. Hughes, and Stanley Reiter, "Aspects of Quantitative Research in Economic History," JOURNAL OF ECONOMIC HISTORY, XX (Dec. 1960), 539-47; Douglass C. North, "Quantitative Research in American Economic History," *American Economic Review*, LIII (Mar. 1963), 128-30; and Robert W. Fogel, "Reappraisals in American Economic History—Discussion," *American Economic Review*, LIV (May 1964), 377-89.

omists playing at history as on the attitudes of economic historians. Whether this bodes well or ill for economic history, I cannot pretend to say. Much depends on just who the "dilettanti" are, for economics proper is not devoid of methodological factions either.[3]

These considerations lend peculiar interest and significance to the volume under review. To be sure, Friedman and Schwartz's *History* merits close attention in its own right; it is not every day, or even every decade, that an outstanding economic theorist joins forces with another able scholar to produce a major work in economic history. But Milton Friedman is not just an outstanding theorist. He is the leading exponent of a radical research methodology which views much of formal economic analysis as "disguised mathematics"; which regards theories as useful only if they "fit as full and complete a set of related facts about the real world as it is possible to get"; which is contemptuous of any test of the validity of a hypothesis other than "comparison of its predictions with experience."[4] And he is also the author or coauthor of some highly impressive testimonials to the virtue of these views.[5] Surely this lends additional allure for both economic historians and their "dilettante" brothers to Friedman and Schwartz's venture into Clio's realm.

II

No brief summary can convey an accurate impression of the range and depth of Friedman and Schwartz's *History*. To be sure, the discussion is highly selective; as the authors state (p. 3): "Throughout, we trace one thread, the stock of money, and our concern with that thread explains alike which episodes and events are examined in detail and which are slighted." Nevertheless, the book reads more like a general economic history than even its authors seem to suppose. And this is as it should be; to distinguish sharply between "monetary" and "other" aspects of the history of a money economy would be artificial as well as misleading.

The book was originally conceived as a single chapter in a statistical study of monetary factors in the business cycle (Preface, p. xxi). It now

---

[3] See H. Laurence Miller, Jr., "On the 'Chicago School of Economics,'" *Journal of Political Economy*, LXX (Feb. 1962), 64-69, and comments by M. Bronfenbrenner and George J. Stigler in the same issue; also G. C. Archibald, "Chamberlin *versus* Chicago," *Review of Economic Studies*, XXVIII (Oct. 1961), 2-28, and later responses by Stigler and Friedman, *ibid.* XXX (Feb. 1963), 63-67.

[4] Friedman, "Marshallian Demand Curve." The quoted phrases are torn out of context from pp. 12, 300, and 9, respectively. Friedman himself would never express views so extreme as these (compare his reply to Archibald [*Rev. Ec. St.*, XXX], pp. 65 ff.)

[5] I refer especially to Friedman, *A Theory of the Consumption Function* (Chicago: University of Chicago Press, 1957); to Friedman and Kuznets, *Income from Independent Professional Practice* (New York: NBER, 1945); and to Friedman and Schwartz, "Money and Business Cycles," *Review of Economics and Statistics*, XLV (Feb. 1963 suppl.), 32-64. But these are just a few choice items in a long and distinguished list.

366   *Robert W. Clower*

covers 860 pages, comprises thirteen chapters and two appendices,[6] and appears in print in advance of the study which gave it birth.

Economic historians will probably find most to arouse their interest in the first few chapters, which cover the relatively tranquil years between 1867 and 1914. Here the authors' central theme is the untrammeled development of the economy in response to the working of natural economic forces, "avarice explaining all, always."[7] The argument is detailed, penetrating, and for the most part convincing. For sheer ingenuity in marshaling evidence, few historical narratives can match Friedman and Schwartz's discussion of "Special Problems Connected with the Greenback Period" (ch. ii, sec. 5), their analysis of the "Great Deflation" (ch. iii, sec. 1), or their account of the Panic of 1907 (ch. iv, sec. 3).

The theme of the middle portion of the *History* (chs. v through xi) is the response of the economy to the vicissitudes of international affairs and domestic politics, with special emphasis on the growing power of the Federal Reserve System as an agent of economic control. Specialists in monetary economics will find these chapters a valuable source of factual and theoretical insight into the working of financial mechanisms. Economic historians are less likely to enjoy or profit from the discussion; too much of it is concerned with technical monetary details and with lengthy accounts of the policy deliberations of the monetary authorities. Like other readers, however, they will be intrigued by Friedman and Schwartz's unconventional views on the "Great Contraction" and other episodes of the interwar period.

The penultimate chapter, on the post-World War II rise in the income velocity of money, seems to be more in the nature of a journal article than a contribution to monetary history, but it is of considerable interest all the same. The final chapter provides a concise but remarkably complete account of the authors' main conclusions.[8]

III

The preceding summary emphasizes the narrative rather than the analytical aspects of the *History*. Appearances to the contrary notwithstanding, the emphasis of the book is the other way around. The authors themselves do not appear to recognize the distinction; indeed,

---

[6] Reference should also be made to the thoughtful and interesting "Director's Comment" by Albert J. Hettinger, Jr., which appears at the very end of the book (pp. 809-14).

[7] I owe this phrase to my erstwhile colleague, Meyer Burstein.

[8] I omit comment on the two appendices, except to say: (1) the statistical work underlying the basic tables in Appendix A and the charts and tables appearing elsewhere in the book is clearly of the highest quality (a full explanation of the estimates prepared by Friedman and Schwartz is to appear in their forthcoming study of "Trends and Cycles in the Stock of Money," another National Bureau project) and (2) the discussion of "the proximate determinants of money" in Appendix B does not add much of value to the argument in the text (most of the relevant information is already given in sec. 4 of ch. ii).

they blend analysis so effectively with narrative that one can hardly tell which of their historical judgments rest on fact and which on theoretical fancy. The difficulty lies, however, not in the authors' exposition, which is generally lucid, but rather in their failure to provide an explicit account of their methodology. My purpose in the pages that follow is to fill this gap.

The essentials of Friedmann and Schwartz's analytical procedure are adumbrated in the opening paragraph of their final chapter (p. 676):

> The varied character of U.S. monetary history [from 1867 to 1960] renders this century of experience particularly valuable to the student of economic change. He cannot control the experiment, but he can observe monetary experience under sufficiently disparate conditions to sort out what is common from what is adventitious and to acquire considerable confidence that what is common can be counted on to hold under still other circumstances.

I interpret this observation to say something as follows. We may view historical time-series observations as rough measures of the values assumed in various intervals of time by the variables of a general dynamic system.[9] If the values of certain variables are observed to follow some regular pattern in relation to one another, we may abstract this pattern from the data and use it as a tentative benchmark to distinguish between "equilibrium" and "disequilibrium" states of the system. The very existence of such a pattern may be taken to mean that the economic system is basically stable.[10] Accordingly, we may assert with some confidence that departures from "equilibrium," as indicated by breaks in the pattern, will tend to be self-restoring, and we may use this stability principle as a basis for predicting the probable behavior of the economy starting from any given initial situation. Moreover, we may attribute obvious deviations from "normal" behavior to various "shocks," some of which can be identified with specific historical events. In this manner, we may assign "causal" significance to particular classes of events— "monetary," "political," "technological," etc.—and perhaps even go so far as to assess the relative importance of each as a source of economic change.

I hope this interpretation does not do serious injustice to the views actually held by Friedman and Schwartz. It portrays with reasonable accuracy a research strategy which seems to me to make some sense and with which I have considerable sympathy. And it is consistent with what I know about the methodological views of the patron saint of "positive economics," Alfred Marshall.[11] The difficulty is to put the strategy to practical use, for it is by no means clear how one is supposed

[9] Compare Friedman and Schwartz, "Money and Business Cycles," pp. 29-63.

[10] At least, for all practical purposes. On this, compare R. L. Basmann, "The Causal Interpretation of Non-Triangular Systems of Economic Relations," *Econometrica*, XXXI (July 1963), 442-43, 453.

[11] See Marshall, "The Present Position of Economics," in *Memorials of Alfred Marshall*, A. C. Pigou, ed. (London: Macmillan, 1925), pp. 166-69; also Friedman, "Marshallian Demand Curve," pp. 89-92.

to distinguish between what is "common" and what is "adventitious," between patterns that are "regular" and patterns that are not.

But here we may draw on "the methodology of positive economics." Clearly, if we are required to judge a theory not by precept but by practice, then we should judge a research strategy in the same way: that is, not by what its exponents say it can do but rather by what it enables them to accomplish. If this is our procedure, then the difficulty mentioned above may be passed over for the time being; a look at the facts may suffice to allay any doubts we have about our ability to "sort out what is common from what is adventitious."

IV

It is common knowledge that changes in money income and employment are more or less closely associated with changes in prices, financial flows, holdings of physical assets, bank deposits, etc. What is not known is the precise character of these associations, their magnitude, reliability, and causal significance. Friedman and Schwartz begin their attack on these problems by studying outwardly relevant time-series data in the hope that these will reveal patterns of association of sufficient clarity to provide a tentative foundation for further analysis.

Referring to the 93-year period from 1867 to 1960, they find that the "stock of money" (defined as currency plus commercial bank deposits) grew from less than $2 billion to more than $200 billion, while income (as measured by Kuznets' unpublished annual estimates of net national product in current prices)[12] grew from less than $6 billion to more than $200 billion (pp. 3-5 and charts 1 and 62). The income velocity of money changed substantially during the period as a whole, falling fairly steadily between 1869 and 1915 (from a value of 4.6 to a value of 2.1), oscillating around an uncertain trend from 1916 to 1946, rising to a level somewhat above that for 1915 during the years 1947-1960. Population more than quadrupled during the same period, per capita holdings of money increased more than thirty-fold, per capita income more than tenfold.

The clearest secular patterns which seem to emerge from the data involve the stock of money, on the one hand, and income and the stock of "high-powered money,"[13] on the other. All three of these magnitudes are found to display strong upward trends, money generally rising faster than high-powered money, high-powered money generally rising faster than income. The suggestion is that rates of growth of the three series have been roughly proportional to one another; but the relationship is far from exact.

---

12 These estimates are available on request from the National Bureau of Economic Research, but are not presented in the *History*, except in charts.

13 Defined as "the total amount of hand-to-hand currency held by the public plus vault cash plus, after 1914, deposit liabilities of the Federal Reserve System to banks" (p. 50).

Friedman and Schwartz's analysis of cyclical variations in the stock of money and in money income produces sharper results. Although the numerical value of income velocity is discovered to vary considerably from one cycle to another, velocity is found to display "a systematic and stable movement about its trend, rising during expansion and falling during contraction" (p. 682). Moreover, observed year-to-year changes in the value of velocity are "less than 10 per cent in 78 out of the 91 year-to-year changes from 1869 . . . to 1960. Of the 13 larger changes, more than half came during either the Great Contraction or the two world wars, and the largest change was 17 per cent" (p. 682).

These results imply a strikingly good correlation between changes in the stock of money and changes in income, comparable in important respects to the familiar time-series correlation between income and consumption.[14] Whatever view one takes of the probable causal significance of this relation, its practical importance cannot be denied. No theory of a money economy which is incapable of generating the kind of behavior required by the correlation can be taken very seriously. Conversely, any theory which is capable of generating such behavior deserves consideration, at least tentatively, as a descriptive and explanatory device. Considered from either point of view, the correlation constitutes a promising point of departure for further research.

V

Friedman and Schwartz's procedure at this stage is to ask, as it were, What is the simplest relation between the stock of money and money income that is capable of rationalizing the behavior patterns suggested by the statistical evidence? It should be emphasized that they do not concern themselves at this point with "causality" or related philosophical issues. Their question relates simply to the behavior of empirical data, not to the behavior of people or markets. How the economic system *really* works is irrelevant; what Friedman and Schwartz want to know is whether the system works *as if* its object were to ensure the maintenance of some "normal" relation between the stock of money and money income.

To cut a long story short, the answer which I interpret Friedman and Schwartz to give to their question is that, to a first approximation, the *normal* stock of money (M_n) and *normal* income (Y_n) are related by an equation of the form $M_n = KY_n^a$, where K is a constant representing the reciprocal of the "normal" income velocity of money, and a is a constant ($a > 1$) representing the "normal" income elasticity of demand for money balances. Of course, the "normal" magnitudes M_n and Y_n are

[14] See Friedman and David Meiselman, "The Relative Stability of Monetary Velocity and the Investment Multiplier in the United States, 1897-1958," *Stabilization Policies* (research study prepared for the Commission on Money and Credit [Englewood Cliffs, N. J.: Prentice-Hall, 1963]), pp. 165-268, especially Charts II-4 and II-6 (pp. 194 and 196). Also, Ando, Brown, Solow, and Kareken, "Lags in Fiscal and Monetary Policy," in the same volume, pp. 14-24.

Robert W. Clower

not directly observable. To connect them with corresponding *measured* magnitudes (M and Y), it is necessary to introduce certain "transitory" variables u_m and u_y, defined by the equations

$$M \equiv M_n + u_m$$

and

$$Y \equiv Y_n + u_y.$$

These identities, together with the initial assumption

$$M_n = KY_n^a$$

imply that the measured stock of money and measured money income are connected by the relation

$$M = K[Y - u_y]^a + u_m.$$

Friedman and Schwartz's inquiry into monetary history is thus directed, in effect, at characterizing the general properties of the transitory magnitudes u_m and u_y, studying their interrelations, and identifying independent variations in each with specific historical events—wars, crises, international gold flows, actions by the Federal Reserve authorities, etc.

They do not couch their argument in these terms; the language and symbols that I am using are mine, not theirs, and so is the interpretation.[15] The purpose of my free translation is to suggest to the reader something that I did not begin to realize until after I started to write this review: that the conceptual framework of Friedman and Schwartz's *History* is virtually indistinguishable from that of Friedman's earlier *A Theory of the Consumption Function*. Once this analogy is grasped, the whole of Friedman and Schwartz's analytical narrative is seen to follow a purposeful pattern; what at first sight seems a slightly untidy argument is instead discovered to be a masterly mosaic of logic and facts.

But is it "history"? Most historians would probably want to reserve judgment about the non-narrative portions of the argument, on the ground that the establishment as distinct from the verification of "laws" of social development is not an essential aspect of history *qua* history. On the other hand, most economists would probably say that the entire argument is strictly history, on the ground that evidence about past human behavior, however important it may be for testing economic hypotheses, is not a necessary, sufficient, or reliable basis for formulating them.

This conflict of viewpoints raises some delicate and controversial issues. To what extent is Friedman and Schwartz's argument directed toward the establishment of causal rather than merely descriptive relations among economic phenomena? Is there any meaningful way to distinguish between the two; that is, what objective criteria, if any, might be used to distinguish between relations that do and relations that do not have causal significance? It seems to me that these issues go to the

---

15 For a very similar symbolic presentation, however, see Friedman and Schwartz, "Money and Business Cycles," pp. 56-58.

heart of the problem with which this review is primarily concerned, which is to assess the "importance" of Friedman and Schwartz's book as a "contribution to knowledge." Accordingly, it is on these issues that I shall mainly focus in the pages that follow.

VI

As I emphasized earlier, Friedman and Schwartz do not initially concern themselves with questions of causality. However, the tenor of their argument gradually runs in that direction until it becomes the dominant note of the book. How do they accomplish this transmogrification? I shall not try to recapitulate the details of their argument, but I shall try to reproduce the main outlines.

The first step in the process is to show that the basic theoretical model is useful for summarizing the salient facts of U. S. monetary history since 1867. To be sure, the procedure used to derive the model in the first place guarantees that its fit to the original money and income series will be reasonably satisfactory; but the model works better than this remark might seem to suggest. Indeed, if one were simply confronted with the model and told to fit it to the data (using moving averages of measured money and measured income as estimates of the corresponding "normal" variables), I daresay he would be amazed at the results.[16]

The second step is to show that where the model does not perform almost perfectly (as during the two depression decades, 1870-1880 and 1930-1940, and during the post-World War II period of rising income velocity), this is attributable not to any basic inadequacy of the model but rather to exceptional variations in the transitory components of money or income, the "causes" of which can be at least tentatively identified. Thus, the imperfections of the model for describing monetary experience during the period 1870-1880 are explained in part by errors in Kuznets' estimates of net national product for this period (pp. 36-41). Similarly, the partial breakdown of the model during the period 1930-1940 is traced to the ineptitude of the Federal Reserve authorities in failing to take adequate measures to stem the tide of the Great Contraction (pp. 693-94). And the failure of the model to account for the rise in income velocity after 1946 is attributed (after lengthy evaluation of other possible explanations, such as rising interest rates, the growth of financial intermediaries, etc.) to "changing patterns of expectations about economic stability" (p. 673).

The third and final step is to conduct some "crucial" thought experiments with historical data, the argument being that "the examination of a wide range of qualitative evidence . . . provides a basis for dis-

---

[16] But perhaps not. On this, see Ames and Reiter's fascinating sampling experiment involving time series drawn at random from *Historical Statistics of the U. S.,* "Distributions of Correlation Coefficients in Economic Time Series," *Journal of the American Statistical Association,* LVI (Sept. 1961), 637-56.

criminating between [alternative] possible explanations of observed statistical covariation [so that one can] go beyond the numbers alone and, at least on some occasions, discern the antecedent circumstances whence arose the particular movements that become so anonymous when we feed the statistics into the computer" (p. 686). This technique is applied to a number of cases (including the Gold Inflation of 1897-1914, the monetary expansions accompanying World Wars I and II, the resumption and silver episodes, and the recessions of 1920, 1931, and 1937). In every instance, it is concluded that "the major channel of influence is from money to business" (p. 694), although "there have clearly also been influences running the other way" (p. 695).

Whether or not one considers the evidence and arguments introduced at each of these steps to be completely persuasive (and I do not), he can hardly fail to be jolted by their cumulative impact (as I was). True, the entire demonstration rests in the final analysis on the assumption that the original theoretical model is basically valid, which is the point at issue. True, it is one thing to use a model to summarize facts, another to use it as a basis for positive judgments about "what might have been" or "what is to be." True, Friedman and Schwartz nowhere provide an explicit statement of the manner in which changes in the stock of money are linked with changes in income.[17] Hence, Friedman and Schwartz cannot be said to have explained the nature of the causal mechanism whose existence seems to be implied by their historical judgments. Nevertheless, they make a case that is not easy to answer, and one which strongly supports the view to which they effectually commit themselves in their final chapter; that is, that *income and prices will typically be found "dancing to the tune called by independently originating monetary changes"* (p. 686, my italics).[18]

Such a conclusion—particularly when it is backed up by over six hundred pages of detailed evidence—is bound to be a bit upsetting to those whose vision of the working of the economic system is informed by neo-Walrasian theoretical conceptions, which is to say, to all but a small handful of contemporary economists.[19] For it is an essential feature

[17] An account of sorts is given in Friedman and Schwartz, "Money and Business Cycles," and criticized in the same issue by Hyman P. Minsky and Arthur Okun (pp. 68-72, 74).

[18] See also Friedman and Schwartz, "Money and Business Cycles"; Milton Friedman, "The Quantity Theory of Money: A Restatement," *Studies in the Quantity Theory of Money* (ed. Milton Friedman; Chicago: University of Chicago Press, 1956), pp. 3-21; Friedman and Meiselman, "Relative Stability," pp. 166-70.

[19] The term "neo-Walrasian" refers to the general point of view underlying such modern classics as Hicks' *Value and Capital* and Samuelson's *Foundations of Economic Analysis*. The distinctive characteristic of this point of view as contrasted with that of Marshall, the neo-Classics, and Friedman and Schwartz, is that market demand and supply relations are explicitly defined in terms of underlying microeconomic decision processes. This aspect of the neo-Walrasian literature stands out with particular clarity in recent contributions to the general equilibrium theory of money. See, for example, Don Patinkin, *Money, Interest and Prices* (Evanston: Row Peterson, 1956); G. C. Archibald and R. G. Lipsey, "Monetary and Value Theory: A Critique of Lange and Patinkin," *Review of Economic Studies*, XXVI (Oct. 1958), 1-22.

both of post-Keynesian income analysis and of contemporary monetary theory that *money does not matter much except in the long run.* More specifically, neo-Walrasians typically argue[20] that, in a closed economy, the absolute levels of money prices and aggregate money income depend *ultimately* on the quantity of *legal tender means of payment* as determined by the fiscal and monetary operations of government; but that the *impact* effects of autonomous changes in the stock of legal-tender money cannot be disentangled from other and equally important sources of economic disturbance—technological, psychological, etc.— not, at least, by visual inspection of historical time-series data and casual study of related events.[21] More pointedly, legal-tender money— which does not include either demand or time deposits—is merely one of many generally acceptable means of payment. The great bulk of objects which people regard as "money" at any given point in time[22] consists of debt instruments, the amounts of which are determined in the short run not by government authorities but by the general public. Facts and arguments to the contrary notwithstanding, therefore, it is absurd to assign a prominent role in cyclical movements to variations in the stock of legal-tender money, and it is even more absurd to treat the total "stock of money," however one might define it, as an independent variable. So the issue is joined.

The difference between Friedman and Schwartz and those whom I have called neo-Walrasians may at first sight appear to turn on questions of fact. If the neo-Walrasians are right (it may be said), they should be able to produce a better explanation of historical experience than that offered by Friedman and Schwartz. If they cannot do this, they should give up the game. But who is to decide if one model is "better" than another? And what does "better" mean if the purposes of alternative models are significantly different—for example, if one model is intended roughly to summarize experience covering nearly a century, and the other is intended to predict with a high degree of accuracy what will happen during a period of a few weeks or months if a certain policy action is taken now? I think there can be no doubt about the answer: *there are no objective standards for evaluating the descriptive*

[20] See M. L. Burstein, *Money* (Cambridge: Schenkman Publishing Co., 1963), pp. 749 ff.; P. A. Samuelson, "Reflections on Central Banking," *National Banking Review*, I (Sept. 1963), 15-28.

[21] For a clear statement of representative views, see H. G. Johnson, "Monetary Theory and Policy," *American Economic Review*, LII (June 1962), 335-84; also, R. G. Lipsey and F. P. R. Brechling, "Trade Credit and Monetary Policy," *Economic Journal*, LXXIII (Dec. 1963), 618-41.

[22] The time qualification is important; for example, in times of prosperity practically any asset may be regarded as "money," whereas in times of "panic" even demand deposits may sell at a discount (compare *History*, p. 161). What constitutes "legal tender" is also a problem: greenbacks were " 'lawful money' and legal tender for all debts, public and private, except customs duties and interest on the public debt, both of which were to be payable in coin," to quote Alonzo Barton Hepburn, *A History of Currency in the United States* (New York: Macmillan Co., 1915), p. 185.

validity of theoretical hypotheses; standards that serve for one purpose or period may not do at all for others. This is quite sufficient to show that the real point at issue cannot be settled by appealing to "facts."

The question whether there exist objective criteria for distinguishing between relations that are "causal" and relations that are "merely descriptive" remains to be decided. This is obviously a matter for philosophers of science rather than for economists. However, since philosophers have now been debating the issue for more than two millenia, we may sensibly infer that "facts" will never resolve it. To date, the only thing on which all philosophers seem agreed is that most scientists have a strong psychological propensity to regard all correlations that are not known to be spurious as manifestations of some underlying causal process. Whether or not this propensity has a solid foundation in fact is beside the point; what is important is that the propensity itself drives scientists to think and act in certain interesting ways.[23]

VII

Thus we come at last to methodological differences as the ultimate basis for the revulsion of neo-Walrasians from the "monetomania" of Friedman and Schwartz. These differences are, I think, greater in practice than they appear to be in principle. No judicious writer on methodology ever takes a completely unqualified stand on any basic issue, knowing full well that some arcanum of science will be dredged up by opponents and used to show him wrong. Real methodological differences are aired in private, usually by groups of people who have fault to find with approaches used by other groups. I propose to be injudicious: to say bluntly and without qualification some things about the methodology of Friedman and Schwartz and that of the neo-Walrasians that I would normally not commit to print.

Friedman and Schwartz, like all other economists, start with certain vague notions about the working of a money economy: banks and businesses act "as if" they want to make money; households act "as if" they want to eat and work; markets act "as if" their object is to arrive at prices that equate demands with supplies. They then proceed *immediately* to give these notions definite form by shaping them in the light of empirical knowledge. There is no sharp distinction in their world between "theory" and "fact"; theory is simply an organized description of consilient inductions drawn from related sets of empirical observations. Nor is there any question of using facts to "illustrate" rather than "test" hypotheses, for this would be to illustrate facts with more facts. Whether or not Friedman and Schwartz regard personal intuitions as "facts" is uncertain; but my hunch is that they do not. If they did, they would have to pay at least some attention to the intuitive plausibility

---

[23] For an elaborate discussion of "causality" and its various behavior manifestations, see Ernest Nagel, *The Structure of Science* (New York: Harcourt, Brace and World, 1961), ch. x.

(that is, "realism") of their assumptions, and this would violate a fundamental tenet of the "methodology of positive economics."[24]

The neo-Walrasians (like Friedman and Schwartz) start with certain vague notions about the working of the economic system. However, these notions are shaped initially not in the light of concrete experience but rather with reference to *stylized facts* (that is, intuition and common sense). There is no pretense of "descriptive realism" in this procedure, but there is a very real concern with the intuitive plausibility of basic assumptions. Personal reflections about one's own objective responses to external stimuli are, after all, as real and reliable as are any observations of external events.[25]

The *crucial* test of the empirical validity of a model, for the neo-Walrasians just as for Friedman and Schwartz, is the conformity of its predictions with experience.[26] But one of the major objectives of theorizing is to avoid having to perform needless experiments. Why put to factual test a model that is logically inconsistent or trivial, analytically unmanageable, intuitively absurd, or devoid of empirical implications even under ideal conditions? Abstractness, elegance, and generality are *not* irrelevant criteria for evaluating the potential empirical fruitfulness of a theoretical model; all have an immediate bearing on one or more of the preliminary tests listed above.

As for the familiar indictment that facts are typically used not to test but merely to illustrate preconceived hypotheses, the neo-Walrasians must certainly plead "guilty"—but only to the specification of being cautious, not to the specification of producing barren abstractions. No doubt most neo-Walrasian models are excessively general (whatever that may mean). The proper way to specialize models is gradually to modify them by reference to results obtained by refined statistical analysis of empirical data *and by reference to other relevant critical procedures*.[27] Economics is an unsettled research science, not a systemized body of established truths. It is still relatively youthful, its subject matter is complex, and its procedure is largely nonexperimental. Progress in shaping economic hypotheses to bring them to bear on concrete problems is bound to be uncertain and slow. Accordingly, neo-Walrasians

---

[24] See Friedman, "The Methodology of Positive Economics," *Essays*, pp. 16-23; and more significantly, *Consumption Function*, p. 231. I should remark explicitly that my interpretation of Friedman and Schwartz's methodological position is based not so much on what they say, here or elsewhere, jointly or singly, as on what they do— and similarly for the neo-Walrasians.

[25] This is an important reason for attaching significance to so-called scientific paradoxes; see my "Permanent Income and Transitory Balances," *Oxford Economic Papers*, XV (July 1963), 177 ff.

[26] I should emphasize once more the inherent ambiguity of the "prediction" criterion (see last paragraph of preceding section). For a concise but exceptionally lucid discussion of the problems involved, see H. Theil, *Economic Forecasts and Policy* (Amsterdam: North-Holland Publishing Company, 1958), pp. 204-7.

[27] On this, see Karl R. Popper, *Conjectures and Refutations* (London: Routledge and Kegan Paul, 1963), ch. i; also K. Klappholz and J. Agassi, "Methodological Prescriptions in Economics," *Economica*, N. S. XXVI (Feb. 1959), pp. 60-74.

may be justly charged with being excessively patient—"like highly trained athletes who never run a race,"[28] but men who are passionately "anxious to do good," who have a "burning interest in pressing issues of public policy, . . . who desire to learn how the economic system really works in order that that knowledge may be used,"[29] are perhaps better employed in politics than in basic scientific research.

These remarks are not intended to settle anything; only to clarify some issues and clear some air. I have so far stressed points of apparent disagreement between the neo-Walrasians and Friedman and Schwartz. I should now like to emphasize two points of fundamental importance on which there is clearly complete accord: first, *the essential art of the empirical scientist is that of inventing conjectures;* second, *this art is bound by no fixed rules.* There are countless "patterns of plausible inference," all potentially fruitful, none capable of *proving* anything.[30] Methodological disputes are generally idle because they are concerned with means rather than ends; the scientific worth of a conjecture does not depend on its methodological pedigree. Methodological differences are nevertheless worthwhile, because diversities of intellectual perspective are a mainstay of vigorous scientific criticism. Whether Friedman and Schwartz are right or wrong, their views, as expressed in the *History* and elsewhere, will invite attention and promote much worthwhile research. Failing the will or the ability to produce equally provocative works, neo-Walrasians will have to take such comfort as they can from the maxim that "the path to useful knowledge is paved with false conjectures."

VIII

As a general rule, every historical narrative may be expected to display one or more instances of each of Wicksell's "faults of dilettantism"; and the longer and more elaborate the narrative, the easier it is likely to be for a critic to spot them. Friedman and Schwartz's *History* is no exception to the rule, but neither is it an easy mark; the range is too great and the target too small for even a diligent critic to accumulate anything but a pitiful score. Nuances aside, I have no fundamental quarrel with any of Friedman and Schwartz's substantive conclusions. My only doubts concern the evidential force and practical significance of some of their historical judgments. The comments that follow are therefore confined to certain general aspects of Friedman and Schwartz's argument that have influenced my assessment of their work.

Research strategies may be considered effective in roughly the same measure as they help us formulate and solve worthwhile problems. The

[28] Samuelson, *Foundations of Economic Analysis* (Cambridge: Harvard University Press, 1947), p. 4.

[29] Friedman, "Lange on Price Flexibility and Employment: A Methodological Criticism," *Essays,* p. 300.

[30] For details, see G. Polya, *Patterns of Plausible Inference* (Princeton: Princeton University Press, 1954).

strategy implicit in "the methodology of positive economics" strikes me as being especially effective for uncovering important empirical regularities, directing attention to useful and intellectually challenging areas of research, and posing problems in a clear and forceful manner. It is not irrelevant in this connection to mention that the consumption function, the accelerator relation, and the "Phillips Curve," were all products of research procedures similar to that espoused by Friedman and Schwartz. By contrast, I cannot recall offhand a single instance in which neo-Walrasian research procedures have yielded *empirical* results of fundamental novelty or importance. Considered from this point of view, the neo-Walrasian approach must probably be adjudged relatively barren.

Of course, procedures that are efficient for formulating problems may or may not be efficient for solving them. As concerns the latter criterion, however, I do not myself see any objective grounds for preferring the strategy of the neo-Walrasians to that of Friedman and Schwartz. It is perhaps more natural to associate modern techniques of econometric research with neo-Walrasian economics; and there can be no doubt about the value of these techniques for evaluating the quantitative significance of regularities discovered by other means. But econometric analysis is hardly a monopoly of the neo-Walrasians.[31]

In the final analysis, the real strengths and weaknesses of the *History* depend not on its authors' research strategy but rather on their inferential tactics. Since my outlook on economics is basically that of a neo-Walrasian (though not, I think, to the point of fanaticism), I should be the last to claim that my appraisal of this aspect of Friedman and Schwartz's book is devoid of bias. Readers may therefore place more than usual credence in my acknowledgement that Friedman and Schwartz's tactical performance is superbly ingenious and effective. This theme merits further elaboration.

Those who view the economic system through neo-Walrasian spectacles will be quick to find fault with such assertions in the *History* as:

. . . the stock of money shows larger fluctuations after 1914 than before 1914 and this is true even if the large wartime increases in the stock of money are excluded. The blind, undesigned, and quasi-automatic working of the gold standard turned out to produce a greater measure of predictability and regularity—perhaps because its discipline was impersonal and inescapable—than did deliberate and conscious control exercised within institutional arrangements intended to promote monetary stability [pp. 9-10];

or,

The monetary collapse [following 1929] was not the inescapable consequence of other forces, but rather a largely independent factor which exerted a powerful influence on the course of events. . . . Prevention or moderation of the decline in the stock of money, let alone the substitution of monetary

[31] However, see Friedman, "Methodology," n. 11, pp. 12-13. For some interesting observations on a related topic, see Polya, *Plausible Inference,* pp. 40-41.

expansion, would have reduced the contraction's severity and almost as certainly its duration. The contraction might still have been relatively severe. But it is hardly conceivable that money income could have declined by over one-half and prices by over one-third in the course of four years if there had been no decline in the stock of money [pp. 300-1];

or, more generally,

While the influence running from money to economic activity has been predominant, there have clearly also been influences running the other way, particularly during the shorter-run movements associated with the business cycle. . . . Changes in the money stock are therefore a consequence as well as an independent source of change in money income and prices, though, once they occur, they produce in their turn still further effects on income and prices. Mutual interaction, but with money rather clearly the senior partner in longer-run movements and in major cyclical movements, and more nearly an equal partner with money income and prices in shorter-run and milder movements—this is the generalization suggested by our evidence [p. 695].

But how does one respond to propositions of this character?

Clearly not by referring to bodies of evidence other than those considered by Friedman and Schwartz, for they have already covered this flank in a prefatory acknowledgment (p. xxii):

A full-scale economic and political history would be required to record at all comprehensively the role of money in the United States in the past century. Needless to say, we have not been so ambitious. Rather, we have kept in the forefront the initial aim: to provide a prologue and background for a [later] statistical analysis of the secular and cyclical behavior of money in the United States, and to exclude any material not relevant to that purpose.

Might one not then respond that to express firm judgments on the basis of such a limited range of evidence is to draw "over-hasty" conclusions? Again the answer must be qualified: first, because most of Friedman and Schwartz's judgments are advanced as "tentative hypotheses"; second, because a glance at the materials actually used to document major analytical themes in the *History* suffices to show that Friedman and Schwartz have spoken disingenuously about "not being so ambitious." Any young historian who managed to display a comparable "lack of ambition" could be certain of immediate professional recognition and renown upon his first venture into print!

Thus one is driven finally to resort to analytical dialectics—to oppose Friedman and Schwartz's judgments by saying that they picture the economic system as "a ship of income afloat on a sea of money." (The simile is not inapt; ocean waves not only influence but are influenced by the motions of a ship, but the ocean is clearly the "senior partner" in long and violent storms.) One can then pour scorn on this view of the world as presupposing that trading is perfectly synchronized in all markets of the economy at every instant of time and that all markets "clear" automatically even over relatively short time intervals. But alas, except that Friedman and Schwartz display a moderate antipathy to

Keynesian economics (see pp. 533-34, 626-27) and nowhere worry seriously about possible direct effects of current market transactions on current demand and supply conditions, this line of argument cannot be sustained either—except by gross prejudice. The *shading* of the argument is in the direction claimed, but the *substance* is not.

I need go no further. My conclusion is that Friedman and Schwartz's conjectures deserve to be taken very seriously indeed. Their book does not pretend to be a definitive account of the monetary experience of the United States (though in fact it comes close to being just that). However, their historical judgments about this history are based on painstaking examination of a fantastically large body of evidence and on thorough, honest, and closely reasoned analysis of its implications. My guess is that subsequent researches, provoked by Friedman and Schwartz's pronouncements, will overturn some of their bolder judgments,[32] but that is another story.

IX

My overall reaction to Friedman and Schwartz's *History* is mixed. Viewed as an intellectual accomplishment, the book has qualities of greatness. The argument is interesting, informative, intricate, and subtle; even a casual reader will recognize the extraordinary keenness of the minds which produced it. Still, the thread of money has strands which even Friedman and Schwartz have no hope of unraveling.

Nor is the volume free of scholarly blemishes. The omission of a detailed bibliography is regrettable, particularly since the authors also fail even to cite such standard works as Hepburn's *History of Currency,* Young's *Analysis of Bank Statistics,* and Harris' *Twenty Years of Federal Reserve Policy.* The book is also marred by a certain flavor of provincialism—cultural and historical as well as technical; this is reflected in the absence from the "Author Index" of such names as Keynes, Robertson, Cassel, Robbins, Wicksell, Giffen, Harrod, and Sayers; a notable dearth of references to specialist works in economic history; and a general absence of what Collingwood would call "historical imagination."[33]

[32] For example, a recent analysis by George Horwich casts serious doubt on the correctness of Friedman and Schwartz's explanation of the persistence of "excess reserves" during the period 1933-39 (*History,* pp. 534 ff.); also on their interpretation of the 1937 contraction (*ibid.* pp. 543-45). See George Horwich, "Effective Reserves, Credit, and Causality in the Banking System of the Thirties," in *Banking and Monetary Studies,* D. Carson, ed. (Homewood, Ill.: D. Irwin, 1963).

In a more general vein, Ando and Modigliani have shown (in a forthcoming paper) that changes in autonomous expenditure, suitably defined, are as closely correlated with changes in income and consumption as are changes in the stock of money, thus casting doubt on the causal significance of the money-income relation on which Friedman and Schwartz place so much emphasis. For background on this, see Friedman and Meiselman, "Monetary Velocity," and Franco Modigliani, "The Monetary Mechanism and Its Interaction with Real Phenomena," *Review of Economics and Statistics,* XLV (Feb. 1963 suppl.), 79-107 (esp. pp. 102 ff.).

[33] R. G. Collingwood, *The Idea of History* (New York: Oxford University Press, 1956), pp. 231 ff.

But the chief faults of the book (from the point of view of a reader) are opacity and lack of direction. These might have been avoided had the authors included an account of the conceptual framework of their argument. The *History* opens with an interesting quotation from Marshall, part of which is pertinent here: ". . . the most reckless and treacherous of all theorists is he who professes to let facts and figures speak for themselves, who keeps in the background the part he has played, perhaps unconsciously, in selecting and grouping them, and in suggesting the argument *post hoc ergo propter hoc*" (*Memorials*, p. 168). Perhaps the most puzzling question posed by the book is: Why did Friedman and Schwartz fail to heed Marshall's implied advice?

The transcendent virtue of the *History* is its unerring vision in searching out important problems and its clear delineation of areas needing further research. The book offers an almost inexhaustible supply of worthwhile conjectures. I have no doubt that it, along with a forthcoming volume on *Trends and Cycles in Economic Activity*, will be the focus of a major share of scholarly research on money and income during the coming decade. For this, if for no other reason, the book must be counted a monumental contribution to positive economics.

ROBERT W. CLOWER, *Northwestern University*

[4]

Snarks, Quarks, and Other Fictions

ROBERT W. CLOWER

University of California, Los Angeles

He had bought a large map representing the sea,
Without the least vestige of land:
And the crew were much pleased when they found it to be
A map they could all understand.

"What's the good of Mercator's North Poles and Equators,
Tropics, Zones, and Meridian Lines?"
So the Bellman would cry: and the crew would reply
"They are merely conventional signs!

"Other maps are such shapes, with their islands and capes!
But we've got our brave Captain to thank"
(So the crew would protest) "that he's brought us the best—
A perfect and absolute blank!"

LEWIS CARROLL, *The Hunting of the Snark*

As an economic theorist, I have long been accustomed to view history in general—and economic history in particular—as an oasis of intellectual renewal in the desert of abstractions that is my normal working habitat. In recent years, however, I have felt a certain unease in the oasis, following the intrusion of large numbers of academic bedouins who not only gabble incessantly and muddy the local springs but also trail sand across the grass—"to make the place look more homey," as they put it. It is easy to see what the oasis has

to offer the bedouins, but what have the bedouins to offer the oasis?
Or to drop the mask of allegory, what has the economic theorist got
to offer the economic historian?

This is not the kind of question that admits of a final answer; it
is more the sort of question one asks when he feels the urge to assert a
position. The position that I wish to assert is fairly conventional:
that the proper relation between economic history and economic
theory—like that between two blind men in search of a bar—is one
of mutual support rather than unilateral guidance. But my reasons
for adopting this position are somewhat unconventional, and that is
what my essay is really about.

I

The attitude of leading economic historians towards economic
theory has been expressed most judiciously, I think, by J. R. T.
Hughes:

> Much has been done in recent years to aid the understanding of eco-
> nomic processes by empirical research in economic history which
> utilizes recent advances in the training of economists. Much could be
> lost, however, if the "new" economic historian failed to mind the
> dictum that in the end, the historian must remain true to the facts. This
> is not an excuse for unimaginative work in economic history, work
> which is not at all informed by theoretical insight. But it is a constraint
> placed by expectations of non-historians upon historians that they, like
> others, should try to pursue truth for its own sake. "No holds barred" as
> a rule of technique is a good rule in the pursuit of truth. Clio is unkind
> to those who confuse ends and means in the pursuit of historical under-
> standing.[1]

On this view, there is no particular reason to doubt that economic
history might be strengthened if its practitioners drew more heavily
on conceptual experiments and modes of analysis suggested by economic theory. With little if any change in perspective, however, one
might find grounds for suspecting that things would work out rather
badly.

The problem at issue is closely analogous to that of deciding
what role mathematics should play in economic theory. The use of
mathematics is no guarantee of good work, and good work can be
produced without using any mathematics at all. Indeed, I should
argue that the law relating quality of mathematical and subject

matter inputs to quality of final output is multiplicative rather than additive; e.g., first-rate economics combined with second-rate mathematics yields second-rate results, second-rate economics combined with second-rate mathematics yields fourth-rate results, and so forth. Applying the same law to the use of economic theory in economic history, we should conclude that no theory is better than bad theory and that second-rate economic history is best left alone.

The inference to be drawn from this is simply that borrowing from other fields can be dangerous. First-rate economic history, like first-rate physics or economics, is unlikely to be produced except by scholars who have immersed themselves in subject matter problems. In general, this will entail quite a lot of serious work in other disciplines. As far as economic history is concerned, however, it is hard to imagine any case for assigning a special role to economic theory that could not be made to apply with equal force to numerous other disciplines. At best, therefore, I see economic theory as one of many subjects that might be expected to play a supporting role in economic history. As a specialist in economic theory, however, I have special misgivings about the probable usefulness of contemporary economic theory even in this role, for it seems to me that the explanatory potential of established economic theory is by no means as great as many outsiders (and not a few insiders) are inclined to suppose.

II

It is not uncommon for economic theorists to assert (or at least insinuate) that the scope of formal economic analysis is limited only by the finiteness of the universe and the genius of economic theorists. Such assertions may contain a grain of philosophical truth, but they are utterly factitious in relation to contemporary practice. In truth, the view of individual and social behavior implicit in established "institutionless" economic theory resembles nothing so much as a worm's view of a fishing expedition—as seen from a can. Advanced economic theory is too arid as well as too abstract to be of any interest or use to an economic historian. Much of the material in elementary economics courses derives from an earlier and less formal tradition, so its relevance is considerable; but its level of sophistication hardly justifies calling it "theory." Between the one extreme and the other lies a vast expanse of unexplored territory that would almost certainly interest the economic historian if he could but discover a path into it. Perhaps a path will one day be found; but if it is, the discovery is more likely to be a result of economic theorists having learned something from economic historians than the other way around.

This brings me to the theme suggested by the headnote to my essay. Besides providing a map, the leader of Carroll's band of Snark hunters furnished his men with a description of their prey: meager and hollow to taste, with a flavor of Will-o'-the-Wisp; slow to take a jest, and no lover of puns; a late riser and erratic eater; a lover of bathing machines; highly ambitious; available in three varieties—those with feathers (who bite), those with whiskers (who scratch), and those that no man has lived to describe (who must be simply horrible!). What has all this to do with economic theory? Regrettably, only too much. It is a fine line, at best, that separates Carroll's description of "warranted genuine" Snarks from the economic theorist's description of "warranted genuine" economic entities—households, firms, labor, capital, money, land, and so forth. As for the Snark-hunters' map—a perfect and absolute blank—it would be hard to provide a more apt description of formal economic theory.

If this comment seems harsh, that is how it is intended—at least insofar as formal theory purports to furnish techniques for describing observable economic experience. I am not asserting that formal theory is inherently useless, for that is not at all what I believe. Rather I am asserting that its usefulness, if any, depends in an essential way on the provision of what might be described as "gearing assumptions" that would lend empirical content to the factually vacuous propositions that constitute its current stock in trade. In this respect, there is no great difference between economic theory and, say, hydrodynamic theory—except that modern hydrodynamicists have supplied relevant gearing assumptions to link "actual" with "ideal" fluids, whereas modern economists have so far been content to dispense with such "complications."

Some examples may be in order at this point. There is a vast literature on monetary economics, and that of three varieties: one is descriptive, and puzzling; another is theoretical, and baffling; a third is concerned with policy, and confusing. Curious though it may seem, the main body of established theory precludes explicit recognition, much less meaningful analysis, of the properties of an economy in which one or more commodities serve a special function as exchange intermediaries.[2] There is even some question whether established theory is capable of describing actual, as contrasted with virtual, processes of market exchange,[3] for the institutional presuppositions on which it rests furnish no hint of what happens after rates of exchange that would serve to clear all markets have somehow been established. In effect, the theory is simply too featureless to support serious analysis of ongoing processes of monetary exchange.

These shortcomings no doubt could be overcome, but only by altering the conceptual foundations of established theory. As matters stand, discussions of monetary policy are necessarily confused because no one can be quite sure what anyone else is talking about. Descriptive discussions of monetary phenomena, historical and otherwise, are correspondingly puzzling because it is never clear how one aspect of experience relates to another. Starting from an essentially *ad hoc* conception of a monetary economy, for example, Friedman and Schwartz have no trouble concluding that the great Depression following 1929 was a result of misbehavior on the part of central bankers.[4] This conclusion—like the argument supporting it—is superficial. The real problem is to account for the apparent failure of the economic system to coordinate the trading plans of individual economic agents. The behavior of the banking system is symptomatic of this failure, but not its cause. That the economic system is not free of coordination problems even in the absence of central banking mistakes becomes evident if one compares the years following 1873 with those following 1929. Apparently the same problems of flawed coordination have plagued the economic system more or less continuously in modern times; but one would hardly get this impression from reading contemporary theory because it does not furnish the tools that would permit serious discussion of such problems.

A more general indication of the vacuousness of economic theory is provided by the wonder with which economists view each new episode of economic history. A recent example has to do with the coexistence of unemployment and inflation, which many theorists seem to think is a peculiar feature of the past few years. A look at the data for the years 1933–1938 would dispel this illusion. A closer look might even lend economic theorists enough sense of historical perspective to make them wonder about the adequacy of their conceptual apparatus.

Other examples of the intellectual poverty of economic theory are provided by the literature on economic growth. The most curious feature of the theoretical portion of this literature is its studied neglect of any but ballistic aspects of the problem. Given certain technological conditions (capital-output ratios, investment-output ratios, etc.) and given certain initial conditions (usually the rate of

growth of the labor force), aggregate output follows a trajectory that
is as inevitable (and economically as uninteresting) as that of a 12-
inch shell fired from a naval cannon. All the same, some of these
ideas have slipped into otherwise promising attempts to describe historical growth processes.

I refer specifically to attempts to account for the outwardly different growth histories of the U.S. and Great Britain in terms of relative capital-labor ratios and corresponding relative scarcities of capital and labor.[5] Apart from the fact that no clear meaning can be attached to the terms *labor* and *capital*, it is not evident that these
magnitudes have any direct bearing on the question even in principle. Surely the real problem is not to catalog the characteristics of
economies that have already become differentiated, but rather to account for the emergence of differentiation in the first place. Why
have some economies suddenly started to grow more rapidly than
others, when at an earlier stage there were no obvious differences in
resource availability or technological knowledge? Unfortunately, the
structure of conventional economic theory has discouraged
economists from even asking questions of this kind.

The reader will have no difficulty supplying further examples in
which restricted vision, associated with the uncritical use of standard
economic theory, has inhibited the imaginative analysis of real
problems; the bedouins of economic theory have left their tracks all
over the professional economic history journals in recent years. To be
fair to the bedouins, it must be said that those who have entered the
historian's realm more as residents than as tourists have generally
behaved rather well. As for the others, it might be argued that their
presence has served to liven up the place. On balance, however, I
doubt if economic history has been helped more than harmed by the
intrusion of these strangers.

III

It is interesting to speculate on the factors that have induced
economic historians to suppose that their discipline might benefit
from greater reliance on formal economic theory. The first explanation that comes to mind would treat the economic historian as a
drowning man clutching at a straw. Economic history, after all, is a
thoroughly messy subject—easily as complicated, slippery, and resistant to conceptual analysis as the toughest parts of sociology or politics. By comparison, economic theory looks—and is—simple, solid,

and analytically tractable. Perhaps the economic historian grasps at economic theory much as the economic theorist, in turn, grasps at mathematics.

A more subtle explanation would treat the economic historian as a man with an inferiority complex who attempts to raise his perceived status by adopting the speech and manners of his superiors. There is probably something in this, for the phenomenon is fairly universal. Harry Johnson once enunciated a Principle of Social Intransitivity, to the effect that each man has good reason to consider himself better than other people. An immediate corollary is that each man has good reason to consider himself inferior to other people. The corollary would explain why physicists occasionally add literary headnotes to their technical papers, why mathematicians occasionally insist that their work is useful as well as fun, why political scientists and sociologists do so much computer-linked research, and indeed, why economic historians do not always shun the company of economic theorists.

A third and really very crude explanation—but one that I am inclined to favor—would treat the economic historian as a man who is prone to the affliction known as "misplacement of concreteness." This affliction manifests itself in an overwhelming urge to explain the inexplicable by giving it a name. Perhaps the classic example is the early medical explanation of the sleep-inducing properties of opium, which consisted in nothing more than calling opium "a soporific." Were it not for this affliction, few religions would prosper, and fewer psychiatrists would manage to make a living. But the affliction is not limited to the humanities and soft sciences. In 1962 the distinguished theoretical physicist Gell-Mann suggested (perhaps somewhat facetiously) that certain anomalous results in high energy physics might be attributable to the existence of strange particles called *quarks* (a name suggested to him by a passage in James Joyce's *Finnegan's Wake*). Whether Gell-Mann himself ever believed in quarks is an open question, but the subsequent history of quark hunting by leading physicists throughout the world leaves no room for doubt about the beliefs of many of his professional colleagues. After five years, during which no one managed to get so much as a sniff of the elusive beasts, the physicist P. G. O. Freund effectively halted the hunt by writing a paper on "The Quark Model" in which he commented as follows:

The quark model has been a major source of meaning for numerous questions that have been raised in hadron physics over the last five years. Satisfactory answers to old questions are also provided by the quark model. This is really quite remarkable, as we know very little about the quarks themselves. We don't know whether there should be three or nine quarks, whether their electric charge should be integral or fractional, whether they carry magnetic charge, whether they are fermions or parafermions, whether they are light or heavy and ultimately whether quarks exist. For reasons that are not too well understood, the predictions of the quark model . . . do not depend on the answer to any of these questions except of course on the existence of quarks. As it turns out, essentially all quark model results . . . can be replicated using only standard dynamical and symmetry arguments, without any reference to quarks. The existence problem is thus circumvented.[6]

I suspect that numerous economic concepts—most of which have names that call forth all kinds of intuitively satisfying associations of familiarity—have found favor among economic historians for no better reasons than those that made quarks popular with many physicists. It is, of course, misguided to confuse emotional comfort with intellectual satisfaction, but that does not prevent the confusion from occurring; it merely inhibits effective solution of real problems.[7] I think that precisely such inhibiting influences have resulted from modern incursions of economic theory into economic history.

IV

Let me now attempt to draw some kind of point from the main threads of the preceding argument. Some historians and many philosophers have argued that historical explanation differs in essential respects from scientific explanation. Some philosophers and many historians have urged a precisely contrary view. The perplexed reader of these mutually opposing arguments may be pardoned for concluding that neither party has quite hit upon the truth. The same reader might also be pardoned for suspecting that both parties have got something wrong. Such, at least, is my suspicion.

What I think is wrong is the presupposition that there exist different kinds of explanation—scientific, historical, religious, etc. It seems to me that all communicable knowledge rests in the final analysis upon persuasive rather than demonstrative argument. This fits very well with popular conceptions of literary history and other humanist disciplines, but not at all well with popular conceptions of mathematics and the hard sciences.

If one delves into the foundations of mathematics, it soon becomes apparent that the essential basis for all of it consists in certain elementary combinatorial propositions about finite sets, the truth of which we are persuaded to believe by the evidence of our senses. The great majority of mathematical propositions are concerned, however, not with finite but with infinite sets, and our only ground for supposing that these propositions are valid is that we already believe in the truth of analogous propositions for finite sets. In effect, mathematics constitutes a single and highly persuasive story about the interesting things that would be true if certain other undemonstrable propositions were themselves true.

The primacy of persuasive argument is less easily recognized in the hard sciences, in part because most hard scientists are so anxious to deny it. As N. R. Campbell has observed:

> Their training ... has impressed on them so firmly that ... everything that can possibly be a matter of personal opinion must be excluded, that they are afraid to admit that anything can properly form part of their study which involves deliberate, though often unconscious, choice.[8]

As T. S. Kuhn[9] and other historians of science have shown, however, it is only in the activities of "normal science"—the elaboration and refinement of established scientific paradigms—that demonstrative modes of argument reign supreme. Matters look entirely different when we consider the major scientific upheavals associated with the names of such men as Copernicus, Galileo, Newton, and Einstein. The seminal ideas of these men were developed and presented within the context of informal explanation sketches, analogous in important respects to the scene-setting prologues that are so common a feature of narrative history. This is not to say that demonstrative forms of argument have played an insignificant role in scientific revolutions, for that would be incorrect. Among other things, such modes of analysis have been invaluable for discovering paradoxes and contradictions in established doctrine, thereby facilitating early recognition of needed modifications in prevailing theories. In all cases of which I am aware, however, background ideas rather than technical expertise have been the prime movers in scientific revolutions. Demonstrative forms of argument have been the chief tools of the men who have elaborated scientific superstructures, but the foundations of the sciences have been set out by men whose talents were primarily those of skillful tellers of fairytales.

Why is the role of narrative and persuasive skills so transparent in economic history and so opaque in mathematics and the hard sciences? The answer lies, I believe, in the fact that economic history is in a more or less constant state of intellectual ferment for lack of any established explanatory paradigm. In effect, every economic historian has to proceed as if he were the Copernicus or Newton of his subject, for he has no actual Copernicus or Newton on which to lean. If every writer of a college text on differential equations or theoretical physics had to begin by explaining and rationalizing his conception of the universe, as is only too often the situation in economic history, we should soon hear a good deal less about the "unscientific" methods of economic history. Most hard scientists and mathematicians are what Keynes would describe as "humble, competent men—on a level with dentists." Their tools of argument and analysis are correspondingly utilitarian and not at all the same as those of the great innovators within their fields. Most economic historians are similarly "humble and competent" types, but their rhetoric is hardly distinguishable from that of the most creative historical writers.

What does all this imply about the nature of historical explanation? Surely not that it relies more heavily on narrative skill than do other supposed forms of explanation—merely that the role of narrative skill in historical research is open rather than disguised. But if this be true, then there is no excuse for economic historians to clutch at the straws provided by other disciplines, to adopt even an unconsciously servile posture in relation to other subjects, or to seek refuge from ignorance in the mindless incantation of familiar sounds. The task of the economic historian is to tell a good story well. If he manages to do just that, then he has done as much as has ever been done by the most creative of thinkers in other fields.

V

Looking back over what I have written, I am reminded of G. H. Hardy's melancholic animadversions on those who write about rather than contribute to a subject: "there is no scorn more profound, or on the whole more justifiable, than that of the men who make for the men who explain. Exposition, criticism, appreciation is work for second-rate minds."[10] Personally, I do not share Hardy's view (which, incidentally, is refuted by his own example); but I think I know why he voiced it. When one writes *about* a subject, one is forced to proceed on the basis of generalities that admit, at best, of persuasive assertion, never of compelling documentation. The result is an argument that, by its nature, strikes its author as disquietingly vague, discouragingly incomplete, and annoyingly pompous. The problem is not that one feels himself to have done something that is fit only for second-rate minds, but rather that one has somehow managed to provide at most a third-rate account of a first-rate problem.

The message I have tried to convey is very simple. I have argued that the essential art of the economic historian, like that of any other creative scholar, is to produce what writers of fiction would call "a damned good yarn." That critical and imaginative use of tools supplied by other disciplines might assist economic historians in this work, I should be the first to agree. That any special reliance can or should be placed on contemporary economic theory, however, seems to me a sentiment open to doubt. To the question, "What has the economic theorist got to offer the economic historian?" therefore, my answer is quite unequivocal, namely, "Nothing in particular, and little in general that the historian cannot better supply for himself." To this I should add that what constitutes a "good yarn" in economic history is best decided by economic historians on the basis of their own criteria of intellectual merit, not by self-appointed experts from other fields whose own subject matter problems are as numerous, as perplexing, and as far from solution as those of the men whom they presume to instruct. Economic historians have their faults, but lack of zeal and aptitude for self-criticism is certainly not among them.

NOTES

Helpful discussions with Peter Howitt, Clayburn Laforce, Axel Leijonhufvud, and Joseph Ostroy are gratefully acknowledged. Not all of the sins committed in this essay are intentional, but all are mine.

1. J. R. T. Hughes, "Fact and Theory in Economic History," in *The New Economic History*, ed. R. L. Andreano (New York: Wiley, 1970), p. 62, Cf. R. W. Clower, "Monetary History and Positive Economics," *Journal of Economic History*, 24 (September 1964), 374–76.

2. R. W. Clower, "Theoretical Foundations of Monetary Policy," in *Monetary Theory and Monetary Policy in the 1970's*, ed. G. Clayton, J. C. Gilbert, and R. Sedgwick (London: Oxford University Press, 1971), pp. 15–17.

3. E. C. H. Veendorp, "General Equilibrium Theory for a Barter Economy," *Western Economic Journal*, 8 (March 1970), 1–3, 21–22.

4. M. Friedman and A. J. Schwartz, *A Monetary History of the United States, 1867–1960*, National Bureau of Economic Research (Princeton: Princeton University Press, 1963), pp. 300–01.

5. For references, see L. E. Davis, " 'And It Will Never Be Literature,' The New Economic History: A Critique," *The New Economic History*, pp. 78–80.

6. P. G. O. Freund, "The Quark Model," *Proceedings of the Boulder Conference on High Energy Physics*, 1969 (Boulder: Colorado Associated Universities Press, mimeographed), p. 565.

7. That there may be important exceptions to this rule is indicated by the apparent successes that microphysicists have achieved by using what are essentially quark-hunting methods of research. See, e.g., N. R. Hanson, *The Concept of the Positron* (Cambridge: Cambridge University Press, 1963). There is widespread dissatisfaction with these methods, however, even among microphysicists. For an account of some of the problems involved, see P. K. Feyerabend, "Problems of Microphysics," in *Frontiers of Science and Philosophy*, ed. R. C. Colodny (Pittsburgh: University of Pittsburgh Press, 1962), pp. 232 ff.

8. N. R. Campbell, *Foundations of Science* (New York: Dover Books, 1957), p. 224.

9. T. S. Kuhn, *The Structure of Scientific Revolutions* (Chicago: University of Chicago Press, 1962).

10. G. H. Hardy, *A Mathematician's Apology* (Cambridge: Cambridge University Press, 1967), p. 61.

[5]

Mathematics and Economics: The Contemporary Prospect*

Robert Clower

The use of mathematics in economics has a long and reasonably honorable history. From the beginning, the question whether pure mathematics should be allowed to play a prominent role in economic inquiry has lingered rather ominously in the background, raising doubts in the minds even of writers who have made important contributions to the basic literature of mathematical economics.[1] However, events in recent years have relegated this particular question to the limbo of academic curiosities. The issue is still debated by students, and it continues to concern many professional economists; but for all practical purposes the question has been answered vigorously and in the affirmative by the appearance in the professional journals of an ever larger number of articles that make use of mathematical symbolism and mathematical ideas.

Under the circumstances, it is rather pointless to discuss the role which mathematics ought or ought not to play in economics. This will be decided on the basis of researches by economists who use mathematics, not by philosophical polemics that condemn the results of entire classes of inquiry even before their results are known. On the other hand, it is not entirely pointless to discuss present realities, the role that mathematics actually does play in contemporary economic analysis, in an attempt to evaluate more or less objectively some of the more important practical consequences of the increasingly quantitative orientation of modern research. Such is the purpose of this paper. Whether we as individuals regard contemporary developments with rapture or regret is largely beside the point. The fact that mathematics is being used in economics to an ever increasing extent is beyond dispute, and the probable consequences of this fact for the future of our discipline merit serious attention accordingly.

BACKGROUND

Viewed in historical perspective, the present situation of economics is a natural by-product of the gradual emancipation

---

* I have to thank my colleagues at Northwestern, graduate students as well as faculty, for many helpful comments and criticisms. The views expressed in this paper are mine alone, however; they do not reflect either the policy of the department which I represent or the consensus of opinion among its members.

[1] See, for example, the preface to the first edition of Marshall's *Principles* (reprinted in all succeeding editions), and Keynes's *General Theory*, pp. 297-98.

37

of the science from its original status as a handmaiden of moral philosophy. The older tradition, which flowered for probably the last time in the work of Marshall, was motivated only indirectly by scientific curiosity. The desire to do good, to educate businessmen, politicians, and the general public in the virtues of free enterprise, the urge to reshape economic institutions in the image of an almost religious vision of the rational society: these were initially the primary goals of economic study. The idea of an empirical science of economics similar in structure to such disciplines as astronomy and mechanics is not altogether absent from the classical tradition, but it does not play a major role in the work of any leading economist until relatively recent times. The precursors of modern economics — writers such as Cournot, Walras, Jevons, Pareto, and Wicksell — although respected by their contemporaries, are honored far more at present and for different reasons than by their own generations.

This does not mean that the older tradition is dead. The capacity of economics to generate moral fervor in the hearts of its devotees is still one of its more prominent and, on the whole, more desirable features. In recent years, however, more and more ethical and logical preconceptions have been brought into the open and subjected to critical examination, and active empirical research has brought about a correspondingly rapid narrowing of whatever areas of economics were once reserved for "eternal truths." If Smith, Ricardo, and Mill were alive today, they would almost certainly be able to follow and appreciate most of the modern literature, and they probably would not be acutely uncomfortable in the presence of their contemporary colleagues. But they would surely be astonished at the turn the science has taken in the direction of mathematical economics and econometrics.

CONTEMPORARY METHODOLOGY OF POSITIVE ECONOMICS

The break with the older tradition is apparent in the prevailing attitude of economists toward economic theory. The accepted philosophy is essentially the same as that of the physical sciences, due allowance being made for differences in detail that arise from differences in subject matter. The existence of certain uniform, albeit highly complicated, relations among measurable phenomena is taken as a point of departure. Nothing definite is supposed to be known about the "true" nature of these relations. Like African tribesmen confronted with a piece of complicated machinery, we are able to detect only the outward signs of the working of inner forces; the underlying mechanism is hidden from sight and might be unintelligible even if it were open to observation. In an attempt to make sense of this chaos of sense impressions, to organize our ideas about objects and events in the real world, we postulate the existence of various imaginary entities, endow them with hypothetical properties, and then deduce by accepted logical procedures the existence of relations among these imaginary objects which would hold *if* reality truly conformed to this particular mental conception of it. If magnitudes described by such a logical system are then identified with measurable properties of observed phenomena, we obtain a concrete interpretation of the logical system, and the system so interpreted is said to constitute a theory of the particular collection of data and relations to which it refers. Finally, if relations among the quantities described in the theory are discovered to hold, within some allowable margin of error, for relations among corresponding measures of observable phenomena, the theory is said to *explain* these phenomena.[2]

On this view, *accurate prediction of observed events is the ultimate criterion of a satisfactory theory,* and empirical relevance becomes an absolute prerequisite of "good" economics. To discover whether the conclusions of a theory are in satisfactory accord with factual knowledge, however, it is first necessary to be sure that the theory itself is internally consistent and logically unambiguous; otherwise there is nothing to test. To state the matter another way, it is essential to distinguish sharply among the casual empirical background, the formal logical content, and the concrete applications of economic theory, and to recognize that there are no definite rules of procedure for linking together these three aspects of theoretical analysis. If intuitive, logical, and factual considerations are mixed together indiscriminately, as is fairly common both in traditional theory and in contemporary literary and mathematical economics, the results can hardly be anything but confused and confusing. To be sure, the practice is sometimes justified on the ground that "it is better to be vaguely

[2] See Milton Friedman, "The Methodology of Positive Economics," in *Essays in Positive Economics* (Chicago: Chicago University Press, 1953), pp. 1-43; T. C. Koopmans, *Three Essays on the State of Economic Science* (New York: McGraw-Hill, 1957), pp. 129-48; A. G. Papandreou, *Economics as a Science* (Philadelphia: Lippincott, 1958). Better and more concise statements of essentially the same point of view are available in writings by noneconomists; see, for instance, W. Feller, *Introduction to Probability Theory and Its Applications* (2nd ed.; New York: Wiley, 1957), pp. 1-6; G. Y. Rainich, *Mathematics of Relativity* (New York: Wiley, 1950), p. 169; M. Richardson, *Fundamentals of Mathematics* (Rev. ed.; New York: Macmillan, 1958), pp. 33-38.

right than precisely wrong."[3] There may be something to this since a precise theory can only be wrong if it is logically inconsistent, and an inconsistent theory is certainly useless. On the other hand, what is vaguely right is thoroughly equivocal and an equivocal theory is, by its very nature, exempt from serious factual or logical criticism. This is not to say that such a theory is necessarily senseless, mistaken, or even devoid of meaning; precisely the contrary *might* be true. Such an issue can hardly be decided until the equivocations of the theory have been removed and its precise formal implications unearthed. The virtue of precision in a theory is, or ought to be, to facilitate the disposal of theoretical rubbish.

RATIONALE OF MATHEMATICAL ECONOMICS

We come now to what is perhaps the most significant feature of current practice among mathematical economists. *Contrary to popular belief, the work of mathematical economists is not essentially different from that of any good literary economist; for it does not involve the adoption of specific problem-solving techniques so much as the application to economics of systematic methods of logical analysis.*

To appreciate more fully what this entails, we may recall that most of the traditional doctrines of mathematics — and the calculus in particular — were developed originally with no real attempt to reduce the fundamentals to a simple collection of axioms. Prior to the present century, a mixture of logic and intuition was the

[3] Compare K. W. Rothchild, "Price Theory and Oligopoly," *Economic Journal*, Vol. 57 (1947), p. 320, reprinted in *A.E.A. Readings in Price Theory* (Homewood: Irwin, 1952), pp. 440-64.

accepted means of developing theorems and this led to difficulties in pure mathematics similar to those which some people now regard as a peculiar affliction of economics, namely, ambiguity, confusion, and consequent distrust of the validity of theoretical results.[4]

This led around the turn of the last century to the development within mathematics of a technique of theory construction specifically designed to guarantee that the basic elements of a logical system were displayed so as to preclude unconscious leaps of the imagination being substituted for acknowledged rules of logic. This technique, now referred to as the *axiomatic method,* is the ultimate standard by which most mathematical economists would judge the adequacy of economic theories. It is also one of the more important sources of inspiration for current research in formal economic theory.[5]

The essence of the axiomatic method is to recognize at the outset of any analysis that certain basic concepts cannot and need not be defined in terms of more elementary notions. Thus, the supposed "definition" of a *point* in geometry as "that which has neither width nor length" is regarded as a picturesque description, rather than a definition in the strict sense. After all, a geometrical point lacks many things besides extension: color, smell, capacity for thought, a happy home life, and so forth. More generally, any word or phrase which has been defined in a strict sense can always be replaced by its defining term; so if all words could be so

defined, then all words could be dispensed with! One is forced to conclude that certain basic words must always remain undefined; that the "meaning" of at least some terms in any analysis must be left to be inferred from the context in which they appear.

Once this basic principle is accepted, it does not matter if words that are used to refer to undefined concepts have intuitive associations for the persons who use them or if different persons have different associations. In adopting the axiomatic method of argument, all such associations are carefully eliminated in actual analysis by simply refusing to know anything at all about undefined concepts except what is explicitly asserted in various initial postulates. Although the undefined concepts thus have no meaning in and of themselves, the postulates impart to them certain generalized "meanings" in terms of permissible mutual interrelationships. That is to say, the set of initial postulates will normally admit of one or more concrete interpretations of the undefined concepts but will firmly and finally exclude certain other interpretations.

Of course, there is nothing in the axiomatic method that guarantees practical usefulness to its results. In the case of pure mathematics, however, the fruitfulness of the axiomatic method has been nothing short of startling; and the informal use of similar procedures in physics, biology, and other sciences has also been highly successful.[6] Among other things, the technique permits an imposing superstructure of propositions to be erected on a very

[4] For further details, see R. B. Kershner and L. R. Wilcox, *The Anatomy of Mathematics* (New York: Ronald, 1950), Ch. 3, particularly pp. 25-27.

[5] See Koopmans, *op. cit.;* G. Debreu, *Theory of Value,* Cowles Foundation for Research in Economics, Monograph 17 (New York: Wiley, 1959), pp. vii-viii.

[6] See J. L. Synge, *Science: Sense and Nonsense* (New York: Harcourt, no date); W. Feller, *op cit.,* Introduction; J. H. Woodger, *The Axiomatic Method in Biology* (Cambridge: Cambridge University Press, 1937); P. Suppes, *Introduction to Logic* (New York: Van Nostrand, 1957), pp. 274-304.

narrow foundation; and because the foundation is explicit, it can be stripped of virtually all ambiguities and made correspondingly amenable to precise communication and criticism.[7] Thus, it is not surprising that economic theorists have been encouraged consciously or unconsciously to make use of axiomatic techniques in economic analysis. This has occurred in an obvious way only in a few areas — notably the theory of consumer behavior and the pure theory of exchange equilibrium[8] — but the point of view adopted in these areas has profoundly influenced theoretical activity in every other branch of economics.

MATHEMATICAL ECONOMICS AND THE LITERARY TRADITION

By its very nature, the axiomatic method is directly applicable only to the formal logical features of a theory. As concerns the selection of basic concepts and the formulation of postulates, intuition necessarily reigns supreme. So far as practical applications are concerned, moreover, there can be no effective substitute for broad experience and solid common sense. Even if an "axiomatic revolution" had already occurred in economics, *these* things would not be changed. Granted that such a "revolution" is now in progress, however, we may draw certain plausible inferences.

In the first place, the "revolution" will be gradual, and the "takeoff," if any, will be delayed for some time, for the construction of fruitful axiom systems in an empirical science necessarily goes hand in hand with the creation of an established body of factual knowledge. Regarded as a preliminary to the development of more efficient procedures of empirical research, moreover, the "revolution" might well turn out to be abortive. What has to be feared is that economic axiomatics may prove so intriguing in its own right that we will never proceed to the point of practical applications; that axiomatics, regarded as a means to the development of a secure theoretical foundation for economic science, will be confused with economic science itself, leading, as Theil has put it, to "the unlimited postulation of irrelevant truth."[9] This is undoubtedly the basis of much of the present distrust of mathematical economists, econometricians, and their work. For as every literary economist knows, and as more than a few mathematical economists have discovered to their sorrow, it is much easier to invent a logically precise model to describe almost any imaginary economic system than to formulate a logically loose model to describe even the simplest concrete situation.

There lies the rub. How much easier to solve imaginary estimation problems than to invent and test a precise theoretical description of some aspect of reality. How much simpler to prove that Marshall must have been the second of two candidates when he won second place in the Cambridge Mathematics Tripos than to carry out a systematic study of the shortcomings of contemporary empirical research. How much nicer, indeed, to discuss the existence and stability of equilibrium under hypothetical competitive conditions than to propose a usable theory of actual commodity markets. Not

[7] For outstandingly clear accounts of the axiomatic method, see R. L. Wilder, *The Foundations of Mathematics* (New York: Wiley, 1952), Ch. 1; and Kershner and Wilcox, *op. cit.*, Chs. 1-6.

[8] Outstanding contributors to this area of economics include Arrow, Debreu, Hahn, Houthakker, Hurwicz, Koopmans, McKenzie, Samuelson, Uzawa, and Wald. For explicit references, see Debreu, *op. cit.*, pp. 103-7.

[9] H. Theil, *Economic Forecasts and Policy* (Amsterdam: North Holland, 1958), p. 4.

that mathematical economists do not concern themselves with practical problems; many do. It has been suggested, however, that the problem of greatest practical significance to the "modal" mathematical economist is the problem of "publish or perish."

If we are seeking grounds for present complaints about the practice of mathematical economists, our search might well begin with a catalogue of potential abuses of the axiomatic method as applied to an empirical science. However, it would be foolish to suppose either that mathematical economists are unaware of these dangers or that mathematical economists are any less concerned than so-called literary economists with the advancement of economics as an applied science. Neither is there any reason to suppose that mathematical economists are less well equipped than their literary brethren for systematic empirical research. This particular line of attack is thus less promising than it looks at first sight.

The root cause of whatever friction exists between mathematical and literary economists is perhaps more easily traceable to the fact that mathematical economists display occasional disdain for the work of their literary predecessors. If literary economists seem to be the main target of critical attacks by mathematical economists, however, that is probably because most of what is both good and bad in modern theory was originally conceived within the literary tradition. Indeed, judging by the extent to which mathematical economists draw their basic hypotheses from received doctrine, it would not be inappropriate to argue that they are, if anything, too diffident toward traditional theory and excessively slow to develop ideas of their own. At the same time, their sharp and sometimes niggling criticisms of

confusions in earlier thought have often appeared to represent a kind of intellectual arrogance, and this may be counted a sin in its own right. The real trouble, however, is surely that mathematical economists and literary economists do not always speak the same language and so communicate rather imperfectly when they communicate at all. Apart from this, the two camps seem to have nothing of substance to quarrel about.

The main burden of the preceding argument is that the advancement of economics as an empirical science requires that its foundations be absolutely secure. This can be accomplished only by distinguishing clearly between logic, intuition, and applications in economic analysis, for only in this way can confusion be avoided between wishful thinking and disciplined analysis. *In principle,* there is no reason why the use of mathematics should be essential for this purpose; systematic thought is presumably systematic thought regardless of the language used to express it. *In practice,* however, ordinary language does not suffice for the development and communication of precise ideas. There would be no end of confusion if legal contracts were written in the language of the man in the street. Historical scholarship could hardly exist if Basic English were the only medium of communication. Statistical analysis would be an impossibly difficult business if the use of symbolic expressions were forbidden. Logic itself — of which mathematics might be considered a special branch — would hardly have progressed beyond the stage at which Aristotle left it were it not for the systematic creation and use of symbolic techniques of expression.

There is no need to pursue the matter further. Logically, an empirical science does not entail the formal or informal use of the axiomatic method; logically, mathematics does not entail the use of abstract symbols. But the practical desirability of linking science with axiomatics, axiomatics with mathematics, and mathematics with abstract symbolism is not open to serious question in this day and age. Issues of "more or less" still arise from time to time, but few people would now be prepared to oppose, on grounds of principle, the use of mathematics in any science.

Even if there is no general opposition to the use of mathematics in economics, we may still expect objections, and strong objections at that, to precise statements of economic theories in which form is confused with substance. This kind of confusion is perhaps more likely to occur in mathematical than in literary analysis, but literary models may suffer from the same defect. What is truly significant in this connection is that, whether a theory is expressed in literary or in mathematical form, persons who are specially equipped to deal with symbolic arguments are likely to be in the best position to appraise its logical validity and potential empirical applications. Ultimately, therefore, the "policing" of economic science — the establishment of minimal standards of professional competence and empirical relevance — is likely to be done by persons who are well versed in the use of mathematics. Indeed, there are obvious tendencies working in this direction at the present time, the strength of which may be expected to increase substantially in the years to come. This will naturally carry with it forces making for even greater use of mathematics in applied and theoretical economic research.

PROBLEMS AND PROSPECTS

The probable consequences of this development are not difficult to foresee.

Already we are beginning to experience important changes of emphasis in teaching and research within the traditional fields of economics. Labor economics, public finance, international trade, economic development, industrial organization, and even the history of economic thought are more and more concerned with problems of theory construction, quantitative measurement, forecasting techniques, and related issues. Courses in elementary statistics are being expanded into sequences of courses leading up to full-scale treatments of econometric theory and practice. Courses in economic theory are being augmented by courses in mathematical economics, activity analysis, linear programming, the theory of games, and so forth.

If this process continues at anything like the pace maintained during the past few years, some fairly serious problems of technological redeployment and even disguised unemployment are likely to emerge. Literary economists will have to learn more statistics and mathematics in order to function effectively in teaching and research; mathematical economists will have to learn more statistics and econometrics to adapt to new standards of empirical relevance in economic theory; econometricians will have to learn more about the real world and concentrate less on the pure theory of statistical estimation. The prospect is not unhappy so far as the future of the discipline is concerned. Bearing in mind the inefficiency and inflexibility of the typical university administrator, however, we may be pardoned a few shudders at the thought of a prolonged period of transition!

Another serious problem, closely related to that just mentioned, concerns the mathematical and statistical training of graduate students. Anyone who has had significant dealings with professional mathematicians knows only too well what a horrible mess they can make of a promising young economist if they are permitted to see too much of him too early in the game; and mathematical statisticians are only slightly less dangerous in this respect. In the absence of a large and well-trained cadre of mathematical *economists* and *economic* statisticians, however, there is little choice. If graduate students do not get inadequate training in mathematics and statistics, they will get the wrong kind — which may be almost as bad. Schools that are fortunate enough to have a strong group of applied mathematicians may do fairly well in this regard; but the typical university is more likely to provide a haven for pure mathematicians, and they are an altogether different breed of animal.

There is no completely satisfactory solution to this problem, but there is some reason to believe that even a partial solution will require increased emphasis on interdisciplinary programs connecting, say, economics with mathematics, with industrial management, and with business economics and industrial engineering. At the present time there is too often a tendency in all of these disciplines to think that every important problem can be solved by calling in occasional specialists or acquiring additional time on a computer. Effective interdisciplinary work could do a great deal to dispel this illusion. To be successful, however, such programs must entail a flow of traffic in more than one direction. Not only must economists treat mathematics, industrial management, and other disciplines as worthwhile sciences in their own right; practitioners of the latter sciences must also come to respect economics for its own sake. The day has passed when a person without training in mathematics and the physical sciences can

be considered to have a "broad" education. The reverse is also true: scholars in the physical sciences need to have a more detailed knowledge of the subject matter and techniques of the social sciences. Of course the prospects for solid interdisciplinary work are not very bright in any case so long as university administrative arrangements artificially separate disciplines into departmental units each of which is forced to consider itself a little "empire." But that is a separate problem.

Another matter of possible concern has to do with the orientation of research in a world of mathematical economists. It is well known that empirical research of any kind is a laborious and time-consuming process; that good empirical research, particularly if it is undertaken by a brilliant scholar, is likely to take a far greater proportion of his active professional life than a piece of theoretical research. It is also likely to require considerably more research money. This might easily lead to a vicious circle in economic research. Being an underdeveloped discipline, economics is badly in need of capital accumulation in the form of an established body of empirical knowledge. At the present time, however, private and social goals are likely to conflict. Even though, as individuals, each of us sees the desirability of doing empirical work, and even though we might feel capable of doing it ourselves, very little thought will suffice to convince anyone who is, at the same time, capable of doing pure theory, that it is in his own interest to think as little as possible about problems of the real world and get on instead with the writing of papers that do not require so much expenditure of time and money — in short, papers on purely theoretical topics.

There is no end of potential papers of

this kind. So long as one is never expected to confront theory with fact, literally any theory is perfectly fair game; and when one model is completed, another can be developed out of the first by adding a few variables, changing a few assumptions, and so forth. Provided this kind of activity is intellectually competent and satisfying, moreover, there is really no basis for objecting to it in principle; who knows what may someday prove to be useful? If enough people do pure theory and do it well, it will naturally come to have a certain generalized respectability in the eyes of the profession at large.

The person who breaks away from this game and engages in empirical research does not need to worry about receiving plaudits from the profession. His energy and spirit of adventure will almost certainly be commended, provided his research is successful. If it is not, however — and there is no reason to believe that empirical research in economics will always be successful any more than it is in the physical sciences — then he may be in trouble. Professional journals are not noted as outlets for unsuccessful research results; and if such research is not recognized in some way, then an individual's time is certainly wasted from the standpoint of the people who control his salary and promotion prospects.

SUMMARY AND CONCLUSION

The ultimate aim of economics, like that of any other empirical science, is accurate prediction of future events. Except within rather narrow limits, such a goal is hopelessly ambitious and can never represent much more than a program of re-search. Regarded as an ideal, however, the goal is worth pursuing, partly for its own sake, partly for the power it may give man over his economic environment. Even if accurate economic prediction is impossible, the attempt to develop useful predictive techniques can be counted upon to yield a large and informative collection of descriptive studies of concrete phenomena. This fact alone is perhaps sufficient to justify the increasingly econometric orientation of contemporary economics.

Wider use of mathematics as a tool for theoretical and empirical research is a natural if not a necessary consequence of this development, and anyone who wishes to retain his standing as a professional economist is therefore well advised to maintain a moderate stock of mathematical artillery, partly for research purposes, partly to fend off possible attacks by second-rate logicians masquerading as brother economists. No doubt there will always be some room on the fringes of the science even for the completely nonmathematical economist. But it is likely to be a case of "standing room only" before many years have passed.

Whither mathematical economics proceeds from this point remains to be seen. Wherever it does go, however, the road is likely to be paved with logical rigor and strewn with the intellectual cadavers of those who are allergic to mathematics. Whether this is a desirable or happy outcome is a separate question. However that may be, those who see in it cause for rejoicing had best look to their economics — they may need it in the near future. Those who shed a bitter tear will do well to look to their mathematics anyhow — unless the age of retirement is fairly near.

[6]

PERMANENT INCOME AND TRANSITORY BALANCES: HAHN'S PARADOX

By ROBERT W. CLOWER[1]

I

1. LIKE fluid dynamics in the nineteenth century, modern economics is a mixture of plausible argument from casual empirical hypotheses and formal reasoning from first principles. This kind of mixture naturally breeds scientific paradoxes—apparent inconsistencies between theoretical results and factual conclusions suggested by experimental data or common sense.[2] Such paradoxes are of practical interest because their solution commonly requires the application of stricter standards of logical rigour (cf. Birkhoff, pp. 3–5, 177–8). This directs attention to weaknesses in existing doctrine and often suggests new avenues of approach to familiar problems.

2. It is symptomatic of the defensive posture which social scientists so often adopt in the company of their physical science colleagues that some economists regard paradoxes as a source of weakness in their discipline. The absurdity of this attitude becomes clear if we reflect that scientific paradoxes arise precisely because scientific theories are not entirely devoid of empirical content. What is to be regretted in contemporary economics is not the plenty but the paucity of well-posed paradoxes.

3. We should expect paradoxes to be especially rare in the more abstract branches of economic theory. It is difficult to arrange a clear confrontation between factual or intuitive knowledge and theories which are aptly characterized as 'explanations of things that can't be observed'. Where anything can happen, nothing should surprise us. In his recent essay on 'Real Balances and Consumption',[3] however, Mr. Hahn has ingeniously provided just such a surprise.

4. *Hahn's Paradox*, as I shall call it, may be put as follows. On the basis of outwardly plausible assumptions, it can be shown that the effect on consumption of a once-over change in an individual's assets is *transitory*.[4] On the same assumptions it can also be shown that the effect on

---

[1] I am indebted to Professor Gorman, Dr. Little, and other members of the Nuffield College seminar in economic theory for helpful comments on an earlier oral version of this paper.

[2] Birkhoff, G., *Hydrodynamics*, 2nd ed. (Princeton, 1960), and Polya, G., *Induction and Analogy in Mathematics* (Princeton, 1954).

[3] Hahn, F. H., 'Real Balances and Consumption', *Oxford Economic Papers*, N.S., June 1962. Subsequent references are by paragraph number.

[4] Archibald, G. C., and Lipsey, R. G., 'Monetary and Value Theory: A Critique of Lange and Patinkin', *Review of Economic Studies*, Oct. 1958.

consumption of a change in the individual's income is *permanent*. Grant that both propositions are valid, and consider a conceptual experiment in which, starting from a position of equilibrium, the individual's holdings of income-earning assets are increased by an amount such that his gain in current and prospective income on asset account just offsets a simultaneous loss in current and prospective receipts from other sources. If the asset effect is transitory, whereas the income effect is permanent, the individual's consumption will ultimately change as a consequence of this experiment, even though his total income—current and prospective—is not affected in any way. We thus arrive at an apparent contradiction between theory and common sense (Hahn, pars. 5–7).[1]

5. What makes Hahn's Paradox significant is that it emerges from a set of ideas about individual behaviour which have long occupied an important place in established theory and have never before led to results so sharply at variance with intuitive knowledge. At the outset, the question arises whether Hahn's Paradox implies the existence of some fundamental weakness in existing theory or merely indicates that dubious economic assumptions have been tacitly introduced into recent discussions of asset-holding phenomena. Hahn contends that the second alternative is correct. Specifically, he argues that in a model of a perfect capital market 'we will be hard put to it to make the asset effect transitory' (Hahn, par. 13); for in such a model

> Any capital sum may be converted into an annuity (by lending) and every annuity can be converted into a capital sum (by borrowing). Hence the choices open to an individual when he experiences an increase in his initial assets are exactly those he would have had, had he experienced a certain increase in his annuity. Thus if the latter raises his consumption in each time interval then so must the former. (Hahn, par. 5.)

Having already demonstrated to his own satisfaction that the asset effect is indeed non-transitory in these circumstances, Hahn concludes that earlier proofs of the transience of the asset effect must involve some questionable assumptions and proceeds to document his conclusion with specific examples.

6. Unfortunately, Hahn's argument contains a logical slip which invalidates most of his later conclusions. His paper begins (pars. 1–4) with a valid proof that in a model of a perfect capital market a once-over rise in real assets will increase consumption in each interval over any *given* planning horizon. He then goes on to assert that this result is at variance with a later result (par. 7) which states that the asset effect is transitory in a model which does not explicitly involve a perfect capital market.

---

[1] This statement of Hahn's Paradox is not to be found in so many words in his paper, but it is clearly implicit in sections I and II.

However, if the term 'transitory' is construed to mean 'vanishing in the limit as time tends to infinity'—which is the way earlier writers (Leser,[1] Archibald and Lipsey,[2] Clower and Burstein[3]), and even Hahn himself (par. 7) have ordinarily construed it—Hahn's assertion is false. On this interpretation the question of transiency turns not on the *state* of consumption at various periods in a given planning horizon, whether finite or infinite, but rather on the *behaviour* of consumption in the limit as time, tending to infinity, steadily shifts the entire planning horizon forward. The effect on consumption of a rise in initial assets may well be positive over any finite interval of time and still vanish completely in the limit as time tends to infinity. Thus the two results which Hahn asserts are at variance with one another are in truth entirely compatible. Hahn's 'indirect' proof that the asset effect is normally non-transitory in a model of a perfect capital market is correspondingly invalid.

7. The preceding argument disposes of Hahn's formal indictment of existing theories and leaves Hahn's Paradox intact. So we come to the main business of this paper, which is to reconsider the entire question. Among other things I propose to show that the asset effect on consumption is in general transitory for all stable decision processes, that Hahn's Paradox appears in a particularly challenging form in a model of a perfect capital market, that the formal source of the paradox lies not in the transience of the asset effect but in the permanence of the income effect, and that the paradox cannot be resolved without modifying certain accepted ideas about the theory of individual choice. Some theoretical and practical implications of these results are discussed briefly at the end of the paper.

8. To give a satisfactory analysis of Hahn's Paradox, we must begin by formulating a model which deals explicitly with income-earning assets as well as consumption flows and stocks of real balances. A fundamental shortcoming of Hahn's approach is that income-earning assets appear explicitly only in his verbal commentary (see the quotation cited in par. 5, above). At the same time, we must keep our model as simple as possible to facilitate recognition of essential ideas which might otherwise pass unnoticed in a notational fog. As far as Hahn's Paradox is concerned, for example, there seems to be no reason to work with multi-period rather than single-period planning horizons. The distribution of planned consumption and asset-holdings over an extended 'future' time interval is no doubt an interesting question in its own right in certain contexts, but it

[1] Leser, C. E. V., 'The Consumer's Demand for Money', *Econometrica*, Apr. 1943.

[2] Archibald, G. C., and Lipsey, R. G., 'Monetary and Value Theory: A Critique of Lange and Patinkin', *Review of Economic Studies*, Oct. 1958.

[3] Clower, R. W., and Burstein, M. L., 'On the Invariance of the Demand for Cash and other Assets', *Review of Economic Studies*, Oct. 1960.

has no obvious bearing on the problem at issue here. The persistence of asset and income effects over time is a question in the dynamics rather than the statics of intertemporal choice.

9. In keeping with the general tenor of Hahn's discussion, let us imagine an economy with only one kind of consumption good and one kind of income-earning asset, namely, bonds which oblige the issuer to pay the holder one unit of consumer goods at the beginning of each market period, in perpetuity. Consider an individual transactor who, at any time t, is free to trade both commodities and bonds in any desired amount at fixed money prices, $\mathbf{p}^t = \mathbf{p} = 1$ and $1/\mathbf{r}^t = 1/\mathbf{r}$, which are (correctly) expected to remain constant throughout all subsequent time. Let x^t, A^t, and M^t denote, respectively, the individual's 'planned' demand in period t for consumer goods, bonds, and money balances. Similarly, let $\mathbf{A}^t$ and $\mathbf{M}^t$ denote the individual's 'actual' holdings of bonds and money balances at the beginning of period t.[1] Since bonds are perpetuities which entitle their holder to one unit of consumer goods at the beginning of each market period, the individual's income on asset account in period t (positive or negative) is numerically equal to his holdings of bonds at the outset of the period (i.e. $\mathbf{p}\mathbf{A}^t = \mathbf{A}^t$). The individual's total income in period t is therefore defined by $\mathbf{y}^t \equiv \mathbf{A}^t + \mathbf{R}^t$, where $\mathbf{R}^t$ denotes the individual's *autonomous income* (i.e. receipts in kind from sources other than bonds, payable, like bond income, at the beginning of each period). Finally, suppose that the choices open to the individual in period t are described by a budget constraint of the form

$$x^t + (1/\mathbf{r})(A^t - \mathbf{A}^t) + (M^t - \mathbf{M}^t) \leqslant \mathbf{A}^t + \mathbf{R}^t, \tag{9.1}$$

and that the individual's decision problem is to choose values $\hat{x}^t$, $\hat{A}^t$, $\hat{M}^t$ of x^t, A^t, M^t which satisfy (9.1) and yield a maximum value of the utility function

$$U = U(x^t, A^t, M^t). \tag{9.2}$$

10. The solution of the decision problem posed above may be assumed to define demand functions for commodities, bonds, and money *in period t*, of the general form

$$\hat{x}^t = \hat{x}(\mathbf{A}^t, \mathbf{M}^t, \mathbf{R}^t, \mathbf{r}), \tag{10.1}$$

$$\hat{A}^t = \hat{A}(\mathbf{A}^t, \mathbf{M}^t, \mathbf{R}^t, \mathbf{r}), \tag{10.2}$$

$$\hat{M}^t = \hat{M}(\mathbf{A}^t, \mathbf{M}^t, \mathbf{R}^t, \mathbf{r}). \tag{10.3}$$

To study the decisions of the individual as a process in time, we have to add to these relations appropriate stock adjustment equations to indicate

---

[1] Throughout the subsequent argument, bold face symbols distinguish 'actual' from 'planned' magnitudes. In particular, all parameters and predetermined variables (including so-called lagged endogenous variables) appear in this way.

the connexion between 'initial conditions' in period $t+1$ and planned asset balances in period t. Specifically, suppose that

$$\mathbf{A}^{t+1} = \hat{A}(\mathbf{A}^t, \mathbf{M}^t, \mathbf{R}^t, \mathbf{r}) \tag{10.4}$$

and
$$\mathbf{M}^{t+1} = \hat{M}(\mathbf{A}^t, \mathbf{M}^t, \mathbf{R}^t, \mathbf{r}). \tag{10.5}$$

Then for arbitrary initial values $\mathbf{A}_0^t$, $\mathbf{M}_0^t$ of $\mathbf{A}^t$ and $\mathbf{M}^t$ at time t_0, and for all values of $t \geqslant t_0$, the recursive system consisting of the five equations (10.1)–(10.5) may be assumed to determine unique values of each of the five 'endogenous' variables $\hat{x}^t$, $\hat{A}^t$, $\hat{M}^t$, $\mathbf{A}^{t+1}$, $\mathbf{M}^{t+1}$ as functions of the 'exogenous' variables $\mathbf{R}^t$ and $\mathbf{r}$. Call this system *Model I*.

11. Model I has a number of interesting properties. We notice first of all that a 'bond-compensated' change in autonomous income in period t, or an 'income-compensated' change in bond holdings (i.e. any change in $\mathbf{R}^t$ and $\mathbf{A}^t$ such that $\Delta\mathbf{R}^t + \Delta\mathbf{A}^t[1+(1/r)] = 0$), will have no immediate effect on the demand for commodities, bonds, or money. In the next period, however, the individual will alter his demand for all three commodities because his initial bond holdings will (by (10.4)) be the same as if nothing had happened in the preceding period, but his autonomous income will, of course, have changed. There is clearly nothing non-transitory about asset effects in this model of a perfect capital market (cf. Hahn, par. 13). We may get a clearer picture of the working of the model if we focus attention on its equilibrium properties. Let $\mathbf{R}^t = \mathbf{R}$ = constant so that Model I may be assumed to define unique 'steady-state' equilibrium values $\bar{x}$, $\bar{A}$, $\bar{M}$, $\overline{\mathbf{A}}$, $\overline{\mathbf{M}}$ of the variables $\hat{x}^t$, $\hat{A}^t$, $\hat{M}^t$, $\mathbf{A}^t$, $\mathbf{M}^t$, all as functions of the parameters $\mathbf{R}$ and $\mathbf{r}$: i.e. $\bar{x} = \bar{x}(\mathbf{R}, \mathbf{r})$, $\bar{A} = \bar{A}(\mathbf{R}, \mathbf{r})$, &c. Assume also that the equilibrium state so defined is dynamically stable; that is to say, for arbitrary initial values of $\mathbf{A}^t$ and $\mathbf{M}^t$, we have

$$\hat{x}^t \to \bar{x}, \qquad \hat{A}^t \to \mathbf{A}^t \to \bar{A}, \quad \text{and} \quad M^t \to \mathbf{M}^t \to \bar{M},$$

all as $t \to \infty$. Thus the asset effect on consumption is strictly transitory if the decision process is stable.[1] Since all equilibrium values depend directly on the autonomous income parameter $\mathbf{R}$, however, the effect of a change in autonomous income on consumption is *permanent*.

12. Hahn's Paradox now arises in a particularly clear way. Suppose that the individual, starting from a position of equilibrium, experiences a decline in autonomous income which is just offset by a simultaneous rise in his bond holdings so that his total income is unaffected. This leaves

---

[1] The purpose of the preceding remarks is not to establish the proposition that the asset effect *must be* transitory. Clearly, the decision process may be unstable, or may converge to a different equilibrium solution, depending on initial conditions (we rule out the latter case by supposing the equilibrium solution is unique). In either case, the asset effect will be non-transitory in an obvious sense. This suggests some interesting possibilities for future research, but we shall not be concerned with these problems (or, indeed, with unstable decision processes) in the present paper.

the individual in a position where he could, if he wished, enjoy the same level of *permanent consumption, x̄,* as before; for bonds are perpetuities and, by hypothesis, $R^t = R$ for all t. According to Model I, however, the individual will choose a lower level of permanent consumption because his autonomous income has been reduced. This result may well appear contrary to common sense. But worse is to come, for Model I implies that the individual chooses his desired level of *permanent income* as well as consumption. (This follows immediately from the definition $y^t \equiv A^t + R^t$ and our earlier assertion that $A^t \to \bar{A}$ as $t \to \infty$; for if $R^t = R$, then as $t \to \infty$, $y^t \to \bar{y} \equiv \bar{A}(R, r) + R$.) Since the choice of a permanent income level depends on the parameter **R** as well as **r**, our model indicates that the individual suffers from a peculiar kind of income illusion which causes him to distinguish between receipts from tradable bonds and receipts from other sources. The common-sense absurdity of this illusion becomes manifest if we suppose that autonomous income receipts represent earnings from an unsaleable collection of bonds which are held in trust for the individual.

13. It should now be clear that Hahn's Paradox cannot be resolved except by altering the basic structure of our model of inter-temporal choice. Hahn's Paradox arises not because the asset effect is transitory, but because the income effect is permanent. What we have to explain is why a change in autonomous income that is offset by a counter-vailing change in bond income should have *any* effect on the individual's consumption, immediately or in the future. In short, why does the demand function for commodities, $\hat{x}(A^t, M^t, R^t, r)$, involve autonomous income as an independent variable?

14. If we approach Hahn's Paradox by the route just suggested, we do not have to look far to find its source. The paradox reflects our failure to deal explicitly with income expectations.[1] No doubt it is possible to argue that perfection in the capital market implies definite income expectations of some kind. But to paraphrase Hahn (par. 8), I cannot believe that this is the kind of assumption an economist would care to make, even if he is concerned to examine a stationary state. If one makes such assumptions at all, he should make them explicitly, not cloak them in vague concepts like 'market perfection' or 'rational behaviour'. Let it be flatly asserted that in Model I we have both a 'perfect' capital market and unspecified income expectations. This commits us to the proposition

---

[1] Hahn puts his finger squarely on this problem in the course of his discussion (par. 8), but fails to follow the problem through. Arguing in terms of a multi-period horizon and beginning from the assumption that 'there is no question of uncertainty' over a given planning horizon, Hahn fails to see that his discussion does not deal with income expectations beyond one horizon, hence, that his own model lacks an appropriate concept of future income in precisely the same sense as the one-period horizon models which he criticizes.

that a steady-state equilibrium is possible in the absence of definite income expectations. We are then encouraged to ask if this proposition makes sense within our model (not in the real world) and, if not, what changes in the structure of the model seem to be called for.

15. The choices open to the individual in Model I are correctly described by the utility function $U(x^t, A^t, M^t)$. In particular, the individual is assumed to choose in period t what his *income from bonds* will be in period $t+1$; for this is clearly what choosing the value of A^t implies. However, the individual is neither assumed to choose nor to be in any position to choose what his *total income* will be in period $t+1$; for the assumption that $\mathbf{R}^t = $ constant *in the model* does not imply that the individual has foreknowledge of this fact. As far as the individual is concerned, receipts of non-interest income in future periods are simply unknown, and these receipts remain unknown regardless of the 'rationality' of the individual or the 'perfection' of the capital market.

16. Even on the most rudimentary view of human learning processes, we cannot fail to recognize that the hypothesis of static income expectations has peculiar merit in a model situation where autonomous income receipts are assumed to materialize period after period in a steady stream (cf. Clower and Burstein, pp. 180–1).[1] In these circumstances, moreover, a theory which implies that the individual regards prospective bond receipts and prospective receipts from other sources as different species of income is clearly suspect. This brings us to the heart of our problem, which is that *no analytical procedure has ever been developed to indicate how income or other kinds of expectations about future events should be introduced into dynamic theories of intertemporal choice.* In this connexion it should be emphasized that the multi-period planning horizon concept is no use at all. This can be seen very easily if one re-defines the variables in Model I as finite-dimensional vectors and makes appropriate alterations in the budget constraint. Hahn's Paradox is still built into the basic structure of the model because there is no way of introducing expectations about autonomous income receipts which accrue beyond a single horizon. The only known way to evade the problem (and it is an evasion) is to work with infinite-dimensional vectors and assume 'perfect foresight' as concerns future income receipts.

17. Most theorists display a strong conservative bias towards proposals which involve systematic meddling with traditional concepts such as the utility function (cf. Patinkin, note D, pp. 413 ff.).[2] Since my proposal for introducing income expectations into the theory of inter-temporal choice involves precisely this kind of meddling, a preliminary defence is in order

[1] See above, p. 179.
[2] Patinkin, D., *Money, Interest and Prices* (Row Peterson, 1956).

at this point. Briefly, it seems to me that our present concept of a utility function has long been outmoded. The concept was developed initially as a convenient device for saying as little as possible about things which economists, like other people, do not wish to dispute, namely, individual tastes. Samuelson once remarked in a witty aside[1] that utility was 'as real to Edgeworth as his morning jam'. The comment would be funnier if modern economists felt that the *utility function* were less 'real' than an engineering production function. My proposal involves nothing more than a frank recognition of the purely *conventional* nature of the utility function concept. Grant that the utility function is a convenient receptacle for vague notions about individual preferences among commodities and the same concept is immediately seen to be an equally convenient receptacle for vague notions about future income receipts and other expectational phenomena.

18. Returning to the problem at hand, let us begin by re-emphasizing (cf. par. **15**, above) that the utility function in Model I already provides a home for income expectations via the inclusion of the bond variable A^t; i.e. this variable is simply a proxy for interest receipts expected to accrue in period $t+1$. If we suppose that the individual's current decisions to consume and hold money balances depend in part on expected future income from bonds, it is natural to argue that other elements of expected future income should also enter the utility function explicitly. Indeed, if there is no reason for the individual to distinguish between one source of expected income and another (due allowance being made for risk, &c.) other elements of expected income should appear as additions to expected income from bonds.

19. We may give formal expression to these views by rewriting the utility function (9.2) as

$$U = U(x^t, M^t, A^t + \hat{R}^t), \tag{19.1}$$

where $\hat{R}^t$ is a parameter representing receipts of autonomous income expected to accrue in period $t+1$. More precisely, we conceive of $\hat{R}^t$ as the individual's subjective estimate at time t of future receipts at time $t+1$, this estimate being obtained by applying some 'rule of inductive inference' to current and past values of the autonomous income variable R^t. Whatever may be the nature of this 'rule of inductive inference', it is appropriate to think of the individual as having a demand for future income y^t defined as the sum of planned income from bonds and expected receipts of autonomous income, i.e. $y^t \equiv A^t + \hat{R}^t$. For any given decision rule, the current value of y^t depends solely on the individual's demand for bonds A^t. Thus, if we suppose that the individual 'demands' future income y^t rather than

[1] Samuelson, P. A., *Foundations of Economic Analysis* (Harvard, 1947), p. 206.

future bond income A^t, we do not in any way imply a change in the *objective* aspects of individual choice; we merely focus attention on the *economic* significance of the choice that is being made. Accordingly, let us adopt just this point of view and rewrite the utility function (19.1) as

$$U = U(x^t, M^t, y^t) \qquad (19.2)$$

to indicate explicitly that the individual's choice set consists of alternative collections of consumption, money stocks, and future income. Similarly, let us make use of the identities $y^t \equiv A^t + R^t$ and $y^t \equiv A^t + \hat{R}^t$ to rewrite the budget constraint (9.1) as

$$x^t + (M^t - \mathbf{M}^t) + (1/\mathbf{r})\{(y^t - \mathbf{y}^t) + (\mathbf{R}^t - \hat{R}^t)\} \leqslant \mathbf{y}^t. \qquad (19.3)$$

20. Maximization of the utility function (19.2) subject to the budget constraint (19.3) may be supposed to define unique solution values of x^t, M^t, and y^t as functions of the parameter $\mathbf{r}$ and the predetermined variables $\mathbf{M}^t$, $\mathbf{y}^t$, and $(\mathbf{R}^t - \hat{R}^t)$. Thus we may write

$$\hat{x}^t = \hat{x}\{\mathbf{M}^t, \mathbf{y}^t, \mathbf{r}, (\mathbf{R}^t - \hat{R}^t)\}, \qquad (20.1)$$

$$\hat{M}^t = \hat{M}\{\mathbf{M}^t, \mathbf{y}^t, \mathbf{r}, (\mathbf{R}^t - \hat{R}^t)\}, \qquad (20.2)$$

$$\hat{y}^t = \hat{y}\{\mathbf{M}^t, \mathbf{y}^t, \mathbf{r}, (\mathbf{R}^t - \hat{R}^t)\}. \qquad (20.3)$$

The demand function for bonds in period t is then defined by combining (20.3) with the identity $y^t = A^t + \hat{R}^t$:

$$\hat{A}^t = \hat{y}\{\mathbf{M}^t, \mathbf{y}^t, \mathbf{r}^t, (\mathbf{R}^t - \hat{R}^t)\} - \hat{R}^t. \qquad (20.4)$$

21. By virtue of the identity $y^t \equiv A^t + R^t$, both of the current income variables A^t and R^t appear implicitly in each of the functions (20.1)–(20.4). Since the variable R^t also appears explicitly in each function, we see that demand behaviour in period t is not invariant with respect to equal absolute variations in R^t and $\hat{R}^t$; i.e. variations in R^t imply variations in all current demands even if simultaneous variations in $\hat{R}^t$ occur such that the value of $(\mathbf{R}^t - \hat{R}^t)$ is unchanged. The presence of the term $(\mathbf{R}^t - \hat{R}^t)$ in the demand functions nevertheless indicates the general way in which demand behaviour is influenced by expected future receipts of autonomous income. Roughly speaking, demand behaviour depends not on the absolute value of autonomous income receipts but on the extent to which such receipts are expected to change between one planning horizon and the next. The demand for bonds is, of course, a clear exception to this rule since it depends directly on the absolute value of the variable $\hat{R}^t$.

22. If we now impose the hypothesis of *static income expectations*, $\hat{R}^t = \mathbf{R}^t$, the term $(\mathbf{R}^t - \hat{R}^t)$ vanishes in (20.1)–(20.4) and the term $\hat{R}^t$ in

(20.4) is replaced by $\mathbf{R}^t$. On this hypothesis, therefore, the demand functions for commodities, money, income, and bonds take the special forms

$$\hat{x}^t = \hat{x}(\mathbf{M}^t, \mathbf{y}^t, \mathbf{r}), \qquad (22.1)$$

$$\hat{M}^t = \hat{M}(\mathbf{M}^t, \mathbf{y}^t, \mathbf{r}), \qquad (22.2)$$

$$\hat{y}^t = \hat{y}(\mathbf{M}^t, \mathbf{y}^t, \mathbf{r}), \qquad (22.3)$$

$$\hat{A}^t = \hat{y}(\mathbf{M}^t, \mathbf{y}^t, \mathbf{r}) - \mathbf{R}^t. \qquad (22.4)$$

As before, a change in either $\mathbf{R}^t$ or $\mathbf{A}^t$ will, in general, alter the demand for commodities and money as well as bonds. However, since the relations (22.1)–(22.3) depend only on the sum of $\mathbf{A}^t$ and $\mathbf{R}^t$, an 'income-compensated' change in initial bond stocks or a 'bond-compensated' change in autonomous income will have *no effect* on the demand for consumption, money balances, or future income. The entire impact of such a change falls on the demand for bonds. Indeed, it is evident from the form of (22.4) that for all values of $\mathbf{A}^t$ and $\mathbf{R}^t$ satisfying the condition

$$\mathbf{y}^t \equiv \mathbf{A}^t + \mathbf{R}^t = \text{constant}, \qquad \Delta\mathbf{A}^t = -\Delta\mathbf{R}^t = \Delta\hat{A}^t.$$

Thus, *the individual adapts completely in the current period to any change in the distribution of income by source which does not entail a change in the current level of total income.* The hypothesis that individual choice depends directly on total future income receipts does not, by itself, lead to this result. 'Income-compensated' changes in initial bond stocks and 'bond-compensated' changes in autonomous income take on a strictly *nominal* character only if we also suppose that income expectations are static.

23. The above conclusions provide a complete solution to Hahn's Paradox. If the individual is subjectively concerned only with total income receipts, and if autonomous income expectations are strictly static, the 'income illusion' described in par. **12** disappears and Hahn's Paradox cannot arise. It is particularly important to observe that our solution of the paradox makes no reference to the dynamics of the decision process. Indeed, our conclusions apply whether or not the individual is assumed to be in asset equilibrium (i.e. whether or not $\hat{M}^t = \mathbf{M}^t$ or $\hat{A}^t = \mathbf{A}^t$). This shows that neither the transiency of the asset effect nor the non-transiency of the income effect has any necessary connexion with Hahn's Paradox (cf. Hahn, par. 13). In the same connexion it is relevant to remark that our solution of the paradox does not presuppose a 'perfect' market for bonds. We assume the existence of bonds, but we do not concern ourselves with the question whether individual plans are realized.[1]

---

[1] In his paper (pars. 9–12) Hahn constructs some examples of market imperfection which may lead an individual to take up a 'second best' equilibrium position, that is, a position defined in terms of an external constraint (e.g. inability to borrow, inability to borrow and lend at the same interest rate). He neatly shows that in these circumstances a once-over change in initial assets may provide only temporary relief, in which case the individual will

24. Let us carry our analysis one stage further by adding the stock adjustment equations

$$\mathbf{M}^{t+1} = \hat{M}(\mathbf{M}^t, \mathbf{y}^t, \mathbf{r}) \tag{23.1}$$

and
$$\mathbf{A}^{t+1} = \hat{y}(\mathbf{M}^t, \mathbf{y}^t, \mathbf{r}) - \mathbf{R}^t \tag{23.2}$$

to the current demand functions (20.1)–(20.4). For purposes of reference, call the resulting recursive system *Model II*.

As in the case of Model I, we may suppose that this system, including the current income identity $\mathbf{y}^t \equiv \mathbf{A}^t + \mathbf{R}^t$, determines unique values of all endogenous variables ($\hat{x}^t, \hat{M}^t, \hat{y}^t, \hat{A}^t, \mathbf{M}^t, \mathbf{A}^t$, and $\mathbf{y}^t$) as functions of the exogenous variables $\mathbf{R}^t$ and $\mathbf{r}$. More strongly, let us suppose that for any fixed value $\mathbf{R}$ of $\mathbf{R}^t$, the system defines a unique equilibrium solution and that this solution is dynamically stable. Inspection of the relations (20.1)–(20.3) then reveals that *the equilibrium demands for consumption, income, and money balances are functions of the rate of interest alone, provided only that the 'rule of inductive behaviour' defining $\hat{R}^t$ is such that $\hat{R}^t \to \mathbf{R}$ as $t \to \infty$. Thus we may write $\bar{x} = \bar{x}(\mathbf{r})$, $\bar{y} = \bar{y}(\mathbf{r}) = \bar{\mathbf{y}}$, and $\bar{M} = \bar{M}(\mathbf{r}) = \bar{\mathbf{M}}$.* The equilibrium demand for bonds, however, is a function of $\mathbf{R}$ as well as $\mathbf{r}$; specifically,
$$\bar{A} = \bar{y}(\mathbf{r}) - \mathbf{R} = \bar{\mathbf{A}}.$$

We conclude that *neither changes in initial assets nor changes in autonomous income have any permanent effect on consumption or final holdings of money balances. Provided that the decision process is stable, all asset effects are transitory, as are income effects on consumption and money balances. The income effect is permanent only with respect to bonds, any change in autonomous income being offset in equilibrium by an equal and opposite change in income from bonds.*

25. It remains to say something about possible practical applications of the models presented in the preceding discussion. Two preliminary problems of interpretation are of immediate relevance in this connexion. The first problem concerns the meaning of the term 'transactor'. Our models assume that the 'transactor' has unlimited life, where 'life' is measured in market periods. This does not preclude any of the more obvious concrete interpretations: 'person', 'household', 'firm', &c. For some purposes, it might be useful to think of the transactor as the set of direct descendants of a particular man ('from rags to riches' in ten generations). Broadly speaking, however, our concept of a transactor is open to as many (or as few) concrete interpretations as are corresponding con-

quickly reassume his initial 'second-best' equilibrium position. Thus, he finds that the asset effect may be 'transitory' in particular instances even if it is permanent in the 'normal' case. In a similar way we might construct examples of market imperfection (e.g. rules that impose firm restrictions on the amount of indebtedness that a transactor can incur, institutional conventions which give rise to 'locked-in' effects) that inhibit the adjustment of asset holdings in response to changes in autonomous income and so cause the income effect on consumption to be permanent rather than transitory.

cepts which appear in other models of individual decision processes. The second problem concerns the speed of adjustment of decision processes. It would obviously be far-fetched to suppose that large changes in asset holdings ever occur in practice over short intervals of time, however much such a result might be desired by the 'individual' concerned. It can be argued, however, that an 'individual's' desire for wealth and income depend in large measure on his background and immediate economic surroundings—even if the 'individual' is a firm or a government agency. If this is so, the kind of changes which would normally concern us need not be all that great. More generally, the models presented in this paper are subject to no practical criticisms which would not apply with equal force to models which are currently used and useful. As Feller has remarked: 'The manner in which . . . theories are applied does not depend on preconceived ideas; it is a purposeful technique depending on, and changing with, experience.'[1] One can never know anything *definite* about the practical usefulness of a model until one has tried to use it.

26. We deal now with some specific cases in which our theoretical findings may be of practical interest. The first case arises from the fact that 'commodity' as distinguished from 'bond' demands in Model II are independent of the distribution of total income among alternative sources. Suppose that we regard the autonomous income variable **R** as a catchall for earnings from business and other 'physical' assets. According to the model, variations in such earnings will have no lasting influence on consumption, but will strongly influence both the current and equilibrium composition of the individual's asset portfolio. This proposition has potential significance as an explanation of the nonconformity of bond prices with other indices of business activity at trade cycle turning points. It also adumbrates a possible alternative approach to some of the 'leverage' and 'cost of capital' problems raised by Modigliani and Miller.[2]

27. The next case has to do with the fact that in Model II the individual chooses his own level of *permanent income* $\bar{y}$, conditional only on tastes and the rate of interest. Since in equilibrium we have $\bar{y}(\mathbf{r}) = \bar{x}(\mathbf{r})$, a similar statement applies to *permanent consumption* $\bar{x}$. One's intuition may boggle at these assertions, but they are valid implications of our model and do no violence to any known set of facts—not even the fact that most of us have smaller incomes and houses than we would like. A common-sense rationalization is provided by remarking that to become wealthier one must save, and to save one must temporarily forego

[1] Feller, W., *An Introduction to Probability Theory and its Application*, vol. 1, 2nd ed. (Wiley, 1957).

[2] Modigliani, F., and Miller, M. H., 'The Cost of Capital, Corporation Finance and the Theory of Investment', *American Economic Review*, June 1958.

consumption. Choosing one's permanent income and consumption thus involves nothing more than the familiar choice between present and future goods.

28. The preceding argument has practical significance for recent studies of consumer behaviour which distinguish between 'permanent' and 'transitory' components of income. The concept of permanent income is defined in these studies (see particularly Friedman)[1] not as a decision variable but as a parameter of choice (determined by past income, present occupation, wealth, family size, age, &c.). Thus it is closely related to the concept of permanent income defined by our Model I (par. 12 above)—a system which, as we now know, contains a built-in autonomous income illusion. Even though the concept so defined is intuitively appealing and leads to models which have some success in explaining observed data, one is inclined to be suspicious of its virtue.

29. Our argument suggests that to regard 'permanent income' as a parameter is unsound in principle; and our models suggest that studies using the permanent income concept might yield better results in practice if closer attention were paid to dynamic aspects of the asset adjustment process. History—particularly American history—provides many examples of 'self-made' men. It would not be surprising if this were the general case. That most of us are poor rather than rich self-made men is beside the point. To say that each man chooses his own permanent income does not mean that every man chooses to become a millionaire— or that those who do achieve their ambition. If there is substance to the view that permanent income is a decision variable rather than a parameter, we should expect the bulk of 'transitory' income (in Friedman's sense) to be saved by individuals whose assets are already growing, i.e. individuals who have not yet reached their desired level of permanent income. Conversely, 'transitory' income should be consumed rapidly by individuals whose assets are approximately stationary, i.e. individuals who have given up the 'intertemporal tussle'.[2] A detailed study of the facts, using the approach suggested, should yield interesting results, particularly if simple hypotheses about the formation of income expectations were tested at the same time.[3]

30. A final practical comment is in order about the interpretation of the utility function on which our solution to Hahn's Paradox depends

[1] Friedman, M., *A Theory of the Consumption Function* (Princeton, 1957).
[2] Strotz, R., 'Myopia and Inconsistency in the Theory of Dynamic Utility Maximization', *Review of Economic Studies*, 1955–6, pp. 165–80.
[3] There is some evidence to show that static expectations are fairly common among transactors in the real world. The broad conclusions suggested by our model do not depend on the satisfaction of this condition, but its failure would seriously diminish the value of our model (or similar constructions) for making specific predictions.

(pars. **16–18** above), and the bearing of this interpretation on the one-period horizon models which have figured so largely in our discussion. Multi-period horizon models are essential for dealing with some problems of economic choice. For studying the dynamics of inter-temporal decision-making, however, their usefulness is open to serious question. Devotees of the theory of rational behaviour find it easy to persuade themselves that there is some magic in working with utility functions and budget constraints that take explicit account of future as well as present alternatives. Adherents to 'dumb beast' theories of decision making[1] should have no more trouble persuading themselves that it is simpler and more realistic to *truncate* the budget constraint at the end of one period and represent whatever the constraint is supposed to say about future income and price expectations by adding appropriate asset, price, and income variables to a one-period utility function. The utility function takes on an entirely different character in the latter case, becoming host to expectations and other phenomena which are normally included in the budget constraint of multi-period models. In principle, the two points of view are entirely compatible. In practice, however, the multi-period point of view distracts attention from problems that have intuitive significance for plain economists and econometricians, and focuses attention on problems that are more interesting to logicians and mathematicians. The multi-period approach also discourages explicit discussion of *disequilibrium* phenomena, the machinery of analysis being so complex that even equilibrium phenomena are sometimes hard to handle. But single-period approach runs serious dangers from implicit theorizing unless it is used with care. No general moral can be drawn, except that neither approach should be adhered to as an article of faith.

[1] The phrase 'dumb beast' is my translation of Simon's notion of the 'adaptive' or 'satisficing' individual. See Simon, H. A., *Models of Man* (Wiley, 1957).

Northwestern University

3

Income, Wealth, and
the Theory of Consumption

Robert W. Clower and M. Bruce Johnson

A theory is a cluster of conclusions in search of a premiss.
N. R. Hanson *Patterns of Discovery.*

The modern literature on household behavior is a fascinating blend of fact, fancy and computer technology, reflecting the mutual interplay of theory and applications that has long distinguished it from most other fields of economic inquiry. It is an impressive literature, considered either as a collection of *ad hoc* rationalizations of apparent empirical regularities, or as a contribution to positive description of household behavior. Yet when all is said and done, it has added remarkably little to our understanding of underlying causal relations.

The explanation lies, we believe, in the historical isolation of consumption theory from developments in closely related branches of general price theory. Perhaps the most notable shortcoming of the literature is its neglect of dynamic interrelations among income, wealth and consumption implicit in the close connection between saving and asset accumulation (Friedman, 1957a, Houthakker, 1961a, pp. 727–30, 735). This is reflected not only in the predominantly statical orientation of theoretical research, but also in the paucity of empirical studies of balance sheet data in conjunction with related income and expenditure statistics. Recent inquiries, by Spiro (1962), by Ball and Drake (1964), and by Houthakker and Taylor (1966), go some way to remedy these deficiencies; but much remains to be done, particularly at the theoretical level, before they are eliminated.

The purpose of the present paper is to carry this work forward—more specifically, to formulate within the framework of conventional demand analysis a dynamic theory of consumption that is consistent with available empirical evidence. Our discussion is divided into three main sections. In Part I (Theoretical Foundations) we outline a microdynamic theory of

45

household behavior, taking our cue from the elegantly simple model set out in Archibald and Lipsey's famous article (1958, pp. 1–23; Lindbeck, 1963) on value and monetary theory. In Part II (Empirical Superstructure) we impose various restrictions on the behavior relations of our model, drawing for this purpose on survey data from the United States and the United Kingdom. In Part III (Statistical Implications) we develop the aggregative consequences of our theory and collate our findings with results reported in earlier studies, particularly Milton Friedman's influential *Theory of the Consumption Function* (1957b). The nature of our subject compels us to devote substantial space to econometric topics. Our primary aim being to elucidate ideas rather than facts, however, we deal with statistical data explicitly only where its introduction serves to guide or illustrate the theoretical analysis.

I. *Theoretical Foundations*

We begin by examining the planning behavior of a household at an instant of time, temporarily setting to one side all questions involving the execution as distinct from the scheduling of economic plans. The argument is later extended to deal with the intertemporal behavior of measurable income, consumption and saving flows. Following a Samuelsonian maxim (1961), we work throughout with a simple and strong theoretical model to avoid obscuring the intrinsic logic of our analysis in a haze of extraneous details.

Household Planning: *Basic Concepts.* In keeping with familiar procedure, we consider a household whose decision problem at any given moment of time is to choose among alternative combinations of desired consumption (c) and desired wealth (w), subject to a planning constraint that depends on the actual wealth ($\underline{w}$) of the household at the same moment (Samuelson, 1961; Rolph, 1954; Chase, 1963). We do not inquire into the motives, rational or otherwise, that underlie household attitudes towards spending and saving, nor do we deal explicitly with factors that might influence such attitudes (e.g. expected prices and rates of return, expected income, age, occupation, family composition, previous purchases of durable goods, etc.). On the contrary, we suppose that the household has a short memory and limited foresight, and we ignore all forces affecting choice that conflict with this point of view (Clower, 1963b; Ball and Drake, 1964). Accordingly, we characterize the household's ranking of alternative wealth-consumption combinations by a preference function of the form

$$u = u(w,c),$$ (1.1)

in which desired wealth and desired consumption appear as the only explicit variables.

Corresponding to (1.1), we define the set of currently admissible wealth-consumption plans by the budget equation

$$c + v(w - \underline{w}) = 0,$$ (1.2)

where v is a given velocity coefficient. The appearance of the parameter v in (1.2) is dictated by the dimensional difference between the flow variable c and the stock variables w and $\underline{w}$. Since no conceivable experiment will enable us to arrive at independent estimates of v and $\underline{w}$, however, we may gain simplicity without loss of empirical content by setting $v = 1$. On this assumption, the budget equation asserts that the planned (instantaneous) rate of consumption at any given date is numerically equal to the difference between desired and actual wealth at the same date.[1]

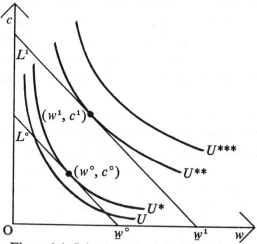

Figure 1.1 Selection of the Optimal Plan

Given the choice alternatives defined by (1.2), we apply the traditional postulate of utility maximization to determine the optimal wealth-consumption combination (w^*,c^*) corresponding to any specified value of actual wealth. This is illustrated in Figure 1.1, where the curves U, U^*, U^{**}, . . ., represent the function $u(w,c)$. If $\underline{w}^\circ$ is the current wealth of the household, the budget line is $L°$ and the optimal wealth-consumption plan, defined by the tangency of $L°$ with the indifference curve U^*, is $(w°,c°)$. Alternatively, if the current wealth of the household is $\underline{w}^1$, the budget line is L^1 and the optimal wealth-consumption plan is (w^1,c^1), and so forth.

Supposing that the decision problem has a unique solution corresponding to any given value of current wealth, we obtain planned consumption at any specified date as a single-valued function of actual wealth at the same date:[2]

$$c^t = c(\underline{w}^t) \, . \tag{1.3}$$

The graph of this function, hereafter referred to as the *consumption locus*, is illustrated in Figure 1.2. Our assumptions impose only one *a priori* restriction on this relation, namely, $c(0) = 0$ (this follows directly from the budget equation (1.2)). Casual empirical considerations suggest that the slope of the consumption locus, that is, the *marginal propensity to consume wealth* (MPCW), is unlikely to be negative; but no such condition is implicit in our model.

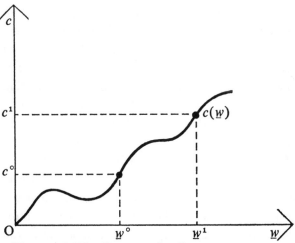

Figure 1.2 The Consumption Locus

The Intertemporal Adjustment Process. The preceding analysis implies that planned consumption at any date t is a function simply of current wealth. This conclusion is in close accord with views advanced on outwardly different theoretical grounds by Milton Friedman (1957b) and by

Modigliani and Brumberg (1954; Farrell, 1959, pp. 687–96). Where these writers regard current wealth as an imperfect proxy for 'permanent' or 'expected' income, however, we regard it as a causal variable in its own right. Correspondingly, where they introduce current income to give operational meaning to the otherwise purely metaphysical concepts of 'permanent' and 'expected' income, we shall introduce it as just one factor (the other being current consumption expenditure) that governs variations over time in objective stocks of household wealth.

Specifically, we assume that *the rate of change of current wealth at any date is equal to the difference between measured income ($\underline{y}$) and measured consumption ($\underline{c}$) at the same date.* Symbolically,

$$d\underline{w}^t / dt = \underline{y}^t - \underline{c}^t . \tag{1.4}$$

This assumption calls for two comments. First, we note that the definition of saving implicit in (1.4) presupposes that assets do not depreciate or appreciate in value, or that exogenous changes in the value of assets are somehow included in measured income and consumption. The second alternative is to be preferred in principle, but the first is easier to manage in practice. For the time being, therefore, we take the easy way out and assume away capital gains and losses. Second, we observe that measured consumption, $\underline{c}^t$, need not bear any simple relation to desired consumption, c^t, at the same date. Again for simplicity, we ignore decision lags and other possible complications and suppose that the value of $\underline{c}^t$ is at all times identically equal to the value of c^t as determined by the wealth-consumption function $c^t = c(\underline{w}^t)$. Given these assumptions, we have only to specify the determinants of measured income before going on to discuss the intertemporal behavior of measured consumption and wealth.

It is customary in discussions of consumer behavior to regard current income as an arbitrary parameter the value of which is determined by social and economic forces over which the individual has no control.[3] We shall adopt the same procedure as concerns one component of total receipts, namely, wage, salary and other *service income*, m^t. Since some portion of household wealth will normally consist of earning assets, we cannot treat rent, interest and other *property income*, n^t, in the same fashion. We shall adopt the simple yet general hypothesis that current property income is a (non-decreasing) function of current wealth: that is,

$$n^t = n(\underline{w}^t) ,$$

4

where $n'(\underline{w}^t)$ is assumed to be non-negative. Total income at any date is then defined as a function of service income and current wealth by the identity

$$y^t = m^t + n(\underline{w}^t) . \tag{1.5}$$

The graph of (1.5) corresponding to a fixed value of service income, $m^t = m$, is illustrated in Figure 1.3 by the curve $y(w)$, henceforth referred to as the *income locus*. The slope of the income locus represents the increase in property income associated with a marginal increment in wealth, that is, the marginal yield, or marginal rate of return, on wealth. The form of the locus will depend on the structure of the household's asset portfolio. For example, if the household holds: (i) only money, the locus will be horizontal; (ii) only perpetual bonds, linear and rising since the slope will represent the coupon rate of return; (iii) money, bonds, and physical assets in varying proportions, non-linear and variable in slope. The greater the proportion of non-earning assets in the portfolio, the smaller will be the marginal rate of return.

We may now characterize intertemporal adjustment processes. The income locus indicates, for each alternative level of current wealth, the maximum rate of current consumption the household can enjoy without drawing on previously accumulated wealth. The consumption locus (reproduced from Figure 1.2 and superimposed on the income locus in Figure 1.3) indicates what the household's actual rate of consumption will be corresponding to any given value of current wealth. The vertical distance between the income locus and the consumption locus measures realized saving; that is, the current rate of change of actual wealth. Thus the income and consumption functions (1.3) and (1.5), combined with the asset adjustment hypothesis (1.4), define a determinate dynamical system in the single variable $\underline{w}^t$ which, starting from any initial value $\underline{w}^t{}_0$ of wealth at date t_0, generates unique values of measured consumption, income, and wealth for all subsequent dates.

Suppose, for instance, that the value of current wealth at some initial data $t = 0$ is represented by the point w° in Figure 1.3; then current consumption and current wealth will initially tend to increase over time at the rate $y^\circ - c^\circ$.[4] With the passage of time, therefore, the actual values of wealth, income, and consumption all will increase as indicated by the directional arrows originating along the perpendicular A° in Figure 1.3.

Alternatively, if the value of current wealth at initial date $t = 1$ is w^1, then consumption will initially exceed income and wealth will tend to decrease over time. The actual values of wealth, income, and consumption will therefore decline with the passage of time as indicated by the directional arrows originating along the perpendicular A^1 in Figure 1.3.

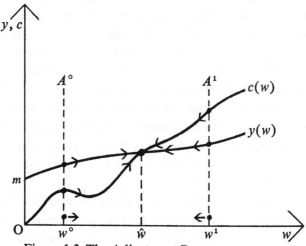

Figure 1.3 The Adjustment Process

In both of these examples, realized saving will converge to zero with the passage of time. That is to say, current wealth will gradually approach a stationary (and stable) equilibrium value ($\hat{w}$ in Figure 1.3) at which current consumption is equal to current income (Spiro, 1962, pp. 339, 342–3). This result holds for all cases in which the consumption locus intersects the income locus from below, provided that only one such intersection occurs for those values of current wealth (e.g. the set $w^1 - w^0$ in Figure 1.3) that are assumed to be admissible. If for some admissible value of wealth the consumption locus intersects the income locus from above, realized saving may or may not converge to zero with the passage of time; for in this case (illustrated in Figure 1.4) one or more of the equilibrium states defined by the consumption and income loci will be dynamically unstable.

Stability Conditions: The Stationary Economy. The exact condition for convergence of the saving process in the neighborhood of any given equilibrium value $\hat{w}$ of wealth is best indicated by approximating the solution of the differential equation

$$dw^t/dt = m+n(w^t)-c(w^t) \qquad (1.6)$$

in such a neighborhood–(1.6) being the general form that the asset-adjustment hypothesis (1.4) takes when $m^t = $ constant. Denoting the marginal rate of return on wealth by $r = n'(\hat{w})$, and the marginal propensity to consume wealth by $a = c'(\hat{w})$, we linearize the income and consumption functions in (1.6) and obtain as our solution

$$w^t = \hat{w}-(\hat{w}-w^\circ)\, e^{-(a-r)t}\,, \qquad (1.7)$$

where w° denotes an arbitrary initial value of w in the neighborhood of $\hat{w}$. Since the term $e^{-(a-r)t}$ governs the convergence of the saving process, we see that *the equilibrium value $\hat{w}$ is dynamically stable if and only if the slope of the consumption locus is greater than the slope of the income locus in the neighborhood of the equilibrium position.*[5] The implications of this condition will be discussed later. However, it should be immediately apparent that convergence of the saving process cannot be taken for granted. Even if consumption is an increasing function of wealth (as seems plausible), household saving will be a permanent phenomenon if the marginal rate of return on wealth is sufficiently large or the MPCW sufficiently small (Liviatan, 1965).

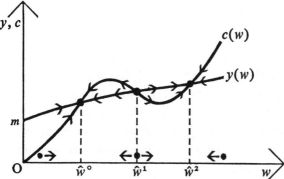

Figure 1.4 Stable and Unstable Equilibria

If the asset-adjustment process is stable, then in the limit as time tends to infinity, consumption will absorb the whole of current income–a proposition which at first sight may seem offensive to common sense.

It would be a serious mistake, however, to discount stability as a practical possibility on this ground. As the illustrative data in Table 1.1 indicate, the convergence of consumption towards income may proceed so slowly in practice as to be observationally unnoticeable – which is to say that observation of the economic system over any *finite* time interval may not provide enough information to enable us to distinguish between stable and unstable asset-adjustment processes.

TABLE 1.1. Time required for 60 per cent completion * of adjustment process, starting at time $t = 0$ ($r = 0.05$)

MPCW	elapsed time
2·00	0·51
1·00	1·05
0·75	1·43
0·50	2·22
0·40	2·86
0·35	3·33
0·25	5·00
0·15	10·00
0·10	20·00

* The exact figure used is 63·2 per cent, corresponding to a value for e^{-x} of 0·368 (i.e., e^{-1}).

Growth, Saving, and the Rate of Return on Wealth. The preceding discussion is applicable only to situations in which the saving process is convergent, and only then on the assumption that the level of service income is fixed. If the saving process diverges for every given value of service income, then *a fortiori* it will also diverge if service income is rising. In neither case can we say anything about the intertemporal behaviour of income, consumption and wealth, except that all will tend to vary with the passage of time.

If the saving process is convergent for every given level of service income, however, definite conclusions can be drawn about the intertemporal behavior of wealth and consumption corresponding to alternative time paths of service income. For instance, if service income varies cyclically (say, as the sine of the time), it can be shown that wealth, total income, and consumption will all vary in a similar fashion – lagging service income by a certain time interval. A more important case for our purposes is that in which service income is assumed to grow over time at a constant exponential rate g; i.e. $m^t = me^{gt}$. If we let $c^t = aw^t$, then the relevant differential equation is $dw^t/dt = me^{gt} + rw^t - aw^t$ which has the solution

$$w^t = \{m/(g+a-r)\}\, e^{gt} + \{w° - m/(g+a-r)\}\, e^{-(a-r)t}. \quad (1.8)$$

The second term in this solution is a transient; hence wealth tends ultimately to grow at the same exponential rate as service income.

Consumption and income must conform ultimately to the pattern set by the growth of wealth. In growth equilibrium, however, there is no tendency for consumption to absorb the whole of income. On the contrary, if we allow sufficient time for transient effects to become negligible, consumption is given by

$$c^t = aw^t = a\{m/(g+a-r)\}\, e^{gt}, \quad (1.9)$$

and gross income by

$$y^t = me^{gt} + rw^t = me^{gt} + r\{m/(g+a-r)\}\, e^{gt}. \quad (1.10)$$

Dividing the first of these equations by the second, we find that

$$c^t/y^t = a/(g+a). \quad (1.11)$$

Thus the *ratio* of measured consumption to measured income approaches a certain constant with the passage of time; but the *absolute* difference between income and consumption increases steadily.

Illustrative values of the consumption/income ratio corresponding to alternative rates of growth and alternative values of a are shown in Table 1.2. The saving-income ratios in the center of the table range from 3 to 12 per cent and probably span most of the cases that are of any practical interest.

It may seem curious that the rate of return on wealth (r) does not play a direct role in the saving process, even in conditions of steady growth. The explanation lies in our earlier decision not to deal with expected rates of return in defining the preference function of the household, for this severs any possible link between growth, realized rates of return, and the marginal propensity to consume wealth. In principle, of course, one should expect prospective yields to have some influence on the MPCW; the question is 'How much influence?' In general there is no reason to suppose that flows of satisfaction yielded by stocks of money, bonds, factories or old masters are different in degree or kind from those obtained by swallowing tranquillizers or feeding children. Apart from the usual motives of straightening out income streams over time, earning income, and providing a hedge against uncertainty (all of which are probably sensitive to yields) a person may hold assets in order to tyrannize his employees or bank manager, impress his neighbors, provide himself and his heirs with the means requisite to a life of noble contemplation, etc. In all circumstances, one is dealing with alternative forms of immediate gratification, many of which may involve appetites too keen to be blunted by variations in yields–certainly not financial yields.

Whether rightly or wrongly, we assume that prospective yields have no significant effect on the general form of the consumption locus. We do not wish to deny that calculating individuals exist. Our position on this as on most other matters affecting household preferences is much like that of Dostoevsky on history.[6]

TABLE 1.2. Growth and the consumption/income ratio

MPCW (a)	GROWTH RATE (g)				
	·01	·02	·03	·04	·05
·05	·83	·71	·63	·56	·50
·10	·91	·83	·77	·71	·67
·15	·94	·88	·83	·79	·75
·20	·95	·91	·87	·83	·80
·25	·96	·93	·89	·86	·83
·35	·97	·95	·92	·90	·88
·50	·98	·96	·94	·93	·91
·75	·99	·97	·96	·95	·94
1·00	·99	·98	·97	·96	·95
2·00	1·00	·99	·99	·98	·98

II. *Empirical Superstructure*

Although our model of the pure theory of household behavior could be extended in a number of directions, our immediate concern will be rather to develop and test relevant implications of the version presently at hand.

The Generalized Stability Hypothesis. It is desirable to proceed as far as possible with a minimal set of special assumptions. This must include the hypothesis that household saving at any *given* level of service income converges to zero with the passage of time; otherwise we cannot say anything useful even about the response of individual households to changes in income and wealth. If we confine attention to a group of households for which this hypothesis is valid, however, then we have only to specify the distribution of service income among households to deduce from our model some conclusions about mutual interrelations among group measures of income, wealth, and consumption.

The implications of these restrictions are more extensive than might be suggested by casual reflection. To suppose that asset adjustment processes are universally stable is equivalent to imposing definite 'laws of motion' on individual households. For to any given vector of service incomes there corresponds a unique and dynamically stable set of equilibrium vectors of household consumption, wealth, and gross income. To assume that the form of the service-income distribution is given, is then equivalent to imposing a kind of 'energy conservation' law on the system of households; for what one household loses, another household must gain.

If we suppose further that all changes in household position within any given service-income distribution occur strictly at random, we may invoke the central limit theorem to assert that unique and stable vectors of measured *mean values* of consumption, wealth, and gross income are defined for any stationary level of aggregate service income.[7] Accordingly, we may think of the individual household as a statistical entity the behavior of which is described in terms of the mean values of the variables that it controls. It is then a straightforward matter to introduce non-random factors into the analysis. Changes in aggregate service income, its distribution remaining the same, clearly will lead to changes in the same direction in the mean values of all individual variables. Less obviously, but just as surely, *specified changes in the statistical characteristics of the service-income distribution income can be shown to imply closely related changes in statistical distributions of mean values of individual variables.* We thus arrive at a theory of the 'dynamics of motion' of a system of households that is closely analogous to classical thermodynamics, the most important element of similarity being that we, like the thermodynamicists, are able to pass from models of individual behavior to models of group phenomena by explicit statistical arguments.

Our method of procedure does not represent a break with tradition; on the contrary, it faithfully reflects the spirit if not the letter of Neoclassical equilibrium analysis (Samuelson, 1947, pp. 21–3; Newman and Wolfe, 1961). It does constitute something of a departure, however, from contemporary modes of macroeconomic analysis, where the common practice is either to ignore individuals altogether or to pass from individual to group phenomena by explicit aggregation.

There is a certain irony here: traditional microeconomic analysis is too sophisticated to be statistically manageable, while contemporary macroeconomics is too naïve to be taken seriously. Our aim in this paper is to steer a middle course between the two extremes: to apply methods suggested by Marshall and Walras to models suggested by Keynes. Whether we have chosen the right course remains to be seen. The only way to assess the factual merit of our theory is to apply it to the real world in the way all useful theories–physical, biological, economic, etc.–are always applied, namely, with a considerable amount of intuition and common sense.

Behavior Relations: Empirical Restrictions. As presently formulated, the empirical content of our model is of the second order of smalls. If we are to use the model to interpret published statistics, we must first set some limits to theoretical speculation by imposing empirically plausible restrictions on the basic behavior relations of our system.

(1) *The Income Locus.* The income locus is in the nature of an objective market constraint. The yield to any given household of a marginal increment in wealth will depend on the structure of its asset portfolio as well as the return on particular items in the portfolio; in principle, therefore, marginal yields may vary significantly among households in a single wealth class. As a practical matter, however, we should not expect this to be of any empirical significance. Studies of the portfolio behavior of households in different income and wealth classes indicate that the percentage distribution of broad classes of financial assets (e.g. money, time deposits, government bonds, corporate securities) is related in a systematic way to total wealth (Atkinson, 1956, 1964). As far as durable goods are concerned, it would appear that the majority of households acquire these in fairly well-defined 'priority patterns' (Pyatt, 1964). If these findings are anything to

go by, we may safely regard the marginal rate of return on wealth as a definite number the magnitude of which depends simply on the total asset holdings of the household. Straightforward measures of average yields by wealth class, together with current information about measured income, should provide an adequate picture of the income locus of a typical statistical household.

Although conclusive evidence on the relation between wealth and yields is not available, such evidence as we have suggests that yields are generally higher the larger the income and asset holdings of the household (Atkinson, 1956, pp. 78–9, 128–31) – which is to say that the typical income locus probably displays *positive* curvature. This is attributable to the (apparently quite uniform) tendency of wealthier households to hold larger proportions of equities as compared with direct debt assets and time deposits and related claims (ibid. pp. 63–85). But the yields earned by even the wealthiest households seldom rise as high as 10 per cent on earning assets[8], and the typical portfolio will also include a substantial quantity of non-earning assets. Accordingly, we are probably safe in supposing that the marginal rate of return on total wealth is, on the average, at most 4 to 6 per cent per annum, and that the same rate applies to all households. The substance of the argument that follows would be much the same whether the marginal rate of return were 10 per cent, 6 per cent or zero; and as long as we deal with rates of this magnitude, the curvature of the income locus is of no consequence.

(2) *The Consumption Locus.* The consumption locus, unlike the income locus, is by its nature subjective rather than objective. Indeed, the term 'consumption locus' is little more than a short-hand expression for a vast complex of social, economic, and psychological factors that determine a household's willingness to abstain from consuming its current wealth. To state the same idea in more operational terms: the consumption locus indicates for each possible level of current wealth what level of current income a household must enjoy to be willing to maintain its present wealth intact. This is clearly a meaningful concept. It may also be useful, provided that the forces it summarizes are relatively impervious to sudden change.

Our only *a priori* information about the consumption locus, given the generalized stability hypothesis and the positive slope of the income locus, is that it passes through the origin of the w–c plane and slopes upward from left to right. We may generate additional information only by carrying out conceptual experiments designed to discover what restrictions have to be imposed on individual consumption loci to produce hypothetical data on wealth and consumption that accord with the available statistical evidence.

Let us begin by supposing that all households have linear consumption loci, but that the slopes of different loci vary randomly from one household to another. Then cross-section data on wealth and consumption corresponding to a given distribution of service income will yield a random scatter of wealth-consumption points. Alternatively, suppose that the slopes of individual consumption loci tend to cluster about a common value. Then a cross-section scatter will be heavily concentrated within a certain pie-shaped area of the $w-c$ plane. More generally, we should expect any clustering of consumption loci (whether the loci were linear or not) to be revealed by cross-section data. Conversely, if an actual scatter of wealth-consumption points displays a definite pattern, we should infer from this that individual consumption loci tend to conform to a similar pattern.

Unfortunately, consumption research traditionally has been directed not towards relations between wealth and consumption, but rather towards relations between income and consumption. We cannot settle the issue before us, therefore, by running a regression of consumption on wealth. For this to be possible, we should require detailed information about household consumption expenditures at various levels of wealth. Such data are not available in any collection of published statistics. For both the United Kingdom and the United States, however, we do have information about mean consumption and wealth at various levels of income (Tables 2.1 and 2.2). For the United States alone, moreover, we have some data on the distribution of income and saving within three broad wealth classes (Table 2.3). A combination of these materials should tell us something about the existence and probable character of the 'modal' consumption locus even though the scatter it produces fails to satisfy conventional criteria of statistical relevance.

For purposes of comparison, we have plotted the data in Tables 2.1 and 2.2 as separate scatters in Figure 2.1. The similarity between the data for the US and UK is obvious. In both countries, mean wealth and consumption are, by and large, positively correlated with mean income. Moreover, consumption tends to increase less rapidly than wealth as income increases (with double-logarithmic scales, this is indicated by the negative curvature of the scatters for low income levels, by a slope of less than unity in the linear sections of the scatters). There is an evident difference between the US and UK scatters at the lower end of the income scale, where the UK data indicate a negative correlation between wealth and consumption. But it would be a mistake to pay any attention to this phenomenon; for we know that there are many households in both countries with negative or zero net worth (e.g. about 35 per cent of UK households, 15 per cent of US households (Lydall and Lansing, 1959, p. 60)), and these simply disappear from the wealth distribution when we classify households by income level. That the resulting loss of information is substantial becomes clear when we reflect that the lowest income brackets in both countries will include large numbers of retired people with substantial accumulations of wealth. This alone would explain the truncation of the two scatters and the negatively-sloped section of the UK relation.

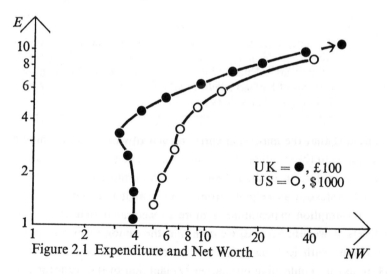

Figure 2.1 Expenditure and Net Worth

The US data on income and saving ratios by wealth classes (Table 2.3) give us a clearer idea of the dispersion of consumption expenditures within different wealth classes. The lowest class in the table (under $1,000) is far enough down the wealth scale to tell us most of what we want to know about the corresponding section of Table 2.1; and the income classifications are sufficiently fine to permit us to gauge the probable distribution of consumption in other sections of the same table.

Income, Wealth, and the Theory of Consumption   61

TABLE 2.1. United Kingdom income units:
mean net worth and expenditure by income classes 1953

income class	gross mean income (£)	mean net worth (£)	mean expenditure (£)
0–99	82	386	101
100–199	146	384	156
200–299	251	356	255
300–399	351	325	347
400–499	466	419	451
500–599	545	563	540
600–699	645	876	646
700–799	742	1372	755
800–899	870	2144	853
1000–1499	1151	3797	1086
1500 and over	2921	16981	2571

Source: Mean gross income and mean net worth are derived from data
presented in K. H. Stern, 'Consumers' Net Worth: The 1953 Savings Survey',
Bulletin of the Oxford Univ. Institute of Statistics, Vol. 18, 1956, p. 12 (table
VII). Mean expenditures are calculated from data on income and saving given
in L. R. Klein, 'Patterns of Savings', *Bulletin of the Oxford Univ. Institute of
Statistics*, Vol. 17, 1955, p. 182 (table IV).

We note first that the maximum entry in each row of Table 2.3 moves
from the lowest to the middle to the highest income class as we proceed up
the wealth scale. Except in the lowest wealth class, moreover, the saving
ratio increases steadily as we move from lower to higher incomes, indicating that consumption expenditure is more concentrated than income at
higher levels of wealth. Second, we note that the saving ratio is negative
for households with less than $3,000 in current income *and* more than
$10,000 in assets, confirming our earlier explanation of the truncation of
the distributions shown in Figure 2.1. Finally, we observe that consumption
is slightly less than income for households with assets under $1,000 *and*
incomes of less than $7,500, which indicates that consumption and income
are distributed in much the same way at lower wealth levels. On this ground
alone, we should be justified in adding some points to the lower ends of the
scatters in Figure 2.1 to indicate that the modal consumption locus extends
back towards the origin.

TABLE 2.2. United States spending units: mean net worth and expenditures by income classes

	1950		
	net	mean	mean
income class	mean income	net worth	expenditure
	($)	($)	($)
under $1,000	655	5,073	1,339
$1,000–1,999	1,601	5,487	1,834
2,000–2,999	2,645	6,538	2,809
3,000–3,999	3,633	7,145	3,691
4,000–4,999	4,617	8,990	4,614
5,000–7,499	6,032	12,076	5,809
7,500 and over	11,573	42,932	9,304

Source: Mean net income and mean expenditure are derived from data given in *Study of Consumer Expenditures Incomes and Savings* (The Wharton School and Bureau of Labor Statistics, Univ. of Penn., 1957), Vol. XVIII, Table 1–1, p. 2. The figures on net worth are calculated from aggregate data given in Raymond W. Goldsmith, *A Study of Savings in the United States* (Princeton: Princeton Univ. Press, 1956), Vol. III, Table W–46, p. 122.

(3) *The Negative Curvature Hypothesis.* Taking account of all the considerations mentioned above, we conclude that there is a definite clustering of consumption loci in the $w-c$ plane, with considerable dispersion of individual loci, however, about the modal locus. We infer from this that the modal locus must exhibit less curvature than suggested by the points plotted in Figure 2.1; for a transfer of retired persons from the lower to the middle and upper ranges of the scatter – a direct implication of classifying these units by wealth rather than income – could hardly help but straighten the scatters as presently shown. At higher levels of wealth, the scatters in Figure 2.1 probably conform more or less closely with the modal locus; for at these levels it is clear that current income imposes no direct constraint on current consumption, hence that the observed relation between wealth and consumption is voluntary rather than forced. Finally, we conclude from the information in Table 2.3 that the locus starts somewhere in the neighborhood of the origin and joins the scatters given by our income-classified wealth-consumption data at the point where they tend to become truncated.

The sum and substance of all this may be put more precisely by saying

Income, Wealth, and the Theory of Consumption   63

TABLE 2.3. Distribution of spending units and saving ratios by asset and income classes (non-moving US spending units, 1960–62)

		MEAN TWO-YEAR INCOME				
number of units	*total assets in 1960*	*under $3,000*	*$3,000 –4,999*	*$5,000 –7,499*	*$7,500 –9,999*	*$10,000 or more*
	under $1,000					
207	A [1]	37 *	30	25	7	1
	B [2]	9·2	3·7	4·8	†	†
	$1,000– 9,999					
422	A	22	18	29 *	19	12
	B	2·5	9·3	10·7	12·2	15·4
	$10,000 or more					
380	A	14	15	25	14	32 *
	B	−8·7	6·6	13·0	17·5	23·6

[1] Indicates percent of units in wealth class with stated income.

[2] Indicates mean saving ratio of units in stated income class.

* Indicates maximum percentage in row.

† Too few cases to present data.

Source: Charles A. Lininger, 'Estimates of Rates of Saving', Survey Research Center, Economic Behavior Program, University of Michigan, mimeograph, p. 11, Table 2.

that the modal w–c scatter, plotted on double-logarithmic graph paper, is probably linear, and that the corresponding least-squares regression line will most certainly have a slope of less than unity. If this guess is correct, then the implied mathematical relationship between consumption and wealth is given by

$$c = hw^b , \qquad (2.1)$$

where h is a positive constant, and b lies between zero and unity.

The graph of the function (2.1) is illustrated in Figure 2.2. In conformity with an old tradition, the relation exhibits negative curvature throughout– suggesting that the marginal urgency of consumption decreases as household wealth increases. In terms of our model, what this means is simply

that the MPCW is a strictly decreasing function of household wealth. As for
the value of *b*, experiments with alternative graphical regressions using the
wealth-consumption data in Tables 2.1 and 2.2 (supplemented by some
freehand plots of points corresponding to lower levels of wealth than any
shown in Tables 2.1 and 2.2) suggest that it is between 0·35 and 0·40 in
both the United States and the United Kingdom, the value almost certainly
being lower in the UK than in the US. This implies a MPCW ($= bc/w$) of
around 0·10 for the wealthiest households in both countries, which agrees
well with marginal c/w ratios calculated from the data in Tables 2.1 and
2.2. The value of *h*, assuming that data are expressed in units of £1,000 or
$1,000, as appropriate, appears to be about 2·6 in the US and 0·33 in the
UK. If we convert pounds into dollars at the official exchange rate of 2·4
dollars to the pound, the UK figure would be about 1·08. This suggests that
British households are vastly more thrifty than US households – or, turning
it around, that British households are habituated to a much lower standard
of living than US households.

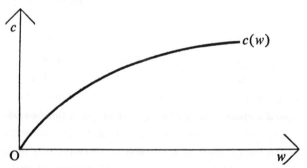

Figure 2.2 The 'Modal' Consumption Locus

From an analytical point of view, the characteristic of the modal consumption locus that merits major emphasis is its negative curvature. If
this restriction is valid, then various implications for observed behavior
follow almost as a matter of course. First, we should expect the wealthiest
households in any society to violate the generalized stability hypothesis;
for at sufficiently high values of *w*, the MPCW will almost certainly be less
than the marginal rate of return on wealth. The validity of this proposition
is supported by Goldsmith's finding that US households with estates valued
at more than $200,000, unlike households with estates valued at $60,000
or less, tend on the average to go on saving and accumulating assets up to

the very end of their mortal existence (Goldsmith, 1956, vol. 1, pp. 222–4). Second, we should expect wealth in any advanced society to be much more unequally distributed than income. In the US and UK, for example, we should expect the distribution of wealth to be roughly proportional to the *cube* of the distribution of income. The validity of this proposition is supported by Lorenz curves of income and net worth for the US and UK in the middle 1950s (Lydall and Lansing, 1959, p. 61). Third, we should expect the marginal propensity to consume windfall gains to vary inversely with the size of the windfall; and this proposition also appears to be supported by the evidence.[9]

III. *Statistical Implications*
We shall focus attention on cross-section regressions of consumption on income, dealing almost as an afterthought with time-series regressions of income on consumption and consumption on wealth. This procedure happens to reflect our opinion of the relative importance of the two topics and emphasizes the area in which we believe we have something essentially new to say.

The bulk of the present literature on household behavior consists of routine exercises in statistical curve fitting. Any number of variables may be (and have been) entered in this game; the payoff in regression coefficients, standard errors, and *t*-statistics is always sufficient to make every player look and feel like a winner. Like any mountain of facts, this one has a certain scientific value, but it has yet to produce more than a molehill of usable knowledge. To make sense of statistical regressions, one must start with a clear conception of the mechanism that is supposed to be generating observations; otherwise one cannot determine whether a given set of results is descriptive of household behavior or is just a piece of arithmetic. More specifically, one must develop from microeconomic considerations an explicit set of statistical relations that permits one to assert in advance which results are and which are not consistent with Basman's 'maintained hypotheses' about household behavior (1963).

Cross-Section Relations Between Consumption and Income. Suppose that we have to deal with a group of households for which the generalized stability hypothesis is valid. In these circumstances, our model determines just one time-invariant reduced-form relation between consumption and income corresponding to any given vector $m = (m_1, \ldots, m_i, \ldots, m_N)$ of

5

individual service incomes, namely, the set of equilibrium consumption-income pairs ($\hat{y}_i, \hat{c}_i$) defined by the equations

$$c_i = y_i = m_i + r\hat{w}_i. \tag{3.1}$$

To any given level and distribution of aggregate service income, $\Sigma_i m_i = M$, there then corresponds a scatter of mean values of the variables c_i and y_i that clusters more or less closely about a 45° line through the origin of the y–c plane. In the discussion that follows, we shall be concerned exclusively with these mean values. To avoid notational frills and error terms, however, we shall denote these means by the same letters as have been used heretofore to represent exact values of household variables.

If we adhere strictly to the assumption that variations in household position within the service-income distribution occur strictly at random, every point in the scatter defined by (3.1) will lie on or close to the 45° line; that is, a regression of c_i on y_i will yield a line that coincides with the latter. In a sense, therefore, the 45° line represents the 'true' long-period income-consumption function for a stationary economy, implying that the long-period marginal and average propensities to consume income are identically unity.

The stationary economy is, of course, a theoretical fiction. As a pedagogical device, however, the concept has its uses, for it enables us to isolate and deal effectively with aspects of behavior that a more realistic analysis would simply obscure. For the time being, therefore, we shall maintain the fiction of stationarity and see where it leads.

(1) *The Stationary Economy*. Recalling Schumpeter's classic account of 'The Circular Flow', we remark first that some changes in household position within the service-income distribution (or to use a more convenient phrase, *income permutations*) may be systematic rather than random even in a stationary state. Life-cycle phenomena (emphasized in the Modigliani-Brumberg model of household behavior) and economic survival processes (emphasized in Friedman's permanent income theory) are cases in point. But one can imagine other 'natural forces' – climatic, technological, political, etc. – that would also induce relatively uniform and persistent flows of households from one level to another within a given service-income distribution. In these circumstances, the number of households in any given income class would never change, but the names of the actual households in any class would change over time. Despite the strict stationarity

of the economy, therefore, few households would ever find themselves in a state of equilibrium.

Households that experienced an increase in measured income would, according to our model, temporarily save a significant proportion of the increment; that is, their consumption would tend to rise by less than their income. Points in the $c-y$ scatter associated with such households would thus lie to the right of the 45° line. Similarly, households that experienced a reduction in measured income would temporarily dissave; their consumption would tend to decline by less than income, producing $c-y$ observations to the left of the 45° line. Extending the argument to households as a group, we infer that the scatter of $c-y$ points, instead of clustering closely about the 45° line, would exhibit considerable dispersion–the exact amount depending on the nature of the forces generating income permutations and the speed with which households adapted to changes in income status.

As long as the level and percentage distribution of aggregate service income are given, what one household gains by an income permutation another household must lose. The effect of any given income permutation process is therefore: (i) to produce dispersion in the $c-y$ scatter; (ii) rotate the scatter to the right or left about its mean point; (iii) a combination of (i) and (ii). In no circumstances can the regression line through the scatter lie entirely to the right or left of the 45° line, for this would imply a general movement of households towards higher or lower levels of service income –a contradiction of our stationarity hypothesis. To determine precisely how an income permutation process will affect the $y-c$ scatter, however, we need to obtain an explicit expression for the regression of consumption on income that will be generated by our model during a unit interval of observation.

By hypothesis, income permutation processes operate continuously. The impact of a particular process during a given time interval will therefore be much the same regardless of what specific stretch of calendar time is chosen as the interval of observation. The disequilibrating force of a particular process will depend, however, on the length of the interval of observation, being generally greater the longer the interval.[10] For the purposes of our analysis, it is convenient to think of the interval of observation as that unit of calendar time in which consumption and income flows are expressed. The effect of an income permutation process on a statistically

representative household may then be expressed in terms of the change in
the average value of its service income during a similar (but not necessarily
contemporaneous) time interval.

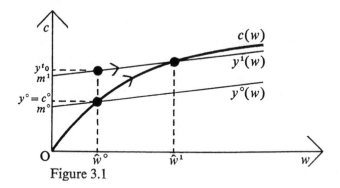

Figure 3.1

This is illustrated in Figure 3.1 where, for the sake of simplicity, we
assume that the household is initially in stationary equilibrium with
$c^\circ = m^\circ + r\hat{w}^\circ$. An increase in service income from m° to m^1 leads to positive
saving, hence to an increase in accumulated wealth and consumption at a
rate per unit time that will depend on the difference between the slopes of
the consumption and income loci. As asserted, the time path of consumption, starting from the initial value c° at, say, date t_0, is defined unambiguously in terms of the change in service income, $m^1 - m^\circ$, and the
properties of the consumption and income loci. Unfortunately, the fact
that consumption at any date $t > t_0$ is related in a definite way to the
change in service income at date t_0 does not mean that the relation can be expressed by a simple formula. Indeed, it cannot be so
expressed; for in general changes in wealth (and consumption) will be
associated with concurrent changes in the MPCW and in gross income.
If our analysis of income-permutation processes is to lead to explicit
regression formulae, therefore, we must first introduce some specialized
assumptions to permit us to establish a simple link between changes in
service income and subsequent variations in consumption expenditure.

We might devise various artful dodges to connect consumption with
service income in an analytically manageable fashion while continuing to
treat gross income and the MPCW as functions of accumulated wealth.

For our purposes, however, it is preferable to adopt a more straightforward and outwardly radical procedure and suppose, first, that $r = 0$, so that gross income is identically equal to service income; second, that the wealth elasticity of consumption is unity, so that the MPCW is a constant. These restrictions do not alter the qualitative characteristics of our model in any significant respect. They do entail potentially significant changes in the quantitative implications of our theory; but whether these are of any practical consequence cannot be decided on *a priori* grounds. Depending on the magnitudes involved, and the applications that we consider, we may discover that even the quantitative implications of our model are in satisfactory accord with the empirical evidence. For the time being, therefore, any misgivings we may have on this score may be held in abeyance. We shall return to the matter after we have developed the statistical implications of our 'special theory' and are in a position to say something definite about its conformity with factual knowledge.

Turning to the task of deriving explicit regression formulae from our model, we begin by assuming that the initial state of the economy at, say, date t_0, is one of stationary equilibrium. Supposing further that $c_i^t = a_i w_i^t$ and $m_i^t = y_i$, we may assert on the basis of the argument in Part I (pp. 46–55) that the consumption of a representative household at the end of a unit time interval starting at date t_0 is given by the equation

$$
\begin{aligned}
c_i^{t_0+1} = c_i' &= a_i w_i^{t_0+1} \\
&= a_i\{ m_i'/a_i - (m_i'/a_i)e^{-a_i}\} \\
&= y_i' - (y_i' - y_i)e^{-a_i},
\end{aligned} \tag{3.2}
$$

where y_i and y_i' denote, respectively, the (average) service income flows of the household at the beginning and end of the interval (i.e. $y_i' - y_i$ represents the change in the average value of the two flows at the beginning of the unit time interval).

Now the least-squares estimates of the slope and intercept coefficients of the regression of consumption on income at date t_0+1 are defined by the usual formulae as

$$
B' = \frac{\Sigma_i(c_i' - \bar{c}')(y_i' - \bar{y}')}{\Sigma_i(y_i' - \bar{y}')^2} \tag{3.3}
$$

$$
A' = \bar{c}' - B'\bar{y}', \tag{3.4}
$$

where barred variables, as is customary, stand for group means. Replacing

c_i' in (3.3) by its equivalent from (3.2), we have

$$B' = \frac{\Sigma_i(y_i'-\bar{y}')^2}{\Sigma_i(y_i'-\bar{y}')^2} - \frac{\Sigma_i(y_i'-\bar{y}')^2 e^{-a_i}}{\Sigma_i(y_i'-\bar{y}')^2} + \frac{\Sigma_i(y_i-\bar{y})(y_i'-\bar{y}')e^{-a_i}}{\Sigma_i(y_i'-\bar{y}')^2}.$$

(3.5)

In general, the weights e^{-a_i} that appear in the last two terms of (3.5) may be expected to vary considerably from one household to another. Referring back to our initial expression for consumption at date $t_0 + 1$, we note that the response of a household to a change in income will be quicker the greater its marginal propensity to consume wealth (a_i), which is to say that households with large MPCWs will contribute relatively little to the dispersion of the $c-y$ scatter. Neither will such households hold large amounts of wealth. It thus seems plausible to argue that our conclusions about the form of the $c-y$ scatter will not be seriously affected if we replace a_i in (3.5) by a wealth-weighted average of MPCWs, namely,

$$a = \Sigma_i(w_i a_i/N).$$

(3.6)

Carrying out the indicated substitution, we rewrite (3.5) as

$$B' = 1 - \left\{ 1 - \frac{\Sigma_i(y_i-\bar{y})(y_i'-\bar{y}')}{\Sigma_i(y_i'-\bar{y}')^2} \right\} e^{-a}$$

$$= 1 - (1-s_y r_y)e^{-a},$$

(3.7)

where r_y represents the coefficient of correlation between the income arrays y and y_i, and s_y represents the ratio of the standard deviation of the array y to the standard deviation of the array y'. Under stationary conditions, however, y and y' differ only in the arrangement of their elements, not in the elements themselves; hence $s_y = 1$ and $\bar{c}_i = \bar{c} = \bar{y} = \bar{y}_i$. Given these restrictions, we obtain the following least-squares estimates of the slope and intercept coefficients of the regression of consumption on income at date $t_0 + 1$:

$$B' = 1 - (1-r_y)e^{-(a)}$$

(3.8)

$$A' = \bar{y}(1-r_y)e^{-(a)}.$$

(3.9)

Like any other correlation coefficient, r_y can only assume values between ± 1. If all variations in income flows are strictly random, $r_y = 1$, and the regression line coincides with the 45° line, as indicated earlier. If income permutations are systematic in their effect, r_y will be less than unity; hence B' will be less than unity and its intercept positive. If all households initially have the same service income, $r_y = 0$ and the slope of the regression line will depend simply on the magnitude of the adjustment coefficient $e^{-(a)}$, being smaller the less the value of the exponent (a).[11] Finally, if income permutation processes produce large-scale flows of households from one end of the income scale to the other, r_y may be negative, in which case the slope of the regression line will be negative.[12]

The last case is no doubt rather fanciful, but it is of some theoretical interest for it indicates, what is not at all intuitively obvious, that even if every household responds positively to an increase in service income, a statistical regression of consumption on income may lead to exactly the contrary conclusion. The case may also be of some practical interest, for something approaching it must happen in any society where retirement incomes are substantially below the average for the society as a whole. Since the number of households that move from gainful employment to retirement during any single year is small relative to the total working population, we should not expect the retirement process to produce a negatively sloped c-y scatter for any large sample of households. However, we should expect to observe a significant flattening of the scatter at the lower end of the income scale (because the asset holdings of retired people tend to be well above the average for low-income households as a group), and perhaps some flattening also at the top (because of increased income among persons who replace those who have retired). Such effects have been observed and noted by Friedman (1957b, pp. 48–51), but accounted for on different grounds (namely, 'nonrepresentativeness of the samples or errors in recorded responses . . .').

The simplicity of our regression formulae makes it possible to determine the precise effects of changes in the parameters r_y and a. For if we differentiate B' and A' partially, first with respect to a, next with respect to r_y, we obtain:

$$
\left.
\begin{aligned}
\frac{\partial B'}{\partial a} &= (1-r_y)a\,e^{-(a)} \geqslant 0 \\[2mm]
\frac{\partial B'}{\partial r_y} &= e^{-(a)} > 0 \\[2mm]
\frac{\partial A'}{\partial a} &= -\bar{y}a(1-r_y)e^{-(a)} \leqslant 0 \\[2mm]
\frac{\partial A'}{\partial r_y} &= -\bar{y}e^{-(a)} < 0 .
\end{aligned}
\right\}
\qquad (3.10)
$$

In plain words, our theory implies a higher slope and a lower intercept the greater the marginal propensity to consume wealth, and the higher the correlation between income arrays at the beginning and end of the period of observation. For later discussion, it is relevant to emphasize here that the effects of fluctuating income (lower value of r_y) are statistically indistinguishable from the effects of increased wealth (lower values of a). Thus 'entrepreneurial' households may exhibit relatively low income-propensities to consume either because of uncertain incomes or because their holdings of assets tend to be large relative to their consumption. Similarly, 'proletarian' households may exhibit relatively high income-propensities to consume either because their incomes are stable or because their holdings of wealth are slight relative to consumption. Though the implications of our theory are definite, therefore, they are not unambiguous in empirical import. One must be correspondingly cautious in applying them to practical problems.

We need not suppose that the MPCW as defined by the index (3.6) is the same for all households. Indeed, if we regard our present model as an approximation to a 'true' model for which the negative curvature hypothesis is valid, then we should expect the average MPCW to be higher the lower the average income of the group of households under consideration. Other things being equal, therefore, the slope derivatives in (3.10) may be taken to imply: (i) that cross-section MPCYs will be smaller the higher the average level of household income; (ii) that households with variable incomes will tend to have lower MPCYs than households with steady incomes. A significant portion of Friedman's analysis in the *Theory of the Consumption Function* is directed towards showing that the second of these implications is empirically valid (see particularly his discussion of farm and non-farm families at pp. 58–69, and of occupation characteristics of families at pp. 69–79). His arguments are compelling, considered in the context of his model (which omits explicit mention of adjustment processes); they are merely suggestive in the context of ours. The first proposition accords well with tradition and common sense and has received contemporary support from many writers (Klein and Liviatan, 1957; Friend, 1957; Mayer, 1963; Friend and Taubman, 1966). Resting as it does on non-linearity assumptions, it is disputed by Friedman–though his own charts of farm and non-farm regressions (p. 59) and of income-change groups (pp. 101 and 105) might be considered to lend firm support to the traditional view. From the standpoint of our model, no judgment is warranted, for in none of the studies that we have examined is proper care taken to ensure that 'other things' are in any degree equal.

One implication of our model that we have not so far mentioned must now be emphasized. We refer to the requirement that mean consumption be equal to mean income for households as a group. With minor exceptions, the mean points of actual consumption-income scatters lie off the 45° line. It could hardly be otherwise, for the world from which our observations are drawn is seldom in a state approaching stationarity. This restriction on our model is easily relaxed, provided that we go no further than supposing that the economy with which we have to deal experiences occasional bursts of growth. Sustained expansions of service income, such as characterize all advanced economies, raise some essentially new problems that require separate treatment. (See below, pp. 77–8).

The effects of once-over changes in aggregate service income may be brought out most clearly by temporarily ignoring income permutation processes. On this understanding, the value of r_y may be set at unity since, with the distribution of service income given, changes in aggregate service income must be accompanied by equal proportionate changes in the service income of every household. The effects of such a change in income can then be taken into account in our stationary regression formulae by re-introducing the relative dispersion coefficient $s_y = \sigma_y / \sigma'_y$. A rise in aggregate income implies a value of s_y less than unity. But changes in s_y affect the slope of the regression line in precisely the same manner as changes in r_y. Thus a rise in aggregate service income must reduce, while a fall must increase, the slope of the regression line. Noting further that the intercept of the regression line is affected in precisely the contrary direction by variations in income, we infer that an increase in income will shift the entire regression line to the right, while a decrease in income will shift it to the left.

We conclude that when changes in aggregate service income are combined with income permutation processes, the relevant least-squares coefficients of the regression of consumption on income are given by

$$B' = 1 - (1 - s_y r_y) e^{-(a)} \tag{3.7}$$

(that is, the general formula given earlier (p. 70)) and

$$A' = \bar{y}(1 - s_y r_y) e^{-(a)}. \tag{3.7'}$$

It is evident from the formal similarity between these relations and the formulae (3.8) and (3.9) that changes in the parameters a and r_y will have much the same effect as before, and, as indicated already, that changes in s_y (corresponding to changes in aggregate income) will affect B' and A' in just the same way as changes in r_y. The inclusion in our formulae of the 'shift factor' s_y significantly modifies our earlier conclusions, however, about the range of admissible values of B'. For suppose that all households experience a sudden decrease in service income; that is, suppose that s_y is substantially greater than unity. Then if r_y is sufficiently close to unity, the bracketed expression in (3.7) may be *negative*, in which case the value of B' will be *greater* than unity. In these circumstances, indeed, the value of B' may be greater than $\bar{c}/\bar{y}$, and both may exceed unity. That is to say, *the group marginal propensity to save may be negative.*

At first glance, this possibility seems as fanciful as our earlier case of a negative marginal propensity to consume. On further reflection, however, it is clear that a negative marginal propensity to save is very likely to turn up among household groups that contain large numbers of newly retired persons or large numbers of newly married couples; for both marriage and retirement may reduce effective household income by as much as 50 per cent in a single year.

A striking confirmation of the results suggested by our model is provided by Malcolm Fisher's cross-section analysis of UK households included in the 1953 Savings Survey of the Oxford University Institute of Statistics, from which the data in Table 3.1 are drawn.[13] Notice that negative marginal propensities to save turn up in almost every age group where we should expect to find them, and are notably absent elsewhere.[14]

The significance of Fisher's findings may be brought out more clearly by a graphical illustration. Suppose that we have to deal with a group of households all of which are initially in stationary equilibrium. Then we may suppose that the corresponding $c-y$ scatter is represented initially by a set of points all of which lie on the 45° line as indicated in Figure 3.2 – each point representing households in a particular income class. Now suppose that every household experiences an equal proportionate decline in service income. Supposing that wealthier households are relatively slower to adapt to the change in income status (as suggested by the negative curvature hypothesis), the $c-y$ scatter will shift leftwards from the 45° line as indicated by the arrows in Figure 3.2. The APCY after the shift

TABLE 3.1. UK spending units: 1953 cross-section marginal and average propensities to save * out of net income

occupation		AGE GROUPS						all ages
		1 (18–24)	2 (25–34)	3 (35–44)	4 (45–54)	5 (55–64)	6 (65 and over)	
Manual	MPSY	·0416	−·0646	·0112 †	−·0013 †	−·1485	−·1542 †	−·0262
	APSY	·0120	−·0075	·0098	−·0019	·0283	−·0990	·0005
Clerical and Sales	MPSY	−·0422	·0867	·0673	·0821	·0104 †	−·0542	·0391
	APSY	·0076	−·0155	−·0483	·0200	·0109	−·0438	−·0086
Managerial	MPSY	−·1165	·1692	·2213	·3063	·1442	−·6166	·2112
	APSY	−·0370	−·0168	·0507	·0574	·0500	−·2731	·0268
Self-employed	MPSY	—	·7141	·2340	·2362	·6039	·3867	·3594
	APSY	—	·1979	·2140	·0103	·3010	·1302	·1607
Retired and unoccupied	MPSY	−·0932	·1576	−·0438	−·4193	−·3614	−·0293	−·1541
	APSY	−·0150	−·0375	−·0014	−·1706	−·1212	−·0905	−·0958
All	MPSY	·0173 †	·1541	·1476	·1591	·0825	−·0493	·1020
	APSY	·0089	·0004	·0283	·0061	·0215	−·0850	·0034

* Saving excludes purchase of consumer durables.   † Denotes standard error exceeds point estimate.

Source: Assembled from data presented in Malcolm R. Fisher, 'Exploration in Savings Behaviour' *Bulletin of the Oxford University Institute of Statistics*, vol. 18, no. 3 (Aug., 1956), Table 2.1 (p. 232), Table 2.3 (p. 236), Table 2.5 (p. 239), and Appendix A (p. 264).

is indicated by the slope of the ray OA, the MPCY by the slope of the line MM'. As indicated, the 'statistical' MPCY exceeds the 'statistical' APCY, and both exceed unity. But note that *no individual household will ever behave as the statistical results suggest*. To suppose that cross-section regressions of consumption on income accurately reflect individual behaviour responses is to commit a gross fallacy of composition.

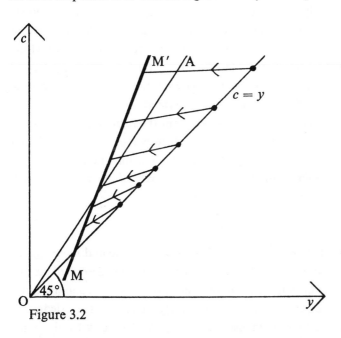

Figure 3.2

(2) *The Nonstationary Economy.* It is evident on *a priori* grounds that estimates of the MPCY based on stationary assumptions will be severely biased unless the state of the economy at the outset of the interval of observation is truly one of stationary equilibrium—biased upward if the economy is growing, downward if the economy is declining. That the amount of the bias may be substantial in practice is indicated by calculating 'typical' MPCYs using direct estimates of r_y suggested by Friedman (0·83 for urban households, 0·69 for farm families), and a value for e^{-a} of 0·82.[15] These calculations yield an MPCY for urban households of 0·86, and an MPCY for farm families of 0·75. A typical value of the MPCY in actual studies of urban families would be about 0·75, and for farm families about 0·60. Thus the bias in our estimates is substantial, and in the anticipated direction.

Income, Wealth, and the Theory of Consumption   77

Whether growth alone can account for the magnitude of the bias is another matter. Recalling our earlier discussion of the effect of growth on the average consumption-income ratio of an individual household, however, it seems plausible to suppose that rates of growth of between 1·5 and 2·5 per cent per annum could produce a reduction of 10–15 per cent in our estimated MPCYs. For if all households in a steadily growing economy had identical MPCWs, the mean point of the cross-section scatter of $c-y$ points would tend at all times to lie on or close to a ray through the origin of slope $a/(g+a)$. Even in the absence of income permutations, therefore, the MPCY would be significantly less than unity for typical values of g and a. A combination of growth and income permutations should thus produce MPCYs that accord closely with actual experience.

Let us check this conjecture by working out the regression implications of a steady-growth model, assuming as before that $y_i^t = m_i^t$ and that $c_i^t = aw_i^t$. Dealing first with a situation in which income permutations are absent, we may describe the equilibrium time path of consumption for a representative household by the relation

$$c_i^t = am_i e^{gt}/(g+a), \tag{3.11}$$

where g denotes the rate of growth of aggregate income and m_i is a given constant. The relation (3.11) defines what might be described as the 'permanent consumption function' of a steadily growing economy. Since the ratio of consumption to income $(a/(g+a))$ is analogous to Friedman's 'propensity to consume permanent income', we denote it by the same symbol in the discussion that follows: that is, $a/(g+a) = k$ (cf. *TCF*, p. 17).

We next introduce income permutation processes by supposing that the base values of individual service incomes vary over time in a systematic way, the distribution of aggregate service income maintaining the same form at all times. Recalling earlier discussion, the consumption of a representative household will be given in this case not by (3.11) but by

$$c_i^t = k\{y_i' - (y_i' - y)e^{-at}\}, \tag{3.12}$$

where $y_i = m_i e^{gt_0}$ and $y_i' = m_i' e^{gt_0}$–the household being assumed to be in growth equilibrium, of couse, at date t_0.

Clearly, the only novel effect of growth is to alter the frame of reference from a stationary to an exponential trend. Indeed, since (3.12) has exactly the same analytic form as the corresponding relation in a stationary economy, we may proceed immediately to write out the implied least-squares regression coefficients:

$$B^* = k\{1-(1-s_y r_y)\,e^{-(a)}\} \tag{3.13}$$

$$A^* = \bar{c}(1-s_y r_y)\,e^{-(a)}. \tag{3.14}$$

These formulae gives the stationary coefficients as a special case, for when $g = 0$, $k = s_y = 1$. In general, however, the MPCY implied by (3.13) will differ significantly from that suggested by the stationary case. If g is positive, for example, then k and s_y will both be less than unity; hence the $c-y$ scatter will be substantially flatter than would be true in a stationary state. Conversely, if g is negative, the $c-y$ scatter will be steeper than in comparable stationary conditions.

Let us now recalculate our theoretical MPCYs, assuming that $g = 0.02$ (approximately the rate of growth of real per capita income in the United States during the period 1900–64). Using the same estimates as before of r_y and e^{-a}, we obtain 0·78 as a typical MPCY for urban households, and 0·68 as a typical MPCY for farm households. These values are close enough to actual experience to be considered acceptable. Indeed, with minor adjustments in r_y to levels that are consistent with alternative estimates suggested by Friedman (1957b, p. 187), our theoretical MPCYs can be made to correspond exactly with observed values in any of the studies discussed by Friedman.

We are now in a position to make a tentative assessment of the empirical consequences of assuming that wealth-elasticities of consumption are unity and that the marginal rate of return on wealth is zero. Briefly, the statistical implications of our model do not appear to be significantly affected by either of these restrictions. The explanation may lie in the facts: (i) that our analysis of cross-section regressions is by its very nature confined to impact effects; (ii) that property income is in practice a negligible proportion of gross income for all but a handful of actual households.

By virtue of (i), what appears to be an extremely rough and ready approximation to an adequate model of household behavior may fail to reveal itself as such simply because we do not pursue the implications of the model beyond a single time interval. As we shall discover at a later point in our discussion, the assumption that wealth-elasticities of consumption are unity appears to be consistent also with empirical evidence on the secular relation between consumption and wealth – an apparent contradiction of our earlier conjecture that the modal consumption locus exhibits negative curvature. For reasons that are not clear, therefore, our 'special theory' seems to possess a higher degree of factual validity than could reasonably have been anticipated on *a priori* grounds.

As for (ii), it may be doubted whether our model would perform well in an analysis of the behavior of relatively wealthy households. Even here, however, it is possible to argue that the *direct* impact effects of changes in non-property income are likely to be so large in relation to the *indirect* effects of induced variations in property income as to preclude accurate identification of the latter in empirical data. The moral would seem to be that, in an inexact science like economics, we have less to fear from quantitative than from qualitative errors in the specification of our theoretical models.

(3) *Wealth and Permanent Income.* There is an evident resemblance between our model of a growing economy and Friedman's permanent income theory. Since Friedman's model is known to be in broad accord with the factual evidence, not only for the United States but for a variety of other countries as well, it is desirable for us to show that our theory is capable of reproducing all of Friedman's results. Otherwise we should have to plod through a vast maze of budget-study evidence the central plan of which has already been provided by Friedman.

The relation between Friedman's model and ours may be brought out most effectively by comparing corresponding formulae for the slope coefficient of the $c-y$ regression line. Friedman's (1957b, p. 32) formula, based on the assumption that mean transitory components of income and consumption are uncorrelated with one another and with corresponding permanent components, is simply

$$b = kP_y,$$ (3.15)

k being interpreted as the propensity to consume permanent income, P_y as the fraction of any difference in measured income that can on the average be attributed to a difference in permanent income. Our formula (3.13), based on the assumption that variations in measured income produce variations in consumption via their effect on current holdings of wealth, is naturally more complex. Thus, we interpret k as measuring the extent to which differences in steadily rising levels of household income are reflected in current holdings of accumulated wealth. Similarly, we interpret the bracketed portion of our slope formula, that is $(1-(1-s_y r_y)\,e^{-(a)})$ as measuring the extent to which differences in stationary levels of household income are associated with differences in current wealth.

Our k, like Friedman's, represents the propensity to consume permanent income; but in our model, the value of k depends on the rate at which income is growing and the speed with which households adapt to resulting trends in absolute income. Our expression $(1-(1-s_y r_y)\,e^{-(a)})$, by analogy with Friedman's coefficient P_y, may be regarded as the fraction of any difference in measured income that is fully reflected in 'permanent wealth'; but in our model the magnitude of this expression depends not only on the correlation between current and past income but also on the rate at which households adapt to changes in absolute income status.

On this showing, the connection between our theory and Friedman's is at best loose and imprecise. However, the matter is not as hopeless as it appears, for Friedman does not in practice rely on his initial definition of b to interpret observed behavior. On the contrary, in all but a minority of practical applications, he assumes that permanent income is defined in terms of measured income by a differential equation of the form

$$dy_p/dt = \beta(y^t - y_p^t)\,,\tag{3.16}$$

where β denotes a given 'speed of adjustment' coefficient (Friedman, 1957b, p. 143). Starting from any initial value y_p^o of permanent income and given any fixed value y^o of measured income, this differential equation has the solution

$$y_p^t = y^o - (y^o - y_p^o)e^{-\beta}\,.\tag{3.17}$$

Thus, if we follow Friedman in supposing that permanent consumption at any date t is given by

$$c_p^t = k y_p^t\,,\tag{3.20}$$

we see that permanent consumption will be correlated with the mean transitory component of measured income if this component differs from zero (Eisner, Friedman and Houthakker, 1958, pp. 974–5, 993).

If this interpretation of Friedman's analysis is correct, then the time path of measured consumption for a representative household – assuming the mean transitory component of consumption is identically zero – is given by

$$c^t = c_p^t = k\{y^o - (y^o - y_p^o)e^{-\beta}\}\,.\tag{3.21}$$

If we interpret y_p^o and y^o, respectively, as measuring the income of the household before and after an income permutation, it is a straightforward exercise to show that the corresponding slope coefficient of the least-squares regression line through the $c-y$ scatter is given not by Friedman's original formula (3.17), but rather by

$$b^* = k\{1-(1-s_y r_y)\, e^{-\beta}\}, \tag{3.22}$$

which is formally identical with our formula for B^* (above, equation (3.13)). Moreover, it includes Friedman's original formula as a special case. For the assumption that mean transitory components of income are zero implies $s_y = 1$, while the assumption that transitory income is uncorrelated with permanent income implies both that $\beta = 0$ and that

$$\frac{\Sigma_i(y_p^\circ - \bar{y}_p)(y^\circ - \bar{y})}{\Sigma_i(y^\circ - \bar{y})^2} = \frac{\Sigma_i(y_p^\circ - \bar{y}_p)^2}{\Sigma_i(y^\circ - \bar{y})^2} = P_y.\,^{16}$$

If these restrictions are imposed, therefore, $b^* = kP_y = b$ as given by (3.17).

Having restated Friedman's permanent income theory in a form suitable for comparison with our model, we may readily establish points of similarity. Our model, like Friedman's implies an observed regression of measured consumption on measured income for which the ratio of consumption to income declines as measured income increases. Our model, like Friedman's, implies that observed cross-section regressions will shift upward in response to an increase in mean measured income; more generally, that regressions in a growing economy will normally lie farther from the origin of the $y-c$ plane the later the date to which they correspond. Our model, like Friedman's, implies that the mean point of observed regressions will typically lie on or close to a ray of slope $k = a/(g+a)$ through the origin of the $y-c$ plane. Contrary to Friedman's stated belief, his model– like ours–is consistent with Fisher's finding that the marginal propensities to save of certain age and occupational groups are negative. In Friedman's model as in ours, moreover, the slope of the $c-y$ scatter may well be significantly flatter at low than at high levels of measured income, reflecting the influence of life-cycle phenomena. In all of these and in many other *qualitative* respects, there is literally nothing to choose between the two theories of household behavior.

Turning to quantitative comparisons, we begin by observing that our model will yield regression results different from Friedman's only insofar as our estimates of a differ from his estimates of β. This being the case, we confine attention to an issue where the relative magnitudes of a and β are of crucial significance, namely, the close correspondence that Friedman (1957b, pp. 190–5) shows to exist between measured income elasticities of consumption and direct estimates of r_y obtained by correlating income arrays for different years. For purposes of exposition, we shall call the numbers a and β *adjustment exponents* since their values determine the magnitude of the adjustment coefficients e^{-x} in the regression coefficients B^* and b^* defined by (3.13) and (3.20).

If we compute the income-elasticity of consumption at the mean point of the $c-y$ regression, the value so obtained is an estimate of the value of the bracketed expressions in (3.13) and (3.20); that is, $\varepsilon_y = 1 - (1 - s_y r_y) e^{-x}$ (cf. Friedman, 1957b, p. 33). The difference between this estimate of the income-elasticity of consumption and the income-correlation coefficient r_y is thus given by

$$\varepsilon_y - r_y = (1 - r_y) - (1 - s_y r_y) e^{-x} .$$

In normal circumstances, however, we should expect s_y to be close to unity, since its value reflects the rate of growth of aggregate income (roughly speaking, $s_y = 1/(g+1)$). Except in unusual circumstances, therefore, the difference between ε_y and r_y should be approximately equal to $(1-r_y)(1-e^{-x})$. Now, this difference clearly will be substantially different from zero unless: (i) income permutations are relatively unimportant (that is, r_y is close to unity); (ii) households adjust very slowly to such income permutations as occur (that is, the adjustment exponent is close to zero). For only in these cases will the slope of the $c-y$ scatter reflect the influence (if any) of income permutations alone–which is what is required if income-elasticities and income-correlation coefficients are to be approximately equal.

As indicated already, the empirical evidence suggests that measured values of elasticities and correlation coefficients are generally very similar. Moreover, both are typically less than unity by a substantial amount. We infer from this that the adjustment exponents β and a must be relatively small (or that our regression formulae are invalid!); for the only alternative is to suppose that s_y is significantly less than unity, and this would require that the rate of growth of aggregate income should typically exceed, say, 10 per cent per annum, which we know to be untrue.

Our estimate of the adjustment exponent a, namely 0·20, is not too large to be consistent with the empirical evidence. Observed differences between elasticities and correlation coefficients are frequently on the order of 0·02–0·04, which is the kind of difference that our model will generate with growth rates of 2 per cent per annum and an adjustment coefficient of $e^{-0.20} = 0.82$. But Friedman's estimate of the probable value of the adjustment exponent β, namely, 0·40–0·70,[17] is much too large to be reconciled with the empirical evidence, for it entails values of the adjustment coefficient $e^{-\beta}$ of only 0·50–0·67. This implies differences between income elasticities and correlation coefficients of 0·04–0·10 for urban households, and differences of 0·15–0·25 for farm households. Our conclusion is that the 'effective horizon'[18] implicit in Friedman's definition of the permanent income concept would have to be considerably longer than the three to five years that he assumes it to be in order to produce anything like the measure of agreement between income-elasticities and income-correlation coefficients that is observed in practice.[19] (The 'effective horizon' implicit in the formula $b = kP_y$, it should be noted, is of infinite length!) Our implicit estimate of the relevant horizon, being based on average rather than marginal consumption-wealth data, may itself be on the small side, and it is nearly 15 years.

The preceding discussion casts doubt on the validity of Friedman's explanation of the temporal relation between consumption and income, for it is largely from his work with time-series regressions of consumption on permanent income that his views about the magnitude of β are drawn. It appears from our analysis that the time-series correlation between permanent income and consumption is spurious: that permanent income is a proxy for a much larger magnitude, namely, household wealth.

This is not the only area where Friedman's theory is open to question; where less idiosyncratic theories – including ours – yield different and rather more plausible results. For example, we should argue that the marginal propensity to save will (other things being equal) tend to decline as we move from lower to higher levels of household income, inferring this result from the negative curvature hypothesis. There is much evidence to support this position, as indicated earlier; but Friedman must oppose it because he assumes that consumption is directly proportional to permanent income.

We should argue that wealth will be distributed much more unequally than income in any advanced society, inferring this from the assumption that the wealth-elasticity of consumption is less than unity and the generalized stability hypothesis (that is, the tendency of consumption to exhaust the whole of income). In the absence of shifts over time in the level of the modal consumption locus, moreover, we should have to argue that the distribution of wealth will tend to become ever more unequal as aggregate real income increases. The validity of the first of these implications is not open to serious argument. As for the second, the evidence suggests no tendency towards greater inequality in the distribution of income or wealth, which suggests that (i) the negative curvature hypothesis is invalid, or (ii) the modal consumption locus is affected in the long run by 'customary' standards of consumption expenditure. We shall consider these alternatives later; here we merely remark that Friedman's model provides no definite link between income and wealth – an absurdity of the first order of magnitude in a theory that purports to say something about saving behavior.[20]

We should argue that receipts of windfall income will, in general, affect consumption in the short run [21] in exactly the same way as an increase in any other kind of income, inferring this from the assumption that current purchasing power consists simply of current wealth, regardless of its original source. There is a large literature on this subject, and all of it seems to support our position (Landsberger, 1966, p. 540; Bodkin, 1966). Friedman cannot accept the obvious conclusion because he assumes that changes in measured income affect consumption only insofar as they produce variations in the household's subjective evaluation of its permanent income – and permanent income is so defined that at most a minor fraction of windfall receipts will in fact be counted as 'permanent'.

We do not ourselves have serious doubts about where the truth lies on any of these issues, for we regard the permanent income theory as a statistically ingenious but economically irrelevant and misleading description of household behavior. A detailed defense of our position is hardly possible without vastly better information about household asset holdings than is presently available. Even without such a defense, however, it is clear from the preceding discussion that our model will perform at least as well as Friedman's in relation to every cross-section problem that is considered by him. For where qualitative properties of consumption-income scatters are concerned, the statistical implications of the two theories are observationally indistinguishable. Moreover, our model is at least as simple and plausible as Friedman's in its theoretical foundations, and definitely richer in testable empirical implications. Without further argument, therefore, we may claim that our theory is at least as good as if not marginally superior to, the permanent income theory.

Time Series Regressions. Our model of household behavior appears to be consistent with available budget-study evidence, which is to say that it describes short-run transition processes with reasonable accuracy. Our only remaining task is to compare the secular implications of the model with time-series data on income, consumption and wealth. To avoid indefinite prolongation of an already lengthy paper, we shall focus attention on evidence concerning the empirical validity of the generalized stability and negative curvature hypotheses, both of which have played an important–but so far untested–role in our discussion of cross-section regressions.

(1) *Theoretical Time Profiles.* In time-series analysis, we are concerned with sums of mean values of household variables or, what comes to much the same thing, with the mean points of cross-section scatters of consumption-income and consumption-wealth data. This being the case, we should not expect MPCYs or MPCWs defined by time-series regressions to bear any close relation to corresponding parameters of cross-section regressions. In a stationary economy that experiences income permutations, for example, the cross-section scatter of $c-y$ points will typically define a definite regression line the slope of which will be interpretable as an MPCY. Time-series data for the same economy will produce a 'scatter' that consists of a single point; no MPCY will be defined or definable. If the same economy experiences occasional bursts of growth, time-series observations will produce a scatter of $c-y$ points the form of which will depend on the precise history of the system and on the rate at which households adjust to changes in income; but the cross-section scatter, apart from periods of transition, will maintain its initial form indefinitely even though its mean point shifts ever upward as aggregate income rises. In these examples, we take it for granted that the generalized stability hypothesis is valid. If asset adjustment processes are typically unstable, then we should not expect cross-section or time-series scatters to exhibit any particular pattern, much less to yield estimated MPCYs or MPCWs that are related in any way.

Granted that we can infer little or nothing about time-series regressions from cross-section regressions, and *vice versa*, our procedure at this point must be to develop the time-series implications of our model without regard to income-permutation and other transition processes. To get quickly to the focal issues posed by our stability and negative curvature hypotheses, we shall deal for the most part with a steadily growing economy. This case is by no means as interesting theoretically as an economy that exhibits fluctuations about a rising trend, but that is a subject that merits (and requires) much lengthier treatment than is possible here.

From earlier discussion, we know that in the special case where wealth-elasticities of consumption are unity, the time paths of wealth, income, and consumption of a typical household in a steadily growing economy are given by

$$w_i^t = me^{gt}\{1/(g + a_i - r_i)\}$$
$$y_i^t = me^{gt} + r_i w_i^t$$
$$c_i^t = a_i w_i^t .$$

Even in this special case, however, we should expect the values of the a_is and r_is to vary with the passage of time – the a_is because of changing standards of taste, the r_is because of changing resources and technology. Moreover, there is good reason to doubt the empirical validity of this description of household behavior even if we could suppose that the structure of the model were invariant with respect to time.

These considerations raise what are probably insoluble problems for precise analysis of the secular implications of our theory – or indeed of any model. We have no real alternative but to suppose that our idealized model provides an adequate approximation to 'true' behavior over moderate intervals of time, and to assume that in these circumstances the variables a_t and r_t can be treated as parameters. On this understanding, we can replace the a_ts and r_ts with corresponding averages (a simple average in case of the latter, a wealth-weighted average in the case of the former) and then sum over the individual decision variables and deal with the resulting aggregates in much the same way as we should deal with their individual components. Needless to say, the inferences that we draw from the resulting mongrelized model are at best plausible; that is, not entirely arbitrary!

If the generalized stability hypothesis holds, the time path of aggregate consumption should be very similar to the time path of aggregate income in a steadily growing economy. Indeed, if wealth-elasticities of consumption are unity, aggregate consumption should be directly proportional to aggregate income, the constant of proportionality being our old friend $k = a/(g+a)$. Common sense and theoretical intuition suggest that a similar relation will hold even if wealth-elasticities of consumption are less than unity, provided that the rate of growth of the economy fluctuates over time between relatively narrow limits, say, $0 < g < 0.05$. For in these circumstances, transient effects will dampen the tendency of the saving ratio to grow larger with the passage of time. The ratio may be expected to vary instead between, say, zero and 0·15, depending on the magnitude of the current growth rate and the size of the average MPCW. We may turn this proposition around and assert with equal or greater confidence that consumption will bear no particular relation to income in a growing or fluctuating economy unless most households in the economy conform to the requirements of the generalized stability hypothesis.

As for the relation between aggregate consumption and aggregate wealth, it should be one of proportionality over relatively long time intervals if wealth-elasticities of consumption are unity and the generalized stability hypothesis is satisfied. If consumption loci typically display negative curvature, however, the consumption-wealth ratio should decline with the passage of time even in an economy that experiences fluctuations around a rising trend. As in the case of the relation between income and consumption, however, we should not expect aggregate wealth to bear any definite relation to aggregate consumption in an economy where few households satisfy the conditions of the generalized stability hypothesis.

The preceding comments would require qualification if the distribution of income were assumed to vary with time; but this does not appear to be an empirically interesting case. Granted that the distribution of income does not alter significantly with the passage of time, we should expect the distribution of wealth to become ever more unequal in a growing economy if the negative curvature hypothesis is valid. Such information as we have suggests that the distribution of wealth has changed relatively little in the US and UK since 1900, but the changes that our theory would suggest might in any case be too slight over periods of one or two generations to be statistically noticeable.

(2) *Observed Time Profiles.* So much by way of speculation. Having indicated in broad outline what time paths we should expect our model to generate, we turn now to historical data for the United States–the only country for which reasonably reliable estimates of household wealth are

available over any considerable period of time. Figure 3.3 shows the time profile of consumption-income points for the period 1900–64, together with the time profile of consumption-wealth points over the period 1945–58 and for selected years prior to 1945 (every year for which household wealth data are available). Since all profiles are plotted on double-log scales, proportionality of variables is implied by a linear relationship of slope +1, and proportionality of variables in different relations by parallel profiles.

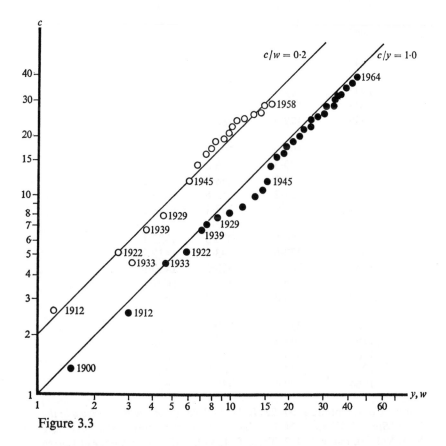

Figure 3.3

That consumption historically has tended to be approximately 90 per cent of income in the United States is well known; the *c–y* profile in Figure 3.3 merely confirms this item of textbook information. It is not perhaps so well known, but is equally true, that consumption historically has tended to be approximately 20 per cent of household wealth (both

TABLE 3.2. Time-series data

	consumption	income	wealth
1900	13·7	15·0	61·5
1912	25·9	30·1	120·7
1922	52·8	59·1	267·4
1929	79·1	83·3	448·1
1933	46·5	45·5	310·6
1939	67·7	70·3	370·8
1940	71·3	75·7	n.a.
1941	81·7	92·7	n.a.
1942	89·3	116·2	n.a.
1943	100·1	133·5	n.a.
1944	109·1	146·3	n.a.
1945	120·7	150·2	622·7
1946	144·8	160·0	678·7
1947	162·5	169·8	752·7
1948	175·8	189·1	799·6
1949	179·2	188·6	821·4
1950	193·9	206·9	920·8
1951	209·3	226·6	993·0
1952	220·1	238·3	1052·2
1953	234·2	252·6	1095·7
1954	241·0	257·4	1198·5
1955	259·5	275·3	1322·1
1956	272·6	293·2	1412·2
1957	287·8	308·5	1450·9
1958	296·5	318·8	1601·8
1959	318·2	337·3	n.a.
1960	333·0	350·0	n.a.
1961	343·2	364·4	n.a.
1962	363·7	385·3	n.a.
1963	383·4	403·8	n.a.
1964	409·4	435·8	n.a.

Source: Consumption, 1900–22: R. W. Goldsmith, *A Study of Saving in the United States* (Princeton, N. J.: Princeton University Press, 1956), Col. 5, Table N–1, Vol. iii, minus Col. 2, Table T–1, Vol. i. 1929–64: *Survey of Current Business*, us Dept. of Commerce, Vol. 45, No. 8 (Aug., 1965), Table 5, line 23, pp. 32–3. Income: 1900–22, Goldsmith, op. cit., Col. 5, Table N–1, Vol. iii. 1929–64, *S.C.B.*, *op. cit.*, Table 5, line 22, pp. 32–3. Wealth: 1900–58, R. W. Goldsmith, R. E. Lipsey, and M. Mendelson, *Studies in the National Balance Sheet of the United States* (Princeton, N J : Princeton University Press, 1963), Tables iii–1d and iii–2, line v, pp. 124–7.

measured in current dollars). This finding constitutes an apparent contradiction of the negative curvature hypothesis. Before commenting on
that, however, it is interesting to notice that the consumption-income ratio
furnished by the data corresponds closely with the figures suggested by our
model. The rate of growth of real per capita income (calculated from a
series prepared by Simon Kuznets) was 0·017 in the period from 1900–29,
0·00 (that is, nil) in the period 1929–39, 0·024 in the period 1946–4, and
0·017 for the entire period 1900–64. Given a value for a of 0·20, these
growth figures imply a consumption-income ratio of 0·92 for the periods
1900-64 and 1900–29, ratio of 0·00 for the period 1929–39, and a ratio
of 0·89 for the post-war period 1946–64. With due allowance for variations
in the consumption-wealth ratio (which has in fact fluctuated over time
by as much as 25 per cent of its maximum value), these computations seem
to lend strong support to the hypothesis that the observed 'constancy' of
the saving ratio reflects nothing more profound than the tendency of
consumption to equal income at every point in time. We certainly should
not expect consumption to display such a regular pattern of behavior
relative to income if the majority of households were unstable accumula-
tors. The empirical evidence thus seems to confirm the validity of the
generalized stability hypothesis.[22]

Returning now to the time profile of consumption-wealth points, we
begin by noting that the apparent constancy of the consumption-wealth
ratio is to some extent an optical illusion. For the one period on which we
have continuous data (1945–58), the ratio dropped from just under 0·22
in 1948 to just over 0·18 in 1958 – a reduction of about 15 per cent in 10
years. Considering the relative magnitudes involved in both terms of this
ratio, the decline indicated might well be considered precipitous–so much
so as to provide strong support for the negative curvature hypothesis.
But this position cannot be defended with any force, for the consumption-
wealth ratio in 1900 was precisely the same as the ratio in 1948, namely,
0·22.

It is difficult to reconcile these contradictory positions without running
into worse problems than are posed by the contradictions themselves. The
evidence from budget-study data is so compellingly in favor of the negative
curvature hypothesis, however, that one or another reconciliation is
almost mandatory. We can think of two rationalizations that seem to us
worthy of serious consideration.

The first rationalization is more in the nature of an evasion than an explanation; it involves the supposition that market forces work in such a way that earning assets are valued at a relatively constant proportion of their income yield. The tendency of consumption to exhaust total income at all times would then link consumption with wealth in a similar fashion, producing relative constancy in the proportions between all three magnitudes–income, consumption, and wealth. There is some evidence that a process of this kind is at work. For if one deflates Goldsmith's wealth data with an index of the prices of capital goods, one finds that the ratio of 'real' wealth to 'real' income declines steadily during the period 1900–58. This means that the price level of capital goods historically has increased more rapidly than the price index implicit in the real income (and consumption) series. If we ask, 'Which way did the *true* ratio of consumption to wealth move ?', our response must be that we simply do not know. For if we allow for quality changes, the relative rise in market prices of capital goods might be considered to reflect accurately the 'service value' of such goods, leaving us with an approximately constant ratio of real consumption to real wealth; or the relative rise in capital goods prices might be considered to represent an understatement of the service value of wealth held by households, in which case we should argue that the consumption-wealth ratio has after all decreased! One is tempted to conclude from all this that the constancy or non-constancy of the consumption-wealth ratio over periods of more than a decade is not an empirically meaningful problem–and, as we noted earlier, the ratio did decline substantially during the one period for which we have continuous data.

The second rationalization does not require us to question the meaning of the raw statistics on wealth and consumption. It involves the supposition that consumption loci shift over time as per capita wealth rises, marginal consumption-wealth ratios becoming greater as standards of living rise. This conjecture bears an obvious resemblance to Duesenberry's famous 'relative income' hypothesis, and might be defended on similar sociological and psychological grounds. Analytically, the conjecture can be expressed by writing the wealth-consumption function as

$$c = hw^b w^{*(1-b)}$$

where w^* represents a suitable index of 'normal wealth' (e.g. the value of $w^*(t)$ obtained from the solution of a differential equation of the form

$$dw^*(t)/dt = \alpha\{w(t) - w^*(t)\}$$

where α is a positive adjustment coefficient ($0 < \alpha < 1$). A relation of this kind between consumption, wealth, and 'normal wealth' would clearly serve to reconcile the negative curvature hypothesis with the secular constancy of the $c{-}w$ ratio, for it effectively implies that the secular wealth-elasticity of consumption is unity. The same relation would also account for the apparent invariance over time of the distribution of wealth, and for differences among countries (e.g. the US and UK) in consumption spending at given levels of wealth. But these and related themes are much too large to be developed in the present paper.

IV. *Concluding Remarks*

Our analysis of the dynamics of household behavior contains numerous loose ends, and may well raise more questions that it settles. Hopefully it has also contributed to improved understanding of the causal foundations and empirical implications of the theory of consumption.

Our central theme throughout has been that statistical findings, in economics as in any other science, have meaning only insofar as they are associated with explicit conceptual experiments. Facts alone can tell us nothing about the mainsprings of consumer choice; we must assert how households behave and leave it to the facts to determine if our assertions are empirically plausible.

A second theme, closely related to the first, is the need to develop the explicit statistical implications of our theoretical models if we are to recognize and profit from apparent anomalies in observed behavior. Progress in an inexact science like economics is hardly possible unless the consequences of our theories are expressed in terms that are qualitatively comparable with the stochastic relationships that constitute our universe of factual discourse. Neither is progress possible, however, if the only 'theory' we ever use is one that says 'Y can be explained by some set of n variables, $x_1, ..., x_y$, and a collection of associated error terms'—which is just about what contemporary econometrics asserts.

A final theme—implicit in every part of our paper—is that household trading on current account cannot be described satisfactorily, much less explained, without explicit reference to related transactions on capital account. Further progress in consumption theory depends crucially on the future availability of information about all aspects of household balance sheets as well as the usual information about current income and expenditure flows.

NOTES AND REFERENCES

[1] It should be emphasized that the variables c and w represent 'virtual' rather than 'real' magnitudes. Thus we can infer nothing directly from (1.2) about the behavior over time of the 'real' variable $\underline{w}$. Planned current consumption constitutes a virtual drain on real wealth at any given date, but this does not mean that real wealth will actually be depleted over time. The behavior of $\underline{w}$ depends, in fact, on a variety of other circumstances (see below, pp. 49–51).

[2] A similar relation can be defined connecting desired with actual wealth: $w^t = w(\underline{w}^t)$. Since desired wealth is defined in our model in terms of actual wealth and desired consumption, however, all relevant information about desired wealth is already embodied in the wealth-consumption relation (1.3). More precisely, if we combine (1.3) with the budget equation (1.2), we have $w^t = \underline{w}^t - c(\underline{w}^t)$. Accordingly, we shall have no occasion to deal explicitly with desired wealth in the remainder of this paper.

[3] In principle, one should no doubt follow general price theory and include factor services as an explicit decision variable in the preference function of the household. To do so raises a number of awkward complications, however, for one then obtains an 'income function' similar to the consumption and wealth functions defined by our model; hence, it becomes necessary either to develop a specific theory about the form of this function, or to assign specific properties to it. The first alternative is disagreeable; the second is logically equivalent to the procedure that is commonly followed. For further discussion of the matter, see Daniel Suits (1963).

[4] Because all variables to which we shall refer from this point onwards are intended to designate 'real' rather than 'virtual' quantities, we no longer use underlines to distinguish 'measurable' variables. Thus w and y, as used in this sentence, are the same variables as were previously represented by $\underline{w}$ and $\underline{y}$.

[5] If we introduce lagged adjustments of measured consumption to desired consumption, depreciation rates, etc., the effect is to complicate the stability condition, perhaps very considerably, by the addition of adjustment coefficients, side restrictions, etc. Provided that rates of adjustment of actual to desired quantities are sufficiently rapid, however, the simple conditions given here remain valid. As for discrete-time models, the stability condition in the simplest case is that $a-r$ be positive and less than 2, with 'cobweb' phenomena occurring if $a-r$ lies between 1 and 2.

[6] '... one may say anything ... that might enter the most disordered imagination. The only thing one cannot say is that it is rational. The very word sticks in one's throat.'

[7] Cf. Arthur Goldberger (1964, p. 122). We are asserting that the values of relevant variables within each of a large collection of service-income classes will tend to be normally distributed, making it possible for us to view the means for each class as definite values.

[8] The highest yields mentioned by Atkinson are on the order of 7 per cent per annum – approximately the same figure as Stigler arrives at for the average rate of return on manufacturing capital in the United States; see G. J. Stigler (1963, chapter 2).

[9] We refer to information supplied in a recent study by Michael Landsberger (1966) of the response of Israeli households to restitution payments from Germany during the two-year period 1958–9. Landsberger designs a statistical experiment that permits us to view each of five groups of households as being essentially similar except for differences in lump-sum receipts of restitution payments. If our assumption about the form of the consumption locus is valid, the logarithms of the MPCWs calculated by Landsberger (shown in his Table 4, p. 539) should vary inversely with the logarithm of the corresponding windfall receipt; for to say that $c = hw^b$ is to assert that $d \log (dc/dw)/d \log w = \log (bc) - \log w$. If the indicated operations are carried out and the resulting data are plotted as a scatter of log MPCW/log w points, four of the observations turn out to lie almost exactly along a straight line of slope -1. The fifth point (corresponding to an MPCW of 1·972) lies well off the line, but involves an MPCW the point estimate of which is not significantly different from values that would put it on exactly the same line as the other four points. We attach no great significance to a correlation that is based on only five observations – but the extent of the agreement between our prediction and the data is too striking to be altogether ignored.

[10] See Friedman (1957b, pp. 188–9). There are no general rules, of course, for some processes may be cyclic, in which case a proper choice of the unit time interval will eliminate all appearance of change.

[11] Note that if $a = 0$, $B' = r_y$; i.e. income permutation explains the whole of scatter. In general, however, $r_y < B'$.

[12] Friedman's (1957b, p. 32) analysis leads to conclusions much like ours, except that in his model the case $r_y < 0$ does not arise. (The reason for this is indicated below, footnote 16.)

[13] We are indebted to James Richmond for calling this study to our attention.

[14] It is not without interest to mention Milton Friedman's reaction to Fisher's results:

> . . . a negative marginal propensity to save contradicts not only the permanent income hypothesis but every hypothesis I know of that has been seriously considered . . . Furthermore, it contradicts a host

of other empirical evidence – the propensity to save as computed from cross section budget study data is almost invariably positive. The clear implication is that there is something wrong with [Fisher's] data (Friedman, 1957a, p. 127).
Friedman attempts to account for the apparent anomalies in Fisher's analysis by suggesting that the 'income units' sampled in the UK survey consist in many cases of what would normally be considered mixed households. Subsequent investigations by Fisher (1957) and Klein (1958) failed to support Friedman's suggestion.

[15] The estimates of r_y are from Table 20, line 5, p. 195 of Friedman (1957b); (they are based on a study by John Frechtling, then a member of the staff of the Board of Governors of the Federal Reserve System). The estimate of e^{-a} is based on a value for a of 0·20 – the *average* consumption-wealth ratio in the US over the period 1900–58.

[16] See Friedman (1957b, pp. 31–2). Note that P_y, unlike r_y, must lie between 0 and 1; it cannot assume negative values.

[17] The estimate of 0·40 is based on time-series evidence and is considered by Friedman (1957b, p. 194) to imply an 'average time lag' – namely 2·5 years – that is longer than the lag appropriate for cross-section analysis. The suggested lag for the latter purpose is 1·5 years, which implies an adjustment exponent of 0·67. Hence the limits indicated in the text, i.e. 0·40–0·70.

[18] Defined by Friedman (1957b, pp. 145,150,1934) as twice the value of the reciprocal of the adjustment exponent (i.e. twice the 'average time lag').

[19] This conclusion is given further support by Margaret Reid's analysis of income-elasticities and income-correlations for a sample of farm households whose average income during the period of observation grew at a rate of approximately 40 per cent per annum – implying a value of s_y of about 0·70. The mean income-correlation coefficient in the sample was about 0·50, while the mean income-elasticity was about 0·40. This *negative* difference is directly inconsistent with the naïve version of Friedman's theory. However, it can be accounted for by our interpretation of his model, provided that the adjustment exponent has a value of something less than 0·15. The Reid data cannot be reconciled, however, with an adjustment exponent of 0·40–0·70, for the smallest of these values would just suffice to make the mean income-correlation coefficient equal to the mean income-elasticity (Friedman, 1957b, pp. 192–4).

[20] Friedman (1957b, pp. 16–17) does permit the ratio of human to non-human wealth to influence the value of k, but this link between wealth and saving is about as substantial as the grin of the Cheshire Cat.

[21] It is important to distinguish between short-run and long-run effects. A windfall, in the nature of the case, cannot support a

permanently higher level of consumption unless it is invested in earning assets. If it is not so invested, consumption will be completely unaffected in the long run. In sharp contrast, a salary increase – if it remains in effect – can be used to sustain a permanently higher level of consumption, either directly by being spent as it is received, or indirectly by being invested in earning assets.

[22] A contrary conclusion is reached by Nissen Liviatan (1965, pp. 225–6) but his analysis rests on the curious assumption that earning assets, unlike money, '. . . are completely illiquid and do not appear . . . as arguments in the utility function' (p. 208). This is equivalent to supposing that the marginal propensity to consume wealth other than money balances is zero. It follows that an increase in holdings of earning assets, however large, will have no *direct* effect on consumption expenditure; such an increase will affect consumption only because it entails an increase in 'permanent' income. Provided that the marginal propensity to consume income from earning assets is less than unity, saving will always be positive as long as households accumulate wealth in the form of earning assets.

Suppose, for example, that household savings are always invested in perpetual bonds that yield, say, 5 per cent per annum in coupon returns. Suppose further that–other things being equal–households invariably save 100 per cent of any increase in bond income. Then bond holdings obviously will increase without limit as time tends to infinity if the accumulation of wealth has no direct effect on consumption expenditure. However, if an increase of £100 in holdings of bonds produces an increase in consumption of more than £5 per annum (a possibility Liviatan does not admit), saving will converge to zero with the passage of time even though the marginal propensity to consume bond income is zero.

As we have remarked on several occasions, the MPCWs of certain households may be less than the marginal rate of return on earning assets. Thus Liviatan's model may provide a fairly adequate description of the behavior of a Scrooge, a Rockefeller, or a Getty. But to suppose that the same model is in any way applicable to a Clower, a Johnson, or to most other non-entrepreneurial and non-miserly households, would be almost as silly as to suppose that earning assets are 'completely illiquid'.

References

Archibald, G.C. and Lipsey, R.G. (1958) Monetary and value theory: a critique of Lange and Patinkin. *Review of Economic Studies* **26**, 1–22.

Atkinson, T.R. (1956) *The pattern of financial asset ownership*. Princeton.

Atkinson, T.R. (1964) Survey of financial characteristics of consumers. *Federal Reserve Bulletin.*

Ball, R.J. and Drake, P.S. (1964) The relationship between aggregate consumption and wealth. *International Economic Review* **5**, 63–81.

Basmann, R.L. (1963) Remarks concerning the application of exact finite sample distribution functions of GLC estimators in econometric statistical inference. *Journal of American Statistical Association* **58**, 943–76.

Bodkin, R.L. (1966) *American Economic Review* **56**.

Chase, S.B., Jr. (1963) *Asset prices in economic analysis*. Berkeley and Los Angeles.

Clower, R.W. (1963a) Classical monetary theory revisited. *Economica* (N.S.) **30**, 165–70.

Clower, R.W. (1963b) Permanent income and transitory balances: Hahn's paradox. *Oxford Economic Papers* (N.S.) **15**, 177–90.

Eisner, R., Friedman, M. and Houthakker, H.S. (1958) The permanent income hypothesis (comments and reply). *American Economic Review* **48**, 972–98.

Farrell, M.J. (1959) The new theories of the consumption function. *Economic Journal* 678–96.

Fisher, M.R. (1957) A reply to the critics. *Bulletin of Oxford University Institute of Statistics* **19**, 179–99.

Friedman, M. (1957a) Savings and the balance sheet. *Bulletin of Oxford University Institute of Statistics* **19**, 125–36.

Friedman, M. (1975b) *A theory of consumption function*. Princeton.

Friend, I. (1957) Some conditions for progress in the study of savings. *Bulletin of Oxford University Institute of Statistics* **19**, 165–70.

Friend, I. and Taubman, P. (1966) The aggregate propensity to save: some concepts and their application to international data. *Review of Economics and Statistics* **48**, 113–23.

Goldberger, A.S. (1964) *Econometric Theory*. New York.

Goldsmith, R.W. (1965) *A study of saving in the United States*. Princeton.

Hanson, N.R. (1958) *Patterns of discovery*. Cambridge, England.

Houthakker, H.S. (1961) The present state of consumption theory. *Econometrica* **29**, 704–40.

Houthakker, H.S. and Taylor, L.D. (1966) *Consumer demand in the United States. 1929–1970.* Cambridge, Mass.

Klein, L.R. and Liviatan, N. (1957) The significance of income variability on savings behaviour. *Bulletin of Oxford University Institute of Statistics* **19**, 151–60.

Kuznets, S. (1961) *Capital in the American economy: its formation and financing*. Princeton.

Landsberger, M. (1966) Windfall income and consumption: comment. *American Economic Review* **56**.

Lindbeck, A. (1963) *A study in monetary analysis*. Stockholm.

Liviatan, N. (1965) On the long-run theory of consumption and real balances. *Oxford Economic Papers* (N.S.) **17**, 205–18.

Lydall, H.F. and Lansing, J.B. (1959) A comparison of the distribution of personal income and wealth in the United States and Great Britain. *American Economic Review* **49**, 43–67.

Mayer, T. (1963) The permanent income theory and occupational groups. *Review of Economics and Statistics* **45**, 16–22.

Modigliani, F. and Brumberg, R.E. (1954) Utility analysis and the consumption function: an interpretation of cross section data. In K.K. Kuruhara (ed.) *Post-Keynesian economics*. London.

Newman, P.K. and Wolfe, J.N. (1961) A model for the long-run theory of value. *Review of Economic Studies* **29**, 51–61.

Pylatt, F.G. (1964) *Priority patterns and the demand for household durable goods*. Cambridge, England.

Rolph, E.R. (1954) *The theory of fiscal economics*. Berkeley and Los Angeles.

Samuelson, P.A. (1947) *Foundations of economic analysis*. Cambridge, Mass.

Samuelson, P.A. (1961) The evaluation of social income: capital formation and wealth. In International Economic Association. *The theory of capital*. London.

Spiro, A. (1962) Wealth and the consumption function. *Journal of Political Economy* **70**, 339–54.

Stigler, G.J. (1963) *Capital and rates of return in manufacturing industries*. Princeton.

Suits, D. (1963) The determinants of consumer expenditure: a review of present knowledge. *In impacts of monetary policy*. Englewood Cliffs.

PART II

MICROECONOMICS

PART II

MICROECONOMIES

Part II: Microeconomics

All but the last of the selections in Part II were published before I had any awareness of the post-1950 Neowalrasian Revolution, though a major contribution to that development (Arrow and Debreu, 'On the Existence of a Competitive Equilibrium') appeared in the same July 1954 issue of *Econometrica* that contained my paper on 'Price Determination in a Stock–Flow Economy' (Chapter 11). All of the papers in this section, including the last, reflect the strong phenomenological orientation that is a hallmark of everything I have ever written in economic theory. I could never take an interest in existence 'proofs' in economics because these logical exercises shed no light on observable phenomena, and so have no probative force in any inductive science. If an ingenious logician some day 'proves' – on 'plausible' assumptions, of course – the *nonexistence* of The Solar System, I will applaud the intellectual performance, but such a proof will in no way disturb me in my enjoyment of a good cigar.

All the 'microeconomic' writings in this chapter precede my first publications in macroeconomics and money; but all of them nevertheless are directly or indirectly outgrowths of a lifelong interest in macroeconomic theory that began with my first reading of Keynes' *General Theory* in 1946. All reflect my concern to 'explain' elementary aspects of everyday experience that are either ignored in or seem flatly incompatible with standard teaching; all reflect my unstated but strongly felt kinship with the man who remarked of an earlier tradition: 'It may well be ... the way in which we should like our Economy to behave. But to assume that it actually does so is to assume our difficulties away.'

[8]

BUSINESS INVESTMENT AND THE THEORY OF PRICE

R. W. CLOWER

State College of Washington

1. Hitherto, most discussions of business investment have been self-contained in the sense that the relation of the theory of investment to the theory of competitive price has received little explicit attention. I propose to investigate this relationship in the present paper. The object of the argument is to indicate some theoretical difficulties which arise when the theory of business investment and the theory of price determination are juxtaposed, and to suggest ways in which these difficulties can be resolved.

2. In existing accounts of competitive business behavior, alternative current economic "plans" of a representative entrepreneur are typically characterized by two sets of functions, each set including, in general, as many relations as there are commodities in the economy: (1) a set of supply functions which relate current flows of outputs to prices and to other parameters, the "other parameters" including such things as anticipated future prices, quantities of various capital goods held by the entrepreneur, etc.; (ii) a set of demand functions which relate current flows of inputs to prices and to other parameters. I shall call these familiar relations *flow supply* and *flow demand functions*, respectively. As far as I am aware, no existing account of the theory of the firm includes, in addition to these flow relations, an explicit set of demand functions for stocks of capital goods in terms of which business investment decisions, that is, decisions to alter business holdings of assets, might be described. Instead, it is usual to suppose that the capital goods which are available to any entrepreneur are fixed quantities in the short run, and to deal with investment in fixed plant, equipment, raw materials, and inventories either by fiat — as when one demonstrates the relation between short- and long-run supply curves — or by *ad hoc* description of typical business responses to profit opportunities. Or to put the matter another way, some of the "other parameters" in the flow demand and supply functions are assumed to represent quantities of capital goods held by the entrepreneur, and the latter parameters are simply juggled about at will.

This familiar textbook treatment of business investment may be objected to on various grounds. For example, the manipulation of capital good parameters seems extremely arbitrary, despite the apparent accord among econo-mists as to which kinds of juggling are realistic. Again, one may ask whether it is logically consistent to postulate pure competition together with the fixity of plant and equipment in the short run. Although the total quantity of any capital good may be fixed in the short run for the economy as a whole, in a competitive system any one entrepreneur should be able to increase or decrease his individual holdings at will by buying from or selling to other entrepreneurs. Of course, this problem does not arise if the theory of the firm is built around decisions affecting a physical plant *at a given location,* and this procedure is almost universally adopted in the literature; but such an approach clearly leaves something to be desired. Finally, a more serious and comprehensive objection to the traditional approach is that it divorces the theory of business investment from the theory of price. This is best demonstrated by noting that if quantities of capital goods are treated as parameters in individual business demand and supply functions, they must be regarded as *given* parameters in market demand and supply functions; otherwise the supply and demand equations which are supposed to determine equilibrium prices are too few in number to accomplish this purpose. But to take capital good parameters as given is equivalent to supposing that *the values of these parameters are imposed from outside the price system.* This result alone seems to provide sufficient grounds for abandoning the usual textbook treatment of the theory of business investment. Once the quantities of capital goods held at an instant of time (for future disposal) are distinguished from the quantities of the same capital goods which are produced or consumed during the current period, it is natural to seek for a description, within the framework of the theory of price, of the determination of the former (stock) quantities as well as the latter (flow) quantities.

3. A different way to deal with business investment within the framework of traditional theory is to assume that the quantity held of each capital good is a function of the input-output plan of the entrepreneur. Instead of treating capital good quantities as independent parameters in the flow supply and demand functions, one may suppose that the values of these parameters depend upon the quantities of inputs and outputs selected by the entre-preneur. The capital good parameters are then suppressed in the flow supply and demand functions and reappear, implicitly at least, as dependent variables in the typical entrepreneur's overall plan. For if the quantity of a capital good which an entrepreneur wishes to hold is a function of his input-output plan, and if the input-output plan in turn depends upon prices, then the quantity held of capital good itself depends upon prices. Relations of the latter kind, that is, functions which relate current holdings of various commodities to prices (and other parameters), I shall call *stock demand functions.*

The introduction of stock demand functions into the theory of the firm seems a distinctly promising procedure since it permits investment phenomena to be brought directly within the framework of the price system without undue artifice or arbitrariness. Certain difficulties remain, however; for if capital good holdings are made to depend upon prices, it appears that the equations which determine market prices are inconsistent. This is readily demonstrated by supposing that k of the commodities in the economy are capital goods which are supplied, demanded, and held solely by firms. Summing over individual flow demand and supply functions for each of these k goods, and equating market supplies to corresponding market demands, one obtains k equations which might be considered to determine the equilibrium values of the k unknown prices of capital goods. Indeed, having discovered sufficient equations to determine prices, one is strongly tempted to stop at this point; however, since by hypothesis capital goods are held as well as produced and consumed, it is necessary to go on to consider the previously mentioned demand functions for stocks of capital goods (of which there are, in general, k for each entrepreneur). Summing over individual stock demand functions for each good, one obtains k market stock demand functions. Moreover, since businesses in the aggregate must hold the entire existing stock of each capital good, and since aggregate stocks are fixed in the short run, each stock demand may be equated to its corresponding stock supply to obtain k additional equations in the k unknown prices of capital goods. Thus, we are confronted in total with 2k equations — k *flow* supply-and-demand functions plus k *stock* supply-and-demand functions—but only k unknown

22

prices. Furthermore, these 2k equations are clearly independent, for while flow demands may be directly related to stock demands, flow supplies can bear no relation whatsoever to *existing* stocks since flow supplies depend upon prices whereas stock supplies are entirely determined by past events. Since the number of independent conditions to be satisfied exceeds the number of prices to be determined, it follows that not all of these conditions can be satisfied simultaneously. This result is valid quite generally. Indeed, we may state that for any economy in which firms hold as well as produce and consume capital goods, the supply-and-demand equations to be satisfied by any set of equilibrium prices appear, in general, to be inconsistent.

4. The economic interpretation of the inconsistency just mentioned is simple; it means that a set of prices at which individuals in the aggregate are willing to hold existing commodity stocks will ordinarily differ from the set of prices at which the current consumption and production of corresponding commodities are equalized, and vice versa. The removal of the inconsistency is more difficult; however, an outline solution to the problem will be offered here.

For present purposes, capital goods are best regarded as commodities which are in fixed supply at any instant of time, the stocks of which may be changing at the same instant as a result of net investment. Now it is only in connection with commodities of this kind — goods which take the form of stocks and of flows simultaneously—that the equations which define equilibrium prices are in general inconsistent. Indeed, the problem of inconsistency arises precisely because a set of prices which equates flow supplies to flow demands, and so establishes flow equilibrium, may not also serve to equate stock supplies to stock demands, and so to establish stock equilibrium. This suggests that the consistency of the equations of price determination can be assured if the concept of equilibrium is properly defined. That this is in fact the case may be indicated as follows.

Assuming that capital goods are in fixed supply at any instant of time, we may suppose that prices at that instant are determined by the sole condition that stock demands are equal to corresponding stock supplies. If the set of prices defined by these stock equilibrium conditions fails to equate flow supplies to corresponding flow demands, the economy may be said to be in *temporary equilibrium,* since at subsequent instants stock supplies will alter in consequence of prevailing gaps between the consumption and production of various capital goods, and a different set of prices will be required to reestablish stock equilibrium. On the other hand, if a set of prices which establishes stock equilibrium also brings flow supplies and corresponding flow demands into balance, the economy may be said to be in *stationary equilibrium.* A graphical illustration may help to clarify these matters. Consider a market for a single capital good and sup-

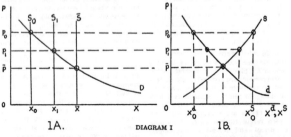

1A.   DIAGRAM I   1B.

pose that at time t_o the existing stock of the good is X_o so that the stock supply curve can be represented by the vertical straight line S_o in Diagram 1A. Assume further that the stock demand curve for the capital good is D in Diagram 1A, that the flow supply and demand curves are s and d respectively in Diagram 1B, and that the D, s, and d curves are given independently of time.

If the price p_o is established in the market, bringing stock supply and stock demand into equality, flow $(x_o{}^s)$ will differ from flow demand $(x_o{}^d)$, and we have a position of temporary equilibrium. For if $x_o{}^s$ and $x_o{}^d$ represent, respectively, total production and total consumption of the capital good during the period $(t_1 - t_o)$, then at time t_1 stock supply will have increased from X_o to, say, X_1, the increase representing the excess of current flow supply over current flow demand. Accordingly, at time t_1 the price at which individuals in the aggregate will be willing to hold the stock X_1 will be P_1, representing a new position of temporary equilibrium. Finally, if price at some unspecified date is established at $\bar{p}$, bringing flow supply and demand as well as stock supply and demand into equality, we have a position of stationary equilibrium. For the price $\bar{p}$ satisfies the stock *and* the flow equilibrium conditions simultaneously so that there will be no tendency for the existing stock or price to change in subsequent periods unless the market situation is disturbed by outside forces. Having adopted the foregoing definitions, the problem of inconsistency is

avoided in situations of temporary equilibrium because flow supply and demand relations are not immediately relevant and may be ignored; *i.e.,* we think of capital good prices as being determined instantaneously by stock supply and stock demand functions alone, and think of *current* flow supply and demand quantities as being determined by the prices thus established. Nevertheless, flow supply and demand relations play an important role in deter-

mining prices at *subsequent* instants of time since changes in stock supplies are governed by flow quantities. In situations of stationary equilibrium, no problem of inconsistency arises because, by definition, all stock and flow equilibrium conditions are satisfied simultaneously.

Since the solution just offered to the inconsistency problem requires one to postulate the short-run domination of stocks over flows, it may not seem entirely satisfactory from a logical point of view except when price determination is described in terms of process analysis. However, because the inconsistency problem arises only in the process analysis case (or in statical versions of this case) this difficulty is only apparent. In a dynamical price system, described by differential rather than difference equations, the only relevant definition of economic equilibrium happens to correspond to our definition of stationary equilibrium; and as I have already noted, in positions of stationary equilibrium the problem of inconsistency is always absent.

5. We have seen that the inconsistency problem can be disposed of by proper definition of equilibrium concepts; it remains to be shown that the definitions suggested lend themselves to the interpretation of empirical evidence. As a practical matter, it is clear that in markets where existing commodity stocks are large in relation to production or consumption flows during any short interval of time, it is reasonable

to ignore flows altogether in the short run. In the major raw material markets, for example, variations in aggregate production and consumption during one or a few days can have little direct effect on current prices. Even in the complete absence of current production, demands can be satisfied temporarily at the current price by drawing on existing stocks; and even in the absence of current consumption, new supplies can be sold temporarily at the current price to firms which hold stocks for future disposal.

Again, in the major security markets, variations in new issues or in retirements of outstanding issues can have little direct effect on current prices, for it is the relation of already outstanding issues to demands to hold such issues for their future income yields, which effectively determines current stock prices and rates of interest. "Productivity and Thrift" are ultimate rather than immediate determinants of security prices.

One could cite further examples indefinitely, for virtually all commodities in the real world exist as stocks and as flows simultaneously. Already, however, it should be clear that the concept of temporary equilibrium has numerous applications in the real world. It is a particularly appropriate concept to apply to the kind of equilibrium which occurs in an economy where capital accumulation is a continuous process. That the concept of stationary equilibrium is also relevant requires no argument.

6. As a by-product of the foregoing argument, I have been led to suggest a partial reformulation of established price theory. It is worth remarking that even when this reformulation is extended to deal with questions of stability as well as with questions of equilibrium, it leaves much of traditional price theory intact. In particular, those portions of established theory which deal with the pricing of goods which are "original and indestructible," or which exist only as services, are not affected. And as any economist can testify from experience, a little judicious implicit theorizing will suffice to bring the pricing of any commodity within the traditional fold. Nevertheless, when explicit theoretical provision is made for the pricing of capital goods, established price analysis can be clarified, extended, and unified to a surprising extent. But this theme is much too involved to be elaborated further at the present time.

7. Before I conclude, one loose end of the preceding discussion should be cleared up. The stock demand functions which appear in the present theory of market price determination are derived by summing over corresponding stock demand functions of individual entrepreneurs. As was noted earlier, however, individual stock demand functions do not appear explicitly in the established theory of the firm. Instead of arising directly out of the familiar assumption of profit maximization, these functions are derived by making the additional and independent assumption that an entrepreneur's holdings of capital goods depend upon his input-output plan. Now, my theory of market price determination clearly would be more satisfactory if it were based upon a theory of the firm in which this arbitrary assumption were absent, a theory in which stock demand functions arose directly out of the profit maximization assumption. Fortunately, such a theory of the firm is readily constructed.

Notice first of all that it is only the *existence* of individual supply and demand functions which is implied by the traditional assumption of profit maximization; the precise *character* of these functions depends upon the nature of the transformation function which confronts the entrepreneur. In established theory, the transformation function is usually assumed to be a purely technical relation connecting inputs and outputs, and no explicit provision is made for the holding of assets of any kind. Hence, the usual sets of supply and demand relations do not include a set of stock demand functions at all. On everyday empirical grounds, however, it is more natural to assume that the transformation function is a relation connecting inputs, outputs and stocks of assets of various kinds. Moreover, since it is absurd to suppose that there is always a fixed technical relation between asset stocks and input and output flows, the transformation relation is best regarded as a *decision function* into which subjective considerations (including price expectations) enter to some extent. If this is granted, then the profit maximization hypothesis stands on precisely the same logical footing as does the utility maximization postulate of preference analysis; *i.e.*, the hypothesis is not directly refutable by appeal to empirical data (although it leads to refutable empirical implications), and the economist need have no immediate interest in the question of why the decision function is what it is. After all, there is no reason why economic science should not bestow upon the businessman the same geniality and sovereignty as it currently bestows upon the consumer!

Modifying the usual definition of net revenue to include the value of net sales of assets, and supposing that the typical entrepreneur maximizes net revenue in this sense, subject to the constraints imposed by a given decision function, one obtains an explicit set of individual demand functions for commodity stocks in addition to the familiar flow supply and demand relations.

This last result completes the immediate investigation. However, it is interesting to notice in passing that when explicit provision is made in the theory of the firm for the holding of commodity stocks, it is no longer possible to deduce that partial demand and supply curves are, respectively, downward and upward sloping! This rather surprising result arises from that fact that commodity stocks may be substitutes instead of complements for input flows of the same commodity (or complements instead of substitutes for output flows); without specifying the form of the decision function, one cannot say *a priori* which situation will prevail. This result is probably of little empirical significance, but it does indicate that there is a definite qualitative difference between the present and established theory.

8. In this paper I have suggested some problems which seem to require further theoretical and applied research, and I have outlined certain methods for attacking the problems indicated. In summary, I have argued as follows. Explicit provision is seldom made in the established theory of the firm for the phenomenon of business investment; as a consequence, the theory of investment is commonly developed in an arbitrary and artificial way, and it is divorced from the general theory of price. However, if one seeks to avoid these shortcomings and attempts to link business investment with price theory by making demands to hold capital goods depend upon prices, the result is the creation of an apparent inconsistency in the equations which determine market prices. The inconsistency can be removed; but in order to do this, one is impelled to generalize the established theory of price to provide explicitly for the pricing of capital goods; and, in turn, one is led to generalize the established theory of the firm in order to provide a more satisfactory microeconomic basis for the generalized theory of price. Because only equilibrium and not stability conditions have been strictly relevant to my immediate theme, I have sketched no more than the bare outlines of these generalized theories. However, they are capable of further development in a variety of directions.

[9]

AN INVESTIGATION INTO THE DYNAMICS OF INVESTMENT

By R. W. Clower*

Partial equilibrium analysis includes some of the most fundamental and well-established ideas in economic theory. Nevertheless, certain aspects of this field—specifically, those portions which deal with the pricing of durable goods—are rather obscure. If one considers a market for services or a market for perishable goods, it is fairly clear what is meant by the familiar statement that "price tends to be established at a level which equates supply and demand." If price were greater than the "equilibrium" level, buyers would be confronted, in effect, with a "queue" of willing sellers; since some sellers would accept a lower price in order to avoid inconvenience (and loss) associated with "queuing," price would tend to fall. If price were less than the equilibrium level, sellers would be confronted, in effect, with a "queue" of willing buyers; since some buyers would offer a higher price rather than "wait their turn," price would tend to rise.

If one considers a market for durable goods, matters are rather different. In this case it is usual to argue that if price were above the level which equates supply and demand, commodity stocks would accumulate; since some sellers would accept a lower price to avoid holding undesired stocks, price would tend to fall. A similar argument is used to show that if price were set temporarily below the equilibrium level, forces would be set in motion which would tend to make price rise. The difficulty in these cases is that it seems equally plausible to argue that if price lies above the equilibrium level, this may be because some individuals *want* to accumulate stocks. Otherwise the phenomenon of investment would be incomprehensible. But does the mere process of investment in stocks imply a tendency for price to fall? Similarly, if price is below the equilibrium level so that demand exceeds supply, it is reasonable to argue that some individuals *want* to disinvest. Does this necessarily imply a tendency for price to rise?

This paper attempts to give precise answers to the above and related questions. More generally, it deals with the pure theory of investment

* The author is assistant professor of economics at the State College of Washington, Pullman.

in a competitive market for a single durable good. The argument is developed in three stages. The factors which govern the price of a durable good at any given moment of time are first outlined. This is followed by an examination of the general conditions governing the course of prices and investment over an interval of time.[1] Finally, some illustrative examples are given to indicate the probable qualitative effects upon the level and time path of prices and investment of changes in various given conditions. It might appear that the pricing of durable goods involves no unfamiliar problems; in general this is not so, but neither does it involve entirely unfamiliar problems. The truth seems to lie between these two extremes. The present analysis, at least, results in a definite blending of traditional and novel ideas.

I. *Price Determination at a Given Moment*

Let us begin by setting out the supply and demand relations which govern current price in a market for a particular kind of durable good.[2] The aggregate stock of a durable good existing at any moment of time is a legacy from the past. It can be altered gradually by future economic activity; but if a sufficiently short time period is considered, additions to, or depletions of, the existing stock during a single period will be negligible.

On the other hand, the aggregate market demand for a durable good at any moment will depend upon current economic decisions. A durable good will be held currently for the sake of its expected future yield of saleable services and/or subjective satisfactions, the precise manner in which an individual (or firm) distributes its resources among various assets being determined by the condition that, at the margin, equal value quantities of different assets shall afford equal value yields. Hence, if productive techniques are specified, and if all expected future prices and the current prices of all other goods are given, the prospective yield of a durable good will be a function of its current price. *Ceteris paribus,* an "economic unit" will ordinarily purchase and hold a larger quantity of a durable good for future use, the lower is its current price in relation to the prices of other assets. Hence, the durable good demand curve of a single economic unit will normally slope downwards from left to right, and similarly for the market demand curve obtained by summing unit demands at each possible price.

Every durable good in the economy must be held by someone; *i.e.,*

---

[1] The first two stages of the argument are summarized in a mathematical note at the end of the article.

[2] Just what specific durable good is selected does not greatly matter for the purposes of this argument; however, the reader may find it helpful at times to think in terms of some concrete commodity, *e.g.,* wheat.

economic units in the aggregate must hold the whole of the existing
stock of a durable good. On the other hand, any one unit is at liberty to
decide for itself—on the basis of relevant market information—what
quantity of a durable good to hold. If these two statements are to be
consistent, however, the current price must be such that individuals in
the aggregate (via interunit exchanges of existing stocks) are *willing*
to hold the whole of the stock outstanding. Thus, through variations in
the current price of a durable good, the freedom of each economic unit
to do as it pleases is rationalized with the necessity for units in the
aggregate to hold a predetermined quantity of each durable good. This
explanation of the pricing of a durable good is illustrated graphically in

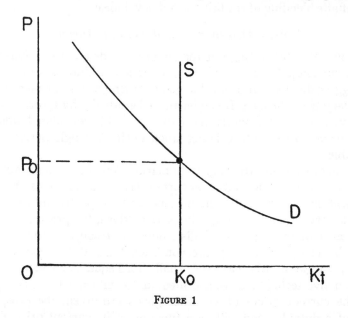

FIGURE 1

Figure 1. The market (stock) supply curve of a selected durable good
is represented by the vertical line, S, the current stock being K_o. The
market (stock) demand curve for durable goods to hold is represented
by D. The current price, P_o, is determined at the intersection of the S
and D curves.

That is about all that needs to be said about the formation of current
market prices of a durable good. However, it should be observed that
because the precise position of the demand curve depends, among other
things, upon expected future prices, and because foresight is unlikely
ever to propose what hindsight knows, the market for any durable good
is necessarily "speculative." Thus, the current market price is a highly
temporary phenomenon.

II. *Conditions Governing Prices and Investment over Time*

The current market price of a durable good may be altered, in the first instance, by a change in demand and supply conditions (prices) in other markets. Again, the current price may vary because of a change in price expectations of dealers in the durable good market. The method of treatment adopted in this discussion does not permit anything new to be said on these matters and they are therefore left to one side for the time being. Finally, the current market price may be affected by changes in the existing stock of durable goods. This possibility merits closer consideration.

A certain portion of the stock of a durable good will disappear during the current period as a result of obsolescence, accidental destruction, and exposure to the elements. In dealing with real-world problems, this kind of "capital consumption" has to be taken into account; however, such matters are not amenable to theoretical treatment and will be ignored in this discussion. I assume, therefore, that durable goods disappear from the economy only through physical wear and tear—the actual "using up" of the services of which durable goods are composed. Thus, in the case of a good which is "original and indestructible," the stock is permanently fixed; its price will be determined according to the principles set out in the previous discussion, and no new issues arise. However, most durable goods are neither original nor indestructible; current stocks may be increased by current production and depleted through current use. Accordingly, what we have to do next is to investigate the conditions governing current levels of gross investment and gross disinvestment in stocks of a given durable good.

A. *Market (Flow) Supply and Demand*

The supply of a new durable good forthcoming into the market during a given period of time (gross investment) is described in terms of an ordinary market (flow) supply curve. Like the demand for goods to hold, the supply of newly produced assets will be a function of current and expected prices. *Ceteris paribus,* suppliers of new durable goods will find it profitable to produce a larger output the higher the current price at which output can be sold; hence, the *flow supply curve* will slope upwards from left to right. Output of the durable good per period will be pushed to the point where the supply price of the marginal producer is equal to the current price as set by the demand for and supply of the current stock of previously produced durable goods. This is illustrated in Figure 2. The industry supply curve of *new* durable goods in the current period is represented by S. The demand curve for newly produced durable goods is represented by D'. The latter curve is infinitely elastic at the level of the current market price since, by hypothesis, the

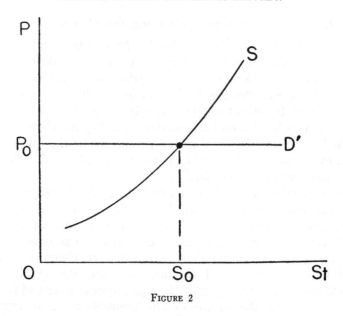

FIGURE 2

market period is so short that current new supply is negligible in relation to existing stocks; *i.e.,* all durable goods which are newly produced
during the period can be added to previous holdings without any noticeable reduction in price. Thus, if the current market price is P_0, the
supply of new durable goods, S_0, will be determined at the intersection
of the S and D′ curves. Notice that the situation depicted in Figure 2—
involving sales by an *industry* to a market in which existing stocks are
large in relation to current new supplies—is closely analogous to the
situation which confronts an individual producer in a market in which
supplies forthcoming from all producers are large in relation to the
production of any one producer.

The quantity of durable goods demanded for current use at various
prices during any given period of time (gross disinvestment) is described in terms of an ordinary market (flow) demand curve. This
curve is to be distinguished sharply from the (stock) demand curve for
durable goods *to hold;* since durable goods are currently held in antici-
pation of possible use during a number of periods, the necessity of this
distinction is apparent. Like any demand curve, the demand for durable
goods for current use will be a function of present and expected future
prices. *Ceteris paribus,* firms will find it profitable to consume larger
quantities of durable goods in the current period the lower their price,
so that the *flow demand curve* will slope downwards from left to right.
Gross disinvestment in the current period will be pushed to the point
on the demand curve where the demand price of the marginal user of

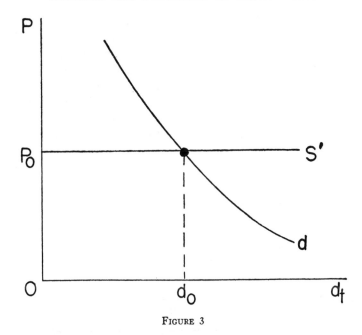

FIGURE 3

durable goods is equal to the current market price. This is illustrated in Figure 3. The market demand curve for "capital consumption" in the current period is represented by d. The supply curve of durable goods for current use is represented by S'. The latter curve is infinitely elastic at the prevailing market price since the market period is so short that current depletion of the existing stock of durable goods can be neglected; *i.e.*, all demands for current disinvestment can be satisfied by drawing on existing stocks without an increase in price. Thus, if the current market price is P_0, the current level of disinvestment, d_0, is determined at the intersection of the d and S' curves.

B. Temporary and Stationary Equilibrium

In order to obtain a more adequate picture of the pricing process in a durable good market, the data given in Figures 1, 2, and 3 need to be considered as a whole;[3] this is done in Figure 4. Figure 4a is a re-

[3] Up to this point, I have attempted merely to restate and clarify received doctrine. Thus, my *stock* demand curve is substantially identical with the familiar *reservation* demand curve concept, and my *flow* supply and demand curves are essentially the same as the familiar *short-run* supply and demand curve concepts. From this point onward, however, there is a definite breach with tradition. In the existing literature, it is almost invariably assumed that supplies of a good are *either* fixed *or* variable, and in any case the process of price determination is always analyzed in terms of one or the other of these two assumptions (see, *e.g.*, George J. Stigler, *The Theory of Price* (Revised Edition), New York, The Macmillan Company, 1952, Chapters 9 and 10). However, durable goods

production of Figure 1 with certain additions which will be mentioned
later. The curve e in Figure 4b represents the *excess flow demand curve*
which is implicit in Figures 2 and 3. This curve is derived by subtracting
flow supply from flow demand at each possible price and plotting the
resulting quantities against price; it shows for each possible price the
corresponding level of net investment (or net disinvestment) which
will occur during a given period. For the moment it is convenient to
assume that the vertical and horizontal scales are the same in Figures

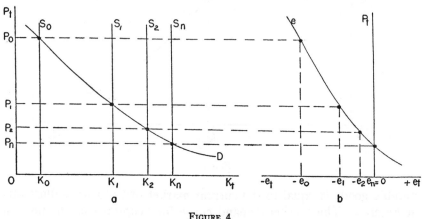

FIGURE 4

4a and 4b (*e.g.*, if 1 inch equals 100 units on the horizontal axis of
Figure 4a, 1 inch equals 100 units *per period* on the horizontal axis of
Figure 4b).

Suppose that at time t_0 the stock of durable goods is K_0 so that
market price is established momentarily at P_0, representing a position
of *temporary equilibrium* such that individuals in the aggregate are
willing to hold the existing stock of durable goods. At this price, excess
flow demand will be negative; hence, net investment will occur during
the initial period. At the beginning of Period 1, therefore, the stock of
durable goods will have risen to $K_1(K_1 = K_0 + e_0)$, and price will fall
to P_1. At the price P_1, net investment (e_1) will still be positive, so that

---

seem to fit both of these supposed alternatives equally well, for *while a typical durable
good is necessarily in fixed supply at any instant of time, existing stocks of the good will
normally be changing at the same instant as a result of net investment or disinvestment.*
Thus, in dealing with durable goods, it is a highly questionable procedure to treat price
determination by stock supply and demand relations and price determination by flow
supply and demand relations as mutually exclusive alternatives. The novelty of the subsequent argument is a direct consequence of denying the mutual exclusiveness of these alternatives. Previous writers have kept both stock and flow horses in their stables, but they
have ordinarily used them to draw different carts; the horses are run in double harness
in this paper.

at the beginning of Period 2 the stock of durable goods will be K_2 $(K_2 = K_1 + e_1)$, price will fall to P_2, *etc.* So long as the market is in a position of flow disequilibrium (*i.e.*, so long as $e_t \neq 0$) this process will continue. In the above example, however, a position of stationary equilibrium will be more nearly approached in each succeeding period; that is to say, there will be a direct, if gradual, movement towards a situation in which the stock of durable goods is K_n, price is P_n, and $e_n = 0$. If this position is eventually attained, price will remain stationary thereafter unless the market is disturbed by changes in factors other than those which are taken as variables in the present discussion. An argument similar to the above clearly applies, *mutatis mutandis,* if one takes as a starting point a price which is such as to induce net disinvestment.

C. *Stability of the Market*

At this point it is natural to ask in what circumstances price, if disturbed, will tend to return to the stationary equilibrium level; *i.e.*, what factors govern the stability of the market? Also, if the market is stable, will the approach towards equilibrium be direct (as in the previous illustration) or are oscillations about the stationary equilibrium price level possible? Two possibilities have to be considered:

1. *Trading activity may occur only at discrete moments in time.* In this case it can be shown (see the Mathematical Note, pp. 78-81) that for linear demand curves, the market will be stable if (a) the stock demand and the excess flow demand curves slope in the same direction (whether positive or negative), and (b) the stock demand curve is less than twice as steep as the excess flow demand curve (both slopes being referred to the quantity axis). Since the slope of the excess flow demand curve is proportionate to the length of the market period (*i.e.*, halving the market period will halve all *per period* quantities), while the slope of the stock demand curve is independent of the market period, condition (b) will always be satisfied if trading dates are sufficiently close together (see the Mathematical Note, p. 79). The time required for the market to approach stationary equilibrium will be less the smaller the absolute difference between the slopes of the stock demand and excess flow demand curves (see the Mathematical Note, p. 79).

Even if the market is stable, it may display damped oscillations about the equilibrium price if the market period is sufficiently long, for damped oscillations will occur if the slope of the stock demand curve is greater than the slope of the excess flow demand curve[4] (Mathematical Note, p. 81). Such a case is illustrated in Figure 5. The curves shown in this diagram are defined in exactly the same way as those in

---

[4] The approach towards equilibrium will be direct if the slope of the stock demand curve is less than that of the excess flow demand curve (Mathematical Note, p. 79).

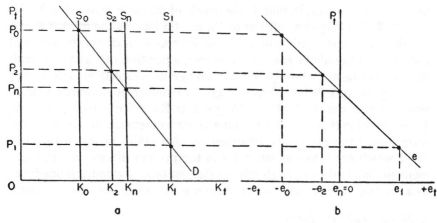

FIGURE 5

Figure 4; but in the present example the excess flow demand curve is less steeply inclined than the stock demand curve. The reader may verify for himself that, starting at the price P_0, both K_t and P_t rise and fall in alternate periods, so that the current price describes a "flat" spiral about the stationary equilibrium price. Basically, this is the same thing as the familiar "cobweb" cycle; but the present is more general than the usual treatment of this phenomenon because no production or trading lags are presupposed and because commodity stocks enter the analysis as an explicit variable.

2. Trading in the market may take place continuously. In this case it can be shown that for linear demand curves the market will be stable only if the stock demand and excess flow demand curves are both downward sloping (Mathematical Note, p. 81). Whether the approach towards equilibrium is direct or oscillatory will depend upon the relative slopes of the two demand curves,[5] and upon the rapidity with which price adjusts to changes in excess *stock* demand. The last mentioned complication is characteristic of a single market involving both stock and flow variables; it does not appear in ordinary partial equilibrium analysis, although it may arise in a different form in ordinary general equilibrium analysis.[6] If the "speed of adjustment" of price is sufficiently rapid, the approach towards stationary equilibrium will always be direct (Mathematical Note, p. 81).

To summarize the results of the preceding sections: The market price of a durable good at any moment is governed by current and ex-

---

[5] Precise conditions for oscillatory behavior are given in the Mathematical Note, p. 81.

[6] *Cf.* P. A. Samuelson, *Foundations of Economic Analysis* (Cambridge, 1948), pp. 263-72.

pected prices taken in conjunction with technical conditions affecting the production of new, and the consumption of previously produced, durable goods. If these conditions are given, the current market price will be established at a level which brings the existing supply of durable goods into equality with the demand for durable goods to hold. If at this "temporary" price the market is in flow disequilibrium (with current production exceeding or falling short of current consumption), the stock of durable goods, and so the "temporary" price, will alter gradually over time. If the market is stable, a position of stationary equilibrium will be approximately attained after the lapse of a sufficient length of time. The nature of the approach towards equilibrium may be direct or oscillatory, depending upon the slopes of the stock demand and excess flow demand curves and (in the case of discrete trading dates) upon the length of the market period or (in the case of continuous trading) upon the "speed of adjustment" of price to changes in excess stock demand.

III. *Adjustment Processes Continuous through Time*

A major shortcoming of modern economic theory is that it does not include a set of analytical tools sufficiently simple and precise, yet sufficiently familiar in terms of traditional ideas, to permit economists to deal effectively with elementary dynamic problems. In the previous discussion an attempt has been made to develop a technique which meets these requirements by generalizing a partial equilibrium model of a durable good market to allow for the simultaneous treatment of stock and flow variables. This generalization adds certain essentially dynamic features to traditional partial equilibrium analysis, thus permitting one to proceed some way towards an explicit characterization, for a single market, of adjustment processes continuous through time. To deal adequately with this topic would require more space than is available here. However, the general method of approach can be made tolerably clear by outlining a few sample analyses of the response of the present model to changes in the demand for final goods, the rate of interest, and technical knowledge. Naturally the discussion that follows is intended to be suggestive rather than rigorous, illustrative rather than comprehensive.

A. *Changes in Demand for Final Goods*

Since any change in the current demand for consumer goods will affect relative prices, it will alter the demand for durable goods to hold. However, a change in demand typically will be spread over a large number of goods, and since durable goods are held primarily for use in the future, the *direct* effects upon a single market of a change in consumer demand are unlikely to be significant in the short run. Nevertheless, if a change in current demand alters expected future prices (*i.e.,* if price elasticities of expectations are nonzero) the demand for durable goods to hold may shift noticeably, in which case there will be important *indirect* changes in current market variables. Indeed, what we have to deal with here is a very general version of the so-called "acceleration principle of derived demand." A diagrammatic illustration will help to clarify the matter. In Figure 6, suppose that the market is initially in stationary equilibrium. Moreover, assume that as a result of an increase in consumption demand there is a 10 per cent increase (at the current price) in the demand for durable goods to hold. This is represented in Figure 6 by a shift in the D curve from D to D*. Current price will rise accordingly, the extent of the increase depending on the elasticity of the D* curve; as the D* curve is drawn in Figure 6, price

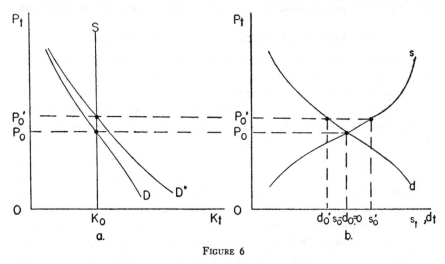

FIGURE 6

will rise to P'$_0$. At the price P'$_0$, however, gross investment and disinvestment are unequal; hence, the rise in price involves an indefinitely large percentage increase in *net* investment (an increase from $s_0 - d_0$ $= 0$ to $s'_0 - d'_0 \neq 0$), while gross investment and gross disinvestment may change by virtually any percentage amount, depending on the respective price elasticities of the s and d curves.[7] In review: an increase in consumer demand which is expected to be permanent will entail "acceleration" or "deceleration" effects upon current activity in a given durable good market. Our analysis indicates that these effects will be more pronounced: (*i*) the greater the initial increase in final demand;

---

[7] The stability of the market in Figure 6 is assured if one supposes that the (per period) quantity scale in Figure 6b is much smaller than the quantity scale in Figure 6a.

(*ii*) the less the degree to which increases in demand affect other markets; (*iii*) the greater elasticities of expectations; (*iv*) the smaller the price elasticity of demand for durable goods to hold; (*v*) the greater the price elasticity of supply of new capital goods; and (*vi*) the greater the price elasticity of demand for current disinvestment. It is worth observing that, in principle, any change in the given conditions of our model will involve acceleration and deceleration effects of the kind just outlined, the magnitude of which will be governed by the above considerations.

An initial change in consumer demand will ordinarily be reinforced by secondary repercussions which are induced by changes in the level of current activity. However, if an initial change in consumer demand is a "once-over" as contrasted with a "continuing" change, and if the market is stable, net investment will, after a time, cease to increase and eventually there will be a return towards a new stationary equilibrium position. Intermittent or continuous changes in demand, on the other hand, may involve permanently nonzero levels of net investment (permanent flow disequilibrium) and continued adjustments in other market quantities. All of this is in conformity with both common sense and established doctrine. The immediate analysis leads to no new results, but familiar conclusions are nevertheless amplified and defined with greater precision.

B. *Changes in the Rate of Interest*

In this section, we suppose that the only securities in the economy are perpetual bonds whose prices all change in the same proportion, so that the phrase "the rate of interest" may be used unambiguously.

A change in the rate of interest, like a change in prices generally, will alter the position of demand and supply curves in every market in the economy; but the main impact of such a change will fall on holders of durable goods, since a change in the rate of interest will alter market appraisals of the discounted (present) value of these commodities. This will entail a change in the current market price, and so a change in current investment and disinvestment. Perhaps the most instructive way to examine this matter is in terms of a "marginal efficiency of capital schedule." *Ceteris paribus*, to every alternative level of the rate of interest there corresponds a demand curve for durable goods to hold. This is illustrated in Figure 7a by the curves $D(r_0)$, $D(r_1)$, and $D(r_2)$, where it is assumed that $r_0 < r_1 < r_2$. If the existing stock of durable goods is, say, K_0, then to each alternative level of the rate of interest there corresponds a definite current price of durable goods, and so a definite level of gross investment and gross disinvestment. This is illustrated in Figure 7b (the effect of changes in the rate of interest upon

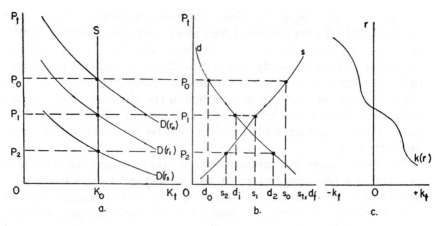

FIGURE 7

the flow supply and demand relations being assumed to be negligible);
here, if the rate of interest is r_0, gross investment and disinvestment are
s_0 and d_0, respectively; if the rate of interest is r_1, gross investment and
disinvestment are s_1 and d_1, etc. Hence, plotting alternative interest
rates against corresponding levels of *net* investment in Figure 7c, we
obtain a curve $k(r)$ which Keynes would call a "schedule of the marginal efficiency of capital." This schedule is defined as of a moment of
time and as of a given stock of durable goods; it shows for each possible
level of the rate of interest the quantity of durable goods, k_t, which
will be added to (or taken from) existing stocks during the current
period. Strictly speaking, it is not an investment *demand* schedule since
its shape and position depend, among other things, upon the shape of
the supply curve of new durable goods.

Is it possible to say anything, *a priori,* about the shape of the schedule
in Figure 7c? Clearly, the schedule will normally be downward sloping;
but otherwise it may have almost any form. If stock demands are highly
responsive to changes in the rate of interest (as will usually be the case
for long-lived capital goods), the marginal efficiency of capital schedule
will nevertheless be highly inelastic if the flow supply and demand
curves are highly price-inelastic (as may or may not be the case for
long-lived capital goods). If stock demands are not responsive to
changes in the rate of interest (as may be the case with inventory stocks
which are held for short periods of time), the schedule of the marginal
efficiency of capital may nevertheless be highly elastic if the flow
demand and supply curves are highly price-elastic, etc. Thus, it does not
seem possible to say very much in general about the impact effects upon
current investment of changes in the rate of interest. As regards the
dynamic properties of a marginal efficiency of capital schedule, however,

it is interesting to note that net investment is *not* related to the *level* of the rate of interest as such, but rather to the difference between the current level of the rate of interest and that rate which would leave the market in stationary equilibrium. That is to say, if the rate of interest were constant at a level which temporarily induced net investment, the schedule of the marginal efficiency of capital would gradually shift to the left with the passage of time until it intersected the r axis at the given rate and net investment had disappeared. Thus, a once-over change in the rate of interest may permanently alter the level of the stock of durable goods and the levels of gross investment and disinvestment; but, *ceteris paribus,* the continuance of nonzero levels of net investment depends upon recurring changes in the rate of interest.[8]

C. *Changes in Technical Knowledge*

A change in technical knowledge affects our model in two distinct ways: via expectations and via changes in productive techniques. The initial impact of a change in knowledge is upon price expectations. In principle, this implies a shift of demand and supply functions in every sector of the economy. Ordinarily, however, one would expect shifts in flow supply and demand curves to be slight relative to shifts in stock demand curves, since the latter relations involve considerations relating to the possibly distant future. If a particular durable good market is originally in stationary equilibrium, a change in technical knowledge will lead to immediate flow disequilibruim; *i.e.,* investment or disinvestment will occur, depending on whether the new knowledge improves or worsens future prospects for the good in question. With the emergence of flow disequilibrium, the change in technical knowledge will give rise to secondary effects in the form of innovations; *i.e.,* the new knowledge will be introduced gradually into the economy in the guise of changes in techniques of production. Innovations will, in turn, lead to further revisions of price expectations which will, in turn, entail further innovations, etc. Moreover, the (flow) supply curve of new durable goods and the (flow) demand curve for previously produced durable goods will shift with changes in productive techniques as well as with shifts in prices in other markets of the economy. However, as in the case of changes in consumer demand and the rate of interest, a once-over change in technical knowledge will be followed (in a stable market) by an eventual return to a new stationary equilibrium position; a permanent condition of flow disequilibrium (economic development) can exist only if changes in technical knowledge are continuing, or at least intermittent.

[8] *Cf.* Hugh Rose, "Demand, Supply and the Price Level in Macroeconomics," *Rev. Econ. Stud.*, 1952-53, XX (1), 6.

MATHEMATICAL NOTE*

1. Consider a market for a single durable good (*i.e.*, assume that current and expected prices of all other goods are given). Denote by $D(p)$ the quantity (stock) of the good demanded to hold at the price p; by S_t the quantity (stock supply) of the good actually held at the beginning of the tth period ($t = 0, 1, 2, \cdots$); by $d(p)$ the quantity (flow) of previously produced units of the good demanded for consumption over a period at the price p; and by $s(p)$ the quantity (flow) of newly produced units supplied to the market over a period at the price p. Then for some initial value S_0 of the stock supply of the durable good, stock supply at the beginning of the nth period is given by

$$S_n = S_0 + \sum_{t=0}^{n-1} [s(p_t) - d(p_t)],$$

where p_t is the price (assumed constant) over the tth period.

As a condition for stock equilibrium in the market at the beginning of the nth period we require that price equate stock supply and demand:

$$D(p_n) - S_n = D(p_n) - S_0 - \sum_{t=0}^{n-1} [s(p_t) - d(p_t)] = 0. \qquad (1)$$

For *stationary* (stock-flow) equilibrium we require also that price equate flow supply and demand:

$$d(p_n) - s(p_n) = 0. \qquad (2)$$

Whether or not (2) is satisfied, (1) suffices to determine the current price p_n of the durable good; since S_n does not depend on $s(p_n)$ or $d(p_n)$, the current price is independent of current levels of flow supply and demand. If both (1) and (2) are satisfied by p_n, then they continue to be satisfied if one takes $p_m = p_n$ for all $m \geq n$.

Now assume that in the neighborhood of some stationary equilibrium price, $\tilde{p}$, $D(p)$ may be expressed as a Taylor series

$$D(p) = D(\tilde{p}) + \Omega(p - \tilde{p}) + [\cdots],$$

while $e(p) = d(p) - s(p)$ may be expressed (using equation (2)) as

$$e(p) = \delta(p - \tilde{p}) - \sigma(p - \tilde{p}) + [\cdots] = \epsilon(p - \tilde{p}) + [\cdots],$$

where

$$\Omega = \frac{dD}{dp}\bigg|_{p=\tilde{p},} \qquad \delta = \frac{dd}{dp}\bigg|_{p=\tilde{p},} \qquad \sigma = \frac{ds}{dp}\bigg|_{p=\tilde{p},} \qquad \epsilon = \delta - \sigma,$$

*This note was prepared by R. W. Clower and D. W. Bushaw, who is instructor in mathematics at the State College of Washington, Pullman.

and $[\,\cdots\,]$ represents terms of degree at least 2 in $(p-\tilde{p})$.

Substituting these expressions into (1), differencing the result in order to rid it of constants, and omitting the nonlinear terms,[9] we obtain

$$\Omega p_t - (\Omega - \epsilon)p_{t-1} - \epsilon\tilde{p} = 0,$$

which gives the market price in the period t as a function of market price in the period $t-1$.

The solution of this linear difference equation for the initial price p_0 is

$$p_t = (p_0 - \tilde{p})\left(1 - \frac{\epsilon}{\Omega}\right)^t + \tilde{p}. \qquad (3)$$

For stability we require that $p_t \to \tilde{p}$ as $t \to \infty$. This will occur if and only if

$$\left|1 - \frac{\epsilon}{\Omega}\right| < 1, \quad i.e. \quad 0 < \frac{\epsilon}{\Omega} < 2.$$

The condition $0 < (\epsilon/\Omega)$ will be satisfied if the stock and excess flow demand curves are both downward sloping (or both upward sloping), otherwise not. Since, as one can easily see, the slope of the excess *flow* demand curve is proportional to the length of the market period, the condition $(\epsilon/\Omega) < 2$ (restricting the *relative* slopes of the stock and excess flow demand curves) will be satisfied if the market period is sufficiently short.

The nature of the approach towards equilibrium depends on the sign of the quantity $[1-(\epsilon/\Omega)]$ in (3); the approach is "direct" $[(p_t-\tilde{p})$ has a constant sign] when this quantity is positive or zero, "spiral" $[(p_t-\tilde{p})$ alternates in sign] when it is negative. It is directly evident from (3) that $p_t \to \tilde{p}$ as $t \to \infty$ more rapidly the smaller $|1-(\epsilon/\Omega)|$.

2. The argument in section 1 of this note is based on the assumption that trading activity occurs only at the beginning of each period. In some respects it is more realistic to suppose that trading is continuous, in which case we arrive at rather different conclusions.

As before, denote by $D=D(p)$ the stock demand function, and by $d=d(p)$ and $s=s(p)$ the flow demand and supply functions respectively (these are now instantaneous rates), where p is the market price. Then for some value a of t, stock supply at time $t(t \geq a)$ is given by

$$S_t = \int_a^t [s(p_\theta) - d(p_\theta)]d\theta,$$

---

[9] We are concerned here only with finding a condition for the stability of the equilibrium price $\tilde{p}$. In such a situation it is permissible to ignore the nonlinear terms. See O. Perron, "Ueber Stabilität and asymptotisches Verhalten der Lösungen eines Systems endlicher Differenzengleichungen," *Journal für die reine und angewandte Mathematik* (1929), CLXI pp. 41–64.

where p_t is the market price at time t.

For equilibrium in the market at the instant of time t we require that

$$E_t = D(p_t) - \int_a^t [s(p_\theta) - d(p_\theta)]d\theta = 0 \qquad (4)$$

and

$$e(p_t) = d(p_t) - s(p_t) = 0. \qquad (5)$$

Condition (4) states that in equilibrium excess stock demand is zero; condition (5) that, in equilibrium, the level of existing stocks displays no tendency to change over time (excess flow demand is zero).

In what circumstances do conditions (4) and (5) determine a position of stable market equilibrium? To answer this question, we assume that the rate of change of price is a function of excess stock demand:

$$\frac{dp_t}{dt} = \phi\left[D(p_t) - \int_a^t [s(p_\theta) - d(p_\theta)]d\theta\right], \qquad (6)$$

where $\phi(0)=0$ and $\phi'>0$. Assume also that in the neighborhood of the equilibrium price $\tilde{p}$, $D(p)$ and $d(p)-s(p)$ have the Taylor series

$$D(p) = D(\tilde{p}) + \Omega(p - \tilde{p}) + [\cdots]$$

and (using equation (5))

$$d(p) - s(p) = (\delta - \sigma)(p - \tilde{p}) + [\cdots]$$
$$= \epsilon(p - \tilde{p}) + [\cdots],$$

where Ω, δ, σ, ϵ, and $[\cdots]$ have the same meanings as in section 1 above.

Differentiating (6) on both sides with respect to t, we obtain

$$\frac{d^2p_t}{dt^2} = \phi'[D(p_t) - S_t] \cdot \left[\frac{dD}{dp}\frac{dp_t}{dt} - s(p_t) + d(p_t)\right]. \qquad (7)$$

Isolating the linear part of the right hand side of (7), we may write this equation in the form

$$\frac{d^2p_t}{dt^2} = K\left[\epsilon(p_t - \tilde{p}) + \Omega \frac{dp_t}{dt}\right] + [\cdots], \qquad (7')$$

where K is some constant, $K = \dfrac{d\phi}{dE_t}\bigg|_{E_t = 0}$

So long as we are interested solely in the qualitative behavior of p_t near the equilibrium price $\tilde{p}$, a well-known theorem from the theory of differential equations[10] assures us that we need to examine only the equation obtained by omitting the nonlinear elements from $(7')$:

$$\frac{d^2 p_t}{dt^2} - K\Omega \frac{dp_t}{dt} - K\epsilon(p_t - \tilde{p}) = 0. \tag{8}$$

The characteristic equation for this equation is

$$\lambda^2 - K\Omega\lambda - K\epsilon = 0; \tag{9}$$

its roots are

$$(K\Omega \pm \sqrt{(K\Omega)^2 + 4K\epsilon})/2.$$

The necessary and sufficient condition for stability is that these roots have negative real parts. This will occur if and only if $\Omega < 0$ and $\epsilon < 0$; these conditions will be satisfied if (i) the stock demand function is downward sloping and (ii) the flow supply and demand functions satisfy the usual Marshallian stability conditions (*i.e.*, the flow supply curve must be upward sloping, or else it must be less steep, referred to the price axis, than the flow demand curve.)

The nature of the approach towards equilibrium will depend on the relative magnitudes of $K\Omega^2$ and ϵ. There are two cases:

Case I. $K\Omega^2 + 4\epsilon \geq 0$. Here the roots of the characteristic equation (9) are real, and we have a stable node; the approach towards equilibrium is direct.

Case II. $K\Omega^2 + 4\epsilon < 0$. In this case, the roots of equation (9) are complex conjugates and we have a stable focus; the approach towards equilibrium is of a spiral (damped oscillatory) nature.

The probability of damped oscillations (Case II) is clearly less the greater K, the "speed of adjustment" of price to changes in excess stock demand.

[10] See, *e.g.*, S. Lefschetz, *Lectures on Differential Equations*. Annals of Mathematics Studies. No. 14, Princeton University (Princeton, 1948), p. 125 ff.

[10]

PRODUCTIVITY, THRIFT AND THE RATE OF INTEREST

1. THIS essay investigates the determination of the rate of interest in a market for a single security. The argument differs from previous treatments of the same topic in that it deals explicitly with both stock and flow aspects of the problem, and does not emphasise one aspect to the virtual exclusion of the other. The discussion is constructive throughout, since I have felt that a running appraisal of previous writings would only obscure the present exposition.

2. For the sake of simplicity, we deal with a market for riskless, perpetual bonds having a par value of $100 and yielding $1 per (some arbitrary) period to bondholders. This implies that the market rate of interest is the reciprocal of the price of bonds, so that the problem of explaining the determination of the rate of interest is effectively transformed into that of explaining the determination of bond prices.

3. The aggregate quantities of various assets existing in an economy in any given period of time are inherited from the past. These quantities can be altered only gradually as a result of future economic decisions, so that if we consider appropriately short time periods, current additions to (or depletions of) aggregate asset stocks can be ignored. On the other hand, the way in which existing stocks are distributed among individual holders (at the end of any period) is determined by current economic decisions. In particular, an individual will distribute his holdings in such a way as to equalise the marginal advantages of holding a dollars' worth of any one asset with the marginal advantages of holding an equal value of any other asset.[1] That is to say, given expected future prices and given the current prices of all other goods, an individual's demand for bonds will be a function of current bond prices.[2] Since, *ceteris paribus*, an individual will generally be more willing to purchase and hold claims to given future interest receipts the lower the current price of bonds in relation to the prices of other assets, the individual demand

---

[1] It should be emphasised that bonds are held rather than used; *i.e.*, while bonds may yield subjective satisfactions as well as interest payments, in every case " yields " are contingent upon possession.

[2] In the case of consumers, it is also implicitly assumed that the individual's asset holdings at the beginning of the current period are given.

curve for bonds will ordinarily slope downwards from left to right. Aggregating individual demands, therefore, we obtain a community demand curve for bonds (to hold) which will also be downward sloping. In general, this curve will be a function of all current prices other than bond prices, of all future prices expected by individuals and of the distribution of assets among individuals at the beginning of the current period.

4. Each bond outstanding in the economy must be held by someone; *i.e.*, the total stock of bonds must be held by individuals in the aggregate. But since any one individual is free to hold or not to hold bonds, as he sees fit, this implies that the market price of bonds must be such that individuals in the aggregate (via inter-personal exchanges of existing bonds) are willing to hold the

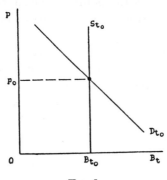

Fig. 1

existing stock. This description of the determination of *current* bond prices is illustrated graphically in Fig. 1. The supply curve of bonds at the beginning of period t_0 is represented by S_{t_0} (the existing stock of bonds being B_{t_0}). The demand curve for bonds (to hold) at time t_0 is represented by D_{t_0}. The price, p_0, at which individuals in the aggregate are willing to hold the existing stock of bonds is determined at the intersection of S_{t_0} and D_{t_0}.

5. The above theory of the *current* rate of interest is all very well as far as it goes; but it does not go very far. I do not mean by this that the theory does not tell us anything about the " nature " of the rate of interest; problems of this sort are not the immediate business of economists in any case. The real difficulty with our theory of the current rate of interest is that it does not permit us to answer questions concerning the economic roles of " productivity and thrift "; that it does not allow us to say anything about the reasons why the rate of interest " is what it is," nor to conjecture what will be the future course of the interest rate over any time interval. However, our theory can

be extended to deal with these problems. Briefly, what we have to do next is to examine those factors which affect the current stock of bonds and the current demand for bonds to hold.

6. The supply of *new* bonds forthcoming into the market during any given period of time will be a function of the same variables as the market demand for bonds to hold (viz., current and expected prices and the current distribution of assets). Individuals will ordinarily be more willing to assume obligations to make given future bond payments the higher the price which can be currently obtained on bond sales; hence, the supply curve of new issues will ordinarily slope upwards from left to right. Given the current market price of bonds as determined by the demand and supply of *old* bonds, sales of new issues (per period) will be pushed to the point on the supply curve where the supply price of the marginal seller of new bonds is equal to the existing market price.[1]

The supply of new issues is only one of the factors affecting the level of current bond stocks; bonds may be destroyed (technically or economically) as well as created. Thus, during any given period, some of the bonds outstanding in an economy will be lost or destroyed, etc. Depletions of this sort will be ignored here. More important, large quantities of existing bonds may be retired by original issuers during any given period. The motives governing reductions in current indebtedness are precisely the same as the motives governing increases in indebtedness, so that an individual will generally be more willing to retire an obligation to make given future interest payments, the lower the price at which the obligation is redeemable. Hence, the demand curve for the retirement of existing bonds (per period) will slope downwards from left to right. Given the current market price of bonds, the retirement of outstanding issues in any period will be carried to the point where the demand price of the marginal redeemer of bonds is equal to the current market price.

The previous argument is illustrated graphically in Fig. 2. Fig. 1 is here reproduced (with certain additions) as Fig. 2a. In Fig. 2b the supply curve of new issues is represented by $s_{(t_1 - t_0)}$, while the demand curve for bonds to retire is given by $d_{(t_1 - t_0)}$. If the current price of bonds is p_0, the quantity of new bonds issued during the current period will be b_0^s and the quantity of bonds retired will be b_0^d.

---

[1] Notice that the demand curve for bonds which confronts the " bond selling *industry* " is analogous to the demand curve as seen by an *individual seller* in a competitive industry.

The supply of new issues may or may not be matched by the demand for bonds to retire. If $b_t{}^s - b_t{}^d = B_{t+1} - B_t =$ the net increase in the stock of bonds in the tth period $= 0$, the current rate of interest will remain unchanged in all future periods unless some outside influence upsets the existing stock and flow equilibrium. If $b_t{}^s - b_t{}^d > 0$, the existing stock of bonds will increase in every subsequent period (and *vice versa* if $b_t{}^s - b_t{}^d < 0$). Thus, when $b_0{}^s - b_0{}^d > 0$, as shown in Fig. 2b, the stock of bonds will increase during period t_0 to, say, B_{t_1}. In period t_1, therefore, bond prices will fall to p_1, new issues will fall to $b_1{}^s$, retirement demand will rise to $b_1{}^d$, and the stock of bonds will increase in period t_1 by $b_1{}^s - b_1{}^d$, etc.[1]

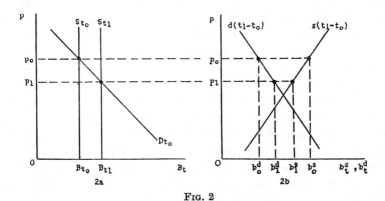

Fig. 2

7. The foregoing analysis provides the necessary tools for a discussion of the effects of " productivity " upon bond prices. If, for example, an increase in productivity (an innovation?) increases the current demand for money to purchase physical assets, this will be partially reflected in the market for perpetual bonds.[2] More precisely, there will be a rightward shift of the supply curve of new issues (greater willingness to borrow) and a leftward shift of the demand curve for bonds to retire (greater willingness to remain in debt). On both counts the time rate of increase of bond stocks $(b_t{}^s - b_t{}^d)$ will rise; but since the current rate of interest is determined independently of the net supply of new issues, it is *a fortiori* independent of current *changes* in the net supply of new issues. Hence, productivity can play no *direct* part in the determination of the current rate of interest.

---

[1] It is implicitly assumed that the effects of increased bond stocks upon the D, s and d curves can be neglected.

[2] " Partially reflected," because the increased demand for money will be spread out over a number of security markets.

However, if changes in productivity affect bondholders' expectations of future prices (thus causing a shift in the D curve in Fig. 2a), productivity considerations will indirectly influence the current rate of interest.

As will be indicated later, in medium and long-run time periods a change in productivity, since it will affect the time rate of change of bond stocks, will partly govern the rate at which the rate of interest changes during various time periods; *i.e.*, productivity considerations eventually help to determine the future course of the rate of interest.

8. Turning now to the economic effects of "thrift," the argument of the previous section applies if a change in thrift leads consumers to increase their current indebtedness. Suppose, however, that the change in thrift involves a decrease in the demand for consumer goods. How will a change of this sort be reflected in the market for perpetual bonds?

A decrease in the demand for consumer goods—the emergence of excess supply in consumer-good markets—implies a change in consumer-good prices, and so a change in demand curves for assets. In particular, a change in consumer-good prices will affect the demand curve for bonds to hold. However, even a large current change in thrift, since its effects will be spread among a myriad of assets, will ordinarily have little effect upon the demand for any one asset. Moreover, in the short run any increase in demands for assets to hold will necessarily be small in relation to total (historically accumulated) demands, so that thrift can play no *direct* part in determining the current rate of interest. As in the case of productivity, the effects of thrift must be cumulated over a medium- or long-run period of time before they can directly influence the course of the rate of interest. However, the current rate of interest will be indirectly responsive to changes in thrift to the extent that such changes alter expected future prices.

9. Thus far, our discussion provides only an outline solution to the problem of what course the rate of interest may be expected to follow over an interval of time. A comprehensive examination of this problem, involving a treatment of interrelations among bond and commodity markets, lies outside the scope of this paper. However, a brief investigation into the dynamics of price determination in our selected bond market (conditions in other markets being held in *ceteris paribus*) can be undertaken here.

Suppose that the bond market is initially in stationary equilibrium, the price of bonds being established at a level such that the quantity of new bonds currently being issued is equal to the quantity of previously issued bonds currently being retired. Then a " once-over " shift in the demand curve for bonds to hold (the *stock demand curve*) will create a condition of flow disequilibrium; new bond issues will currently exceed or fall short of bond retirements, and the current stock of bonds and the price of bonds will change in every subsequent period during which flow disequilibrium persists. At this point, therefore, the following questions naturally arise : Will the price of bonds gradually return to the stationary equilibrium level so that the bond market will be stable ? If the market is stable, will the approach towards equilibrium be direct, or will it be characterised by oscillations of the current price about the stationary price level ? What factors will govern the length of time which must elapse before stationary equilibrium conditions are re-established ? In order to give clear-cut answers to these questions, we must first define an *excess flow demand curve* for bonds; this is a relation which shows, for each possible price of bonds, the amount by which the existing stock of bonds will increase or decrease during the current period (*i.e.*, when excess flow demand is positive, the stock of bonds will decrease during the current period; when excess flow demand is negative, the stock of bonds will increase during the current period). Such a curve is implicit in Fig. 2, above; it may be obtained explicitly by subtracting the supply of new issues from the demand for bonds to retire at each possible price, and relating the resulting *net* figure to its corresponding price.

Now, it can be shown that [1] :

(i) the bond market will be stable if the slope of the excess-flow-demand curve is less than twice the slope of the

---

[1] For small deviations from the stationary equilibrium price, p_0, the price of bonds at time t is given by the linear difference equation

$$p_t = \left(1 - \frac{e_{p_0}}{D_{p_0}}\right)P_{t-1} + \frac{e_{p_0}}{D_{p_0}}P_0$$

where e_{p_0} and D_{p_0} are the respective slopes of the excess-flow-demand and stock-demand curves in the neighbourhood of the equilibrium price. The solution of this equation may be written

$$p_t = p_0 + (\bar{p} - p_0)\left(1 - \frac{e_{p_0}}{D_{p_0}}\right)^t$$

where $\bar{p}$ is some arbitrary initial price. For stability, therefore, it is necessary and sufficient that:

$$\left| 1 - \frac{e_{p_0}}{D_{p_0}} \right| < 1,$$

or that $-1 < 1 - e_{p_0}/D_{p_0} < 1$. These conditions will be satisfied if $e_{p_0}D_{p_0} > 0$, and $e_{p_0} < 2D_{p_0}$. The nature of the approach towards equilibrium depends upon the size of e_{p_0}/D_{p_0}; the approach is direct if $e_{p_0}/D_{p_0} \leqslant 1$, oscillatory if $e_{p_0}/D_{p_0} > 1$. Obviously $p_t \to p_0$ more rapidly as $t \to \infty$, the smaller is $(1 - e_{p_0}/D_{p_0})$.

stock-demand curve (*both slopes being referred to the price axis*);

(ii) price will oscillate about the equilibrium price level if the slope of the excess-flow-demand curve is greater than the slope of the stock-demand curve;

(iii) price will approach the equilibrium level directly if the slope of the excess-flow-demand curve is less than the slope of the stock-demand curve;

(iv) the approach towards equilibrium will be less rapid the greater the difference between the slopes of the two demand curves.

It would require more space than is available to demonstrate all of these results in non-symbolic terms [1]; however, a typical

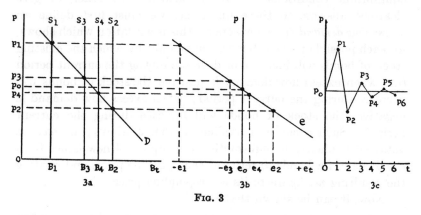

FIG. 3

diagrammatic example of the second result is presented in Fig. 3. The S and D curves shown in Fig. 3a are defined in precisely the same way as the corresponding curves in Fig. 1, above. The curve e in Fig. 3b is the excess-flow-demand curve for bonds; notice that it is drawn more steep (with reference to the price axis) than the stock-demand curve in Fig. 3a. For the purposes of this discussion, we assume that the horizontal scale is the same in the a and b parts of Fig. 3 (*e.g.*, if 1 inch equals 1,000,000 bonds on the horizontal axis of Fig. 3a, 1 inch equals 1,000,000 bonds *per period* on the horizontal axis of Fig. 3b).

The market illustrated in Fig. 3 will be in stationary equilibrium if excess flow demand is equal to zero; *i.e.*, if price is p_0 so that $e_t = e_0$. If the stock of bonds in the initial period is B_1, however,

---

[1] Strictly speaking, our results hold only in the case of straight-line demand curves; but they are approximately true for more complicated curves so long as one deals with " prices " and " slopes " in the neighborhood of the stationary equilibrium price.

and if the stock-demand curve is D, the price of bonds will be p_1, e_t will be equal to $- e_1$, and the market will be in a state of flow disequilibrium. During period 1, therefore, the stock of bonds will increase by e_1 so that, at the beginning of period 2, B_t will have risen from B_1 to B_2 ($B_2 = B_1 + e_1$). Hence, price in period 2 will be p_2 (which lies below the equilibrium price, p_0), and in this period the stock of bonds will *decrease* from B_2 to B_3 ($B_3 = B_2 - e_2$). In period 3, therefore, price will be p_3 (which lies above p_0, but below p_1) and the stock of bonds will increase during the period from B_3 to B_4 ($B_4 = B_3 + e_3$). Price in period 4 will be p_4 (below p_0 but above p_2); hence the stock of bonds will decrease, etc. A time series illustrating the dynamic behavior of price in this model is shown in Fig. 3c; the approach towards the equilibrium price is oscillatory but damped. By using an argument similar to the above, the reader may easily convince himself of the validity of the remainder of the results set out earlier.

Now, the possibility of unstable or oscillatory market behavior cannot be ruled out on *a priori* grounds. However, in most real-world bond markets, the market period—the time which must elapse between the establishment of a price and its possible subsequent alteration—is likely to be very short; indeed, it may be no more than a matter of minutes in the case of highly organised markets. In such cases the excess-flow-demand curve will normally be extremely flat (referred to the price axis) relative to the slope of the stock-demand curve; this is because the slope of the former curve decreases as the length of the market period decreases, while the slope of the latter curve is independent of the period of analysis—a typical stock–flow relationship. Hence, to the extent that the four rules set out earlier can be applied to the real world, a bond market is not likely to be unstable in practice, nor even oscillatory, simply by reason of its structural properties; a movement away from stationary equilibrium is likely to be followed by a slow, but persistent and direct, return movement. The causes of the violent fluctuations which are sometimes observed in practice are probably to be sought in sudden changes in price expectations, or in changed conditions in markets which are less well behaved than security markets.

The foregoing discussion deals with the effects of " once-over " shocks to our model. More complicated situations are encountered in practice; *e.g.*, changes in productive techniques occur almost constantly, and individual expenditure patterns are subject to ceaseless development over time. If considerations of this sort are introduced into the model, it is apparent that its behavior will be different from that outlined above.   Bond prices will still *tend* towards a stationary equilibrium level, but the stationary equilibrium position will itself shift with the passage of time so that the market may " develop " indefinitely; in particular, the location of the stationary equilibrium price at any moment will depend in an essential way upon those forces of " productivity and thrift " which are negligible in the short run. This leads to the conclusion that the significance which one is justified in attaching to the factors of productivity and thrift depends primarily upon one's point of view.   The forces underlying price determination in a bond market certainly cannot be appreciated in their entirety by looking simply at the day-to-day operations of the market; a sense of perspective is required which only the passage of time can provide.

10. If the present analysis seems novel in certain respects, this is because it deals simultaneously and explicitly with both stock and flow aspects of the determination of bond prices.   The end result of this generalisation of established analysis is a more complicated, but also a richer and perhaps more realistic, theory of interest.   Moreover, since the present method of approach can be extended to deal with the pricing of monetary and physical assets generally, some of the ideas and conclusions of this paper may be more widely applicable than is apparent at first glance. As it stands, however, the present essay is merely an introduction to a comprehensive treatment of the general theory of capital.

R. W. CLOWER

The State College of Washington,
Pullman, Washington, U.S.A.

[11]

PRICE DETERMINATION IN A STOCK-FLOW ECONOMY

By R. W. Clower and D. W. Bushaw

1. introduction

In recent years economists have devoted considerable attention to special problems involving stock-flow relationships.[1] Thus far, however, attempts to study such relationships within the framework of the general theory of price determination have been few in number and highly restricted in scope.[2] The object of the present paper is to fill at least part of this gap in the existing literature. It is a study in the pure theory of market price determination in a stock-flow economy—an economy in which the typical commodity is simultaneously produced, consumed, *and* held for future disposal by economic units.

We begin by formulating a stock-flow model of the pricing system. Equilibrium and stability conditions which are appropriate to this and to a closely related model which has been outlined by Professor Samuelson are then obtained. Next we indicate how the more familiar existing theories of price determination may be derived as special cases from the stock-flow model, and the latter theory is shown to be essentially different from the former theories. Finally, we deal briefly with the relative merits of a stock-flow model, in comparison with less complex theories, as a device for interpreting empirical data.

2. assumptions and definitions

Consider a money economy comprising n commodity markets. Denote by p_i $(i = 1, \cdots, n)$ the current money price of the ith commodity. Taking all expected future prices as given, write $d_i(p_1, \cdots, p_n)$ for the flow demand function, $s_i(p_1, \cdots, p_n)$ for the flow supply function, and $D_i(p_1, \cdots, p_n)$ for the stock demand function of the ith commodity. It is convenient to suppose that commodity stocks can be increased only by new production and decreased only by actual consumption or depreciation;[3] hence for some value t_0 of t, the stock supply of the ith commodity at time t is defined by

$$S_i \equiv S_i^0 + \int_{t_0}^{t} (s_i - d_i) \, dt,$$

where S_i^0 is the stock of the ith commodity at time t_0. Also define the *excess stock demand* functions

$$(1) \quad X_i(p_1, \cdots, p_n ; t) \equiv D_i(p_1, \cdots, p_n) - S_i^0 + \int_{t_0}^{t} x_i(p_1, \cdots, p_n) \, dt$$

$$(i = 1, \cdots, n),$$

---

[1] See, e.g., the extensive literature on the "acceleration principle."

[2] See, however, Clower [3] and [4] for discussions of certain partial equilibrium aspects of stock-flow analysis.

[3] Thus flow demand includes "wear and tear," but decreases in capital stocks due to obsolescence, accidental destruction, Acts of God, and the like, are excluded.

328

where $x_i(p_1, \cdots, p_n) \equiv d_i(p_1, \cdots, p_n) - s_i(p_1, \cdots, p_n)$ is the *excess flow demand* for the ith commodity. Finally, assume once for all that the functions now defined have all subsequently required continuity and differentiability properties.

The basic assumption of the present analysis is that the time rate of change of price for any of the n commodities is a function of the excess flow and excess stock demands for that commodity; i.e., we postulate the existence of a dynamical system having the general form

$$(2) \qquad \frac{dp_i}{dt} = f_i(x_i, X_i).^4$$

In general, the functions f_i may be nonlinear. However, we shall assume: (a) $(\partial f_i/\partial x_i)^2 + (\partial f_i/\partial X_i)^2 > 0$ for all values of x_i and X_i, and (b) $f_i(0, 0) = 0$ $(i = 1, \cdots, n)$. It follows from (a) that in a sufficiently small neighborhood of any fixed values $\bar{x}_i$ and $\bar{X}_i$ of x_i and X_i, the functions f_i can be approximated arbitrarily well by linear expressions

$$f_i(\bar{x}_i, \bar{X}_i) + \alpha_i(x_i - \bar{x}_i) + \beta_i(X_i - \bar{X}_i),$$

where at least one of the constants α_i, β_i is not zero for each i. Since we shall be concerned entirely with the local behavior (behavior in the small) of the system, and in fact in some neighborhood of $\bar{x}_i = 0$, $\bar{X}_i = 0$, we therefore (recalling the condition (b), above) take

$$(3) \qquad\qquad f_i = \alpha_i x_i + \beta_i X_i \qquad\qquad (i = 1, \cdots, n)$$

at the outset. These functions are subject to the sole requirement: *for each i, either $\alpha_i \neq 0$ or $\beta_i \neq 0$ or both*. Indeed, for the system (2)–(3), if it were true that $\alpha_i = 0$, $\beta_i = 0$ for some i, then p_i would be constant and could be regarded as an implicit parameter in the flow supply and stock and flow demand functions of the other commodities.

A commodity for which $\alpha_i = 0$ will be called a *stock-oriented* commodity, and one for which $\beta_i = 0$ a *flow-oriented* commodity.

3. EQUILIBRIUM

Suppose that in the neighborhood of a certain set of prices $(p_1^0, \cdots, p_n^0)$, the functions x_i and D_i admit the power series expansions

$$(4) \qquad x_i = x_i^0 + \sum_j a_{ij}(p_j - p_j^0) + [(p_1 - p_1^0), \cdots, (p_n - p_n^0)],$$

$$(5) \qquad D_i = D_i^0 + \sum_j b_{ij}(p_j - p_j^0) + [(p_1 - p_1^0), \cdots, (p_n - p_n^0)].$$

---

[4] More generally, one might assume that the price of the ith commodity depends upon excess demands for commodities other than the ith. This would introduce no essential new difficulties into the mathematics, but it would make the economic content of our results unnecessarily obscure without appreciably increasing their realism. *Cf.* Samuelson [17], pp. 274–5.

Here, and elsewhere below, the symbol $[r, s, \cdots, v]$ indicates 0 or some power series in the variables $r, s, \cdots, v$ starting with second degree terms; $\sum_j$ indicates the sum over all values of j from 1 to n.

If we define the new variables q_i by

(6) $$\frac{dp_i}{dt} = q_i$$

we have, using equations (1)–(6),

(7) $$\frac{dq_i}{dt} = \beta_i x_i^0 + \sum_j \beta_i a_{ij}(p_j - p_j^0) + \sum_j (\alpha_i a_{ij} + \beta_i b_{ij})q_j$$
$$+ [(p_1 - p_1^0), \cdots, (p_n - p_n^0); q_1, \cdots, q_n] \qquad (i = 1, \cdots, n).$$

These equations, together with equations

(2') $$\frac{dp_i}{dt} = \alpha_i x_i + \beta_i X_i \qquad (i = 1, \cdots, n)$$

form the system with which we have to deal.

If the set of prices $(p_1^0, \cdots, p_n^0)$ is to give equilibrium at the instant t_0, we must have

$$\frac{dp_i}{dt} = 0, \qquad \frac{dq_i}{dt} = 0 \qquad (i = 1, \cdots, n)$$

at that instant.[5] Thus, from (7) and (2'), the set of prices $(p_1^0, \cdots, p_n^0)$ gives equilibrium at time t_0 if and only if

$$\alpha_i x_i^0 + \beta_i X_i^0 = 0$$
$$\beta_i x_i^0 = 0,$$

where $X_i^0 = X_i(p_1^0, \cdots, p_n^0; t_0)$. These equations are in turn equivalent to the condition

(8) $$x_i^0 = X_i^0 = 0 \text{ if } \beta_i \neq 0, \qquad x_i^0 = 0 \text{ if } \beta_i = 0.$$

In words, the necessary and sufficient conditions for equilibrium are that both excess stock demand and excess flow demand vanish for any commodity which is not flow-oriented, and that excess flow demand vanishes for any flow-oriented commodity.

If k of the commodities are not flow-oriented, (8) contains $n + k$ equations for the n unknowns $(p_1^0, \cdots, p_n^0)$, so that equilibrium prices may seem to be

---

[5] These conditions are both necessary and sufficient for equilibrium. That they are necessary is clear; they are also sufficient, for once these conditions are satisfied, successive differentiation of the equations (7) with respect to t, combined with substitution from the equations $dp_i/dt = 0$, $dq_i/dt = 0$, shows that *all* the derivatives of q_i (and therefore all those of p_i) $(i = 1, \ldots, n)$ must vanish.

overdetermined; but this is not so. To make this point clear, consider the case in which all commodities are stock-oriented ($\alpha_i = 0$ for all i); then the condition for equilibrium is that the $2n$ equations

$$x_i^0 = 0, \qquad X_i^0 = 0 \qquad\qquad (i = 1, \cdots, n)$$

be satisfied. If a set of prices $(p_1^0, \cdots, p_n^0)$ satisfies the equations $x_i^0 = 0$ but not the equations $X_i^0 = 0$ at a certain instant, prices will be changing at that instant in accordance with (2'), so that the economy certainly cannot be in equilibrium. Whether or not the prices so changing will ultimately approach an equilibrium state, and whether or not this equilibrium state will be represented by the same prices $(p_1^0, \cdots, p_n^0)$ are essentially questions of stability; such questions are discussed in the next section. On the other hand, if a set of prices satisfies the equations $X_i^0 = 0$ but not the equations $x_i^0 = 0$, then, although by (2') the derivatives dp_i/dt $(i = 1, \cdots, n)$ vanish *at that instant*, the values of the functions X_i^0 will be changing; immediately after, therefore, the equations $X_i^0 = 0$ will cease to hold, and any semblance of equilibrium will disappear. Thus, even though it is possible to distinguish situations of "apparent equilibrium" (stock *or* flow, but not stock *and* flow "equilibrium") involving the satisfaction of one of the sets of equations $x_i^0 = 0$, $X_i^0 = 0$, but not both, it is not possible to attach any significance to such situations in a dynamical system of the kind considered here (*cf.* Brunner [2], pp. 247–8).

4. STABILITY: SUFFICIENT CONDITIONS

We now seek conditions under which an equilibrium state determined by (8) will be stable. We take stability to mean what Professor Samuelson has called *perfect stability of the first kind in the small* (Samuelson [17], pp. 261–2), or what others (*e.g.* Malkin [12], pp. 3–4) have more succinctly called *asymptotic stability*: if, for whatever reason, prices are slightly displaced from their equilibrium values, they will tend to return to these equilibrium values in the absence of further disturbances.

Let $(p_1^0, \cdots, p_n^0)$ be a set of equilibrium prices. For convenience we define the new variables $P_i = p_i - p_i^0$, $Q_i = dp_i/dt = dP_i/dt$. In vector notation, the equations (6)–(7) may be written

(9)
$$\begin{cases} \dfrac{dP}{dt} = Q \\[2mm] \dfrac{dQ}{dt} = \mathbf{A}P + \mathbf{B}Q + [P_1, \cdots, P_n; Q_1, \cdots, Q_n], \end{cases}$$

where $\mathbf{A} = (A_{ij})$, $A_{ij} = \beta_i a_{ij}$, $\mathbf{B} = (B_{ij})$, $B_{ij} = \alpha_i a_{ij} + \beta_i b_{ij}$, and P and Q stand for the column vectors with components P_i and Q_i respectively. In the remainder of this section and in the next we shall assume that $\beta_i \neq 0$ $(i = 1, \cdots, n)$; some of the consequences of dropping this restriction are discussed in sections 6 and 7 below. As is well known, the stability or instability of the equilibrium state $P = 0, Q = 0$ for (9) is implied by that for the corresponding linearized system

(10)
$$\begin{cases} \dfrac{dP}{dt} = Q \\ \dfrac{dQ}{dt} = \mathbf{A}P + \mathbf{B}Q, \end{cases}$$

to which we therefore confine our attention henceforth. The matrix of coefficients in (10) is

$$\begin{pmatrix} \mathbf{0} & \mathbf{I} \\ \mathbf{A} & \mathbf{B} \end{pmatrix}$$

where $\mathbf{0}$ and $\mathbf{I}$ are, respectively, the zero and unit matrices of order n.

The necessary and sufficient condition for stability in a system like (10) is that all the characteristic roots of the coefficient matrix have negative real parts. Our immediate problem is to find conditions on the matrices $\mathbf{A}$ and $\mathbf{B}$ under which this condition holds. A similar problem has been dealt with by Routh (Routh [16], Chapter VII) in a physical context; his work provides the basis for the results stated and proved as Theorems 1, 2, and 3, below.

We first note that the system (10) can be rewritten as a second order vectorial differential equation

(11)
$$\frac{d^2 P}{dt} - \mathbf{B} \frac{dP}{dt} - \mathbf{A}P = 0.$$

This is essentially the system (7) linearized. The characteristic equation common to (10) and (11) is

(12)
$$| \mathbf{I}\lambda^2 - \mathbf{B}\lambda - \mathbf{A} | = 0,$$

where the matrices $\mathbf{A}$, $\mathbf{B}$, and $\mathbf{I}$ are defined as before.

THEOREM 1. *If the matrices $\mathbf{A}$ and $\mathbf{B}$ are negative definite, every real root of (12) is negative.*

PROOF. Let λ be a real root of (12), and let M be a corresponding (real) characteristic vector. This means

(13)
$$(M)\lambda^2 - (\mathbf{B}M)\lambda - (\mathbf{A}M) = 0.$$

Taking the scalar product of both sides of (13) with M, we get

$$(M'M)\lambda^2 - (M'\mathbf{B}M)\lambda - (M'\mathbf{A}M) = 0,$$

where the prime indicates transposition, as usual. Since the matrices $\mathbf{A}$ and $\mathbf{B}$ are negative definite, all of the coefficients in this quadratic equation are positive and the real root λ can only be negative.

COROLLARY. *If all roots of* (12) *are real* (*i.e., if no solutions of* (10) *or* (11) *have oscillatory components*), *the negative definiteness of* **A** *and* **B** *is a sufficient condition for stability.*

THEOREM 2. *If the matrices* **A** *and* **B** *are negative definite and the matrix* **A** *is symmetrical, every root* (*real or complex*) *of* (12) *has a negative real part.*

PROOF. We now allow the root $\lambda = \sigma + \tau i$ of (12) to be complex, and again let M be a corresponding (possibly complex) characteristic vector. If we take the scalar product of both sides of (13) with $\bar{M}$, the complex conjugate of M, we obtain

$$(14) \qquad (\bar{M}'M)\lambda^2 - (\bar{M}'BM)\lambda - (\bar{M}'AM) = 0.$$

Taking complex conjugates on both sides of (14) gives

$$(15) \qquad (M'\bar{M})\bar{\lambda}^2 - (M'B\bar{M})\bar{\lambda} - (M'A\bar{M}) = 0.$$

We now divide through in (14) by λ, in (15) by $\bar{\lambda}$, and add; this gives

$$(\bar{M}'M)\sigma - \tfrac{1}{2}(\bar{M}'BM + M'B\bar{M}) - (\bar{M}'AM)\,\frac{\sigma}{\sigma^2 + \tau^2} = 0$$

(the symmetry of **A** is used at this point). If we put $M = U + iV$, the real part of this last equation can be written

$$(\bar{M}'M)\sigma - [U'BU + V'BV] - [U'AU + V'AV]\,\frac{\sigma}{\sigma^2 + \tau^2} = 0.$$

The negative definiteness of the matrices **A** and **B** again implies that all the coefficients are positive, so that σ must be negative.

COROLLARY. *A sufficient condition for stability is that* **A** *and* **B** *be negative definite and* **A** *be symmetrical.*

THEOREM 3. *If the matrix* **B** *is negative definite and both the matrices* **A** *and* **B** *are symmetrical, then every complex* (*i.e., nonreal*) *root of* (12) *has a negative real part.*

PROOF. Let λ and M be as defined in the preceding proof, with $\tau \neq 0$. If both **A** and **B** are symmetrical, the coefficients in (14) are all real, even though M has complex components; thus $\bar{\lambda}$ is the other root of (14), and by an elementary theorem from algebra we have

$$\lambda + \bar{\lambda} = 2\sigma = \frac{\bar{M}'BM}{\bar{M}'M} = \frac{U'BU + V'BV}{\bar{M}'M}.$$

This last quantity is negative if **B** is negative definite.

COROLLARY. *If no roots of* (12) *are real* (*i.e., if all the solutions of* (10) *and* (11) *are of an oscillatory nature*), *then a sufficient condition for stability is that* **A** *and* **B** *be symmetrical and* **B** *be negative definite.*

The three corollaries above provide the stability conditions which we set out to establish.

The economic interpretation of the conditions of negative definiteness and symmetry in the corollaries to Theorems 1, 2, and 3 presents some difficulties. We note first that the constants a_{ij} and b_{ij} represent, roughly speaking, the slopes of the excess flow demand and the stock demand functions with respect to the various prices. In fact,

$$a_{ij} = \partial x_i / \partial p_j, \qquad b_{ij} = \partial D_i / \partial p_j,$$

these derivatives being evaluated at the equilibrium state in question. In particular, $a_{ii} = \partial x_i / \partial p_i$ is the rate of change of the excess flow demand for the ith commodity with respect to the price of that commodity (other prices being held fixed) and as such can normally be expected to be negative. To say that the matrix (a_{ij}) is negative definite would then be to say that the excess flow demand for each commodity varies in the normal way with respect to its own price ($a_{ii} < 0$—this being necessary for negative definiteness), and that "cross effects" (represented by the elements a_{ij} where $i \neq j$) in the aggregate do not counteract these direct effects (cf. Hicks [6], pp. 316–17; Samuelson [17], p. 141). A similar line of reasoning would apply to the matrix (b_{ij}). However, we are dealing in the general case not with these simple matrices, but with the matrices

$$\mathbf{A} = (\beta_i a_{ij}), \qquad \mathbf{B} = (\alpha_i a_{ij} + \beta_i b_{ij}).$$

Here the constants α_i, β_i are *coefficients of price flexibility* (cf. Lange [10], p. 95); they represent, in some sense, the "speeds of adjustment" of prices, for from (2') one can see that

$$\alpha_i = \frac{\partial}{\partial x_i} \left(\frac{dp_i}{dt} \right), \qquad \beta_i = \frac{\partial}{\partial X_i} \left(\frac{dp_i}{dt} \right),$$

the derivatives again being evaluated at equilibrium. Normally all of the constants α_i and β_i may be expected to be positive. Thus in order to interpret the negative definiteness of $\mathbf{A}$ one must modify the above discussion to take the constants β_i into account, for instance by regarding each of the "slopes" a_{ij} for the ith commodity as being weighted by the corresponding flexibility coefficient β_i. $\mathbf{B}$ is more complicated still, but it can be viewed as the sum of the two matrices $\mathbf{A}_1 = (\alpha_i a_{ij})$ and $\mathbf{B}_1 = (\beta_i b_{ij})$, which are subject to the same kind of interpretation as $\mathbf{A}$; and if $\mathbf{A}_1$ and $\mathbf{B}_1$ are both negative definite, their sum $\mathbf{B}$ is negative definite (but not conversely).

It should be remarked that conditions of negative definiteness were to be expected; they suggest analogies with the investigations of Samuelson ([17], pp. 269–73), and Lange ([10], pp. 94–7) into the stability of equilibrium in flow-oriented commodity markets.

The symmetry conditions which appear in the corollaries to Theorems 2 and 3 also have counterparts in the investigations of Samuelson and Lange, but it does not seem possible to interpret these conditions in an intuitively plausible fashion. Hence, one is tempted to conjecture that such conditions may be dispensed with altogether, *e.g.*, that the mere negative definiteness of **A** and **B** may imply stability. That no general theorem to this effect can be established is shown by the following example.

Example A. Let $n = 2$, and let the matrices **A** and **B** be as follows:

$$\mathbf{A} = \begin{pmatrix} -4 & 6 \\ 1 & -4 \end{pmatrix}, \qquad \mathbf{B} = \begin{pmatrix} -4 & 1 \\ 6 & -4 \end{pmatrix}.$$

It is easy to verify that both of these matrices are negative definite. However, in this case the equation (12) becomes

$$\lambda^4 + 8\lambda^3 + 18\lambda^2 - 5\lambda + 10 = 0,$$

and the presence of the negative coefficient -5 indicates that the equation has at least one root (necessarily complex, in view of Theorem 1) with a positive real part. Thus the equilibrium state is unstable.

Example A, together with a host of other unsuccessful attempts by the authors to dispense with symmetry assumptions, leads us to doubt whether any very general sufficient condition for the stability of (12) can be formulated without using symmetry conditions in one form or another. It is worth noticing, however, that if **A** and **B** have off-diagonal elements which are sufficiently small relative to the diagonal elements (so that in a certain sense the matrices **A** and **B** are *almost* symmetrical), negative definiteness will suffice for stability, even in the presence of complex characteristic roots; for in this special case we may approximate (12) by an equation in which **A** and **B** become symmetrical (in fact, diagonal) negative definite matrices, whereupon Theorem 2 guarantees that all roots of the approximating equation will have negative real parts. Since the roots of a polynomial equation depend continuously on its coefficients, this means that the original equation (12) will also have roots of the same kind, and stability follows.

Other special assumptions about the relative magnitudes or about the signs of the constants α_i, β_i, a_{ij}, b_{ij} may lead to similar conclusions (see, *e.g.*, Metzler [13], pp. 282–90); but since information is not available which would enable us to decide which such assumptions are realistic, we shall not pursue the subject further here.[6]

All of the conclusions in this section have been based so far on Liapounoff's "first method" for investigating stability (see Malkin [12], p. 4), *i.e.*, they depend ultimately on the fact that solutions of the system (10) can be explicitly computed. It should be pointed out that Liapounoff's "second method," which

---

[6] One reader has conjectured that stability may occur if the matrices **A** and **B** are negative definite and all off-diagonal elements have identical signs (i.e., if all commodities are either gross substitutes or gross complements). That this cannot be so in the case where all goods are gross substitutes is shown by Example A, where all off-diagonal elements are positive and yet stability does not occur. Since the characteristic equation which appears in Example A is not affected by a change in the signs of all off-diagonal elements, neither is stability assured in the case where commodities are assumed to be gross complements.

depends on establishing the existence of certain functions associated with a system like (10), is also available and is sometimes more powerful than the "first method." By way of illustrating this remark, we now give an alternative proof of the corollary to Theorem 2, based on the following form of a theorem due to Liapounoff (see Malkin [12], pp. 5–6):

If there exists a continuous function $V(P, Q)$ which

(a) *vanishes when $P = Q = 0$,*

(b) *is positive definite, and*

(c) *has a total derivative dV/dt with respect to t which is nonpositive, then the equilibrium state $P = Q = 0$ is stable.*

If **A** and **B** are negative definite and **A** is symmetrical, such a function is provided by

$$V(P, Q) = Q'Q - P'AP.$$

This function clearly satisfies (a) and (b), and since its derivative (computed using (10)) is $dV/dt = 2Q'BQ$, it also satisfies (c).

5. STABILITY: NECESSARY CONDITIONS

When $n = 1$, the sufficient conditions in the corollary to Theorem 2 are also necessary. In this case the matrices **A** and **B** reduce to scalars A_{11} and B_{11} ; the symmetry condition is vacuously satisfied, and the negative definiteness condition is met if A_{11} and B_{11} are negative.[7] We have discussed this case for a stock-oriented commodity at length elsewhere (Clower [4]).

However, when $n \geqslant 2$, the conditions in the corollaries to Theorems 1, 2, and 3 are not necessary. This is shown by the following examples.

Example B. Let $n = 2$, and let

$$\mathbf{A} = \begin{pmatrix} -1 & 3 \\ 0 & -1 \end{pmatrix}, \qquad \mathbf{B} = \begin{pmatrix} -2 & 6 \\ 0 & -2 \end{pmatrix}.$$

Neither of these matrices is symmetrical or negative definite; but all of the roots of (12) have negative real parts, being in fact equal to -1, and stability of a strong (non-oscillatory) type occurs. This shows that the conditions in the corollaries to Theorems 1 and 2 are not necessary for stability.

Example C. Again let $n = 2$, but reverse the roles of **A** and **B**; *i.e.*, take

$$\mathbf{A} = \begin{pmatrix} -2 & 6 \\ 0 & -2 \end{pmatrix}, \qquad \mathbf{B} = \begin{pmatrix} -1 & 3 \\ 0 & -1 \end{pmatrix}.$$

Then the roots of (12) again have negative real parts; in fact, they are double roots with the values $(-1 \pm \sqrt{7}\, i)/2$. Thus stability again occurs. This shows that the condition in the corollary to Theorem 3 is not necessary.

[7] In this particular case, for given functions d_1 , s_1 , and D_1 , the characteristic equation has real roots if the flexibility coefficients α_1 and β_1 are sufficiently large (provided that $| \alpha_1/\beta_1 |$ is not too large). This suggests that when $n > 1$, if prices are sufficiently flexible, all roots of (12) may be real, in which case Theorem 1 would suffice to establish stability.

Necessary and sufficient conditions for (12) to have only roots with negative real parts are available in the form of the Routh-Hurwitz test determinants (*cf.* Samuelson [17], p. 430 ff.), which can of course be computed explicitly in any concrete case. However, these determinants for (12) depend in an extremely intricate way on the elements of the matrices **A** and **B**, so that their general theoretical usefulness is slight.

6. A RELATED STOCK-FLOW THEORY

So far as we are aware, the only previous analysis of stability conditions in a stock-flow system is by Professor Samuelson (Samuelson [17], pp. 268-9, 275-6). Samuelson's investigations concern a system of the form (2′), but in which all stock demands are independent of prices and in which the constants $\dot{\alpha}_i$ and β_i are independent of i:

$$(16) \qquad dp_i/dt = \alpha x_i + \beta \left[D_i - S_i^0 + \int_{t_0}^{t} x_i \, dt \right] \qquad (\alpha > 0, \beta > 0).$$

Because the functions D_i are constants, $b_{ij} \equiv 0$ $(i, j = 1, \cdots, n)$. Accordingly, our matrices **A** and **B** become $\beta(a_{ij})$ and $\alpha(a_{ij})$ respectively, and the hypotheses in Theorems 1, 2, and 3 may be restated as hypotheses on the matrix (a_{ij}). In particular, Theorem 2 states that stability occurs when (a_{ij}) is symmetrical and negative definite; Theorem 3 adds nothing to this, but Theorem 1 states that negative definiteness alone is sufficient for stability if all the characteristic roots are known to be real. That these conditions are still not necessary is shown by Examples B and C, Section 5.

Samuelson has conjectured (Samuelson [17], p. 276, ftn. 20) that the stability of equilibrium for the extreme cases (I) $\beta > 0, \alpha = 0$ and (II) $\beta = 0, \alpha > 0$ may imply stability for all intermediate cases $(\alpha > 0, \beta > 0)$. Actually, stability in the extreme case (I) implies stability in case (II), as we shall see.

In case (I) the characteristic equation (12) becomes

$$| I\lambda^2 - \beta(a_{ij}) | = 0,$$

so that, as Samuelson shows (Samuelson [17], p. 275), stability occurs if and only if the characteristic roots of $\beta(a_{ij})$ (*i.e.*, of (a_{ij}) itself) are real, negative, and distinct. The stability that occurs here is not the asymptotic stability we have been considering, but what Samuelson calls *stability of the second kind*: the general solution consists not of exponentially damped functions, but of almost periodic functions which, although they do not approach the equilibrium values, remain in a small neighborhood of those values. It is important to realize that, in general, (even when $n = 1$) the fact that a linearized system like (10) displays stability of the second kind enables one to conclude nothing whatever about stability or instability of either kind in the original nonlinear system (9).[8]

---

[8] The vexing question of deciding what happens in the nonlinear system when the linear system has stability of the second kind has been a favorite subject for mathematical investigation recently, particularly in the Soviet Union. See, for example, Nemyckiĭ and Stepanov [14], pp. 123-133.

Thus, in order for the characteristic-root approach to be at all relevant, we must assume that the systems (9) and (10) coincide, an assumption which in the case under consideration is equivalent to the assumption that the excess flow demands are exactly linear, at least in the neighborhood of equilibrium under consideration. Under these circumstances Samuelson's conditions for stability (of the second kind) in case (I) (*i.e.*, that the characteristic roots of (a_{ij}) be real, negative, and distinct) are indeed necessary and sufficient. However, the necessary and sufficient condition for stability (of the first kind) in case (II) is that the solutions of

$$| \, \mathbf{I}\lambda \, - \, \alpha(a_{ij}) \, | \, = 0$$

have negative real parts, and this condition will surely be satisfied if the "case (I)" conditions on the characteristic roots of (a_{ij}) are satisfied.

Let us assume, therefore, that Samuelson's conjectured condition for stability in (16) is satisfied: the characteristic roots of (a_{ij}) are real, negative, and distinct. If (a_{ij}) is symmetrical, this implies that (a_{ij}) is negative definite, and Theorem 2 shows that stability does indeed occur in all intermediate cases ($\alpha > 0, \beta > 0$). But Theorem 2 tells more, for it makes no assumption about the distinctness or reality of the roots. In any case, we may conclude: *When (a_{ij}) is symmetrical, Samuelson's conjecture is correct.*

7. RELATION OF EXISTING THEORIES TO THE STOCK-FLOW MODEL

The more familiar existing theories of price determination are closely related to our stock-flow model. This is readily seen as follows.[9]

(i) *Pure flow theories.* Suppose that all commodities are flow-oriented, *i.e.*, that in (3), $\beta_i = 0$ for all i. Then it is clear from (2') and (8) that the excess stock demand functions are altogether irrelevant to the determination of prices. Indeed, stocks disappear from the model entirely, and we have a *pure flow theory.* This model, consisting of the differential equations

$$dp_i/dt = \alpha_i x_i \qquad (\alpha_i \neq 0, i = 1, \cdots, n),$$

with equilibrium conditions

$$x_i^0 = x_i(p_1^0, \cdots, p_n^0),$$

is a dynamical counterpart of the familiar Walrasian general equilibrium theory. The matrices **A** and **B** of section 4 become **0** and $(\alpha_i a_{ij})$ respectively, and the characteristic equation (12) becomes

$$| \, \mathbf{I}\lambda^2 \, - \, (\alpha_i a_{ij})\lambda \, | \, = \lambda^n \, | \, \mathbf{I}\lambda \, - \, (\alpha_i a_{ij}) \, | \, = 0.$$

[9] Throughout this section we continue to assume that the various functions f_i are linear and satisfy the other conditions set out in Section 2. As before, this may be regarded as the result of linearizing some nonlinear functions f_i in a neighborhood of an equilibrium state.

The n-tuple root 0 of this equation is present because of the now redundant differentiation leading to the equations (7). The relevant roots are the others, *i.e.*, the roots of

$$(17) \qquad\qquad | I\lambda - (\alpha_i a_{ij}) | = 0;$$

if these roots have negative real parts we have stability. By modifying the proof of Theorem 2 slightly, we obtain

THEOREM 4. *If the matrix* **B** *is negative definite, every root of the equation* $| I\lambda - \mathbf{B} | = 0$ *has a negative real part.*

PROOF. Let $\lambda = \sigma + \tau i$ be a root of this equation, and let $M = U + Vi$ be a corresponding characteristic vector; then

$$M\lambda - \mathbf{B}M = 0.$$

Taking the scalar product with $\bar{M}$ on both sides we obtain

$$(\bar{M}'M)\lambda - (\bar{M}'\mathbf{B}M) = 0.$$

The real part of this equation is

$$(U'U + V'V)\sigma - (U'\mathbf{B}U + V'\mathbf{B}V) = 0,$$

and since the negative definiteness of **B** implies that the coefficients of this equation are positive, σ must be negative. This result, which does not involve symmetry conditions in any form, does not appear to have been stated previously in the economic literature.

COROLLARY. *If* **B** *is negative definite, equilibrium in the pure flow theory is stable.*[10]

A simple way to see that the general stock-flow theory and the pure flow theory lead to essentially different results is to note that for stability in the stock-flow theory the $2n$ roots of (12) must have negative real parts, while in the pure flow theory the same condition is required of only n numbers, namely the n roots of (17). One can also note the difference in the number of equilibrium conditions.

(ii) *Pure stock theories.* Now suppose that $x_i \equiv 0$, *i.e.*, either no commodities are produced or consumed in the economy, or the consumption and production of each commodity are equalized independently of price movements. This implies that the integral in (1) vanishes, *i.e.*, that the stock supply of each commodity is fixed. Then the system (2') can be written in the form

$$(18) \qquad\qquad dp_i/dt = \beta_i(D_i - S_i^0) \qquad\qquad (i = 1, \cdots, n),$$

---

[10] This corollary may also be proved directly using Liapounoff's Theorem. The linearized vector differential equation for the pure flow model is $dP/dt = \mathbf{B}P$, and Liapounoff's theorem becomes: *If there exists a continuous function* $V(P)$ *which* (a) *vanishes when* $P = 0$, (b) *is positive definite, and* (c) *has a nonpositive total derivative* dV/dt, *then the equilibrium state* $P = 0$ *is stable.* Such a function is here provided by $V(P) = P'P$, the derivative of which is $dV/dt = 2P'\mathbf{B}P$.

with the equilibrium conditions

$$X^0_i = X_i(p^0_1, \cdots, p^0_n) = 0.$$

This represents a *pure stock theory* of market price determination; it is a general dynamical counterpart of such models as those of Wicksell ([18], Part I), Marshak and Makower ([11], pp. 282–88), and Boulding ([1]). It is clear from a comparison of equations (18) with those for the pure flow theory that the two theories are formally identical.[11] For (18) the relevant matrix is $(\beta_i b_{ij})$, whose characteristic roots must have negative real parts for stability. Again, a sufficient condition for this to happen is that the matrix $(\beta_i b_{ij})$ be negative definite.

It should be noted that the pure stock theory (where $x_i \equiv 0$) is not a special case of the general stock-flow theory in the same simple sense as is the pure flow theory (where $\beta_i \equiv 0$). For if one assumes that all commodities are stock-oriented ($\alpha_i \equiv 0$ for all i) one obtains a model quite different from the pure stock theory; in particular, in a theory based on the stock-orientation hypothesis the equilibrium conditions (8) become

$$X^0_i = x^0_i = 0 \qquad\qquad (i = 1, \cdots, n);$$

and since in general $x_i \neq 0$, these are essentially stronger conditions than those in the pure stock theory.

(iii) *Partial stock-flow theories.* Finally, suppose that for each i either $\beta_i = 0$ or $x_i \equiv 0$; *i.e.*, suppose that market decisions regarding any particular commodity involve *either* the production and consumption *or* the holding of stocks of that commodity, *but not both*. Then the system (2′) takes the form

$$dp_i/dt = \alpha_i x_i \qquad \text{for some values } i_1, i_2, \cdots, i_k \text{ of } i,$$

$$dp_i/dt = \beta_i X_i \qquad \text{for all other values } i_{k+1}, \cdots, i_n \text{ of } i$$

The corresponding equilibrium conditions are $x^0_{i_p} = 0$ ($p = 1, \cdots, k$), and $X^0_{i_p} = 0$ ($p = k + 1, \cdots, n$). This represents a *partial stock-flow theory* of price determination, and is a dynamical version of the models which underlie recent writings in monetary theory in which stocks of money and bonds are treated as parameters but all ordinary commodity variables are regarded as stocks or as flows (see Keynes [7], Chapter 18; Klein [9], pp. 192–96; Patinkin [15]). This

---

[11] This does not mean that the choice between a stock and a flow theory is a matter of indifference. In dealing with the pricing of bonds, for example, it is necessary to recognize from the outset that the ownership of bonds is a special instance of the holding of commodity stocks. Hence, the only way in which a valid flow theory of bond prices can be constructed is to suppose that price is determined solely by the excess demand for *changes* in the total stock of bonds, which is to suppose that stocks *qua* stocks are completely irrelevant to the price determination problem. However, the last-mentioned supposition would be difficult to reconcile with everyday observation of the operation of major security markets. Hence, most economists would probably accept a stock (or stock-flow) theory of bond prices in preference to a flow theory. Compare the discussion of these matters by Klein ([8]), Fellner and Somers ([5]), and Brunner ([2]). Also see Clower ([3]).

system is also formally equivalent to the pure flow theory, the relevant matrix being that which has as its i_pth row

$$\alpha_{i_p} a_{i_p 1} , \cdots , \alpha_{i_p} a_{i_p n} \qquad\qquad (p = 1, \cdots , k)$$

$$\beta_{i_p} b_{i_p 1} , \cdots , \beta_{i_p} b_{i_p n} \qquad\qquad (p = k + 1, \cdots , n).$$

The difference between the pure flow, pure stock, partial stock-flow and stock-flow theories is vividly illustrated by the following example.

Example D. Let $n = 2$, and postulate a pure flow model ($\beta_1 = \beta_2 = 0$) for which a certain set of prices (p_1^0, p_2^0) satisfies the equilibrium conditions $x_1(p_1^0 , p_2^0) = x_2(p_1^0 , p_2^0) = 0$. For the sake of simplicity, assume that $\alpha_1 = \alpha_2 = \alpha > 0$; and suppose that the excess flow demand functions are such that the matrix **B** is

$$\mathbf{B} = \alpha(a_{ij}) = \alpha \begin{pmatrix} -4 & 6 \\ 1 & -4 \end{pmatrix}.$$

This matrix is negative definite for any positive value of α; accordingly, under the pure flow hypothesis the equilibrium state (p_1^0, p_2^0) is stable. Next assume that stock supplies at a certain instant t are such that the same prices (p_1^0, p_2^0) satisfy the stock equilibrium conditions $X_1(p_1^0, p_2^0; t_0) = X_2(p_1^0, p_2^0; t_0) = 0$. Instead of postulating a pure flow model, we now postulate a pure stock model ($x_1 \equiv x_2 \equiv 0$) in which $\beta_1 = \beta_2 = \beta > 0$, and in which the stock demand functions are such that the relevant matrix ($\beta_i b_{ij}$) is

$$\beta(b_{ij}) = \beta \begin{pmatrix} -4 & 1 \\ 6 & -4 \end{pmatrix}.$$

Since this matrix is negative definite also, we may conclude that in this pure stock model the equilibrium state (p_1^0, p_2^0) is again stable. Finally, postulate a stock-flow theory with both goods stock-oriented ($\alpha_1 = \alpha_2 = 0$)[12] and assume that the prices (p_1^0, p_2^0) satisfy both of the above equilibrium conditions and thus truly represent a stock-flow equilibrium state; assume further that $\beta_1 = \beta_2 = 1$. Then the characteristic equation is

(12) $|\, \mathbf{I}\lambda^2 - \mathbf{B}\lambda - \mathbf{A} \,| = 0,$

where

$$\mathbf{A} = (a_{ij}) = \begin{pmatrix} -4 & 6 \\ 1 & -4 \end{pmatrix}, \qquad \mathbf{B} = (b_{ij}) = \begin{pmatrix} -4 & 1 \\ 6 & -4 \end{pmatrix}.$$

But **A** and **B** are precisely the matrices of Example A, section 4, and we recall that (12) with these matrices has some roots with positive real parts. Thus, the equilibrium is unstable. Accordingly, we have an example of a two-commodity

---

[12] This assumption is made as a matter of convenience rather than necessity. The result obtained below can be made to hold for the general as for the present special case.

model with given functions D_i, d_i, s_i ($i = 1, 2$) for which a certain equilibrium state is *stable* under pure flow or pure stock hypotheses, but *unstable* under stock-flow hypotheses. Nothing could make clearer the limitations of arbitrarily postulating a pure flow, pure stock, or partial stock-flow theory when genuine stock-flow relationships may be pertinent.

8. CONCLUSION

Since the primary object of economic theory is to provide a general frame of reference to assist in organizing and deriving knowledge about the real world, it is important that theories be formulated in such a way as to make allowance for factors which are likely to be of crucial significance. Now, everyday observation suggests that in the domain of actual economic experience, a commodity is more likely to appear as a stock *and* a flow simultaneously than as a stock alone or as a flow alone. For although one can find concrete examples of flow markets (e.g., markets for direct labor services), and perhaps stock markets also (e.g., markets for "old masters"), most markets will come within the stock-flow category (including all markets for durable manufactured goods, most farm product markets, housing markets, security markets, foreign exchange markets, etc.).[13] From the very outset, therefore, there is a presumption in favor of a stock-flow theory over a pure stock theory or a pure flow theory. Whether or not this presumption is decisive, however, depends on the extent to which the logically simpler pure stock and pure flow theories provide an adequate basis for the interpretation of empirical phenomena—on the extent to which stock-flow relationships can be ignored or else dealt with implicitly in terms of the simpler models.

The preceding argument seems to shed some light on this question. If it *were* the case that stock-flow relationships could be safely ignored, our discussion might have been expected to support this surmise by indicating that the insertion of stock-flow relationships into a model would effect no essential changes in its character. But our analysis leads in fact to precisely the contrary conclusion. This is illustrated most clearly by Example D, section 7, which shows that the suppression of stock-flow relationships in favor of a pure stock or pure flow theory may lead to conclusions which are *qualitatively* inconsistent with the conclusions to be obtained from the more complete model.

This result should not be unexpected, for in a stock-flow economy a flow or a stock theory is inherently incomplete. A flow theory may or may not ignore the existence of stocks, but it leaves the dynamics of stock holding altogether out of account. A stock theory errs in the opposite direction: it does not reckon with the mechanism which governs the level of production and consumption flows. Moreover, one cannot escape from these difficulties by simply juxtaposing stock and flow models (using one to explain "stock" prices, the other to explain "flow"

---

[13] Whether or not the theoretical system set forth in this paper provides an adequate description of price behavior in actual stock-flow markets is, of course, a separate question which can be decided only on the basis of empirical studies.

prices), for the result is simply a theory which, as regards any single commodity, has all the shortcomings of its constituents.

We are thus led to the inference that an effective general model for the study of price determination and kindred questions, whatever other characteristics it may have, should be a genuine stock-flow model. Moreover, since in practice some commodity markets may be flow-oriented, others stock-oriented, etc., an acceptable stock-flow theory should comprehend flow, stock, and partial stock-flow theories as special cases. This paper has attempted to initiate the systematic investigation of models which satisfy both of the above requirements.

The State College of Washington

REFERENCES

[1] BOULDING, K. E., "A Liquidity Preference Theory of Market Prices," *Economica*, Vol. XI, May, 1944, pp. 55–63.

[2] BRUNNER, KARL, "Stock and Flow Analysis: Discussion," ECONOMETRICA, Vol. 18, July 1950, pp. 247–51.

[3] CLOWER, R. W., "Productivity, Thrift and the Rate of Interest," *Economic Journal*, March, 1954, pp. 107–115.

[4] CLOWER, R. W., "An Investigation Into the Dynamics of Investment," *American Economic Review*, March, 1954, pp. 64–81.

[5] FELLNER, WILLIAM, and HAROLD M. SOMERS, "Stock and Flow Analysis: Comment," ECONOMETRICA, Vol. 18, July 1950, pp. 242–45.

[6] HICKS, J. R., *Value and Capital*, second edition, Oxford University Press, 1946, 340 pp.

[7] KEYNES, J. M., *The General Theory of Employment, Interest, and Money*, New York, Harcourt, Brace, and Co., 1935, 403 pp.

[8] KLEIN, LAWRENCE R., "Stock and Flow Analysis in Economics," ECONOMETRICA, Vol. 18, July 1950, pp. 236–41.

[9] KLEIN, LAWRENCE R., *The Keynesian Revolution*, New York, The Macmillan Company, 1947, 218 pp.

[10] LANGE, OSCAR, *Price Flexibility and Employment, Cowles Commission Monograph No. 8.*, The Principia Press, Inc., Bloomington, Indiana, 1944, 114 pp.

[11] MARSHAK, J., and H. MAKOWER, "Assets, Prices, and Monetary Theory," *Economica*, Vol. V, August 1938, pp. 261–288.

[12] MALKIN, I., "On the Stability of Motion in the Sense of Lyapunov," *Recueil Mathématique [Matematičeskiĭ Sbornik]* N.S. 3(45), 47–100 (1938), American Mathematical Society Translations, No. 41, 1951, 68 pp.

[13] METZLER, LLOYD A., "Stability of Multiple Markets; The Hicks Conditions." ECONOMETRICA, Vol. 13, October 1945, pp. 277–92.

[14] NEMYCKIĬ, V. V., and V. V. STEPANOV, *Kačestvennaya Teoriya Differencial'nyh Uravnenii* (Qualitative Theory of Differential Equations), second edition. Moscow and Leningrad, 1949, 550 pp.

[15] PATINKIN, DON, "A Reconsideration of the General Equilibrium Theory of Money," *Review of Economic Studies*, Vol. XVIII (I), 1949–50, pp. 42–61.

[16] ROUTH, E. J., *Dynamics of a System of Rigid Bodies, Part II*, sixth edition, London, The Macmillan Company, 1905, 484 pp.

[17] SAMUELSON, PAUL A., *Foundations of Economic Analysis*, Harvard University Press, 1948, 447 pp.

[18] WICKSELL, KNUT, *Lectures on Political Economy, Vol. 1*, English translation by E. Classen, London, Routledge and Sons, 1934, 299 pp.

COMPETITION, MONOPOLY, AND THE THEORY OF PRICE

By

R. W. CLOWER *

THIS essay provides a geometrical supplement to an earlier mathematical analysis in which it is shown that the gulf separating accepted modern theories of competitive and non-competitive price determination can be bridged from either side. The basic problem is to construct the approaches to the "bridge", for the gulf itself is largely illusory.

Let us begin by considering a familiar Marshallian "short-period" competitive market characterized by the supply and demand curves shown as s and d, respectively, in Figure 1.

Equilibrium price, $\bar{p}$, is of course defined by the intersection of the supply and demand curves. But this says nothing about the determination of *current* price, which may or may not be equal to $\bar{p}$. This shortcoming may be remedied either by restating the problem in explicitly dynamical terms (describing the time rate of change of price as a function of net demand at any given price), or by adding economic content to the statical model. Since the implications of the former procedure are already well-established, we shall adopt the latter procedure here.

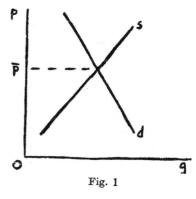

Fig. 1

First, it is necessary to assign definite responsibility for the setting of current price to a specific unit of economic decision : *viz.*, to the the "market authority" or, more shortly, the *marketee*. Since the marketee (whether "he" is a person, a committee, or a mechanical device) cannot

---

* Professor, Hailey College of Commerce, Lahore.

be expected to know with certainty the exact shape and location of the supply and demand curves, it is necessary further to suppose that demand and supply conditions are *estimated* and that these estimates are used as a basis for setting current price.

Suppose, initially, that the estimates in question may be represented by the curves S and D in Figure 2, while the "true" supply and demand

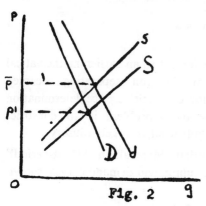

Fig. 2

curves are represented, as before, by s and d. Provisionally it may be presumed that, in setting current price, the marketee is guided by the postulate of *zero net sales* i. e., he may be assumed to set current price at a level which, according to the relevant demand and supply estimates, will equalize quantities currently demanded and supplied. *Current price* is in fact defined as that price at which the *marketer* (not the *market*)

is in equilibrium with *estimated* net sales equal to zero. But if the marketee sets current price at p¹ in Figure 2, which is the price at which estimated supply and demand are equal, the market will not be in equilibrium ; for *realized* net sales cannot be zero except at the higher price p̄. In short, the marketee's estimates will not be consistent with observed results. If we are to retain the view that current price is set by the marketee, therefore, some provision must be made for the revision of demand and supply estimates.

To simplify subsequent graphs, let us first restate the entire problem in terms of the marketee's *estimated net sales* and "*true*" *net demand*. Figure 2 may thus be redrawn as illustrated in Figure 3, where E is the marke-

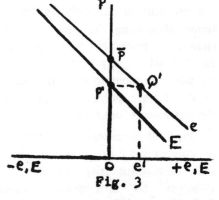

Fig. 3

tee's estimated *net sales curve* (D-S at each alternative level of price) and e is the "true" *net demand curve* (d-s at each alternative level of price). *Current price* is defined by the intersection of the price axis and the curve E, while *market equilibrium price* is defined by the intersection of the price axis and the curve e. If current price is set at p^1, therefore, current net demand will be e^1 rather than zero, and the marketee will know that he has made a mistaken estimate of demand. He will also know, however, that the point Q^1 lies on the "true" net demand curve, for this is an observable point at the price p^1. Thus it is reasonable to suppose, initially at least, that the marketee's current sales estimates will be revised to include this observed point. That is to say, if current net sales are e^1 at the price p^1, the estimated net sales curve selected by the marketee will be other than E and will be such as to pass through Q^1.

But any point on the curve e *might* represent an observable price-sales point. Hence, from a statical point of view, it is necessary to postulate the existence of an estimated *net sales field* comprising the aggregate of all net sales curves which intersect the curve e at any point. Such a net sales field or, more shortly, *sales field* is illustrated in Figure 4, where E1, E2, and E3 are representative sales curves in the sales field and e is the net demand curve, as before. It will be seen that the current price may be set anywhere, depen-

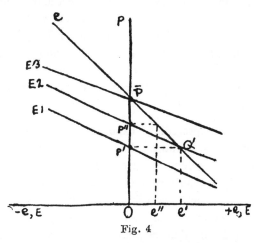

Fig. 4

ding upon which sales curve in the sales field is currently relevant. Suppose, for example, that the curve E1 were relevant at some initial instant of time. Then current price would be set at p^1 (satisfying the zero net sales postulate) and current net demand would be e^1. The marketee would then know that the sales estimates defined by E1 were partially incorrect (for the observed point Q^1 is not included among them), and he would revise his sales estimates accordingly, selecting E2 (which passes through the point Q^1) instead of E1. If current price were then set at p^1, in accordance with the sales estimates defined by E2, however, realized net sales would still differ from zero; hence, yet another sales curve would be selected, etc. Market equilibrium could occur, indeed, only if the sales estimates of the marketee were ultimately given by the curve E3 ; for the current price $\bar{p}$ is the only price at which estimated *and* realized net sales are both zero.

It might happen, however, that the price $\bar{p}$, were selected at a time when the marketee either held unwanted commodities or at a time when he wished to acquire further stocks. In the first case, the marketee would purposely underestimate net sales possibilities and so set a price at which demand temporarily exceeded supply ; in the second, he would purposely overestimate net sales possibilities and set a price at which supply temporarily exceeded demand. That is say, the sales curve E 3 would not be selected by the marketee unless he were just willing to hold the quantity of commodity stocks which he currently possessed.

In summary, if current estimates of net sales are known to be partially incorrect, the marketee will revise these estimates ; and even if current estimates are known to be correct (correct in the sense that current net (estimated) sales and current net demand are equal), these estimates will not be used in setting current price if to do so would preclude desired adjustments in the marketee's holdings of commodity stocks.

The preceding exposition is conducted in time steps, suggesting a dynamical rather than a statical view of the pricing problem ; but this is merely to give the argument greater intuitive meaning. Statically considered, any price is a possible current price since any sales curve might be relevant at any time. If some particular sales curve is known to be relevant, therefore, current price is determined by the condition that estimated net sales be zero. At any given time, however, there can be only one price ; hence, market equilibrium price is defined by *two* conditions : that *estimated* net sales be zero, and that *realized* net sales be zero also. However, if it is assumed, as above, that the marketee himself initiates price changes so long as he is not satisfied with his current stock holdings, then the condition that realized net sales be zero implies the satisfaction of the condition that estimated net sales be zero i. e. if the marketee is not satisfied with his current stock, price will purposely be set so that realized net sales are *not* zero. Hence, the condition, *viz.*, that net demand be zero, is both necessary and sufficient to determine market equilibrium price. Our model thus leads to precisely the same final conclusions as the Marshallian model ; but it leads there via a route (*viz.*, the determination of current price) which has considerably greater empirical content than the initial model.

So much for the competitive "approaches". Let us turn now to the monopoly side of the "gulf".

The first thing which strikes one here is the perfect contrast with the competitive situation ; for the problem of *current* price setting is already solved, while the problem of determinig market *equilibrium* is essentially untouched . More specifically, the monopolist is assumed to select current price and output in accordance with the principle of profit maximization, acting with reference to a given subjective sales curve. Just as in the case of a competitive marketee, however, it may happen that current price is such that consumers are (i) not willing to purchase the whole of the monoplist's current output, in which case he will be forced to hold stocks of finished commodities or (ii) consumers may be willing to purchase more than the monopolist's current output, in which case he will have to sell from stocks or sell short. Of course, this cannot happen in the usual text book models of monpoly, because there it is assumed that the monopolist's sales curve coincides everywhere with the consumer demand curve. But such an assumption is no more admissible for a monopolist than for a competitive marketee. As Hicks has put it, "Is not the slope of the......demand curve confronting a...monopolist conjectural too ?" Hence, we may reject the textbook assumption out of hand.

If the monopolist does miscalculate consumer demand for his pro- duct, it is reasonabe to suppose that he, like the competitive marketee, will revise his current sales estimates, choosing a (subjective) sales curve which passes through the currently observed price-sales point. This implies, as before, the existence of a subjective *sales field* consisting of the aggregate of all possible sales curves. Current price output may then be set at any point along a particular sales curve at which mar- ginal revenue is equal to marginal cost. Hence, the locus of all such possible current price-output points (one for each alternative sales curve in the sales field) constitutes a *monopoly supply curve*. The monopoly supply curve will lie to the left of the marginal cost curve if, as is usually assumed, all sales curves in the field are downward sloping. This is illustrated in figure 5, where the curves A1, A2, and A3 represent alternative sales curves in the sales field. MC is the marginal cost curve, d is the consumer demand curve, and SC is the monopoly supply curve (relevant portions of alternative marginal revenue

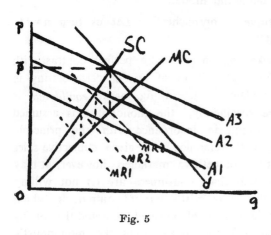

Fig. 5

curves are shown as MR1, MR2, MR3). Text book monopoly theory assumes that the sales *field* is represented by a single sales *curve viz.*, the consumer demand curve ; hence, the monopoly supply curve reduces to a single point. We are dealing here with a more general case.

Now, any price represents a possible current price, depending upon which sales curve happens to be relevant. But market equilibrium can occur only at the point where the monopoly supply curve SC intersects the consumer demand curve d (notice the perfect analogy with the Marshallian market !) ; for only at this point can it be true that the output at which profit is currently maximized is also the output at which demand is currently equal to quantity supplied. But this price will be chosen only if the monopolist is just satisfied with his current holdings of commodity stocks ; otherwise, like the competitive marketee, he will over or underestimate demand purposely, and so set a higher or a lower price, depending on whether he wishes to fill depleted inventories (by restricting consumer demand) or rid himself of unwanted stocks (by extending consumer demand).

The problem of monopoly equilibrium may now be phrased in the same terms as those used to describe the determination of market equilibrium in a competitive market. That is to say, we can deal with net sales (consumer demand less monopoly supply at each alternative price) and so consider the monopolist in the same light as a competitive marketee ; i. e., price is selected by the monopolist in accordance with the postulate of zero net sales. Except that the subjective net sales fields are likely to differ in the two cases, therefore, it is obvious that the problem of price determination under monopoly is precisely identical with the corresponding problem under conditions of pure competition. At first sight this is rather a startling conclusion ; for one does not expect to bridge a gulf without ever having to build over water. The conclusion becomes no more than a matter of common sense, however, if one notices that *the responsibility for making demand estimates and for adjusting commodity stock holdings must be borne by someone in every market.* The purely competitive seller merely shifts this responsibility to the competitive marketee ; but the monopolist, since he is both the seller and the marketee, must bear the responsibility himself. The *marketee function*, in itself, however, is precisely the same in monopolistic as in competitive markets : in all cases, *price changes are simply a means of adjusting stock holdings or for avoiding adjustments which would have to occur in the absence of price changes.*

Once the marketee function is distinguished clearly, it is apparent that the monopolist as a seller or *marketor* acts in substansially the same manner as a purely competitive seller. The only difference between the two is qualitative ; *i. e.*, the monopolist's sales field consists of sales curves all of which are not perfectly elastic, implying a supply curve different from MC (Fig. 5). If all the sales curves were perfectly elastic, as in the case of a competitive seller, then the monopolist's supply curve would coincide with his marginal cost curve (just as if he were a purely competitive seller) and market price under monopoly would be precisely the same as under pure competition *i. e.*, equal to marginal cost.

The idea that there is something fundamentally different about a monopoly and a competitive market is therefore mistaken. It is a mere illusion which follows from the failure to recognize that the *marketee* function must be undertaken by some economic unit in every market. Heretofore this fact has not been recognized in monopoly theory because it has been supposed that the monopolist knows the form of the "true" demand curve ; the marketee function (i. e. stock adjustment) simply does not exist in this case. And the marketee function has not been recognized in the case of pure competition because the statical problem of the determination of current price has not been analyzed with sufficient care.

Once the marketee function is recognized, all distinctions between competitive and non-competitive market situations—other than qualitative —disappear immediately. In particular, the so-called problem of "conjectural interdependance", involving uncertainty on the part of one seller (or buyer) about the indirect effects upon demand (or supply) of his own price-output decisions, becomes simply a special aspect of demand (supply) uncertainty in general. The monopolist, the duopolist, the oligopolist, *and* the competitive marketee, all have to take into account the indirect as well as the direct effects of alternative possible prices which they might set. But this merely affects the form of the subjective sales fields ; it does not mean that the sales fields are undefined. Then, since subjective sales fields may vary widely from one economic unit to another ; even if the units in question confront precisely the same objective market situation, it follows that the effects of conjectural interdependence are likely to vary as much from one competitive market to another as from one oligopolistic market situation to another ; and these effects will always influence the determination of equilibrium price inasmuch as they will influence the form and position of monopoly (and perhaps competitive) supply and demand curves.

The implications of the above argument should be clear : *the mechanical aspects of price determination processess are always the same regardless of market structure considerations.* Thus, any single-product oligopoly situation (monopoly, bilateral monopoly, duopoly, price leadership, etc.) can be described by a statical model which is formally analogous to a model of an isolated competitive market for a single commodity ; any two-product oligopoly situation can be described by a statical model which is formally analogous to a competitive model involving two interrelated commodity markets, etc. By recognizing the existence of stock adjustment processes (which, it should be emphasized, are already implicit in traditional theory), and by dealing with these phenomena explicitly, the gulf between the theories of competitive and non-competitive price may not only be bridged ; it can be filled. What have been thought to represent separate branches of economic analysis are thus seen to be no more than parts of a more general, unified theory of price determination.

In the more general theory, all "theories" of price which use traditional method of analysis appear as special cases. Traditional monopoly theory, and all modern theories of monopolistic (imperfect) competition, appear, also however, as empirical absurdities ; for all of these "theories" involve the tacit assumption that non-competitive marketee *do not* revise their sales estimates in the light of realized results. Such an assumption remove these theories just as far from the world of reality as it is possible to go, a not uncommon fate of supposedly "realistic" theories which are formulated without paying adequate attention to the logical consistency of the resulting models.

[13]

5. *Toward a Generalized Theory of Price Determination.* It is taken for granted in Chapters Five and Six and in preceding sections of this chapter that economic units (consumers and businesses) act competitively in the sense that commodity prices are regarded as given parameters, and are in fact set equal to market prices so that any quantity can be acquired or disposed of at prevailing "market" rates. These assumptions permit important analytical simplifications; but it remains to be shown that the resulting gain in theoretical manageability is sufficient to offset the associated loss of realism. This question can be decided only by dealing explicitly with individual and market behavior under conditions less restrictive than those given above.

A partial answer to the question is provided in this and the following section; "partial," because we deal in detail only with the behavior of individual sellers each of whom is assumed to produce and offer for sale in a single market units of a homogeneous product, and because the total cost of each seller is regarded as a given function of output. The purpose of these restrictions is to reduce the task of exposition to manageable proportions. As it happens, nearly all of the conclusions reached can be generalized to apply to consumers as well as to businesses, to multiple commodity models, and to situations in which other than purely competitive behavior occurs on both sides of a given market; so despite certain limitations the discussion does not lack generality in any significant sense.

Let us begin by relaxing the "competitive" hypothesis that each seller can always dispose of any desired quantity of output at some going "market" price. As noticed earlier (Chapter Two, Section 6), this hypothesis is hardly ever satisfied in actual practice, even in supposedly competitive markets; i.e., in concrete situations, individual sellers (or their agents) normally act as independent price setters for their own offers of outputs, and they may easily miscalculate the true extent of demand for their product at prevailing prices, at least momentarily. The analytical import of this is simply to require that we deal with both output *and* sales variables together with *individual* prices, rather than confine attention solely to output variables and to a single "market" price.

To put matters another way, the state at any instant of the present model is described by specifying the values of the *output* quantities x_i ($i = 1, \ldots, n$, depending on the number of sellers), the *sales* quantities x_i^*, and the sale prices p_i^*; our immediate task is to impose appropriate restrictions on these variables to determine their behavior over time and, as a special instance of this, to provide equilibrium criteria for the market in question. Let us proceed by dealing in turn with each of four closely related matters: sales adjustment, price adjustment, sales estimation, and output adjustment.

Sales Adjustment. Define *effective price* to buyers by the identity

$$p^* \equiv \mathrm{Min}(p_1^*, \ldots, p_n^*) \; ;$$

i.e., suppose that prospective buyers wish to deal with the seller(s) offering the lowest price at any instant. Next, consolidate the planned purchases of buyers (this is a convenient, not a required simplification), denote the resulting aggregate *planned demand* variable by d and suppose that the value of d is determined at any instant by the value of p^* in accordance with a functional identity

$$d \equiv d(p^*) .$$

Now it is known as a matter of everyday observation that *actual* purchases by buyers in any market may differ from aggregate planned purchases, even over fairly long periods of time; but there is good reason to suppose that buyers try to adjust actual purchases over time in such a way as to lessen any existing difference between planned and actual purchases. If aggregate actual purchases at any instant are denoted by x^* ($\equiv \sum_{i=1}^{n} x_i^*$, since aggregate purchases are simply the obverse of aggregate sales), this may be expressed by the more precise assumption

$$\frac{dx^*}{dt} = A[d(p^*) - x^*] \quad (A > 0) ,$$

where A is a constant "adjustment" coefficient. However, this is of very limited value in describing the behavior of the *individual* sale variables, x_i^*; for while the latter may be expected to move in much the same way as aggregate sales *if the sale prices of all sellers are identical*, it is simply a matter of common sense to admit that the sales of any one seller may react in a very different fashion indeed if his current sale price differs appreciably from the sale prices of other sellers. Accordingly, let us recognize but idealize this aspect of experience by supposing that

(5.1) $\quad \dfrac{dx_i^*}{dt} = A_i[d(p^*) - x^*] + B_{i1}(p_1^* - p_i^*) + \ldots + B_{in}(p_n^* - p_i^*)$

$$(A_i, B_{ij} > 0) ,$$

where A_i and B_{ij} are constant "adjustment" coefficients. Then, among other things, the sales of the ith seller will increase if aggregate sales are increasing (with all prices identical), or will increase at the expense of other sellers if his own sale price is less than that of any other seller, etc.

From (5.1) it follows directly that the sales of the ith seller will be stationary *if* (*i*) planned demand is equal to aggregate sales and (*ii*) the sale prices of all sellers are equal; in symbols,

(5.2) $\begin{cases} d(p^*) - x^* = 0 \\ p_1^* = p_2^* = \ldots = p_n^* . \end{cases}$

Moreover, all sale variables will be stationary at the same time *only if* these conditions are satisfied. For suppose that all $dx_i^*/dt = 0$ even though (5.2) is not satisfied (this apparently might happen because for certain values of i, the terms on the right-hand side of [5.1] might be such that positive and negative items just offset each other). Then the terms with coefficients A_i will all have the same sign or will be zero. In the latter case, there will be at least one seller, say the kth, whose sale price is greater than that of any other seller; so all of the terms with coefficients B_{kj} will have a *negative* sign. But this contradicts the assumption that all $dx_k^*/dl = 0$, so we may confine attention to the case in which the terms in (5.1) with coefficients A_i are nonzero. Again, there will be at least one seller (the kth) whose sale price is greatest and also at least one seller (the lth) whose sale price is least; hence, all of the terms in (5.1) with coefficients B_{kj} will be *negative* while all terms with coefficients B_{lj} will be *positive*. But the terms with coefficients A_k and A_l are necessarily of the *same* sign, so if $dx_k^*/dl = 0$, then $dx_l^*/dl \neq 0$, and *vice versa*, which is again a contradiction. Therefore, $dx_i^*/dl = 0$ for all values of i *only if* all of the conditions (5.2) are satisfied simultaneously.

The economic sense of the price equality requirements in (5.2) is evident (the concept of a market is often "defined" by these conditions); as concerns the meaning of the first equation, however, a geometrical interpretation may be in order. Consider a hypothetical situation in which the actual sales of all sellers but the ith are fixed $(x_j^* = x_j^{*0}, j \neq i)$; then for the sales of the ith seller to be stationary, it is necessary that the value of p_i^* be set such that

$$\left[d(p_i^*) - \sum_{j \neq i} x_j^{*0} \right] - x_i^* \equiv \delta(p_i^*) - x_i^* = 0,$$

where the expression in brackets, δ, represents the "statical" demand function for the product of the ith seller (i.e., planned market demand less the sales of all other sellers). Thus, measuring values of δ and x_i^* horizontally, values of p_i^* vertically, any point (x_i^*, p_i^*) in Figure 5.1 (e.g., $[x_i^{*0}, p_i^{*0}]$) represents a potentially *observable* quantity-price combination; but such a point is an admissable *equilibrium* combination only if it lies on the curve δ (as is true for the point $[x_i^{*1}, p_i^{*1}]$); otherwise not. A change in the value of any sales variable other than the ith will of course lead to a "shift," either to the right or to the left, in the position of the δ curve (e.g., from δ to δ' in Fig. 5.1); but the *form* of the curve δ is always exactly the same as that of the planned market demand curve so it is not affected by changes in the value of any sale variable.

Price Adjustment. Granted that current sales *may* differ from current output for a particular seller, it is a shade unrealistic to suppose that output is always equal to planned sales (current sale offerings); for if at any moment actual stock holdings differ from desired stock holdings (and this can hardly fail to happen if sales can differ from output), planned sales may be expected to differ from current output by a certain amount of planned investment or disinvestment in stocks. However, we shall not deal explicitly with this complication; indeed, we shall simply ignore the presence of stocks and of desired changes in them. At the same time, we shall assume that each seller attempts to avoid differences between sales and output with a view to maintaining constant whatever level of stocks he happens to hold at any instant.

Unwanted changes in stocks may be avoided in a wide variety of ways in any concrete situation: output may be adjusted directly to match sales; prospective buyers may be exhorted to purchase or not to purchase from a particular seller; sales by rival sellers may be influenced intentionally by

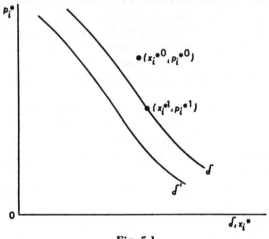

Fig. 5.1

political and other "nonmarket" activities of one or more other sellers; etc. Here, however, attention will be confined for the sake of simplicity to the balancing of output and sales via price adjustments; *nor is this at all unrealistic, for price adjustment is used to some extent in every actual market, including those in which other factors are perhaps more decisive.*

In analytical terms, we shall suppose that the behavior of the sale price of the ith seller is governed in every case by the condition

$$(5.3) \quad \frac{dp_i^*}{dt} = F_i(x_i^* - x_i) \quad (F_i > 0),$$

where F_i is a constant "adjustment" coefficient. This hypothesis is directly consistent with our earlier discussion of competitive price determination, and it does not contradict accepted views regarding price behavior in other than purely competitive markets. Moreover, it leads directly to the plausible equilibrium requirements

$$(5.4) \quad x_i^* - x_i = 0 \quad (i = 1, \ldots, n);$$

i.e., the ith sale price will be stationary if and only if sales are equal to output.

The Estimation of Current Sales Prospects. With the above restrictions on the behavior of the various sale and sale price variables in our model, it only remains to describe the behavior of the output variables, x_i. Now from our earlier discussion of sales adjustment, it is clear that the concept of "actual demand for the product of an individual seller" can be given no clear meaning in theory or in fact except when certain very special conditions are satisfied by the sale variables of other sellers. The practical implication of this is that current sales prospects are necessarily estimated by individual sellers; they cannot be known *ex ante*. In a moment, we shall wish to describe output adjustment as a function of estimated profit; since current profit prospects depend directly on estimates of current prices and sales, however, a brief digression is necessary at this point to discuss the general character of the current sales estimates of individual producers.

The main obstacle to be overcome in constructing a theory of sales estimation is to establish a definite and sensible link between estimates and observable facts; otherwise, the theory could have no operational significance, no empirical implications. To be sure, it can be stated immediately—as a formal matter—that the *highest price* at which the ith seller estimates that a given level of output can be sold at any instant will be a function of current and past values of all sale variables, of all sale price variables, and of the ith output variable (the current and past outputs of other sellers may or may not be known to the ith seller); i.e., *highest estimated price* (or simply *estimated price*), denoted by p_i, may be represented symbolically by

$$(5.5) \quad p_i(t) \equiv p_i[\overset{t}{\underset{-\infty}{x_i}}; \overset{t}{\underset{-\infty}{x_1^*}}, \ldots, \overset{t}{\underset{-\infty}{x_n^*}}; \overset{t}{\underset{-\infty}{p_1^*}}, \ldots, \overset{t}{\underset{-\infty}{p_n^*}}; t].$$

Unfortunately, the definition (5.5) is too general to be of any immediate use; to make progress, some rather far-reaching restrictions must be imposed on (5.5) to obtain a simpler and more specific view of the data upon which estimated price depends and the nature of the dependence.

First, notice that the effect of (5.5) is to assert that estimated price depends on a learning process the *content* of which may change from instant to instant as the seller has new experiences; this is the implication of the inclusion of *past* together with *current* values of the various variables, and the implication is strengthened by the explicit presence in (5.5) of the time variable, t. Since little or nothing is known about such learning processes, however, and, more particularly, since one can only speculate about the factors which lead sellers to revise their over-all views of market conditions, it is just as well to subsume the entire content of the learning process in the form of the functions (5.5) rather than to attempt to state any general rules about the dependence of p_i on past experience. Analytically, this amounts to the substitution for (5.5) of the alternative function

$$(5.5') \quad p_i(t) \equiv p_i(x_i; \ x_1^*, \ldots, x_n^*; \ p_1^*, \ldots, p_n^*),$$

which involves only current values of the relevant variables. In other words, it is assumed that the ith seller takes currently observable information into account in estimating current sales prospects; but his general views on the

nature of this dependence are already fixed by past experience and by subjective "hunches" about that experience and are not subject to change in
the light of new data the implications of which are, in the nature of the
case, somewhat ambiguous. This view is not at all plausible if it is considered to describe the behavior of a seller over a long interval of time; but
it seems fairly realistic in reference to short time periods, and it may be accepted on a provisional basis accordingly.

Second, while knowledge about the behavior of other sellers (given by the
values of the quantities x_j^*,p_j^* [$j \neq i$]) may be of some slight significance in
estimating p_i, it cannot play a critical role unless the ith seller has definite
information about over-all market demand conditions; and it is highly unrealistic to suppose that any seller knows very much about this! Hence, it is
permissible to carry out a further specialization of (5.5), this time substituting for (5.5′) the relation

$$(5.6) \quad p_i \equiv p_i(x_i,x_i^*,p_i^*) \; .$$

This function will serve as a basis for the whole of our subsequent discussion of sales estimation; for convenience, it will be assumed to be single
valued, continuous, and to possess continuous first derivatives with respect to each of its variables.

It is not advisable to place any definite *quantitative* restrictions on
the functions (5.6) at this stage; the views of individual sellers, since they
depend upon subjective interpretations of possibly very different objective
experiences, are likely to vary a great deal in practice, and it is as well to retain this aspect of the real world in our theoretical deliberations. However,
there is one *qualitative* restriction which it does seem safe to impose on
(5.6); viz., the requirement

(5.7) *For all values of x_i and x_i^* satisfying the condition $x_i = x_i^*$,*
$$p_i \equiv p_i^* \; .$$

The reason for defining p_i in terms of the requirement (5.7) is to ensure that
the subjective sales estimates of the seller are never directly contradicted
by current observation. That is to say, since any currently observed pair of
values of x_i^* and p_i^* indicates unmistakably the quantity of output that
can be sold at one particular estimated price at the moment of observation,
it is natural to require that the estimated sales curve include the same point.

A statical illustration of the preceding comments is given in Figure 5.2,
where quantities of output and sales are measured horizontally and values
of price and estimated price are measured vertically. To the given observable point x_i^{*0},p_i^{*0} there corresponds the estimated sales curve $R_A{}^0$,
which indicates the highest level of price (average revenue) which the seller
estimates will be associated with each alternative level of output (planned
sales); one of the output-estimated price points thus specified coincides
with the point (x^{*0},p^{*0}) from which the curve $R_A{}^0$ is extrapolated. Since the
given observable point is essentially arbitrary from a statical point of view,

however, the function defining p_i must be represented geometrically by an entire family or *field* of such estimated sales curves, one curve for each possible sale-sale price point (no two curves in the field can intersect because the function [5.6] is single-valued). Thus, the estimate curve $R_A{}^0$ in Figure 5.2 is defined by the point $(x_i{}^{*0}, p_i{}^{*0})$, the estimate curve R_A' is defined by the point $(x_i{}^{*'}, p_i{}^{*'})$, and so forth. However, an unlimited number of different sale-sale price points may of course define the same estimated sales curve (e.g., the curve R_A' in Fig. 5.2 is defined by the point $[x_i{}^{*''}, p_i{}^{*''}]$ as well as by the point $[x_i{}^{*'}, p_i{}^{*'}]$). In particular, it is conceivable that in a single seller market where buyers adjust purchases instantaneously to

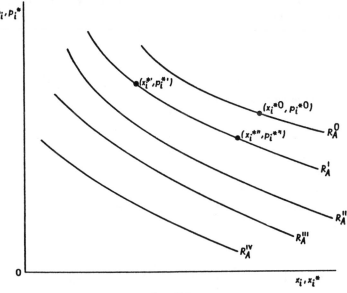

Fig. 5.2

planned demand, the seller might discover the "true" planned market demand curve for his product, in which event the sales field would degenerate to a single curve—the same curve being defined by *every* admissable observable point; this is, in fact, the assumption upon which traditional monopoly theory is founded.

Output Adjustment. Given the estimated sales function of the ith seller, we may proceed to deal with the behavior of output much as in Chapter Six (Section 11). First, denote the *total cost* of the ith seller by C_i and let the value of C_i be determined by the value of x_i at any instant in accordance with the identity

$$C_i \equiv C_i(x_i) .$$

Next, let *estimated net revenue* at any instant be defined by

$$R_i \equiv p_i(x_i, x_i{}^*, p_i{}^*)x_i - C_i(x_i) ,$$

so that *estimated marginal net revenue* is defined by

$$R'_i = p_i(x_i, x_i^*, p_i^*) + x_i\left(\frac{\partial p_i}{\partial x_i}\right) - C'_i,$$

where $C'_i \equiv dC_i/dx_i$. Finally, assume that at any instant output varies directly with estimated marginal net revenue. In symbols,

$$(5.8) \quad \frac{dx_i}{dt} = H_i R'_i \quad (H_i > 0).$$

As a further condition for market equilibrium, it is then necessary that, for arbitrary values of x_i^* and p_i^*, the value of the variable x_i be such as to satisfy the equation

$$(5.9) \quad p_i(x_i, x_i^*, p_i^*) + x_i\left(\frac{\partial p_i}{\partial x_i}\right) - C'_i = 0 ;$$

i.e., for the output of the ith seller to be stationary, estimated marginal revenue must be equal to marginal cost.[4]

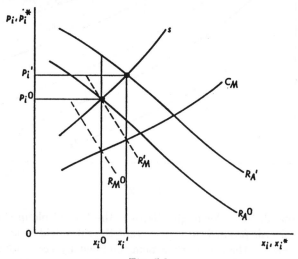

Fig. 5.3

This statical requirement is illustrated in Figure 5.3, with reference to a single seller where, as before, values of x_i and x_i^* are measured horizontally and values of p_i and p_i^* are measured vertically. To any given set of values of x_i^* and p_i^* there corresponds one and only one estimated sales curve and one and only one estimated marginal revenue curve (the latter curve is derived from the estimated sales curve and shown in dotted lines in Fig. 5.3). The intersection of any given estimated marginal revenue curve with the

---

[4] Here, and in all that follows, it is taken for granted that only those values of x_i for which net revenue is estimated to be nonnegative are admissible as equilibrium values of output.

marginal cost curve C_M then defines a particular level of equilibrium output which is associated, via the given estimated sales curve, with a particular level of estimated price. Thus, if the relevant marginal revenue curve is R_M^0 in Figure 5.3, the corresponding value of equilibrium output and the associated value of estimated price are x_i^0 and p_i^0, respectively; if the relevant marginal revenue curve is R_M', the corresponding equilibrium values of x_i and p_i are x_i' and p_i', etc. Allowing the variable parameters x_i^* and/or p_i^* to assume all possible values, therefore, and plotting corresponding values of equilibrium output against associated values of estimated price, a *supply curve* is obtained such as that illustrated by s in Figure 5.3. Any point is an admissable equilibrium output-estimated price combination if it lies on the supply curve s; otherwise not.

An interesting special case is that in which the estimated price function (5.6) takes the special form

$$(5.6')\quad p_i \equiv p_i^* ,$$

so that the estimated sales field is composed entirely of horizontal straight lines as shown in Figure 5.4. In this instance, each estimated sales "curve"

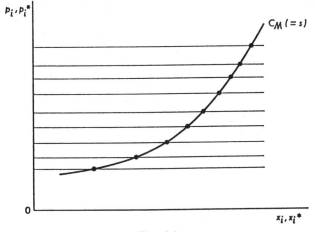

Fig. 5.4

is defined by a particular value of p_i^* independently of the value of x_i^* (i.e., the slope of the line is known to be zero relative to the quantity axis so the line as a whole is determined by its price intercept); hence, estimated marginal revenue is identically equal to estimated price regardless of the value of x_i; this means that the supply curve, s, coincides everywhere with the marginal cost curve, C_M (provided, of course, that the sales field is everywhere well defined).

The case described by the condition (5.6') may be characterized by saying that the sales estimates of the seller are *parametric* or, more conveniently in some instances, by saying that *pricing* is parametric. Otherwise, we may speak of *nonparametric sales estimates* or of *nonparametric pricing*. Of course, parametric pricing is associated only with selling under conditions of pure competition in the existing economic literature; but there is no *a priori* reason why such behavior cannot occur in a one-seller market since even in this case there may be fierce competition in a relevant sense among sellers in different but closely related markets. In any event, the preceding remarks are significant because they show that the theory of sales estimation asserted by (5.6) and (5.7) is already implicit in a special form in the accepted theory of purely competitive selling ([5.7] is satisfied vacuously when p_i is defined by [5.6']).

EXERCISE

5.1. If $p_i \neq p_i^*$ when $x_i = x_i^{*0}$ (where x_i^{*0} and p_i^{*0} are particular current values of x_i^* and p_i^*), would it be possible to test empirically any specific hypothesis about the dependence of p_i upon certain past and current values of x_i, x_i^*, and p_i^*?

5.2. If all estimated sales curves in the estimated sales field are downward sloping, where does the supply curve *s* lie in relation to the marginal cost curve? What is the situation if all the estimated sales curves are upward sloping?

5.3. As a general rule, sellers probably cannot be presumed to estimate sale prospects involving quantities or prices which differ greatly from those which they have actually experienced in the recent past. What would this imply about the domain of definition of estimated sales curves? What would it imply about the definition of the supply curve where sales estimates are parametric? (Hint: Would the supply curve still coincide *everywhere* with the marginal cost curve?)

6. *A Unified Theory of Price and Quantity Determination.* Combining the behavior equations (5.1), (5.3), and (5.8), we obtain a model of an *n*-seller market in which pricing is nonparametric; viz.,

$$(6.1) \begin{cases} \dfrac{dx_i^*}{dt} = A_i[d(p^*) - x^*] + B_{i1}(p_1^* - p_i^*) + \ldots + B_{in}(p_n^* - p_i^*) \\ \qquad\qquad (A_i, B_{ij} > 0, \quad i = 1, \ldots, n) \\ \dfrac{dp_i^*}{dt} = F_i(x_i^* - x_i) \quad (F_i > 0, \quad i = 1, \ldots, n) \\ \dfrac{dx_i}{dt} = H_i\left(p_i + x_i\dfrac{\partial p_i}{\partial x_i} - \dfrac{dC_i}{dx_i}\right) \quad (H_i > 0, \quad i = 1, \ldots, n), \end{cases}$$

where, as before, $p^* \equiv \text{Min}(p_1^*, \ldots, p_n^*)$, $x^* \equiv \sum_{i=1}^{n} x_i^*$, and the estimated price functions $p_i \equiv p_i(x_i, x_i^*, p_i^*)$ are defined to satisfy the condition (5.7). Now, since the model (6.1) comprises $3n$ independent differential equations in the $3n$ independent variables $x_1, \ldots, x_n, x_1^*, \ldots, x_n^*, p_1^*, \ldots, p_n^*$, it may without difficulty be regarded as a determinate system. To study its dynamical properties explicitly, however, would require a separate volume. Moreover, our object in the present analysis is merely to discover the extent to which competitive hypotheses (specifically, the assumption of parametric pricing) can serve to describe market situations in which pricing is *non-parametric*; and from this standpoint the dynamical model (6.1) has already served its purpose by providing a capacious grab bag out of which may be snatched a wide variety of *quantitatively* different statical models.

Let us proceed by considering first the special case of *monopoly*, defined by the condition $n = 1$. In this instance, $p_1^* = p^*$, and the system (6.1) takes the simple form

$$(6.2)\begin{cases} \dfrac{dx_1^*}{dt} = A_1[d(p_1^*) - x_1^*] \\[2mm] \dfrac{dp_1^*}{dt} = F_1(x_1^* - x_1) \\[2mm] \dfrac{dx_1}{dt} = H_1\left(p_1 + x_1\dfrac{\partial p_1}{\partial x_1} - \dfrac{dC_1}{dx_1}\right), \end{cases}$$

whence market equilibrium is defined by the conditions

$$(6.2')\begin{cases} d(p_1^*) - x_1^* = 0 \\[2mm] x_1^* - x_1 = 0 \\[2mm] p_1 + x_1\dfrac{\partial p_1}{\partial x_1} = \dfrac{dC_1}{dx_1}. \end{cases}$$

Expressed geometrically (Fig. 6.1), the sales of the monopolist will be stationary only if p_1^* and x_1^* are such that the point with these numbers as its co-ordinates lies on the planned demand curve $d(p_1^*)$, the output and estimated price of the monopolist will be stationary only if the point with corresponding co-ordinates lies on the monopoly supply curve s (defined as in the preceding section), and the sale price of the monopolist will be stationary only if these two points coincide, so that output and sales are equal. Moreover, sales, output, and price will all be stationary *if* all three of these conditions are satisfied simultaneously. Therefore, market equilibrium is defined by the intersection of the supply curve s with the demand curve d in Figure 6.1—a result which is remarkably similar to that which defines market equilibrium price in an isolated competitive market![5] Indeed, if we impose the special *quantitative* restriction on the estimated price function that $p_1 \equiv p_1^*$ (so that $\partial p_i/\partial x_i \equiv 0$), market equilibrium in (6.2) even im-

---

[5] A similar illustration holds for the case of traditional monopoly theory, except that in this model the sales "field" coincides with the planned market demand curve so that the monopoly supply "curve" degenerates to a single *point* which "intersects" (i.e., lies on) the planned market demand curve by hypothesis. Sale and price adjustment problems are essentially nonexistent in this instance. Analytically, the first requirement in (6.2') is gratuitous since it is assumed that $x_1^* \equiv d$ (instantaneous adjustment of purchases with changes in price); and while both of the remaining conditions might still be considered to be relevant, it is in fact usual to assume that $x_1 \equiv x_1^*$, which means that the dynamical restriction on dp_1^*/dt in (6.2) has to be replaced by the essentially statical requirement $p_1^* \equiv f(x_1)$, where f is the function inverse to d. Thus, attention is ultimately focused on the problem of output adjustment alone.

plies equality of marginal cost and price, and the analogy already noted is strengthened further. To be sure, it is customary to regard competitive supply and demand schedules as relations which indicate the actual amount of a commodity that will be offered for sale or demanded to purchase at any given price; but this is valid only on the assumption that actual output and purchases adjust instantaneously to their equilibrium values at any instant. And even in this case, supply and demand functions can be legitimately regarded as "partial" equilibrium requirements, precisely as is done in the present analysis. It only remains to be seen, therefore, whether the analogy

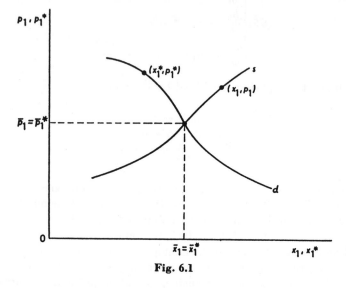

Fig. 6.1

between parametric and nonparametric pricing established in the case of monopoly can be established in more general instances.

If $n = 2$, the system (6.1) describes a general *duopoly* model, and may be written in full as

$$(6.3)\begin{cases} \dfrac{dx_1{}^*}{dt} = A_1[d(p^*) - x_1{}^* - x_2{}^*] + B_{12}(p_2{}^* - p_1{}^*) \\[2mm] \dfrac{dx_2{}^*}{dt} = A_2[d(p^*) - x_1{}^* - x_2{}^*] + B_{21}(p_1{}^* - p_2{}^*) \\[2mm] \dfrac{dp_1{}^*}{dt} = F_1[x_1{}^* - x_1] \\[2mm] \dfrac{dp_2{}^*}{dt} = F_2[x_2{}^* - x_2] \\[2mm] \dfrac{dx_1}{dt} = H_1\left(p_1 + x_1\dfrac{\partial p_1}{\partial x_1} - \dfrac{dC_1}{dx_1}\right) \\[2mm] \dfrac{dx_2}{dt} = H_2\left(p_2 + x_2\dfrac{\partial p_2}{\partial x_2} - \dfrac{dC_2}{dx_2}\right); \end{cases}$$

so market equilibrium is defined by the conditions

$$(6.3')\begin{cases} d(p^*) - x_1^* - x_2^* = 0 \\ p_2^* - p_1^* = 0 \\ x_1^* - x_1 = 0 \\ x_2^* - x_2 = 0 \\ p_1 + x_1\dfrac{\partial p_1}{\partial x_1} = \dfrac{dC_1}{dx_1} \\ p_2 + x_2\dfrac{\partial p_2}{\partial x_2} = \dfrac{dC_2}{dx_2}. \end{cases}$$

Expressing these conditions geometrically but in an order the reverse of that in which they appear, we see first that the outputs of the two duopolists cannot be stationary unless the values of the output and estimated price variables of each duopolist are co-ordinates of points which lie on the respective supply curves s_1 and s_2 in Figure 6.2. Furthermore, since the

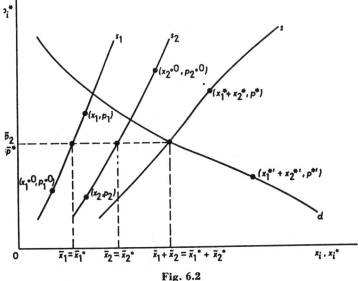

Fig. 6.2

price of each duopolist will vary over time unless his sales are equal to his output, and since the equality of output and sales implies the equality of sale price and estimated price (by [5.7]), it follows that for equilibrium to occur the sale price and sales of each duopolist must be such that the point with corresponding co-ordinates also lies on the appropriate supply curve. Next, since the sales of both duopolists will vary unless their respective sale prices are equal, equilibrium requires that aggregate sales together with the common value of the two sale prices be such that the point with corresponding co-ordinates lies on the *market supply curve s* in Figure 6.2, which is defined by simply adding the individual supply curves laterally.

Finally, aggregate purchases and the sale price of the duopolists must be such that the point with corresponding co-ordinates lies on the planned market demand curve, *d*. Hence, precisely as in the case of monopoly, market equilibrium is defined by the intersection of the market supply and demand curves *s* and *d* in Figure 6.2. As before, moreover, marginal cost will be equal to sale price for both duopolists in the case of parametric price estimates.

Now it should be evident that the above duopoly model is representative of the general case in every important respect. Regardless of the number of sellers in a given market, and regardless of their estimates of sale prospects, individual supply curves can always be defined and added laterally to obtain a market supply curve. The intersection of this curve with the planned market demand curve indicates the point at which aggregate equilibrium output is equal to aggregate sales at a common sale price, and individual equilibrium sales and output can then be read off from the individual supply curves which lie behind the market relation. And this is precisely the same procedure as one has to follow in dealing with the theoretical description of purely competitive selling. To be sure, it is usual in the latter case to suppose that sales and output are always identically equal for each seller so that some of the requirements which we have imposed as *equilibrium* conditions are there built into the basic structure of the model. What we have accomplished in the preceding analysis, therefore, is to outline a unified statical "supply and demand" theory of quantity and price determination which is valid *regardless of market structure considerations*. Different market models are obtained by imposing alternative *quantitative* restrictions, either on sales estimates or on the number of sellers involved in the market, but all of the models thus obtained are *qualitatively* identical.

EXERCISE

6.1. (Cournot's theory of duopoly.) Assume that two duopolists, each the proprietor of a mineral spring from which water can be obtained without cost, aim independently at maximizing their respective profits, given any (postulated) value of the other duopolist's sales, and given full knowledge of the planned market demand function for their (identical) products. More precisely, let the market demand function for the output of the two duopolists jointly be given by

$$x = x_1 + x_2 = -p + 6,$$

so that the sales curve for the product of the *i*th duopolist is

$$p = 6 - x_i - x_j{}^*$$

where $x_j{}^*$ is a parameter representing the sales of the other duopolist. Given that the profit function of the *i*th duopolist is $R_i = x_i(6 - x_i - x_j{}^*)$, determine the supply curve of each duopolist analytically, represent your findings graphically, and show that market equilibrium is defined by the intersection of the consumer demand curve with the curve obtained by adding the quantity supplied by each duopolist at alternative levels of price. Compare and contrast your findings with those for a comparable competitive model.

7. *Monopoly and Competition: An Appraisal.* At this point it would be possible to deal at some length with questions which arise in connection with the statement of the model (6.1). For example, can the model be extended to deal with multiple market monopoly situations (monopolistic competition)? Is full allowance made for the presence of "conjectural interdependence" among sellers (i.e., for the fact that the actions of one seller may induce reactions by others)? Is it true, as suggested on numerous occasions in the preceding discussion, that "objective" market structure considerations do not play a controlling part in deciding whether sales estimates will be parametric or nonparametric? Will price behavior depend on such factors as the subjective cost of changing decisions, on institutional and legal restrictions, and similar things when sales estimates are parametric just as it does when sales estimates are nonparametric? Is the qualitative behavior of prices and quantities likely to be much the same from a dynamical point of view regardless of the character of sales estimates? And so forth, with virtually no limit. However, apart from noting that it would be possible to justify or to defend strongly an affirmative answer to each of the above queries, we shall turn immediately to the matter of using the analysis, as it now stands, to answer the original question raised at the beginning of Section 5.

In this connection, the preceding argument appears to support three general conclusions:

(*i*) The complexity of our unified model, which is itself greatly simplified in important respects, suggests that a comprehensive statement of the theory of nonparametric price and quantity behavior would be an extremely lengthy and difficult task, and would yield an unwieldy tool for applied analysis. Moreover, the complexity of a general dynamical theory of nonparametric pricing would probably have to be seen to be believed. Thus, in the absence of overwhelming arguments to the contrary, there seems to be every justification for the procedure adopted in the text by which nonparametric sales estimates are ignored. This is not to say that the formulation of a completely general theory would be pointless; such an undertaking would undoubtedly yield many interesting and useful results. But for reasons suggested below, the ultimate outcome of such an inquiry would probably be merely to increase the flexibility and to enrich the content of accepted competitive price theory, the latter being used for dealing with most practical problems, the general theory being used as a subsidiary frame of reference against which to check the appropriateness of applications involving the explicit use of "nearly" competitive models.

(*ii*) The fact that one can describe both "competitive" and "monopolistic" varieties of individual and market behavior in terms of a single model, allowance being made for quantitative differences, indicates that no compelling arguments can be advanced in favor of dealing, as a general rule, with "monopolistic" rather than with "competitive" models. Competitive hypotheses, since they are readily expressed to allow for the existence of alternative sets of demand estimates, are already considerably more general in this respect than the hypotheses underlying traditional monopoly theory (which involves only a single set of estimates; i.e., a single estimated demand curve); and the same observation applies to most "monopolistic" (nonparametric pricing) models which are considered in the economic literature. Moreover, the *methods of analysis* adopted in competitive price theory are immediately applicable to the analysis of any concrete situation (this remark is supported by the fact that, in every instance, whether competitive or not, one has to deal with much the same kind of equations, supply and demand functions, etc.). Thus, it is not difficult to show that duopoly is formally similar either to a competitive market in which there are only two sellers or to a system of two (related) competitive markets (depending on whether the commodities sold by the duopolists are or are not regarded as identical by buyers); and similarly for other oligopoly or oligoposony situations. In effect, therefore, competitive hypotheses, if appropriately elaborated, may always be regarded as workable approximations, suitable for most theoretical and for nearly all practical purposes.

(*iii*) Finally, our argument suggests that all differences between competitive and other formal theories of price determination are reducible in a logical sense to postulated differences in the subjective beliefs of the economic units which participate in any given market. This begs the question of the precise way in which the subjective beliefs of economic units (i.e., estimates of demand and supply conditions generally) are determined. Intuition suggests that "objective" market circumstances have much to do with this; but the problem of linking "beliefs" with "facts" cannot be attacked properly using armchair methods. To make any progress in this area, explicit models must be formulated and tested in the light of behavior observed in actual markets. At bottom, however, the problem of describing the formation of current demand estimates under other than competitive hypotheses is similar to that of describing the formation of future price anticipations under competitive hypotheses. Regarded as subjects of empirical research, problems of a particularly difficult and intricate character are involved in both instances. In any event, the problems in question fall within the scope of theoretical economics only to a very limited extent; they belong essentially to the realm of applied economics.

To the question, "Does the loss of realism associated with the adoption of competitive hypotheses more than offset the resulting gains in theoretical manageability?", the above considerations appear to support a negative reply. In fact, there appears to be no appreciable loss of realism associated with the adoption of competitive hypotheses; hence, there are no very substantial disadvantages to be set off against the admitted advantages of competitive assumptions. In short, the general presumption that competitive hypotheses are inadequate to describe other types of market situations is only a presumption; its validity cannot be demonstrated because the presumption does not appear to be correct. What is true is that accepted statements of competitive price theory are themselves inadequate in certain important respects; but that is altogether a different matter.

8. *Conclusion*. The view of an economic system which emerges from the discussion in this and preceding chapters is analogous to a scale drawing of an intricate piece of machinery accompanied by blueprints which describe the working of various internal gears and pulleys. Such a picture represents an obvious oversimplification of economic activity as we experience it in everyday life, where fitfully human things overlie and modify profoundly the mechanistic elements which have been the main concern of this study. While our analysis may be useful for studying and interpreting many important aspects of behavior in the real world, therefore, this can be true only to a limited degree.

Perhaps the most obvious and important nonmechanical elements to be taken into account (among those to which it is possible to attach a label at all) are governmental and political activity, activities leading to the creation and destruction of units of economic decision, and activities involving the development of new consumer tastes and new business techniques. In principle it is of course possible to study the economic effects of these activities in terms of the comparative statics of a general equilibrium system, or, more generally, in terms of the *comparative dynamics* of a general dynamical system (describing changes in the motion or behavior over time of an economic *system* resulting from various "once-over" changes in initial conditions or in the functional structure of a model—cf. P. A. Samuelson, *Foundations of Economic Analysis* [Cambridge: Harvard University Press, 1947], pp. 351–53). As a practical matter, however, it is clear that the activities in question are to some extent related to happenings in the strictly economic sector of the economy; i.e., the effects in question work in two or more directions, not in one direction only. This is particularly clear as concerns the creation and destruction of economic units and the development and introduction of new techniques, although even here the connection is extremely complicated. If a change in taste has the effect of making the expenditures of a consumer consistently exceed his income, the consumer may die; but he may also beg, borrow, or steal additional funds or, more likely yet, curtail his fancies to suit his purse. Similarly, a change in technique which increases the profits of certain firms and threatens other firms with bankruptcy may easily encourage further changes in technique among the threatened firms. The difficulty in these and in other cases of the kind, however, is to discover a way in which to relate "economic" to "legal," "political," "institutional," "psychological," and "biological" factors. These considerations naturally lead to the study of questions which are far wider in scope than any considered in this book—to what one writer has called ". . . the majestic problems of economic development." The general principles underlying study of this kind may be clarified, however, by reference to the same principles which guide one in analyzing market behavior.

To investigate the properties of an isolated market, one formulates a model involving, say, a single variable u_1 together with any number of parameters which are held constant by the assumption of *ceteris paribus*. The model may be expressed, under appropriate circumstances, as a functional equation of some kind (perhaps a statical, perhaps a dynamical equation) having the general (symbolic) form

$$f_1(u_1; a_1, \ldots, a_m) = 0,$$

in terms of which most of the actual analysis is to be conducted. Having pursued the examination of such a model as far as seems worth while, however, one is immediately prompted to ask what effects will follow if one or more of the parameters, $a_1, \ldots, a_m$, previously held constant, are permitted to vary. This leads directly to questions in comparative statics or comparative dynamics, and, in turn, to the statement of more general models described by systems of equations in which *quantities previously regarded as parameters are treated as explicit variables*. That is to say, one is led to consider systems of functional equations having some such symbolic expression as

$$(8.1) \quad f_i(u_1, \ldots, u_n; a_n, \ldots, a_m) = 0 \quad (i = 1, \ldots, n),$$

where $u_i = a_{i+1}$ in terms of the simple one-variable model mentioned above. To be sure, if one continues to proceed in this fashion indefinitely, he will eventually convert into variables all parameters which are clearly "economic" in character, without, as a rule, having satisfied himself that his knowledge of economic phenomena is at all complete even in a theoretical sense. Eventually, therefore, it will seem desirable to treat various governmental and institutional quantities, etc., *as explicit variables, $v_1, \ldots, v_q$*, within the framework of more general models represented symbolically in the form

$$f_i(u_1, \ldots, u_n; v_1, \ldots, v_q; a_{n+q}, \ldots, a_m) = 0,$$

where $v_i = a_{n+i-1}$ in terms of the original one-variable model. In this way, provided that one is sufficiently ingenious in quantifying "noneconomic" parameters and expressing them as explicit variables in various functional equations, the range of subjects upon which precise methods of analysis can be brought to bear might be extended almost indefinitely.

[14]

SOME THEORY OF AN IGNORANT MONOPOLIST [1]

ALTHOUGH no one doubts the importance of limited information and uncertainty as factors affecting the management decisions of actual business firms, economists have long been reluctant to introduce such complications into traditional models of price and output determination. To the extent that learning and uncertainty phenomena have been considered at all, they have been studied mainly in the context of recent developments in the mathematical theory of games of strategy; and results reached via this route have had little if any effect upon the thinking of the majority of professional economists, most of whom continue, as before, to think and work in terms of models which presuppose a world of perfect information, perfect certainty and instantaneous response to changing circumstances.

The purpose of this paper is to initiate a redress of the balance: to encourage study of learning processes and delayed responses *within the framework of traditional economic theory*. The paper is directly concerned only with certain natural and potentially fruitful dynamical generalisations of traditional monopoly theory, but it has implications for every branch of established price theory. The discussion rests more on plausible than on demonstrative reasoning, and the mathematical argument is correspondingly elementary. However, some of the economic considerations which motivate the formal analysis are fairly subtle and are developed, accordingly, with more than usual care.

I. THE KNOWLEDGEABLE MONOPOLIST: STATICS

In keeping with the spirit, if not the letter, of traditional theory, consider a market in which, during any specified period of time, t, the quantity of *output* $x(t)$ of a particular commodity is produced by a monopoly firm and offered for sale to a group of prospective buyers at the unit *price* $p(t)$. Assume that *market demand* (monopoly *sales*) in the same period, denoted by $D(t)$, is a given function of price: $D(t) = D[p(t)]$; and suppose that *total costs* incurred by the monopolist in producing and selling the quantity $x(t)$ are given by a function $C(t) = C[x(t)]$. Assume also that the function D has a

[1] A complete list of acknowledgments would be embarrassingly long, but it would be indecent to ignore the obligations which I owe to my colleagues R. B. Heflebower, A. A. Charnes, Alvin L. Marty and Mitchell Harwitz, to Alan Walters of the University of Birmingham and to Arnold Zellner of the University of Washington. I am grateful also to the Graduate School of Northwestern University for partial but generous financial support. The research underlying this paper was undertaken for the project on *Temporal Planning and Management Decisions Under Risk and Uncertainty* at Northwestern University, under contract with the U.S. Office of Naval Research (contract Nonr—1228(10), Project 047–021). Reproduction of this paper in whole or in part is permitted for any purpose of the United States Government.

unique inverse, F, and provisionally define the *profit function* of the monopolist to be

$$R(t) \equiv F[x(t)]x(t) - C[x(t)] \qquad (0 \leqslant R(t))$$

(this function being presumed to be continuously differentiable). Finally, let the output of the monopolist in period t be set at any value of $x(t)$, in the domain of definition of the profit function, which satisfies the " maximum profit " condition

$$(1) \quad F[x(t)] + x(t)F'[x(t)] - C'[x(t)] = 0;$$

and let the price of the monopolist in period t be determined by the " market clearance " requirement

$$(2) \quad p(t) - F[x(t)] = 0.$$

Provided the profit function has a unique maximum value (this will henceforth be taken for granted), the conditions (1) and (2) then determine unique *equilibrium values* $\bar{x}$ and $\bar{p}$ of output and price which the monopolist will select and maintain in any and every market period. For purposes of reference, call the system (1), (2), *Model I.*

The preceding remarks provide a complete and accurate account of the essentials of traditional monopoly theory.[1] If the exposition has less " sparkle " than the usual classroom discussion of the same topic, that is probably because the typical instructor adds dynamical and other " frills " to his account of the statical theory. Among other things, it is usual to ask such questions as: " What happens if the monopolist makes a mistake and sets his output at some level other than $\bar{x}$? " Strictly speaking, however, it is not legitimate to ask this kind of question in the context of the model described by (1) and (2). For these equations (and the assumptions underlying them) assert unequivocally that *the monopolist has no choice:* either values of output and price $\bar{x}$ and $\bar{p}$ satisfying Model I exist and are set accordingly; or such values do not exist, in which case monopoly output and price are not specified by the model. To make the question meaningful, it is necessary to relax the assumptions of the theory, tacitly if not explicitly.[2] Let us relax them explicitly.

II. The Knowledgeable Monopolist: Dynamics

Let condition (2) in Model I be retained, but replace (1) by the alternative requirement

$$(3) \quad x(t) - x(t-1) = \lambda\{F[x(t-1)] + x(t-1)F'[x(t-1)] - C'[x(t-1)]\},$$

where λ is a positive constant; *i.e.,* suppose the output of the monopolist varies from one period to the next in direct proportion to the difference

---

[1] Compare J. R. Hicks, " Annual Survey of Economic Theory: Monopoly," *Econometrica*, Vol. III (1935), pp. 2–4.

[2] See, *e.g.*, the discussion of " stability " at pp. 3–4 of the Hicks article just cited.

between " marginal revenue " and " marginal cost." To determine output in any period t, it is only necessary to adjoin to (3) an initial condition specifying the value of output in the preceding period; equation (3) then generates a well-defined time series in $x(t)$ and the " market clearance " condition (2) may be used to obtain a corresponding time series in $p(t)$. Call the system described by (2) and (3) *Model II.*

It is now possible to pose the question stated earlier, for Model II does not *require* that output be set at some equilibrium value $x = \bar{x}$ as is the case in Model I. Of course, if output should just happen to be set at the value $\bar{x}$, the expression in braces in equation (3) will be zero and output will not change over time; *i.e.*, $\bar{x}$ is a stationary solution of (3) (which means that Model II is *statically equivalent* to Model I). If output is initially specified to have a value different from $\bar{x}$, however, output (and price) will vary in every subsequent period of time in accordance with (2) and (3). In the neighbourhood of an equilibrium point $(\bar{x}, \bar{p})$, for example, variations in output, starting from some initial value x_0 of x are approximately described by the equation

$$x(t) = \bar{x} + (x_0 - \bar{x})[1 + \lambda(F' + F'' - C'')]^t.$$

From this it is easy to verify that, except for special functions F and C, or special values of the " adjustment coefficient " λ, the approach to equilibrium is always gradual, may be oscillatory, and never terminates; also, that output will tend toward its equilibrium value over time for most " plausible " choices of the functions F and C, provided λ is not too large.

Model II is more interesting in several respects than Model I; in particular, since it is capable of generating states $[x(t), p(t)]$ other than the single equilibrium state $[\bar{x}, \bar{p}]$, it is potentially referable to empirical data sets of the kind which one associates with " going concerns " in the real world. Since it is still a rather dull affair, however, another " classroom " question is in order. Let it be the following: " What happens if the position of the market demand curve shifts? "

From one point of view, this question presents no new problem. Starting from a situation of monopoly equilibrium, and assuming that a shift in the demand function occurs, we have simply to deal with the question " What happens if the output of the monopolist is not set at the equilibrium level? " For the original value of output is simply one of many non-equilibrium values after the shift in demand occurs. In this respect, Model II is more satisfactory than might have been supposed at first sight.

From another point of view, however, the model gets into difficulties. So long as one deals with a fixed demand function, it is reasonably sensible to suppose that the profit and price calculations of the monopolist are made with reference to this function; one has merely to assume that the model applies to a situation in which, following various trial-and-error experiments with different prices, the monopolist knows the precise character of market demand (at least within some relevant range of price and output quantities). If the demand function is not assumed to be fixed, however, Model II would seem to have definite *empirical* relevance only on a *recurrent* basis; *i.e.*, it would be devoid of practical interest, following any shift in demand, until it could be supposed that a " sufficiently long " interval of time had elapsed to permit the monopolist to discover the new position and properties of the demand function.

Now, a model of the latter type is rather awkward to justify; but if one is to retain Model II, the only obvious alternative to some kind of " recurrent validity " hypothesis is to suppose that the monopolist has *correct a priori knowledge* about market demand in every period of time. Since this postulate imputes a highly artificial type of omniscience to the monopolist, however, it can easily prove more embarrassing than the assumption it is designed to replace. On this view, it seems desirable to seek a generalisation of Model II. A " knowledgeable monopolist " is clearly just a theoretical curiosity; it is time to see whether an " ignorant monopolist " might not be something more.

III. The Ignorant Monopolist: Naïve Strategy

As a preliminary to the development of a more general model, return for a moment to the " recurrent validity " theme and assume that, *although the position of the demand function shifts from time to time, its general form remains always the same.* Specifically, assume that the function is always representable as a straight line of constant slope, say

$$(4)\quad D(t) = ap(t) + b,$$

where $a < 0$ and the constant b is a " shift parameter." If the demand function is assumed to shift not too frequently (no more often, say, than every three market periods), it is then permissible to argue that the monopolist will acquire *correct information* about the *slope* of the function from *ex post* price and sales data (the three-period scheme allows time for two consecutive observations so that a conjecture concerning slope can be made, and then time for a final observation to " confirm " the conjecture!). This having been accomplished, the monopolist's only remaining problem is to find the *position* of the demand function in different periods of time. In the latter connection, however, it is possible to argue that the monopolist—having settled on a definite slope—will *estimate* the current position of the demand function on the basis of recent sales experience—say by reference to sales and price in the immediately preceding market period. But this, added to our earlier assumptions, is formally equivalent to postulating the existence of a (linear) *conjectural demand function* of the form

$$(5)\quad E(t) = a\{p(t) - p(t-1)\} + D[p(t-1)],$$

where the symbol $E(t)$ denotes *conjectured sales* (in period t).[1] Then, since the coefficient a in (5) is assumed to have the same value as the corresponding coefficient in (4), it follows that the *conjectural demand function in period t* is identically the same as the *market demand function in period $t - 1$*. Hence, if the revenue function in Models I and II is replaced by a " conjectural " revenue function involving the inverse of the conjectural demand function (5), monopoly output and price behaviour following a shift in market demand may still be analysed in terms of our earlier discussion. It is only necessary to argue as if shifts in the market demand parameter, b, occur one period later than is actually the case. In particular, the conditions for market equilibrium in Models I and II are entirely unaffected by the suggested substitution of a " conjectural " for an " objective " profit function.

Suppose, however, that the monopolist is less clever than the preceding discussion suggests, or that shifts in the market demand function occur so frequently that no amount of ingenuity permits the monopolist to obtain *correct* information about the form of the market demand relation. Specifically, suppose the monopolist believes the market demand function is linear when it is actually non-linear. Suppose, also, that the conjectural demand function of the monopolist is still given by (5). Then the position of the conjectural demand function in any given period is no longer determined simply by the position of the market demand function in the preceding period; its position depends also upon the behaviour of market price. To be sure, the conjectural demand function in period t will always coincide *at a single point* with the market demand function in period $t - 1$; but unless the two functions coincide everywhere (which cannot happen on our present assumptions) a change in price (resulting, *e.g.*, from a change in output) leads to a shift in the conjectural demand function even though the position of the market demand relation is fixed.

It follows from this that the output and price behaviour of an " ignorant " monopolist (*i.e.*, a monopolist who manages to make only a " reasonable " guess about the form of the market demand function) cannot be described by working with the simple " lagged " version of Model II described above.

Let us carry out a modification of Model I to allow for the presence of a minimal degree of ignorance and see where it leads. First, replace the function F (which indicates the maximum unit price at which prospective buyers *will* purchase any given level of output) by an appropriate con-

---

[1] The notion of a " conjectural," or " imagined " demand, or " demand as seen by the seller," is, of course, a standard feature of traditional theories of oligopoly and pure competition; and it has been applied before to problems of monopoly. See Sidney Weintraub, " Monopoly Equilibrium and Anticipated Demand," *Journal of Political Economy*, 1942, pp. 427 ff.: N. Kaldor, " Market Imperfection and Excess Capacity," *Economica*, 1935; R. Triffin, *Monopolistic Competition and General Equilibrium Theory*, pp. 62–6; Bushaw and Clower, *Introduction to Mathematical Economics* Chapter Seven, Sections 4–5; S. Thore, F. Billstrom and O. Johansson, " Models Involving Monopolistic Strategies for Price and Supply," *Report 2 of the Uppsala Econometric Seminar* (mimeographed, no date); Cyert, Feigenbaum and March, " Models in a Behavioral Theory of the Firm," *Econometrica*, October 1958, pp. 611–12 (abstract).

jectural price function.   In the present context, the "appropriate" concept is evidently a function which indicates the maximum unit price at which the monopolist *conjectures* that buyers will purchase any given level of output. Denoting the conjectural price variable by $e(t)$, therefore, and recalling that the conjectural demand function is defined by (5), the relevant conjectural price function is

$$(6) \quad e(t) = p(t-1) + k\{D(t-1) - x(t)\},$$

where $k \equiv -(1/a) > 0$.   The "profit maximisation" requirement in Model I is then replaced by the condition

$$(7) \quad p(t-1) + k\{D[p(t-1) - 2x(t)\} - C'[x(t)] = 0,$$

while the "market clearance" requirement is replaced by its "conjectural" equivalent

$$(8) \quad p(t) - p(t-1) - k\{D[p(t-1)] - x(t)\} = 0.$$

The system (7), (8)—call it *Model III*—describes the behaviour of what might be called an "ignorant but opinionated" monopolist.   The precise position and form of the demand function is conjectured "with certainty" at the beginning of any given period on the basis of sales and price data in the immediately preceding period.   Just as in Model I, monopoly output and price are then assumed to be set in period t at certain unique "momentary equilibrium" values, $\tilde{x}(t)$ and $\tilde{p}(t)$ in order to yield a *conjectural* "profit maximum" and achieve *conjectural* "market clearance."   And this procedure is assumed to apply in every market period regardless of the fact that, in general, *sales* conjectured by the monopolist, corresponding to any selected value of price, differ from *sales actually realised*.[1]

The working of Model III is illustrated in Fig. 1, where D represents the market demand function, C_m represents the marginal cost function, e is a line having the same *slope* as the conjectural price function and S describes the *conjectural supply function* of the monopolist,

$$\tilde{x}(t) = S\{\tilde{p}(t); (p(t-1) + kD[p(t-1)])\},$$

defined implicitly by equations (7) and (8).   Sales are initially assumed to be set at the level D_0 corresponding to the price p_0; the conjectural price function at the *beginning* of period t_1 is therefore represented by e_1.   The value $\tilde{x}$ of output which "momentarily" maximises conjectured profit in period t_1 is then $\tilde{x}_1$, as defined by the intersection of e_1 with the conjectural supply curve S (where "conjectural marginal revenue" is equal to "marginal cost").   The value $\tilde{p}$ of price at which it is conjectured that the

---

[1] This "portrait of a monopolist" is very similar to the "portrait of a monopolistic competitor" as drawn by Professor Chamberlin in his *Theory of Monopolistic Competition* (see, particularly, pp. 89–93).   Indeed, it is possible to regard Model III as a basis for construction of a theory of multiple-market monopoly systems which are formally identical to systems considered by Professor Chamberlin, except that they do not depend on artificial "symmetry" conditions and can be considered to apply to "small-group" as well as "large-group" systems.   But it is not within the scope of this paper to pursue the matter further.

market will be cleared in period t_1 is similarly defined as $\hat{p}_1$. At the price $\hat{p}_1$, however, sales in period t_1 are $\hat{D}_1$ rather than D_0; so the conjectural price function at the beginning of period t_2 is represented by e_2 instead of e_1. Hence output in period t_2 increases to the level $\tilde{x}_2$, while price rises to $\hat{p}_2$. And so the process continues, with consequences indicated by following the " zig-zag " line $ABCD$ . . . As in the case of Model II, the adjustment

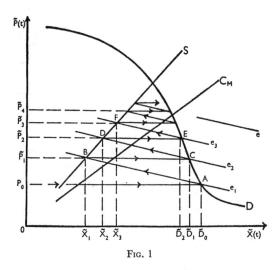

Fig. 1

process does not terminate, but the motion illustrated in Fig. 1 clearly tends toward the "true" equilibrium point $(\bar{x}, \hat{p})$—where the conjectured position [1] of the price function is consistent with realised results.

Analytically, the behaviour of "momentary equilibrium" output in the neighbourhood of an equilibrium point $(\bar{x}, \hat{p})$ is described by

$$(9) \quad x(t) = \bar{x} + (x_0 - \bar{x})\{(k/a + 1)(1 - k/(2k + c))\}^t$$
$$(a < 0 < k; \ 1/a = F'[\bar{x}], \ c = C'[\bar{x}]),$$

which indicates that the motions of the system are " direct " and stable (as illustrated in Fig. 1) if $k \leqslant -a$, " oscillatory " and either stable or unstable if $k > -a$. Examples of the last two possibilities are illustrated in Fig. 2. The analogy with familiar " cobweb " models is amusing as well as instructive.

Model III has a number of intriguing features. In the first place, it permits monopoly equilibrium to be defined by the intersection of " curves of demand and supply." [2]   Even more significant is the fact that the dynamical

---

[1] Notice that market equilibrium does not require the *slope* of the conjectured price function to bear some definite relation to the *slope* of the demand function; merely that the equilibrium values of output and price should satisfy both relations simultaneously.

[2] Compare Chamberlin's discussion of the case of traditional monopoly theory at pp. 12–16 of the *Theory of Monopolistic Competition*; also E. R. Hawkins, " Note on Chamberlin's Monopoly Supply Curve," and " Reply " by Chamberlin, *Quarterly Journal of Economics*, 1939, pp. 641 ff.

(and so the comparative statics) properties of the model can be analysed in " supply and demand " terms using strictly traditional techniques of analysis.[1] This is most easily seen by working with a model in which

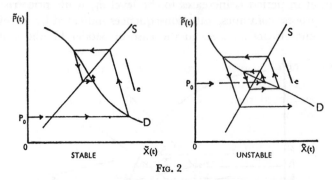

STABLE   UNSTABLE

FIG. 2

units of measurement are chosen to make the equilibrium point $(\bar{x}, \bar{p})$ coincide with the point $(0, 0)$. For, in this case, (9) implies that

$$\tilde{x}(t-1) \equiv \tilde{x}(t)/\{(k/a+1)(1-k/(2k+c)\} \equiv K\tilde{x}(t),$$

which means that the behaviour of "momentary equilibrium" price (as given by (8)) may be described in the alternative form

$$(10)\quad \Delta\bar{p}(t) \equiv \bar{p}(t) - \bar{p}(t-1) = k\{D[\bar{p}(t-1)] - K\tilde{x}(t-1)\}(k > 0).$$

And (10) asserts that price variations are directly proportional to *market excess demand*. The analogy with price behaviour in a competitive model requires no further emphasis.

IV. QUASI-SOPHISTICATED STRATEGIES

Although Model III is similar in many respects to a simple dynamical model of a competitive market, the analogy is not perfect. The clearest expression of a basic difference is probably provided by noting that Model III makes no provision for the possibility that the price conjectures of the monopolist may be *parametric*; in every case it is assumed that the coefficient k in the conjectural price function is strictly positive, which implies that the value of conjectured price, $e(t)$, depends on the value assigned to the output variable $x(t)$—that is to say, the price conjectures of the monopolist are *nonparametric*. Indeed, if these conjectures are assumed to be parametric in Model III (*i.e.*, if it is assumed that $k = 0$), (9) yields the value x_0 of $\tilde{x}(t)$ *for all values of t*, and (10) asserts that $\Delta\bar{p}(t) \equiv 0$! This makes nonsense of the entire model.

It is instructive, however, to explore the consequences of this situation a little further. Assume, therefore, that $k = 0$ in Model III, that $\tilde{x}(t_0) = x_0$ and $\bar{p}(t_0) = p_0$, but that $D[p_0] \neq x_0$ (x_0 and p_0 being given constants).

[1] For a description of the more usual situation in models of this kind, see Bushaw and Clower, *Introduction to Mathematical Economics*, pp. 186–7, 190–92.

Then, although the actual sales of the monopolist differ from desired sales (*i.e.*, output) in every period, the implication of Model III is that output and price will be maintained indefinitely at their initial levels, x_0 and p_0. Notice, however, that everything would be well *if the coefficient k in the conjectural price function were not also used as the " adjustment coefficient " in* (10). Specifically, if some positive constant, α, were substituted for k in (10), output variations would be governed by " marginal cost-price " considerations (the assumption $k = 0$ causes no trouble in (7)); and price variations would be governed by straightforward " market clearance " considerations. Moreover, this would seem to be a desirable solution on other grounds. There is no reason to assume that the monopolist is so naïve as to believe that his price conjectures in *any* given period will be correct; and in the absence of such an assumption, it is gratuitous to suppose that price is set *in every* period on the basis of the conjectural price function. It would be just as appropriate to describe price movements in terms of a strictly pragmatic "trial-and-error" process, as suggested above. Following the same line of argument, neither is there any reason to assume that output is set *in every period* to maximise conjectural profit as *currently* conceived; gradual adjustment " in the light of current conditions," as implied by one of the assumptions in Model II, would be an equally legitimate and in some ways a more satisfactory assumption.

In the light of the preceding remarks, it is in order to consider first the model

(7) $p(t - 1) + k\{D[p(t - 1)] - 2x(t)\} - C'[x(t)] = 0$

(11) $p(t) - p(t - 1) = \alpha\{D[p(t - 1)] - x(t - 1)\}$ $(\alpha > 0)$,

which is simply Model III with a " price adjustment equation " in place of the " market clearance requirement " (8).

Equilibrium conditions for this model are precisely the same as for Model III, namely,

(7') $p + kD[p] - 2kx - C'[x] = 0$,

and

(8') $D[p] - x = 0$;

but the dynamical characteristics of the system are rather different.

This is conveniently illustrated in Fig. 3, where the curves D, S and e are defined precisely as in Fig. 1, and α is assigned the value $\alpha = 1/2$. Starting from values p_0, D_0 and x_0 of price, sales and output in period t_0, output in period t_1, denoted by $\tilde{x}_1$, is defined by the intersection of the curves e_1 and S. Price in period t_1 is determined, however, by the requirement (11); *i.e.*, $p(t_1) = p_0 + \frac{1}{2}(D_0 - x_0) = p_1$.[1] In period t_1, therefore, sales are D_1 and

---

[1] The " tilda " is dropped from the variable p in the present model because the values of $p(t)$ generated by (11) may not (and ordinarily will not) be " momentary equilibrium " values; *i.e.*, if a value $\tilde{x}(t)$ of x which satisfies (7) and a value of $p(t)$ which satisfies (11) are both inserted into (8') the resulting expression is not *identically* zero.

the conjectural price function at the beginning of the next period is e_2 (the " zig-zags " of Model III disappear because of the independence of price adjustment and price conjectures). Accordingly, output in period t_2 is $\tilde{x}_2$, price is given by $p_1 + (D_1 - \tilde{x}_1)/2 = p_2$ and so forth. In the present case,

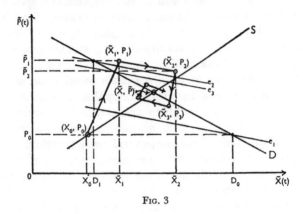

FIG. 3

the point $(\tilde{x}(t), p(t))$ " spirals " toward the equilibrium point $(\tilde{x}, \tilde{p})$; however, unstable " spirals " and stable and unstable " direct " motions are also possible.[1]

An even simpler graphical description of the model results if the now perfectly legitimate assumption is made that $k = 0$. The conjectural price function then becomes $e(t) = p(t - 1)$, and (7) is replaced by the simpler requirement $p(t - 1) - C'[x(t)] = 0$. Hence, output, price and sales adjustments can be described in terms that are formally identical with the usual text-book discussion of the adjustment of supply, demand and price in a purely competitive market.[2]

The system (7), (11) is a distinct improvement over Model III from the standpoint of potential empirical applications. Models which yield abrupt changes in the values of theoretical variables are hard to reconcile with

---

[1] The characteristic equation of the linearised counterpart of (7), (11) is

$$f(r) \equiv \begin{vmatrix} r - \alpha/a - 1 & \alpha \\ k/a + 1 & -r(2k + c) \end{vmatrix} = 0, \, (1/a = F'[x]; \, c = C'[\tilde{x}])$$

which is a *quadratic*. The corresponding equation for Model III, however, is

$$f(r) \equiv \begin{vmatrix} r - k/a - 1 & k \\ k/a + 1 & -(2k + c) \end{vmatrix} = 0,$$

which is *linear*. This " explains " the qualitative difference between the motions generated by the two models.

[2] What is even more surprising, J. N. Wolfe, of the University of Toronto, tells me that he has come across a case in Canada, involving monopoly suppliers of road-construction materials, which might be considered to fit this " competitive monopoly " model! Needless to say, I don't believe him.

known sets of economic data; hence it is desirable to avoid building models in which " cobweb " phenomena are, so to speak, part of the basic structure. Model (7), (11) is not altogether free of this defect, but because of the presence of the coefficient α in equation (11), it can always be made to yield a " smoother " time series than Model III for given functions C, D and a given value of k. Besides adding an element of flexibility to an otherwise rigid model, moreover, the presence of the coefficient α in (11) divorces the problem of estimating the coefficients of the conjectural price function from the problem of estimating the coefficients of the price-adjustment equation. Finally, the model describes " hit and miss " price behaviour of a kind which one might well find in a " going concern "; this means that fewer questions would have to be begged before attempting to use the model to interpret concrete situations.

Comments similar to the above apply with equal or greater force to the model described by

(11) $p(t) - p(t - 1) = \alpha\{D[p(t - 1)] - x(t - 1)\}$ $(\alpha > 0)$

(12) $x(t) - x(t - 1) = \beta\{p(t - 1) + kD[p(t - 1)] - 2kx(t - 1)$
$\qquad\qquad\qquad\qquad - C'[x(t - 1)]\}$ $(\beta > 0)$,

which is obtained from the preceding model by substituting an " output adjustment equation " for the " maximum profit " condition (7). The resulting system is still relatively simple from a formal point of view,[1] but it can be used to describe quite complicated patterns of price, output and sales behaviour. Because it portrays the monopolist as a *profit seeker* rather than a *profit maximiser*, moreover, it is an improvement on earlier models from a casual empirical point of view.

Indeed, if the model (11), (12) is generalised slightly to make allowance for the possibility that the monopolist varies output in direct response to changing demand conditions, it leaves little to be desired as an elementary description of the mechanics of monopoly output and price adjustment in a world of limited knowledge.   This generalisation is accomplished very easily by adding an extra term to the right-hand side of (12), to obtain

(12′) $x(t) - x(t - 1) = \beta\{p(t - 1) + kD[p(t - 1)] - 2kx(t - 1)$
$\qquad\qquad - C'[x(t - 1)]\} + \gamma\{D[p(t - 1)] - x(t - 1)\}\}(\beta, \gamma > 0).$

While the model described by (11) and (12′) is then equivalent, *from a statical point of view*, to all of the Models III, (7)–(11), and (11)–(12), its qualitative dynamical properties are in better accord with everyday experience.   Formal analysis of these properties is left to the interested reader,

[1] The characteristic equation of the linearised version of (11), (12) is

$$f(r) \equiv \begin{vmatrix} r - \alpha/a - 1 & \alpha \\ -\beta(k/a + 1) & r + \beta(2k + c) + 1 \end{vmatrix} = 0,$$

where a and c are defined as before.   Compare the corresponding equation for the system (7), (11) given in footnote 1, p. 714.

however, with the warning that the task is difficult and not particularly instructive.[1]

IV. CONCLUSION

Ignorance about demand conditions is a ubiquitous feature of market life in the real world. Whatever its source—whether it arises from competition among sellers, lagged response of buyers to changing prices, exogenous changes in tastes, techniques, government policies, etc.—it is a factor to be reckoned with in any attempt to describe observed output and price behaviour. Moreover, the phenomenon of demand ignorance implies—in a plausible if not in a demonstrative sense—the existence of learning and response mechanisms through which output and price decisions arrived at on the basis of provisional conjectures are revised in the light of realised results and ultimately reconciled with experience. The purpose of this paper has been to provide an intuitively plausible and logically coherent description of some particularly simple mechanisms of this kind.

In this connection, it is worth emphasising that the orientation of the preceding analysis is not entirely philosophical. On the contrary, the argument has been influenced at every stage by tacit recognition of the fact that the lack of provisionally plausible theoretical models of other than " purely competitive " markets has long been a major obstacle to systematic empirical study of the production and marketing activities of individual business firms. Whether any of the models outlined above can be used to obtain fruitful results in this area is, of course, another question. It may be noted, however, that most of these models have the econometrically convenient properties of linearity and identifiability. Also, most of them owe their existence to an earlier (and unsuccessful) attempt to reconcile traditional monopoly theory with factual descriptions of the behaviour of " monopolistic " firms in the United States.[2] Finally, preliminary analysis of price, sales, output, and inventory data obtained from a selected sample of major U.S. firms has yielded results which are sufficiently promising to encourage deeper and more systematic studies in the same direction. While the immediate emphasis of the present paper is theoretical, therefore, its original sources, current uses and ultimate aims are all distinctly practical.

R. W. CLOWER

Northwestern University,
Evanston, Illinois

---

[1] The relevant characteristic equation (cf. footnote 1, p. 715) is

$$f(r) \equiv \begin{vmatrix} r - \alpha/a - 1 & \alpha \\ -\beta(k/a + 1) - \gamma/a & r + \beta(2k + c) + \gamma - 1 \end{vmatrix} = 0,$$

[2] A particularly instructive study of this kind is by Edmund P. Learned, " Pricing of Gasoline: A Case Study," *Harvard Business Review*, Vol. XXVI, November 1948, pp. 723–56.

[15]

Reprinted from PROCEEDINGS OF THE THIRTY-FOURTH ANNUAL CONFERENCE OF THE WESTERN ECONOMIC ASSOCIATION, 1959.

OLIGOPOLY THEORY: A DYNAMICAL APPROACH

R. W. CLOWER

Northwestern University

The purpose of this paper is to sketch a theory of oligopoly which is broadly consistent with traditional doctrine yet sufficiently general to include both established monopoly theory and the accepted theory of pure competition as special cases. The central theme of the argument is that, whether sellers are one, many or few, market performance characteristics cannot be inferred from market structure considerations alone; that market behavior depends in every case upon certain more or less arbitrary "rules of inductive behavior" as well as the objective milieu in which sellers operate.

The analysis is novel in only one important respect; namely, elementary learning processes are given explicit recognition within the foundations of price theory. Such processes have been largely ignored in traditional equilibrium analysis, largely, I suspect, because issues of this kind simply do not fit into a statical frame of reference.[1] Matters are altered

[1] Cf. Robert Triffin, *Monopolistic Competition and General Equilibrium Theory* (Harvard, 1941), p. 66.

considerably, however, if rudimentary dynamical elements are introduced into traditional price theory; learning processes are then seen to have not only a natural but a necessary place within the main body of the discipline. Such, at least, will be my contention in the discussion that follows.

I

Let us begin by imagining an organized auction market in which units of output produced by sellers during any given market period are pooled together and sold at the beginning of the next period, using the services of an independent auctioneer whose sole task is to discover and announce a unit price at which buyers in the aggregate will be just willing to "clear the market" of existing supplies. Assuming that market demand is a single-valued and continuous function of market price, we may then state that *price in any given period is determined by aggregate output in the immediately preceding period.*

The existence of this dynamical lag implies that production decisions have to

be made by producers before anything definite is known about the price at which outputs can actually be sold; which is to say that *no seller confronts an objectively determined average revenue function.* Hence, even if total costs are given for each producer as a smooth and continuous function of output, the usual criterion of profit maximization cannot be used to characterize seller behavior. With respect to traditional assumptions about market structure and seller motivation, therefore, the present model is basically indeterminate regardless of the number of sellers involved.

II

The obvious way to remove this indeterminacy is to assume that each seller confronts some kind of *subjective* average revenue relation, defined so as to give the seller's *estimate* of market price in any given period as an explicit function of *ex post* price and quantity data.[2] This permits a (subjective) *profit func-*

[2] See, e.g., N. Kaldor, "Mrs. Robinson's 'Economics of Imperfect Competition,'" *Economica*, August, 1934, pp. 340–41.

16

219

tion to be defined for each seller and the usual profit maximization postulate may then be applied to describe the determination of outputs — and so the determination of market price — in any given period.

The difficulty with this procedure is that it is purely formal. The specification of literally any price estimation mechanism will yield a determinate model; the real problem is to formulate determinate models which make sense from a casual empirical standpoint. This is not quite the same thing as to say that price estimation procedures should conform to some sort of rational ideal. In particular, we cannot require that all sellers in a given market follow exactly the same estimation procedure, for this would imply the existence of some kind of logical connection between facts of market experience and subjective interpretations of these facts, which would be completely contrary to common sense.[3] All that we can sensibly require is that each seller should follow a "reasonable" price estimation procedure, meaning by this that, whatever procedure is adopted, it should never yield estimates of price which are flatly inconsistent with actual experience.

This condition is much too broad to provide positive guidance as far as the construction of specific estimation procedures is concerned; but it suggests one general criterion which every estimation procedure should satisfy. Specifically, every procedure should be such that, if market price and output happen to remain constant for an indefinitely long interval of time, then price as estimated by the seller should approach the actual market price in the limit as time becomes infinite; otherwise a stationary equilibrium state might involve an actual market price which differed from price as estimated by sellers, which would contradict the "reasonableness" criterion just mentioned. The same criterion also suggests that price estimates obtained by any procedure should be interpretable in a probability sense as estimated *mean* values rather than precise forecasts; but this is more a matter of empirical than of theoretical content. The preceding comments do little to restrict the range of potentially admissible estimation techniques, and in other circumstances it might be desirable to carry matters further by imposing additional criteria such as "simplicity," "accuracy," and the like. I am concerned only with the statement of a generalized theory of oligopoly, however, not with the statement of a definitive theory, and under these circumstances an exhaustive account of the implications of the "reasonableness" criterion is unnecessary.

[3] Cf. Martin Shubik, *Strategy and Market Structure* (Wiley, 1959), pp. 163-5.

III

Returning now to the main thread of the argument, a specific price estimation procedure remains to be introduced in order to arrive at a model of oligopoly which will justify my initial claims. Before making definite proposals in this regard, however, certain heuristic preliminaries are in order. First, it seems natural to suppose that a "typical" seller will sooner or later develop a "feel" for the market in which he operates; that he will form some conjecture as to the influence which he is able to exert upon market price through his own actions; that he will acquire some idea of the way in which competing sellers (if any) can be expected to behave in various circumstances; that he will develop some more or less accurate notions about the way in which his own situation is influenced by conditions in other markets, and so forth. The "feel" in question may be largely unconscious, and in any case it cannot be presumed to lead to dogmatic price forecasts.

Second, it seems sensible to suppose that recent events will dominate the thinking of a typical seller and, in particular, that there will be a tendency to regard prevailing prices or prevailing price trends as being more or less permanent in the absence of definite reasons for believing the contrary.

Finally, it seems natural to suppose that a typical seller will tend to follow any given estimation procedure that happens to be adopted so long as it yields results that are roughly in accord with realized experience. "Satisfactory" rather than "optimal" results, to use terms suggested by Simon,[4] are all that a reasonable seller can hope to achieve.

One might suggest a great variety of price estimation functions all of which would be consistent with the requirements suggested by the preceding comments. The simplest kind of function to use, however, is one whose form is specified in advance (in accordance with the idea that the seller develops a "feel" for general market conditions), and whose position in any given market period is estimated by reference to actual experience in the preceding period. To take a specific example, assume that the typical seller estimates that the price which he can expect to realize in any period is a linear function of the quantity of output which he offers for sale in the same period. The *form* of the price estimation function is then characterized by a single parameter representing its slope. Similarly, the *position* of the function in any period is characterized by specifying a single point through which it must pass, namely, the point whose coordinates represent present sales and market price in the immediately preceding period.

This is illustrated in Figure I where the output, x(t), and sales, q(t), of an individual seller in period t are measured horizontally while market price,

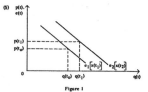

Figure 1

p(t), and estimated market price, e(t), are measured vertically. Given that the sales of the seller in some initial period, say period t_o, are represented by $q(t_o)$, and market price in the same period by $p(t_o)$, the estimated price function of the seller at the beginning of the next period, period t_1, is represented by the line $e_1[x(t_1)]$. Then if sales in period t_1 (equal to output in period t_o) are given by $q(t_1)$ while market price is represented by $p(t_1)$, the estimated price function at the beginning of period t_2 will be $e_2[x(t_2)]$ instead of $e_1[x(t_1)]$, and so forth. In the special case where the slope of the estimated price function is identically zero, the position of the function is determined simply by the value of market price in the preceding period. This is illustrated in Figure 2.[5]

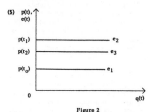

Figure 2

These are merely illustrative examples: thus, while I shall adhere in what follows to the assumption that the position of the price estimation function is always fixed according to the simple procedure outlined above, for the sake of greater generality, I shall usually regard the function as being nonlinear rather than linear in form.

IV

Let us deal now with some specific models, starting with a case in which the

[4] See Herbert A. Simon, *Models of Man* (Wiley, 1957), pp. 270-71; also March and Simon, *Organizations* (Wiley, 1958), pp. 140-41.

[5] In the first of these cases, it is convenient to say that the price estimation process is *nonparametric* since the seller's estimate of price is a function of current output. Similarly, since estimated price is independent of output in the second case, the price estimation process is said to be *parametric*.

number of sellers is extremely large. On this supposition, provided that the distribution of outputs among individual sellers is not too asymmetrical, it is plausible to assume that each seller will discover as a matter of experience that variations in market price are not related in any obvious way to variations in his own output. This is not a logically demonstrable proposition, but it is more or less acceptable on commonsense grounds; and if it is accepted, then it follows that the price estimation function of each seller will be independent of output — that is to say, price estimates will be parametric (see Figure 2, above). The position of the function in any period will therefore be determined, in accordance with the procedure mentioned earlier, by market price in the preceding period; i.e., each seller will regard the prevailing market price as a "reasonable" estimate of what the market price will probably be in the following period. Applying the usual assumption of profit maximization, it follows from this that each seller will select a level of output for which marginal cost is equal to the prevailing market price. The price actually realized at the beginning of the next period may differ from the price originally anticipated, and if this happens, each seller will revise his estimate of what price will be in the next period, select a different level of output, and so on, perhaps indefinitely. However, if a price is ultimately established at which aggregate output is such that buyers are just willing to clear the market, then this price will be maintained indefinitely unless a change occurs in objective demand conditions. Thus the statical properties of the present model are precisely the same as those of the accepted theory of pure competition.

Turning to the other extreme, suppose that we have to deal with a single-seller market — monopoly in the literal sense of the term. If objective demand conditions remain always the same from one period to another, then it is not implausible to suppose that the seller will sooner or later arrive at a perfectly accurate idea of the nature of the demand function confronting him, at least within a limited domain of output and price combinations. And in these circumstances it is legitimate to suppose that the price estimation function of the seller will coincide with the inverse of the market demand function.[5] If the seller then selects a level of output for which marginal revenue, as calculated from this function, is equal to marginal cost, the output will in fact be sold at the price

originally estimated. Thus the seller will never have any occasion to revise his estimate of demand. The present model is formally equivalent, therefore, to the traditional theory of simple monopoly.

If objective demand conditions vary from one period to another, however, then as a general rule the seller cannot be expected to arrive at a correct conjecture as to the form or position of the market demand function. Suppose, nevertheless, that some kind of conjecture is actually made. Then if output is set in any given period so as to equate estimated marginal revenue with marginal cost, the price realized in the next period will normally differ from the price originally anticipated, and the seller's estimate of the position of his average revenue function will have to be revised. This process will continue indefinitely unless and until the position of the function is such that the quantity of output offered for sale can in fact be disposed of at the price anticipated by the seller. Such a position of equilibrium can be attained, however, at any level of output less than or equal to the competitive level at which marginal cost is equal to price. Everything depends on the nature of the seller's subjective estimate of demand, and this may bear little relation to actual demand conditions. We arrive, therefore, at a model of monopoly which is much less specific in its implications than is traditional doctrine, but also much less artificial. It is of no use at all for *prescriptive* purposes, but may have *descriptive* potentialities — a statement that has to be exactly reversed in order to apply to traditional monopoly theory.[7]

V.

The analogy between this generalized monopoly model and traditional oligopoly theory is fairly obvious. In both instances, it is necessary to impose additional assumptions in order to arrive at specific results. Indeed, the analogy can be carried further if we notice that the phenomenon of conjectural interdependence represents nothing more than a particular kind of ignorance and uncertainty. Just as a monopolistic seller may make an incorrect conjecture as to the way in which conditions in his market are influenced by the behavior of sellers in *other* markets, so any one seller in a market where the total number of sellers is small may fail to forecast correctly how his own situation will be affected by the behavior of other sellers in the *same* market. Up to this point, indeed, I have no particular bone to pick with existing oligopoly theories nor anything particular to add to them. When it

comes to the matter of introducing additional assumptions to achieve determinacy, however, I part company with most previous writers.

It seems to me that there is no essential difference, in principle, between a multiple-seller market in which objective demand conditions never change and a single-seller market in which demand conditions vary over time in a more or less random fashion. In both instances, the crucial issue is this: will the output decisions of a typical seller be governed by arbitrary rules of thumb, by security motives, political considerations, moods of optimism and pessimism, legal and institutional arrangements, etc., at Triffin and others would seem to have it,[8] or will the typical seller use what evidence he can command as a basis for "reasonable" decision making? Needless to say, my own predilection is for the latter alternative; and I think this point of view is supported by reference to the behavior of actual business firms.

If this point of view is adopted, we are led to a theory of oligopoly in which each seller confronts a subjective average revenue function defined by reference to previous market experience and subject to revision over time in the light of realized results. This yields a determinate dynamical model with properties similar to those of the generalized monopoly model outlined above.[9] The model may also be regarded, however, as a simple generalization of our earlier competitive model. For, however many sellers are assumed to operate in a particular market, one or more of them may come to believe that they can affect market price by varying their own output offerings; and if this is the case, then it does not matter whether or not the belief is correct in fact. Aggregate output will tend to be smaller and market price will tend to be higher than the competitive level. The familiar purely competitive model is converted, in fact, into an oligopolistically competitive model which has all the same *qualitative* features but which generates *quantitatively* different types of behavior.

This kind of result is no doubt more plausible when there are two, three, or ten sellers than when there are two, three, or ten hundred; but this does not affect the logic of the matter. In every instance, market performance depends in a critical way upon the subjective interpretation of market experience by individual sellers, and models which are determinate in the usual sense cannot be obtained in any case without introducing "extra" institutional assumptions.

---

[5] The price estimates of the seller will usually be nonparametric (see Fig. 1, above) but all observable price-sales points will lie on a single curve according to our present assumptions.

[7] For a detailed account of these matters see R. W. Clower, "Some Theory of an Ignorant Monopolist," *Economic Journal*, December, 1959.

[8] See Triffin, *op. cit.*, pp. 70–71, 78.

[9] For an extended account of a continuous time version of this model, see Bushaw and Clower, *Introduction to Mathematical Economics*, pp. 185–92.

VI

Historically, much has been made of the indeterminacy of oligopoly models as compared with the determinacy of monopoly and pure competition. Determinacy being regarded as a virtue in theoretical models, moreover, countless writers have applied themselves to the task of constructing oligopoly theories which have this desirable property. Granted that this is one way of unifying the various branches of price theory without destroying the entire body of traditional doctrine, the question remains whether it is a satisfactory procedure; and most modern economists would undoubtedly answer the question in the negative.

The only alternative seems to be the one suggested in this paper, namely, to unify existing theories by recognizing that all of them are equally "indeterminate" in the absence of specific assumptions about the way in which market participants learn from experience. This is not an easy alternative to swallow because it creates unity only by extending the analytical chaos of existing oligopoly theories into realms which have hitherto been regarded as fairly orderly. Since closer inspection of traditional theories indicates that their "orderliness" is, in any case, contrived rather than natural, this particular disadvantage is probably less serious than it appears at first sight. The basic argument in favor of approaching price theory from a broader point of view, however, is that such a procedure directs our attention to areas of inquiry which are interesting for their own sake and which may bear fruit in connection with economic forecasting — presumably the ultimate goal of the positive side of our science.

[16]

Chapter 5

TRADE SPECIALISTS AND MONEY IN AN ONGOING EXCHANGE ECONOMY

Robert W. CLOWER and Daniel FRIEDMAN*

The fact surely is that in modern (capitalist) economies there are, at least, two sorts of markets. There are markets where prices are set by producers; and for those markets, which include a large part of the markets for industrial products, the fixprice assumption makes good sense. But there are other markets, 'flexprice' or speculative markets, in which prices are still determined by supply and demand ... What we [as macroeconomists] need is a theory in which both fixprice and flexprice markets have a place.

Hicks (1974, pp. 23–24)

1. Introduction

Even in 'flexprice' markets, some sort of institutional structure is necessary to transform amorphous 'supply and demand' into publicly announced prices and real-time transactions. The fictitious institution known as the 'Walrasian auctioneer' — an external agent who elicits excess demand schedules from all transactors, aggregates them, and computes and announces market-clearing prices, but ignores the assignment[1] of actual exchange partners — is a great convenience to theorists but provides little insight into the performance of actual flexprice markets, such as those for metals, grains, or financial assets. In actuality price announcements and arrangements for transactions in these markets are typically made by *trade specialists* of some sort, such as brokers, dealers or middlemen.

To what extent do ongoing markets organized by trade specialists yield Walrasian outcomes? In particular, do relative prices tend towards competitive (i.e., Walrasian) equilibrium values? In a decentralized monetary economy with markets organized by trade specialists, does the price level adjust proportionately with the stock of money? If one can't obtain positive answers to these questions, a considerable part of received economic theory becomes doubtful. On the other hand, if positive answers are forthcoming, one is then

---

*Department of Economics, University of California, Los Angeles, CA, and Economics Board of Studies, University of California, Santa Cruz, respectively.
[1]A non-trivial problem even at known market-clearing prices, see Ostroy and Starr (1974).

better equipped to proceed with Hicks's suggestion for reconstructing macro-economic theory.

In seeking answers to these questions, we focus in this paper on how the transactions structure (trading specialists and money) affects the existence, efficiency and dynamic stability of equilibrium in a many-goods economy. Consequently, we offer only a cursory treatment of other possibly important aspects of markets. We will take as given the existence and general characteristics of the specialist traders who maintain inventories and adjust prices, and we shall ignore such interesting issues as why specialists exist in some markets but not in others,[2] and how they acquire and process information.

For simplicity our models employ strong but standard assumptions on household preferences (mostly to avoid the nuisance of 'corner solutions') and are set in discrete time. Likewise, we omit production from consideration and do not deal explicitly with uncertainty or intertemporal choice. Finally, we omit some formal details and proofs [the interested reader can find these in Friedman (1982ab)].

After a brief review of the standard discrete time Walrasian model of pure exchange in section 2, we present our basic conceptual experiment for the exchange and price adjustment process, and indicate how specialists can be introduced into the formal model. We then describe the dynamics of the resulting economy in the neighbourhood of equilibrium. This microdynamic barter model (MBM) is reminiscent of earlier treatments of multiple-market dynamic price adjustment processes [Samuelson (1947, pp. 269 ff), Clower and Bushaw (1954)], but it has a more explicit conceptual basis and yields slightly sharper conclusions.

Section 3 outlines a more elaborate model, featuring monetary exchange. We argue that certain undesirable features of the barter model can be removed if we introduce a medium of exchange, and we then outline how a monetary microdynamical model (MMM) can be formalized. Section 4 analyzes the adjustment properties of our model following moderate 'shocks', both real and nominal. It turns out that fairly mild conditions suffice for the economy to be stable and for money to be neutral. Finally, section 5 of the paper discusses some shortcuts we have taken, some implications of our model, and directions for further work.

2. The standard Walrasian model and a barter microdynamic model

Our benchmark is the standard discrete time Walrasian model. It consists

---

[2]Also, one notes that specialists play slightly different roles in different markets. For instance, in foreign exchange markets, brokers don't hold inventory ('open positions') but dealers do; brokers are price takers in lumber markets [Balderston and Hoggatt (1962)] but price makers in grain markets. We will employ a fairly general specification of the specialist's role in the present study.

of a finite set of households indexed $j = 1, \ldots, n$, each characterized by unchanging preferences U^j over the periodic endowments $s^j(t)$ in a finite number of goods $i = 1, \ldots, l$ (none of which is stored). Via the standard[3] constrained optimization problem, we arrive at the vector of net trades $x^j(t)$ $= d^j(t) - s^j(t)$ desired by household j, once prices $p(t)$ are specified. By construction, the budget constraint (or Say's principle)

$$p(t) \cdot x^j(t) = \sum_{i=1}^{l} p_i(t) x_i^j(t) = 0,$$

holds for each household j. Walrasian equilibrium (WE) may then be defined as a price vector $p(t)$ and a set of desired net trades (i.e., excess demand vectors) $x^j(t)$ corresponding to $p(t)$ such that the net trades balance, i.e., sum to the zero vector $x^T(t) \equiv \sum_j x^j(t) = 0$. Well-known theorems assert the existence and Pareto-efficiency of WE under quite general assumptions regarding preferences and endowments. Under more restrictive assumptions, one can establish the uniqueness of WE [up to a scale factor in p; see Arrow and Hahn (1972)].

We are now ready to introduce trade specialists — agents who maintain stocks of inventory from which they can accommodate households' desired net trades, and who adjust prices so as to maintain control over their inventory. In our underlying conceptual experiment, each period t represents a market day. In the morning of day t, the specialists post prices $p(t)$ computed on the previous evening as described below. Households observe these prices, receive their endowments, and compute their desired net trades $x^j(t)$ as in the Walrasian model. In the afternoon, the households show up in no particular order at the market place with the goods they wish to 'sell' (those for which the desired net trade is negative) and shopping lists of goods they wish to 'buy'. After checking that the value of goods to be bought is no greater than the value of goods to be sold, the specialists allow a household to enter the market. In the market, there are l storage bins, one for each good. Each household places its 'sold' goods in the appropriate bins and withdraws its 'bought' goods from their bins, in the desired quantities (we assume away possible outages for the moment). When these transactions are complete, the household leaves the market place. In the evening, households consume their goods and enjoy their leisure. Specialists note how the *ending* level in each bin $S_i(t + 1)$ differs from (a) the *beginning* or previous level $S_i(t)$, and (b) the *desired* level for the next day $D_i(t + 1)$. They then decide on the price adjustment for the next day, $\Delta p_i(t) = p_i(t + 1) - p_i(t)$ according to some given rule based on these differences.

---

[3]Throughout this paper we assume for convenience that households satisfy standard strong assumptions to guarantee an interior solution $d^j(t)$ to the optimization problem that is a differentiable function of its parameters, e.g., the assumptions $s^j \gg 0$, U^j smooth, strictly convex and monotone, and a strong boundary condition, suffice.

To formalize this story, we can retain the Walrasian specification of households, and reinterpret the goods as non-perishable, the specialists having unique access to a storage technology (assumed costless in this section). Collectively, specialists observe the aggregate excess (flow) demand vector[4] $x(t) \equiv x^T(p(t)) = S(t) - S(t+1)$ and know their own excess (stock) demand vector $X(t) \equiv D(t+1) - D(t)$. Other information available to specialists can be incorporated in specifying desired stock holdings D. Therefore it is reasonable and quite general to specify the price adjustment rule for the ith good as $p_i(t+1) = p_i(t) + f_i(x(t), X(t))$. If f_i depends only on the ith components of x and X (i.e., if the specialist for good i looks only at his own bin, and not at excess demand for goods $j \neq i$), then the pricing rule f_i is called *simple*; otherwise we call f_i *sophisticated*. In any case, a specification of specialist behavior via f_i and D_i completes the formal model, which we shall refer to as a *Microdynamic Barter Model* (MBM). We now turn to dynamics.

In general, a discrete-time *dynamical process* is a rule that assigns the next period's state as a function of this period's state. In the present instance, the *state* on day t of our barter model consists of a pair of positive vectors $p(t)$ and $S(t)$, specifying prices and initial inventories. Given today's state $(p(t), S(t))$, we obtain tomorrow's state $(p(t+1), S(t+1)) = F(p(t), S(t))$ from the household sector's (Walrasian) excess demand vector $x(t) \equiv x^T(p(t))$ and the pricing rules f; viz., $p(t+1) = p(t) + f(x(t), X(t))$ and $S(t+1) = S(t) - x(t)$. For the rest of this paper, we will assume that D is positive and constant,[5] that $f(0,0) = 0$ (i.e., if purchases equal sales and actual inventories equal desired inventories, the prices don't change), and that each f_i is twice differentiable and non-degenerate at $(0,0)$; thus one obtains a tractable closed model.

The appropriate notion of equilibrium for such a MBM is that of a rest state, i.e., a state $(\bar{p}, \bar{S})$ such that if $(p(0), S(0)) = (\bar{p}, \bar{S})$, then $(p(t), S(t)) = (\bar{p}, \bar{S})$ for all $t \geq 0$. It is easy to see that a necessary and sufficient condition is that $(\bar{p}, \bar{S})$ is invariant under F, i.e., $F(\bar{p}, \bar{S}) = (\bar{p}, \bar{S})$; we refer to such states as (Barter) Steady-state Equilibria (BSE). A fixed point theorem could be invoked to prove existence of BSE, but we think it more edifying to establish a 'correspondence principle'. Each MBM contains within it a Walrasian model (viz., its household sector) and it is not hard to see that the WE of this Walrasian model stand in 1:1 correspondence with BSE of the MBM. The argument is simply that if in the MBM inventories are all at desired levels, and prices at WE values so desired net trades aggregate to zero, then prices will remain steady and so will inventories; hence, we have a BSE. On the other hand, if we are at a BSE, then inventories remain

---

[4]That $X^T = S(t) - S(t+1)$ assumes no stock outages; presumably $D(t)$ is chosen largely to make outages extremely unlikely. We will assume away outages for the next few paragraphs.

[5]This is not as severe a restriction as it might seem. One can show that a model with D_i depending on last period desired purchases and sales [probably the most relevant information, see Friedman (1982b)] yields a model that is essentially equivalent to one with constant D_i.

constant, so (outages aside) we must have desired net trades which aggregate to zero; hence, we have a WE. Thus existence and efficiency[6] of BSE are inherited from the Walrasian model.

A more difficult and perhaps more important task is to find conditions that guarantee the stability of BSE. Stability is clearly a crucial issue: if a BSE isn't stable, then it has little economic significance in an economy subject to even the mildest of shocks. We say that a BSE $(\bar{p}, \bar{S})$ is *globally stable* if, for an arbitrary initial state $(p(0), S(0))$, we have $p(t) \to \bar{p}$ and $S(t) \to \bar{S}$ as $t \to \infty$. If this convergence holds only for initial states in some neighbourhood of the BSE, it is *locally stable*.

Global stability is too much to hope for in our barter model for two reasons. The first has to do with the indeterminancy of the price level. Since p is never unique in the Walrasian model, there can be no unique BSE; but it is easy to see that the definition of global stability entails uniqueness. This problem can be eliminated at the cost of minor technical complications by an appropriate normalization of p. The second difficulty is more fundamental: our dynamical process is not well defined if outages occur, i.e., if $x_i^T(t) > S_i(t)$ for some good i. Such states can't always be avoided; indeed, one would *expect* an outage in good i if the initial price $p_i(0)$ is sufficiently low. Hence our process is not even globally defined, much less globally stable. On the other hand, it is clear that outages won't occur if we begin in a sufficiently small neighborhood of a locally stable BSE.

Local stability of a BSE $(\bar{p}, \bar{S})$ evidently depends on the price elasticities of aggregate demand at $\bar{p}$ as well as on the price adjustment rules; the former can be represented by the matrix A of partial derivatives of aggregate excess (flow) demand with respect to prices, evaluated at $\bar{p}$,

$$A = \left(\frac{\partial x_i^T}{\partial p_k} \bigg|_{p = \bar{p}} \right).$$

We have been able to prove two stability results for our microdynamic barter model. Apart from some technical qualifications having to do with price level indeterminancy, the first says that if we allow sophisticated pricing rules, then specialists can (locally) stabilize *any* BSE at which the A-matrix is non-singular. The second result says that if the Hicksian matrix A is symmetric (or nearly so) and negative definite at a BSE then simple pricing rules (in fact, wide families of simple pricing rules) can ensure the local stability of the BSE. Negative definiteness of A has been a well-known condition for stability results in economics since Samuelson (1947). It may be interpreted as the requirement that own price effects are normal and not counteracted by cross-price effects. Near symmetry may be thought of as

[6]That is, households' marginal rates of substitution all coincide with relative prices.

small income effects. Non-singularity is a much weaker condition that may be interpreted as saying no bundle of other goods is a perfect substitute for any given good.

To summarize, our MBM has several attractive features. By introducing only the single institution of trade specialists, we are able to come up with an ongoing process in which notional trading plans can be realized through logistically plausible transactions and in which prices can be adjusted over time in a simple fashion. The steady states of our process correspond precisely to the equilibria of our Walrasian benchmark, and these steady states are locally stable under a wide range of intuitively plausible conditions.

The MBM with sophisticated price adjustment rules can be viewed as a concrete version of the 'central supermarket' model of Clower–Leijonhufvud (1975), and provides strong verification of the conjecture (p. 186) 'Except in circumstances where trader reactions to price variation are both erratic and violent ... it should be possible for the trade coordinator to devise some strategy of price adjustment that would ensure stability'. Indeed, we are able to prove that our specialists can manage even 'erratic and violent' reactions; all we require (given our standard assumptions on preferences, etc.) is that traders regard the goods as distinct.[7]

However, our MBM still has several major defects. We have already noted that outages can be expected if the economy is perturbed too far from equilibrium, but the logic of our model precludes any simple way of dealing with outages. The usual household constrained maximization problem (whose solution yields desired net trades) is inappropriate if desired trades might not be realized. Hence there is no direct way to define F globally. Another defect is that our barter exchange process is centralized, in that we require the services of some specialist to check that each household takes away goods from the marketplace whose value does not exceed the value of goods brought to the marketplace. Also, the maintenance of some fixed price level would seem to require the efforts of a specialist who looks at all prices and renormalizes them. Thus even with simple pricing rules, the MBM can't really be decentralized.

3. A monetized microdynamic model (MMM)

We are hardly the first to find that money can solve many of our problems (at best we can claim that our problems are novel). The introduction of a commodity called 'money' (or 'cash') as the medium of exchange and as a store of value allows us to define an exchange process that is more

---

[7]More precisely, that A has maximum rank. In defining A, we use strong standard assumptions on preferences to ensure the differentiability of demand functions. If one is willing to tolerate more complicated statements and proofs, there seems to be no obstacle to relaxing these assumptions.

decentralized than our barter process and that can be defined globally. The key point is that in monetized exchange, each transaction is quid pro quo; that is, each component of a household's net trade is accompanied by an offsetting cash flow. Given quid pro quo, we need no longer postulate a centralized checkpoint for verifying households' budget constraints. Likewise outages need not upset household plans to any great extent, so we can hope to define a dynamical process globally. There is also reason to believe the price level will take care of itself, at least in the long run.

Let us first see that happens to our conceptual experiment when we introduce money. As before, specialists post prices for their goods each morning. Households receive their daily endowments of goods, check their cash balances carried forward from the previous day, and plan today's purchases and sales. To ensure that their plans are robust with respect to possible disappointments due to outages, we impose a *finance constraint* that the value of each household's purchases does not exceed its cash balances.[8] Consequently we need not and do not require the budget constraint that the value of planned purchases do not exceed the value of planned sales of goods.

In the afternoon, householders travel around to various specialists, buying and selling goods for money at the posted prices. Each specialist accommodates his customers if possible, but turns away buyers if and when his bin of goods is empty, and sellers if and when his cash balances are exhausted. In the evening, households consume their purchases and any unsold endowments, and update their cash balances. Specialists check their bin levels and compute price adjustments as in the previous model.

It turns out to be convenient for modeling purposes to complicate this conceptual experiment a bit. Specialists may charge a 'spread' between buying and selling prices; specifically, the price p_i^+ at which a household can purchase a good may exceed the price p_i^- at which it can sell that good by some fixed percentage $\sigma_i > 0$. We also allow for the possibility that specialists may return 'excess' cash at the end of the day to 'shareholder' households.

We now sketch how this story can be formalized. Each household (index j suppressed for the moment) is characterized by an endowment of goods $s = (s_1, \ldots, s_n)$, and by preferences described by a (Patinkinesque) utility function U defined over consumption $d = (d_1, \ldots, d_n)$ and net cash income y, with current prices p and cash balances M possibly serving as shift parameters. The commodity M differs from the n 'goods' commodities in that it can be stored by households, and is neither produced nor consumed. U is

---

[8]The finance constraint can be rationalized with a Kohn (1981) story that households consist of a wife (who, for a change, let's say, sells labor or other goods) and a husband (who does all the shopping); the assumption that the husband and wife do not meet during the working day yields the finance constraint. One should also note that a finance constraint is more natural than a budget constraint in a continuous-time setting.

assumed homogeneous of degree zero in the 'nominal' variables y, p and M. An example, which we call the Modified Cobb–Douglas (MCD)[9] is

$$U(d, y; M) = \sum_{i=1}^{l} a_i \log d_i + y/M,$$

where $\sum_i a_i \leqq 1$, $a_i > 0$.

The household chooses its desired consumption $d^*(t)$ by maximizing U subject to the finance constraint $m^+ \leqq M(t)$, where

$$m^+ = p^+ \cdot (d-s)^+ = \sum_{i=1}^{l} p_i^+ \max\{0, d_i - s_i\}$$

is the planned gross expenditure required to obtain d, given ask prices $p^+(t)$ and endowment s. The household's desired net trade is then $x^*(t) = d^*(t) - s$. *Actual* net trade $x(t)$ may differ from $x^*(t)$ if outages occur; in this case some given rationing rule determines $x(t)$.[10] Realized net income for a household then consists of dividends received from specialists less net expenditures, i.e., $y(t) = \pi(t) - m_+(t) - m_-(t)$, where dividends $\pi(t)$ are described below,

$$m_+(t) = p^+ \cdot x^+(t) = \sum_{i=1}^{l} p_i^+ \max\{0, x_i\}$$

is realized gross expenditure, and the absolute value of

$$m_-(t) = p^- \cdot x^-(t) = \sum_{i=1}^{l} p_i^- \min\{0, x_i\}$$

is realized gross sales revenue. End of period cash balances for the household then are (reverting now to the use of the household index j) $M^j(t+1) = M^j(t) + y^j(t)$.

We also need to characterize specialists' behavior with respect to cash balances, $M_i(t)$. The specialist's actual net cash revenue in period t is

$$NCR_i(t) = p_i^+(t) \cdot x_i^{+T}(t) + p_i^-(t) \cdot x_i^{-T}(t).$$

---

[9]Those who don't like to see cash balances M look 'bad' should feel free to use the utility function $V = (M/P)U$, where P is some appropriate price index; U and V yield the same demand functions.

[10]We won't need to employ specific rationing rules in this paper, but certain extensions of our analysis (e.g., to effective demand failures) would require them. Basically, any rationing rule will do, as long as (a) it doesn't provide incentives for households to misrepresent their desired trades (thus rationing proportional to x^* is not acceptable), (b) no component of x exceeds that of x^* in absolute value, or differs in sign, and (c) $x = x^*$ if feasible. An example of an acceptable rule is 'rationing by priority': households with lower indices j are allowed to transact first.

Occasional rationing ensures that $M_i(t) + NCR_i(t) \geq 0$ for all t. Presumably, NCR will ordinarily be positive, since $p_i^+ \geq p_i^-$, while $x_i^{+T} \simeq |x_i^{-T}|$ near equilibrium. Hence we need some rule for distributing excess cash accumulated by specialists. We hypothesize that there is some desired cash balance $M^*(t)$ for each specialist i, possibly depending on prices and purchases and sales volume, and that balances in excess of $M^*(t)$ are paid out to shareholders (households).

$$\pi_i(t) = (M_i(t) + NCR_i(t) - M_i^*(t))^+,$$

so next period's cash balance

$$M_i(t+1) = M_i(t) + NCR_i(t) - \pi_i(t),$$

is bounded between 0 and $M^*(t+1)$. Finally, we close the MMM by assuming some fixed share distribution $\theta_i = (\theta_i^1, \dots, \theta_i^n)$, where $\theta_i^j \geq 0$, $\sum_{j=1}^n \theta_i^j = 1$, and $i = 1, \dots, l$.

Hence,

$$\pi^j(t) = \sum_{i=1}^l \theta_i^j \pi_i(t)$$

is the dividend payment received by the jth household.

We shall retain the assumptions on the price-adjustment rules f_i from the previous model, and also postulate (for decentralization) that each is *simple*.

We noted at the beginning of this section that certain problems regarding household behavior can be solved by the introduction of money. On the other hand, money can create new problems, in this case for specialists. The quid pro quo nature of monetary exchange allows us to regard each specialist as an autonomous agent, attempting in some sense to maximize profits. (Thus, for instance, D_i might best be thought of as arising from balancing marginal inventory storage costs against the marginal convenience yield of inventories in facilitating trade.) To properly pose an optimization problem for specialists, however, requires a lot of structure — inventory storage costs, outage penalties, information structures, stochastic specification of household arrivals and desired trades, etc. — that is extraneous to our present purposes. Hence we content ourselves here with the plausible but general rules listed above, and refer the interested reader to Friedman (1982b) for further discussion and a derivation of rules conforming to present assumptions from a simplified (but still fairly messy) optimal control problem.

4. Local dynamics

The monetary model laid out in the previous section gives rise to a dynamical system that differs in crucial ways from that of our MBM. First, a *state* of our MMM is now a *trio* of non-negative vectors p, S and M, where p and S are as in the MBM and $M = (M_1, \ldots, M_I, M^1, \ldots, M^n)$ represents the distribution of the economy's stock of money among specialists and households. Our specifications evidently yield a *globally* defined dynamical system G, with $(p(t+1), S(t+1), M(t+1)) = G(p(t), S(t), M(t))$. Note that G conserves the *total money stock* $M_T^T(t) = \sum_{i=1}^{I} M_i(t) + \sum_{j=1}^{n} M^j(t)$, i.e., $M_T^T(t) = M_T^T(0)$ for all $t \geq 0$. A *steady-state equilibrium* for our monetized model (MSE) is a fixed point $(\bar{p}, \bar{s}, \bar{M})$ of G.

One can again use a 'correspondence principle' to establish the existence of such equilibria, although the matter is more delicate than before. From E_0, a given MMM with $\sigma = 0$, one can extract a Walrasian model by suitably restricting the domain of the household utility functions, while retaining the household endowments. For each WE price vector $\bar{p}$ of that Walrasian model, one can find vectors $\bar{M}$ and $\bar{S}$ such that $(\bar{p}, \bar{S}, \bar{M})$ is a no-rationing MSE of E_0, and employs the same net trades as the WE. Let E_σ be a MMM exactly like E_0 except that $\sigma > 0$. One then can find a no-rationing MSE of E_σ corresponding to $(\bar{p}, \bar{S}, \bar{M})$. For $\sigma = 0$, these MSE are 'efficient' in the sense that all households have the same marginal rates of substitution of goods for income and these coincide with prices, i.e., $MRS_{iy}^j = \bar{p}_i$ for all j and i. For $\sigma > 0$ we only have approximate efficiency in the sense that $\bar{p}_i \equiv \bar{p}_i^- \leq MRS_{iy}^j \leq \bar{p}_i^+ = (1 + \sigma_i)\bar{p}_i$.

Taking these existence and efficiency results as established, we shall be concerned for the rest of this section with the dynamics of an MMM, E, in a neighborhood of $(\bar{p}, \bar{S}, \bar{M})$, a no-rationing[11] MSE. In particular, we will investigate conditions under which the economy returns to our MSE following various types of 'shocks'. By a *temporary real shock*, we mean an exogenous shift at $t = 0$ in the inventory stocks; i.e., initial conditions for the dynamics are $p(0) = \bar{p}$, $M(0) = \bar{M}$, but $S(0) \neq \bar{S}$. A *permanent* real shock would consist of a change in household endowments or preferences (or perhaps a change in specialists' markup). We can describe such a shock by means of initial conditions that may have constituted an MSE for the original pre-shock economy, but are not an MSE of our given (post shock) economy, E. That is, for a permanent real shock, we generally have $p(0) \neq \bar{p}$, $S(0) \neq \bar{S}$ (perhaps), and $M(0) \neq \bar{M}$, although $M_T^T(0) = \bar{M}_T^T$. The MMM economy E is *locally stable* at $(\bar{p}, \bar{S}, \bar{M})$ if $(p(t), S(t), M(t)) \to (\bar{p}, \bar{S}, \bar{M})$ as $t \to \infty$ for all sufficiently mild[12] real shocks.

[11] That is, $x^* = x$ at $(\bar{p}, \bar{S}, \bar{M})$. It turns out that MSE with rationing $(x^* \neq x)$ are also possible.
[12] Technically, 'mild' means there is some given open neighborhood N of $(\bar{p}, \bar{S}, \bar{M})$ such that $(p(0), S(0), M(0)) \in N$.

Again, the local stability analysis for E is similar to that for a corresponding MBM but a bit more delicate. In general, stability of a MSE requires that the 'real sector' of the economy be stable, i.e., the pricing rule stabilizes demand in the sense of section 4 above, given the matrix[13]

$$A_\sigma = \left(\frac{\partial x_i^{*T}}{\partial p_k^-} \bigg|_{p=\bar{p}} \right).$$

Restricting our attention to simple pricing rules, we must therefore rule out aggregate demand functions that yield eigenvalues of A_σ with positive real part — roughly speaking, we rule out the possibility that there is a basket of goods with the Giffen property.

Stability of the real sector does not suffice, however. If the composition of aggregate demand responds sensitively to the distribution of M_T^T, we could have a self-reinforcing process wherein an initial shock causes a shift in demand, which induces a shift in income that intensifies the demand shift as cash balances adjust. The simplest way to eliminate this possibility is to assume that distributional effects are small, i.e., x^T is relatively insensitive to small changes in M, for M_T^T fixed.[14] Finally, to avoid price level stickiness due to reallocations of M_T^T from households to specialists (or vice versa), we make the convenient assumption[15] that specialists' desired cash balances are proportional to their prices, ceteris paribus. We refer to this as *homogeneous desired balances*. This assumption will serve its purpose if specialists have positive payout in equilibrium, i.e., if $\sigma \gg 0$.

Given these additional conditions, an extension of the local stability proposition for the MBM may be established. Specifically,[16]

Proposition 1 (Local stability). A no-rationing steady-state equilibrium $(\bar{p}, \bar{S}, \bar{M})$ of an MMM economy E_σ with $\sigma \gg 0$, is locally stable if the following conditions are satisfied:

(a) *The pricing rule f is stabilizing given A_σ,*
(b) *distributional effects are sufficiently small, and*
(c) *specialists have homogeneous desired balances.*

A similar analysis applies to nominal shocks. An exogenous shift at $t=0$ in the distribution of cash balances or in prices is a *temporary nominal shock*,

---

[13]A_σ is not well defined on a set of measure zero in M and p, a fact we can safely ignore here. See Friedman (1982ab).
[14]Distributional effects will be *zero* under many common assumptions, e.g., identical homothetic preferences.
[15]It appears that in the absence of this assumption there may be shifts in the MSE, greatly complicating the statement of propositions 1 and 2.
[16]Propositions 1 and 2 below are proved in Friedman (1982ab, proposition 5).

i.e., $p(0) \neq \bar{p}$, $M(0) \neq \bar{M}$ but $S(0) = S$ and $M_T^T(0) = M_T^T$. A nominal shock is *permanent* if $M_T^T(0) \neq \bar{M}_T^T$. The local stability result above establishes that mild temporary nominal shocks have only transient effects, but the case of permanent nominal shocks requires a little further analysis.

Given that specialists and households have homogeneous cash balances (the latter being a consequence of the maintained assumption of degree zero homogeneity of preferences), it is easy to see that we have money neutrality in the sense that $(c\bar{p}, \bar{S}, c\bar{M})$ is a MSE if $(\bar{p}, \bar{S}, \bar{M})$ is, for any $c > 0$. However, even an equiproportionate change in cash balances does not result in an *immediate* shift to the new MSE; unless we suspend our price adjustment rules,[17] the best we can hope for is that $p(t) \to c\bar{p}$ as $t \to \infty$ following an exogenous shift of $\bar{M}$ to $c\bar{M}$ at $t = 0$. The more interesting case of a permanent nominal shock which is *not* equiproportionate must a fortiori be analyzed in asymptotic terms.

Let $(\bar{p}, \bar{S}, \bar{M})$ now refer to an MSE of E *before* the shock, and for some $c > 0$ suppose the shock consists of an increase in the total money stock of $(c-1)100\%$, i.e., $M_T^T(0) = c\bar{M}_T^T$, with distribution arbitrary. We say that the *asymptotic neutrality property* (ANP) holds if $(p(t), S(t), M(t)) \to (c\bar{p}, \bar{S}, c\bar{M})$ as $t \to \infty$; i.e., if all nominal quantities respond in proportion to the change in the total money stock. Hence our neutrality property is an equilibrium relationship whose validity depends on the stability properties of the economy. Recall that even to obtain stability with respect to real shocks, we required mechanisms that remove 'distortions' in the distribution of the money stock. Hence it is not surprising that these same mechanisms also ensure ANP.

Proposition 2 (Local asymptotic neutrality). *Conditions (a)–(c) of proposition 1 guarantee that ANP also holds for mild permanent nominal shocks at a no-rationing steady-state equilibrium $(\bar{p}, \bar{S}, \bar{M})$ of an MMM economy E_σ with $\sigma \gg 0$.*

Corollary. *The equation of exchange $M_T^T V = PT$ holds asymptotically with constant V and T under the conditions of the propositions.*

The argument for the corollary is as follows. Let $\bar{x}$ be the vector of transactions occurring at $(\bar{p}, \bar{S}, \bar{M})$; for arbitrary x and p, define the index numbers $P = p^+ \cdot \bar{x}^{+T} / \bar{p}^+ \cdot \bar{x}^{+T}$, $T = \bar{p}^+ \cdot x^{+T} / \bar{p}^+ \cdot \bar{x}^{+T}$ for prices and trans-actions, and let $V = (M_T^T)^{-1}$. Following a nominal shock, if ANP holds, we asymptotically reach a new equilibrium $(\bar{p}, \bar{S}, \bar{M}) = (c\bar{p}, \bar{S}, c\bar{M})$. But $\bar{M}_T^T V = \bar{M}_T^T / \bar{M}_T^T = c$, $\bar{T} = 1$ since $\bar{x} = \bar{x}$ (due to homogeneity of demands in M and p),

---

[17]It might make sense to suspend the rules if the precise nature of a forthcoming shock were common knowledge; we prefer to keep the rules and regard the shock as a surprise, the nature of which is only gradually realized.

and $P = (c\bar{p}^+) \cdot \bar{x}^{+T} / (\bar{p}^+ \cdot \bar{x}^{+T}) = c$. Hence we have $\bar{M}_T^T V = \bar{P} T = c$ for constant V and T at the new equilibrium as long as ANP holds.

Our neutrality result is reminiscent of that of Howitt (1974). He posited a price adjustment rule that depended only on excess flow demands in a model without explicit inventories, and hence had rationing except at equilibrium. Under the strong assumption of gross substitutes [see Arrow, Block and Hurwicz (1959), Howitt (1974) extended this assumption to include a real balance effect] and an assumption on the rationing scheme (or alternatively that there were no distribution effects), he used a system of differential equations approximating his model's discrete time dynamics and demonstrated global asymptotic neutrality. Our proposition 2 can be viewed as an extension of Howitt's result to an economy with a more general price adjustment process and weaker assumptions on excess demand. We obtain only local neutrality because our assumptions allow for multiple equilibria.

5. Discussion

We have shown that it is possible to model a logistically plausible exchange process in which trading plans can normally be realized even when the plans are not mutually consistent. We have also specified decentralized real-time adjustment processes for prices and stocks of goods (and money), and explained some simple stability and neutrality results. Before presenting some final perspectives, a brief discussion of some of our modeling short-cuts may be in order.

In our models we employed only one specialist for each good. We really have in mind a situation in which many specialists compete in selling each good (or closely related goods), so arbitrage would enforce essentially unified prices. In that case, any spread $\sigma > 0$ should reflect specialists' costs of storing and transacting. It is not easy to model these activities explicitly, especially if the economy as a whole is adjusting, but it would be desirable to derive specialists' desired inventory levels, cash balances, and pricing rules from optimizing behavior in a continuous time stochastic setting. Friedman (1982b) begins this task.

As a second shortcut, we have followed Patinkin in putting money (cash income in our case) directly into the utility function. Of course, we really believe that households value current income only to the extent that it enhances future consumption opportunities. It does so in our model for two logically distinct reasons: cash is the only store of value for households and, given the finance constraint and updating rules for $M(t+1)$, it should be regarded as the sole means of payment. Again it would be desirable to pose an appropriate intertemporal stochastic optimization problem that incorporates these roles, whose solution would yield indirect single period utility functions of the sort we have postulated.[18]

[18]See Howitt (1974) and Grandmont (1984) for a discussion of these matters.

We do not believe, however, that the local dynamics we have discussed here are at all sensitive to our shortcuts. Our existence results are obtained from quite general 'correspondence' principles, and the local stability and neutrality results arise from a study of the *linearized* total excess demand, pricing rules, etc. at a steady-state equilibrium. Given the quite general specification of these functions, it seems clear that they will include the linearized versions of functions derived from more fully articulated optimization problems.

Our analysis generally supports the view that the basic (static) Walrasian model is a reasonable approximation to the long-run tendencies of an ongoing 'flexprice' market organized by trade specialists. Of course, our propositions apply only to 'mild shocks' that do not cause any outages (inventory stock outages or cash outages) and consequent rationing. The MMM admits adjustment paths (following 'severe shocks') that exhibit these inefficiencies over a prolonged transitory period,[19] so the model can exhibit something akin to Leijonhufvud's (1973) 'effective demand failures' and 'corridor effects'. We have not emphasized such phenomena here because we believe that a proper understanding of them requires an examination of 'fixprice markets' (such as that for labor) and more sophisticated financial arrangements than direct cash-for-goods spot markets. Clearly much work remains to be done before one can construct a theory of the sort called for by Hicks, but in describing the dynamic interactions of individual agents in terms of a simple institutional structure, we believe we have taken a crucial first step.

[19]Preliminary results suggest that these effective demand failure equilibria can be asymptotically stable if $\sigma = 0$, but are unstable if $\sigma \gg 0$. Hence the presumption is that our economies *eventually* return to some sort of no-rationing MSE following severe shocks.

References

Arrow, K.J. and F.H. Hahn, 1972, General competitive analysis (Holden-Day, San Francisco, CA).

Arrow, Block and Hurwicz, 1959, On the stability of competitive equilibrium, II, Econometrica 26, 522–552.

Balderston, F.E. and A.C. Hoggatt, 1962, Simulation of market processes (University of California Press, Berkeley, CA).

Clower, Robert W., 1967, A reconstruction of the microfoundations of monetary theory, Western Economic Journal 6, 1–9.

Clower, Robert W., 1975, Reflections on the Keynesian perplex, Zeitschrift für Nationalökonomie 35, no. 1, 1–24.

Clower, Robert W., 1977, The anatomy of monetary theory, American Economic Review 67, no. 1, 206–212.

Clower, Robert W. and D.W. Bushaw, 1954, Price determination in a stock-flow economy, Econometrica 22, no. 3, 328–343.

Clower, Robert W. and Peter W. Howitt, 1978, The transactions theory of the demand for money: A reconsideration, Journal of Political Economy 86, 449–466.

Clower, Robert W. and Axel Leijonhufvud, 1975, The coordination of economic activities: A Keynesian perspective, American Economic Review 65, no. 2, 182–188.

Friedman, Daniel, 1982a, Two microdynamic models of exchange, UCLA mimeo., April, forthcoming in Journal of Economic Behavior and Organization.

Friedman, Daniel, 1982b, Specialist optimization problems, UCLA working paper, July.

Grandmont, J.M., 1984, Money and value (Cambridge University Press, NY).

Hicks, J.R., 1974, The crisis in Keynesian economics (Blackwell, Oxford).

Howitt, Peter, 1974, Stability and the quantity theory, Journal of Political Economy 82, no. 1, 133–151.

Kohn, Meir, 1981, In defense of the finance constraint, Economic Inquiry, 19, no. 2, 177–195.

Leijonhufvud, Axel, 1973, Effective demand failures, Swedish Economics Journal, March.

Ostroy, Joseph M. and R. Starr, 1974, Money and the decentralization of exchange, Econometrica, 38, 233–252.

Patinkin, D., 1956, Money, interest and prices (Harper and Row, New York).

Samuelson, Paul A., 1947, Foundations for economic analysis (Harvard University Press, Cambridge, MA).

PART III

MACROECONOMICS

Part III: Macroeconomics

These selections are in strict chronological order and, except for introductory (1975) essay, all were written and published after I retired from UCLA and took up my present duties at The University of South Carolina. Like the microeconomic essays, and for precisely the same reasons, these selections reflect my exclusive interest in (some might say obsession with) phenomenologically- rather than a methodologically-based economic theory.

17

Zeitschrift für Nationalökonomie 35 (1975), 1—24
© by Springer-Verlag 1975

Reflections on the Keynesian Perplex

By

Robert Clower*, Los Angeles, Calif., U. S. A.

(Received February 12, 1975)

> The Jury had each formed a different view
> (Long before the indictment was read),
> And they all spoke at once, so that none of them knew
> One word that the others had said.
>
> Lewis Carroll, *The Hunting of the Snark*

Critical commentaries on the present state of the arts in economic theory have been appearing with increasing regularity in the professional literature during the past few years[1]. Of course, different writers have voiced very different grounds for discontent. One finds modern theory logically pretentious; another deplores its lack of conceptual unity; another faults it for ideological bias; another for lack of social relevance; another for empirical aridity; another for philosophical shallowness; and so on ... and on, and on. Indeed, the only ascertainable element of unity in the cacaphony of complaint is the conviction apparently shared by all writers that the presently lamentable state of economic theory is not attributable to the intractability of the problems addressed by economists. On first reflection, then, one is tempted to ascribe contemporary discontents to the regrettable but notorious proclivity of economists mutually to

---

* Professor of Economics, University of California. An earlier version of this paper was presented at a meeting of the Austrian Economics Association on March 19, 1974, at which time the author was Visiting Professor at the Institute of Advanced Studies, Vienna.

[1] A full list of contributions to this literature would fill several pages. Here it must suffice to mention only some of the more notable items, namely Hicks (1967 and 1974), Arrow (1967), Hahn (1970 and 1973), Leontief (1971), Shubik (1970), Robinson (1974), Kaldor (1972), Davidson (1972), Kornai (1971), Leijonhufvud (1973), Ostroy (1973), Becker (1974), Johnson (1974).

2   R. Clower:

disparage each others' pursuits[2]. Second thoughts, however, suggest
that the true source of dissatisfaction lies deeper.

Popular opinion and television news commentators to the contrary notwithstanding, professional economists are no more prone
to idle disputation over the fundamentals of their discipline than are
their counterparts in other fields. To be sure, economics has never
lacked for critics since Adam Smith elevated it to the status of a
separate discipline in 1776. All the same, the first concerted attack
on prevailing orthodoxy by an acknowledged leader *from within*
the economics profession was that mounted by J. M. Keynes in the
1930's — the so-called Keynesian Revolution. As is now generally
acknowledged, the Keynesian Revolution was abortive[3]. Its intended
target was the foundations of received doctrine[4]. Its main impact,
however, has been not upon the foundations but rather upon the
superstructure of economic theory[5]. Thus, what now appears to some
as the outbreak of a novel strain of intellectual disorder is, in truth,
nothing more than a renewal in unfamiliar guise of the same malaise
that Keynes sought unsuccessfully to diagnose and treat some
forty years ago[6].

Such, in brief, is my explanation of the presently unsettled and
uncertain state of economic theory. My purpose in the pages that
follow is to elaborate upon this theme. Much of the discussion is
correspondingly retrospective in orientation. In the concluding sections of the paper, however, I shall go beyond the question, "How
did we get where we are?", and attempt to deal constructively with
the currently more important question: "Where do we go from
here?"

I. Keynes and the Neo-Classics

The intellectual authority of Neoclassical economics and, more
specifically, of Marshall and his school had ceased to have significant
pragmatic justification long before Keynes came on the scene. The
rapid pace of European and American industrialization and urbani-
zation in the century preceding World War I and, accompanying

---

[2] Cf. Edgeworth (1925), Vol. 1, p. 11 and Vol. 2, p. 285; Leijonhufvud (1973*), pp. 327—328.

[3] The reasons are fully documented in Leijonhufvud's influential
writings (Leijonhufvud, 1967, 1968, 1969, 1973).

[4] See the Preface to Keynes (1936); also Keynes (CW), *13*, pp. 485—487.

[5] See the observations by Leontief in Harris (1947), p. 240; also
Clower (1965) and Leijonhufvud (1967).

[6] Cf. Leijonhufvud (1973), pp. 28—29.

Reflections on the Keynesian Perplex   3

that, the growing role of governmental intervention in social and economic affairs had, by 1920, created a world in which the equilibrium and stability presuppositions of established economic theory — the essential basis for traditional indifference to questions about short-run adjustment processes — were palpably anachronistic. Professional awareness of the growing discrepancy between presumption and reality it most clearly apparent in the business cycle literature of the era, but is reflected also in the burgeoning literature of institutional economics[7], in Knight's classic *Risk, Uncertainty and Profit,* in the famous *Economic Journal* debate of the 1920's on economic progress and increasing returns[8], in the growing literature critical of pure competition[9] and, perhaps most significantly, in the scientifically escapist literature of welfare economics inaugurated by Pigou (when one can find nothing new to say about *what is,* one's fancy easily turns to *what ought to be*)[10]. In plain truth, Neoclassical economics furnished no tools to analyze the overall working of an ongoing economic system[11]; at best, it furnished methods to investigate the behavior of particular markets *within* an ongoing system that could itself be regarded as self adjusting and strongly stable.

So the stage was set for Keynes' *General Theory* well before its appearance in 1936[12]. More accurately, the stage was set not for Keynes and *his* message, but rather for the rapid decline of Marshall and his school and a long-overdue redirection of economic analysis along lines suggested sixty years earlier by Leon Walras. The history of the Keynesian Revolution — more particularly, the reasons why it effectively fizzled out — can be fully appreciated, therefore, only by viewing it as an episode within a broader and ultimately more influential series of doctrinal developments which, for reasons that will soon become evident, I shall refer to as the *Neo-Walrasian Revolution.*

It is customary (and, I think, correct) to regard the *General Theory* as an attempt to construct a theoretical model that would serve to rationalize Keynes' deeply felt conviction that modern capitalist economies tend to adjust *slowly and imperfectly* towards a state in

[7] In the U. S., one thinks mainly of the work of Veblen and Commons in this connection. In Europe, the same kind of work would be called "historical" or "sociological" economics.

[8] For references, see Kaldor (1972).

[9] See Samuelson (1972), pp. 18—51.

[10] Cf. Johnson (1974), p. 5.

[11] Cf. Keynes (1936), p. 260.

[12] See Winch (1969) for more elaborate documentation of this theme.

4   R. Clower:

which all productive resources are fully employed[13]. One might also regard the *General Theory* — and many have so regarded it — as an attack not merely upon the implicit stability presuppositions but also upon the explicit behavioral assumptions of Marshallian *partial process analysis*[14]; but to so regard it would, I believe, be an egregious error. Keynes' intention surely was not to deny the essential validity of Marshall's conception of the economic process. Keynes must rather have intended to offer the world an analytically manageable aggregative version of the kind of *general process analysis* that Marshall himself might have formulated had he ever felt a need explicitly to model the working of the economic system as a whole.

Of course, Marshall never did feel any such need. On the contrary, he went out of his way to deny the practical usefulness of such models in the then existing state of economic science. Marshall's thinly disguised contempt for the work of his distinguished contemporary, Walras, provides evidence enough of his attitude in that regard[15]. Apart from a few scattered remarks in the text and appendices of the *Principles,* Marshall furnished no clues about his own conception of general process analysis. That Marshall had pondered the problem cannot be doubted. That he rejected Walras' formalistic approach to the problem cannot be doubted either[16]. Of all this, Keynes must surely have been aware. We may be quite certain, therefore, that Keynes did *not* view the analysis of the *General Theory* as "Variations on a theme of Walras"[17].

------

[13] The alternative interpretation, to the effect that Keynes sought to deny the existence of *any* forces making for adjustment towards a state of full employment, finds no support in documents published in Keynes (CW), Vols. *13* and *14*. On this, see Patinkin (1975).

[14] I owe the term "process analysis" to my colleague Leijonhufvud. The term is more accurately descriptive of Marshall's method than the more familiar term, "equilibrium analysis".

[15] This observation is based on correspondence between Walras and Marshall reproduced in Jaffee (1965). See also the references to Walras cited in the index to Marshall (1920).

[16] Marshall (1920), pp. 850—852.

[17] A letter from Keynes dated December 9, 1934, (to be published by Hicks in a forthcoming volume of essays in honor of Georgescu-Roegen) is of interest in this connection. It says in part:

"There is one small point which perhaps I may be able to clear up ... You enquire whether or not Walras was supposing that exchanges actually take place at the prices originally proposed when those prices are not equilibrium prices. The footnote which you quote [Keynes refers to p. 345 of Hicks (1934)] convinces me that he assuredly supposed that they did

II. Hicks and the Neo-Walrasians

How is it possible, then, to maintain that developments set in motion by the publication of the *General Theory* can be fully appreciated only by viewing them as part and parcel of a Neo-Walrasian revival? To answer this question, we must think ourselves back, as it were, to the intellectual milieu into which the *General Theory* was projected.

In the mid-1930's, general equilibrium theory was for most economists merely a label for a collection of propositions about the mutual interdependence of economic activities the precise details of which were not worth knowing. The theory then had none of the authority it has since acquired; indeed, it was commonly regarded as little more than an academic exercise in the counting of equations and unknowns even by the elite few who knew something of its details[18]. As for the mass of economists, to them it made as little sense to question the existence of the price system as to question the existence of the universe; why bother to "prove" what was already obvious to anyone with eyes to see? To the rule of ignorance or indifference, however, there were numerous exceptions (especially outside Cambridge, England), and the most notable of these — particularly as concerns the history of the Keynesian Revolution — was J. R. (now Sir John) Hicks.

Hicks began his university career as a mathematics scholar, but turned to economics at the end of his first year at Oxford[19]. Perhaps

---

not take place except at the equilibrium prices. For that is the actual method by which the opening price is fixed on the Paris Bourse even to-day. His footnote suggests that he was aware that the Agents de Change used this method and he regarded that as the ideal system of exchange to which others were approximations. [...]. On page 364 I should readily agree that you prove that Walras' theory of capital is no more open to objection than the usual theory and, indeed, that it is much the same thing. All the same, I shall hope to convince you some day that Walras' theory and all the others along those lines are little better than nonsense!"

Of course, how Keynes *viewed* his book is one thing, what he *wrote* in it is another. On a literal reading of the *General Theory*, it is hard to avoid the impression that the central core of the analysis is just a carelessly executed version of a few-commodity Walrasian model. Thus there is merit in Grossman's contention (Grossman, 1972) that Keynes was a "Keynesian" in the modern sense of that term.

[18] Cf. Hicks (1939), p. 60.

[19] Biographical information is drawn from various sources including personal conversations with Sir John, but comes mainly from Hicks' Nobel Lecture (1973*).

because he never enjoyed the "advantages" of a formal training in economics (his tutor at Balliol College was a military historian!), Hicks approached the study of economic phenomena with a freedom from preconceived ideas and a freshness of outlook that distinguished him sharply from most of his contemporaries. Moreover, he had special gifts as a linguist and powerful mathematical ability. Encouraged to read Pareto's work on general equilibrium theory by a London School of Economics colleague in the late 1920's, he later turned his attention to Walras and other continental writers and, shortly after, began work on *Value and Capital* (published in 1939), the book that was to become the starting point for virtually all subsequent developments of Neo-Walrasian general equilibrium theory.

In common with other leading contributors to the early Neo-Walrasian literature, Hicks began with what seems in retrospect a grossly exaggerated notion of the conceptual purview of general equilibrium theory; *everything* of significant economic interest was — or seemed to be — suitable grist for the Neo-Walrasian mill[20]. So it is not surprising that Hicks, in his 1936 review of the *General Theory* for the *Economic Journal*[21], should have interpreted Keynes' work not as a generalization of Marshallian partial process analysis but rather as a special case of the Neo-Walrasian theory that he was then himself engaged in writing out. The review was not a great success[22]. Some of the Keynesian wine simply did not go well in Walrasian bottles. Keynes himself was particularly annoyed by Hicks' suggestion that the distinction between liquidity-preference and loanable-funds theories of the rate of interest could be reduced to an arbitrary choice between two analytically equivalent ways of writing down the excess demand equations of a general equilibrium system. But Hicks, satisfied with the essential "rigtness" of his vision, continued thinking along the same lines and later produced a disguised Neo-Walrasian version of the Keynes model that not only met with Keynes' quick approval[23] but also established the conceptual framework for virtually all subsequent theoretical contributions to so-called Keynesian Economics. I refer, of course, to Hicks' celebrated paper, "Mr. Keynes and the Classics"[24], the

---

[20] Cf. Samuelson (1974), p. 8.

[21] Hicks (1936), p. 246.

[22] Cf. Hicks (1973), pp. 8—9, and Hicks (1974), pp. 6—7.

[23] See Hicks (1973), pp. 9—10.

[24] This appeared originally in *Econometrica*, 1937, but is conveniently reproduced in Hicks (1967), pp. 126—142.

publication of which marked the beginning of what I have elsewhere called the Keynesian Counterrevolution[25].

No doubt the Neo-Walrasian Revolution might have proceeded along much the same lines that it later followed even without the additional impetus that Hicks imparted to it by explicitly linking his lucid and scholarly account of general equilibrium theory with the rather unscholarly but vastly exciting and "socially relevant" analysis of Keynes' *General Theory*. In my opinion, however, the Neo-Walrasian revival of interest in general equilibrium theory might well have foundered at an early stage on the same reef of professional indifference that sank the original Walrasian ship except that on this occasion the navigators of the vessel could claim that a prime object of their voyage was to sound and chart the newly discovered Keynesian seas[26]. But that is pure conjecture. In actual fact, the links that Hicks forged to connect Keynes' ideas with Neo-Walrasian theory were avidly grasped and held on to by the profession at large, and were not seriously questioned thereafter until Hicks himself raised doubts about their solidity in a review of Don Patinkin's *Money, Interest and Prices* in 1957[27]. As a consequence, what is now called "Keynesian Economics" owes as much or more to the author of *Value and Capital* and "Mr. Keynes and the Classics" as to the author of the *Gerenal Theory of Employment, Interest and Money!*

III. Keynes and the Keynesians

To appreciate the full irony of Hicks' transmogrification of Keynes' analysis, we must look more closely at the conceptual experiments that implicitly underlie the Keynesian and Neo-Walrasian theories, for only in this way can we distinguish clearly between *what the two theories appear to say* and *what they are actually talking about*.

As emphasized above — and as is now generally recognized[28] — Keynes' basic conception of the organization and working of the economic system was Marshallian rather than Walrasian[29]. In the

---

[25] Clower (1965).

[26] See Hicks (1939), pp. 4—5.

[27] Hicks (1957), p. 278. See also Hicks (1974), p. 7.

[28] Useful discussions of this aspect of Keynes' work may be found in Davidson (1972), Patinkin (1975), and Leijonhufvud (1974).

[29] The sharp distinction between Marshall and Walras implied by the terms "Marshallian" and "Walrasian" cannot be justified by reference to their respective writings. The terms provide convenient labels, however,

Marshallian scheme of thought (as in earlier Classical doctrine) the central task of economic science is to provide an intellectually satisfying account of the coordination of economic activities in an ongoing economic system comprised of business firms and households whose informational links with one another are provided by markets in which dealers of various kinds — visible counterparts of Adam Smith's "invisible hand" — stand ready continuously to trade goods for money or money for goods on terms that each trader varies independently in response to forces that impinge directly upon his own working stocks of money and commodity inventories[30].

On this view, the details of individual behavior are too complex to admit of literal modelling, and are of dubious interest in any case since the focus of theoretical analysis is not upon the isolated actions of particular primary agents (households, firms, etc.) but rather upon the average or representative behavior of groups of primary agents as perceived by dealers in different markets. Discussion of standard microtheoretical problems of household and business behavior — by Marshall as well as Keynes — tends accordingly to be vague and, by contemporary standards, unsatisfactory[31]. In Marshallian analysis, economic agents are conceived to be not so much rational as reasonable. Individuals fumble and grope rather than optimize[32]. They are presumed to know little and care less about efficiency except as competition forces them to attend to it. The coordination of economic activities is carried out *within* particular markets by traders (manufacturers and bankers as well as wholesalers, brokers, and retailers) who either do the task effectively or drift into bankruptcy. As for the coordination of activities *among* markets, since that is not anyone's specific concern it may or may not be done well.

The contrast between the Marshallian conception of economic activity and that underlying the Neo-Walrasian literature could hardly be more stark. Neo-Walrasian analysis has no use for the bumbling oafs that populate a Marshallian world. Instead of markets organized to suit the requirements of disparate groups of specialized traders, Neo-Walrasian analysis works with just one grand trading center

---

for two fairly distinct doctrinal perspectives that have played a prominent role in post-Keynesian writings. Cf. Friedman (1953), pp. 89—92; Clower and Due (1972), pp. 22—25.

[30] Cf. Clower and Due (1972), Chaps. 2 and 3; Marshall (1919), Book 2, Chaps. 5—8; Whitaker (1974).

[31] Cf. Samuelson (1972), pp. 22—24.

[32] For further elaboration on this theme, see Leijonhufvud (1975).

where, thanks to the freely provided services of a *deus ex machina* called "the auctioneer", multilateral trades of anything for everything else are potentially open to every economic agent on terms of exchange that are known in advance of any actual trade. The only visible players on the economic stage are primary production and consumption units. The action revolves around alternative conceptual experiments that usually end happily with a scene in which, following many trials and tribulations, the auctioneer (who does his acting off stage) announces to the players that he (or she, or it) has finally managed to discover a set of exchange rates that ensures the collective compatibility of individual production, consumption and trading plans[33]. The curtain then falls, leaving the audience to wonder how, when (and, indeed, if) scheduled trades are subsequently executed[34].

On this view, the rationality of economic agents may be taken for granted, for price information is not only complete but also costless to obtain, and quantity information is irrelevant to anyone but the auctioneer. Optimality and efficiency of individual plans is guaranteed (more accurately, defined) by conventional maximization postulates in conjunction with appropriate subsidiary assumptions about technology and preferences. As for the coordination of economic activities, that is not so much a question to be investigated as a proposition to be proved. That the economic system "works" may be taken for granted, for how could it fail to work when every relevant aspect of individual behavior is costlessly monitored and controlled by a central coordinator[35]?

At first sight, the Marshallian and Neo-Walrasian schemes of thought appear to be utterly incompatible. In truth, they *are* incompatible except in the very special case where attention is restricted to Marshallian states of long-run equilibrium. In this special case, as Schumpeter brilliantly demonstrated more that a half-century ago[36], general equilibrium analysis can be considered to provide an accurate *partial* description of selected aspects of an ongoing economic system. Flow demands equal flow supplies. Commodity and money inventories fluctuate, but *average* values are stationary over any extended interval of time. Prices of particular commodities are the

---

[33] Cf. Newman (1965), pp. 84—86; Howitt (1973*), pp. 489—496.

[34] On this, see especially Veendorp (1970), pp. 3—5, and Ostroy and Starr (1974), pp. 1093—1094.

[35] Cf. Clower and Leijonhufvud (1975).

[36] Schumpeter (1949), Chapter 1.

same for all transactors; and though money changes hands with every exchange transactions, trade proceeds much as if goods were being traded directly for goods without the intervention of money. But this special case is of no use for analyzing short-run disequilibrium adjustment processes; it is useful only for distinguishing between states of the economy that satisfy given criteria for long-run equilibrium and states of the economy that do not. To argue that Neo-Walrasian theory has any bearing on the observable behavior of an economy actually in motion, we should have to regard it as providing a *complete* description of *actual* behavior rather than a *partial* description of *virtual* behavior — and that we surely cannot do. Strictly interpreted, Neo-Walrasian theory is descriptive only of a fairytale world of notional economic activities that bears not the slightest resemblance to any economy of record, past, present or future. It is science fiction, pure and simple — clever and elegant science fiction, no doubt, but science fiction all the same.

IV. The Present Perplex

Granted that the conceptual background of Keynes' work is wholly Marshallian, how is it that Hicks, Samuelson, Lange, Modigliani, Metzler, Patinkin, and most other early interpreters of "the economics of J. M. Keynes" could not only overlook the inherent irrelevance of Neo-Walrasian modes of thought to the questions raised by Keynes, but could also affirm, at least tacitly, the validity of a precisely contrary view? The answer is, I think, straightforward: the logical and empirical implications — and so also the conceptual limitations — of Neo-Walrasian theory were simply not clear to anyone until after the Neo-Walrasian Revolution had pretty well run its course. In the interim, it was only natural for economists generally to proceed on the presumption that general equilibrium theory had no inherent limitations. After all, even quite specialized economic models generally admit of a variety of alternative interpretations; that is to say, it is usually possible to add new variables and behavior relations without having completely to reconstruct the logical foundations of the original model. In mathematics, axiom systems that possess analogous properties are said to be *noncategorical*[37]. That any even moderately "general" economic model should be anything but *noncategorical*, therefore, would hardly occur naturally to any but a very perverse mind. That the elaborate Neo-Walrasian model set out in Hicks' *Value and Capital* might fail

---

[37] See Kershner and Wilcox (1950), pp. 230—231.

Reflections on the Keynesian Perplex 11

to satisfy this condition would have seemed correspondingly incredible to any sensible person at the outset of the Neo-Walrasian Revolution.

It is an open question, indeed, whether the restrictive character of Neo-Walrasian theory would be clearly recognized even today had not the development of the Neo-Walrasian Revolution followed a particular course. Economics is difficult enough without borrowing additional trouble by constantly questioning its conceptual foundations. In this instance, however, there was no need to borrow trouble; trouble came knocking at the door as a direct consequence of an early division of the Neo-Walrasian literature into two relatively distinct branches, both emanating from intellectual roots planted by J. R. Hicks.

The first branch — which starts from Hicks' *Value and Capital* — includes work by such writers as Samuelson, Hurwicz, Arrow, Debreu, McKenzie, Scarf, Hahn and Negishi[38]. It is concerned with the purely logical task of establishing sufficient conditions for the notional "existence and stability"[39] of competitive equilibria in formal systems satisfying the usual assumptions of Neo-Walrasian theory including, specifically, the assumptions of (i) no disequilibrium trading and (ii) no explicit treatment of money[40]. That this line of research had at most a peripheral bearing on any real-world problem was, I think, taken for granted by all who contributed to it, if not by all who read it[41]. The second branch — which starts from Hicks' "Mr. Keynes and the Classics" — is familiarly associated with such names as Lange, Samuelson, Hansen, Modigliani, Tobin, Metzler, Eisner and Patinkin[42]. It deals with the relatively practical task of constructing analytically manageable aggregative models of a monetary economy that will serve not only for purposes of doctrinal exegesis but also as useful guides to applied research and to the formulation of desirable government policies of economic coordination and control. That this line of research had a direct

---

[38] For references, see Negishi (1962), pp. 666—669; also Newman (1965), pp. 124—125.

[39] As Newman has observed (1965, p. 106), the term "convergence" would be more appropriate than the term "stability" in this context. For a colorful but highly instructive account of the process, see Burstein (1968), pp. 201—202.

[40] See Debreu (1959), p. 28; Hahn (1973), pp. 15—16; Veendorp (1974), p. 82, and references cited there.

[41] Cf. Hahn (1973), pp. 3—6.

[42] For references, see Clower (1969), hp. 344—346.

and immediate bearing on real-world problems was, I think, never seriously doubted by anyone who contributed to it, though certainly some who read it (most notably, Milton Friedman) had very serious doubts indeed[43].

The two branches of literature converged in the middle 1950's — and produced a collision of ideas that shattered earlier illusions about the "generality" of Neo-Walrasian general equilibrium theory[44]. The subject matter content and potential empirical significance of the second branch of literature seemed evident. It purported explicitly to deal with an economy that bore at least a family resemblance to economies of record. The subject matter content and significance of the first branch was by no means transparent, but one thing was clear: *the mathematical structure of the models appearing in it was identical with that of models appearing in the second branch.* The conclusion was then inescapable: *either* (i) the assumptions underlying the first and more formal branch of literature were unduly restrictive *or* (ii) serious second thoughts were in order concerning the empirical and doctrinal relevance of the second line of inquiry.

I need not trace the details of the reconsideration that followed from this conclusion[45]. The outcome of the investigation is adequately reflected in the final chapter of Arrow and Hahn's recent and authoritative *General Competitive Analysis* where it becomes evident that the existing body of Neo-Walrasian theory rests upon assumptions that preclude its use for explicit analysis of either disequilibrium trading processes or monetary exchange[46]. Contrary to earlier presumptions, the theory does not admit of a variety of essentially different interpretations. It is categorical rather than non-categorical — closed to extension in certain crucial directions including, specifically, those directions that would permit explicit formal analysis of Keynesian short-run adjustment processes. But these are precisely the kind of processes about which economists must be able to speak with scientific authority if their science is to be anything more than a body of idle speculation and a breeding ground for charlatans and quacks. Hence, the present perplex in economic theory; for if Neo-Walrasian theory is bankrupt — as, for practical purposes, it most surely is — then where do we go from here?

---

[43] Cf. Johnson (1961 and 1971); Friedman (1953), pp. 277—300.

[44] See especially Hicks (1957), Clower (1965), Hahn (1965), Barro and Grossman (1971), Leijonhufvud (1969).

[45] See Leijonhufvud (1969), Hines (1971), Weintraub (1974).

[46] Arrow and Hahn (1972), pp. 366—369.

V. Reconstructing the Foundations

The crucial flaw in Neo-Walrasian theory, as revealed especially by recent work of Ostroy[47], lies in its silence concerning the logistics of exchange — the absence of an explicit account of the execution as distinct from the scheduling of commodity trades. This flaw is an indirect consequence of the standard Neo-Walrasian assumption that trading plans (and actions, if any) are mediated by some kind of central coordinator; for though this assumption does not logically preclude further discussion of the logistics of exchange[48], it effectively sweeps the problem under the rug and so encourages its continued neglect. Accordingly, it appears that a sensible first step towards the formulation of an acceptable theory of an ongoing economy is to dispense with the assumption of a central coordinator and to suppose instead that trade among individual economic agents is a strictly "do it yourself" affair[49]. This procedure is bound to be a hard pill for some to swallow. Without a central coordinator, hitherto harmonious intellectual reveries about smoothly interlocking individual economic activities become waking nightmares. *Who trades what, for which, with whom, where, and when?* At first sight, these questions may well seem to pose insoluble conundrums; but if that were so, how could the same questions be answered in real life, as they most assuredly are?

As Ostroy and Starr (1974, pp. 1097—1098) have shown, a formal solution to these conundrums may be obtained by supposing that some individual agents hold sufficiently large stocks of commodity inventories to permit them to act as exchange intermediaries. This is, of course, the procedure implicitly followed by Marshall in his account of the role of middlemen as links between producer and consumer (Marshall, 1919, pp. 278—280). But it is one thing to be assured that the conundrums at issue can be resolved in principle, another to persuade ourselves that the solution indicated will emerge as a matter of course in an economy where trade is initially organized on a "do it yourself" basis. Specifically, can it be shown that, in such an economy, "natural economic forces" will induce some individual agents to accumulate commodity inventories and to act as middlemen in trades involving other economic agents?

A full answer to this question would require far more space than is available here. Briefly and somewhat loosely, the answer is

---

[47] Ostroy (1973). Also see Veendorp (1979), Kaldor (1972, p. 1248) and Ostroy and Starr (1974).

[48] Cf. Clower and Leijonhufvud (1975).

[49] Cf. Walker (1970), Ostroy (1973).

that middlemen traders will emerge *only if* (but not necessarily *if*) search and other costs associated with trade between individuals are not only positive but also independent (at least in part) of the amounts of commodities traded[50]. Provided that certain other intuitively plausible conditions are met (in particular, that subjective rates of time preference are relatively low for some individuals), it can then be shown that otherwise unexploitable gains from trade can be realized if some individuals accumulate stocks of tradeable commodities and proceed to act as exchange intermediaries[51]. It is a short step from this conclusion to the conjecture that some agents will decide to play just such a role, but a formal proof of this conjecture has yet to be found. As of the present time, therefore, the proposition that a class of middlemen traders will emerge naturally out of a situation in which trade is initially carried out on a strictly individual basis must be regarded as simply a plausible conjecture[52].

For the sake of argument, suppose that the conjecture is true, i. e., suppose that natural economic forces gradually cause an economy without organized facilities for trade to evolve into a "middleman economy" with such facilities. Even so, it does not follow that the organization of trading activity in such an economy will be recognizably "monetary" in character[53]. The development of such highly specialized forms of market organization cannot be accounted for without introducing additional (and very strong) assumptions about technology, preferences, and the physical characteristics of different commodities[54]. At first sight, this result may seem to pose

---

[50] See Clower (1969), pp. 7—14; Hirshleifer (1973), pp. 138—139; Ostroy and Starr (1974), pp. 1110—1111.

[51] An ingenious formal proof is provided by Chuchman (1974). The reasoning underlying Chuchman's argument is a natural continuation of earlier work in search and information theory by Stigler (1961), Hicks (1967), Alchian (1969) and others. See also the recent paper by Lee (1974).

[52] Personally, I doubt if a general proof of the conjecture is possible. If necessary conditions can be provided for a broad enough class of special cases, however, these may serve collectively as an effective substitute. In the latter connection, papers by Reiter (1959 and 1959*), Foley (1970), Niehans (1971), Hahn (1971), Grandmont and Younes (1972), Karni (1973), Mortensen (1973), Kurz and Wilson (1974), and Jones (1975) merit special notice.

[53] On the definition of a "monetary" economy, see Clower (1967 and 1969) and Benassy (1975). Chapter 2 of Flannery and Jaffee (1973) is also of interest in this connection.

[54] Cf. Brunner and Meltzer (1971); Clower and Leijonhufvud (1975).

some very awkward problems. For analytical purposes, however, explicit recognition of monetary considerations is a matter of convenience rather than necessity. In all essential respects, the performance characteristics of an economy in which goods are traded directly for goods through facilities provided by inventory-holding middlemen are qualitatively indistinguishable from those of a strictly monetary economy. That conventional economic wisdom has for so long encouraged us to cling to a contrary belief is attributable, I suspect, to its consistent refusal to deal explicitly with *any* kind of ongoing economic system, monetary or otherwise. In the discussion that follows, I shall proceed generally on the assumption that we have to deal with a world of organized barter. Since monetary exchange is, in any case, merely a special kind of organized barter, this procedure should cause no problems.

A full account of the characteristics of a middleman economy or, more generally, of what I shall refer to henceforth as *Neo-Marshallian* theory, is out of the question here. To focus upon any particular formal model would be a mistake in any event, for that would divert attention from the foundations of Neo-Marshallian theory, which are fundamental, to its superstructure, which is incidental. As for the foundations, the following sketch, though desperately incomplete, hopefully will serve as a working guide not only to the basic structure but also to the potential empirical implications of Neo-Marshallian models considered as a class.

For simplicity of exposition, I shall proceed on the assumption that the typical middleman or "shopkeeper" [55] holds inventories of, and operates a market for, *every* commodity traded in the economy. It might seem more plausible to imagine instead that each shopkeeper deals only with certain *subsets* of commodities; but that procedure (which, in the limit, includes the special case of monetary exchange) would merely complicate the form of the subsequent argument without altering its substance, so we lose nothing by leaving intuition to languish at this point.

Given the arrangements just stipulated, let us further imagine that each shopkeeper decides independently the *terms* on which he stands ready to trade various commodity pairs[56], while each trader (some of whom will be shopkeepers acting in another capacity)

---

[55] This terminology is suggested by Howitt (1974), p. 135.

[56] The word "terms" refers not only to rates of exchange between commodity pairs, but also to trading (rationing) rules, delivery arrangements, etc. Cf. Howitt (1974).

decides independently what *quantities* to trade with various shop-keepers. Thus, the economy is *decentralized* in the strictest sense of that term. Supposing that individual traders and shopkeepers seek always to exploit potential gains from trade, however, strong forces making for order will be constantly at work within the system. Specifically, since individual traders have an incentive to search out and trade with those shopkeepers that currently offer relatively favorable terms of trade, rates of exchange set by different shop-keepers will tend toward equality over time. Shopkeepers that are slow to fall into line will be drained of stocks of some commodities, swamped with stocks of others, and so forced eventually either to conform or to close up shop. For analogous reasons, brokerage and other trading fees charged by different shopkeepers will tend toward equality over time at levels that permit representative shopkeepers to earn no more than a normal rate of return on their average holdings of commodity inventories (trade capital).

Explicit modeling of this kind of economy is not a simple matter. It seems natural, and involves no loss of essential generality, to sup-pose that rates of exchange of all shopkeepers will be expressed in terms of a common unit of account, the unit being a standard quantity of one of the commodities traded in the system. We might then sup-pose that the prices of all other commodities (i. e., rates of exchange with the standard commodity) will be varied by each shopkeeper in response to his own conception of the adequacy of his existing stocks in relation to present and prospective sales. This would lead us to describe price behavior not in terms of familiar first-order difference or differential equations involving *flow* excess demands but rather in terms of second or higher order equations involving distributed lag functions of past purchases and sales, i. e., *stocks* as well as *flows*. However, since each shopkeeper would be free to establish his own set of price-adjustment procedures, and since these procedures would depend upon costs of holding inventories, costs incurred in adjusting prices, expectations of future market conditions, and so forth, price behavior might follow very different patterns even in outwardly similar markets. Much simplification would be possible if, following Marshall, we could assume that prices set by different shopkeepers tended almost instantaneously to equality, for then we might view the economy as if it contained just one great market; but that pro-cedure would entail a type of implicit theorizing that is best avoided[57].

---

[57] An alternative if somewhat artificial procedure is to postulate ex-plicitly that a central "trading warehouse" is established by "social compact"; see Clower and Leijonhufvud (1975).

This very cursory account of the problem of modelling shop-keeper behavior provides no more than a glimpse of the tip of an iceberg of analytical complications, but hopefully it will serve to indicate the general milieu within which individual traders in a Neo-Marshallian world must be presumed to formulate their plans.

Dealing next with the behavior of individual traders, we may suppose that their choice alternatives are defined, in general, in terms of a matrix of price vectors, one vector for each shopkeeper in the system. Each trader must then decide not only with which shop-keepers to trade but also the *timing* of trips to different shops; for the existence of positive transaction costs (a basic presumption underlying the existence of shops) implies that individual traders as well as shopkeepers will hold positive commodity inventories, which implies, in turn, that trades will occur at discrete points rather than continuously in time. To suppose that these considerations might be dealt with explicitly in a *manageable* formal model would, I suggest, be grossly to underestimate the complexity of the problem[58]. As high-energy physicists have had to settle for quantum-theoretic descriptions of subatomic phenomena, so economists probably must settle (at least provisionally) for some kind of surrogate, statistical description of transactor behavior in an ongoing exchange economy[59].

Granted that individual traders independently decide when and what to trade with specific shopkeepers, commodity stocks held by different shopkeepers will vary randomly with time, for traders in a shopkeeper world are similar in important respects to particles in Brownian motion. Since shopkeepers could never know for sure whether perceived trends in activity were transitory or permanent, we should not expect changes in prices, much less accompanying changes in the distribution of trades and traders among shopkeepers, to reflect *prevailing* economic conditions at all accurately. On the contrary, we should expect current conditions to influence overall economic activity only after what Professor Friedman, in another context, has described as "long and variable lags". For example, prices of some commodities might be rising even when flow excess supplies of the same commodities were positive and stocks were

---

[58] Cf. Howitt and Clower (1974), p. 4.

[59] This need not and should not involve any relaxation of established standares of theoretical discourse. If Neo-Marshallian process analysis is to be of any permanent value, it must ultimately be expressed in precise and mathematically rigorous terms in keeping with the fruitful tradition established by Hicks, Arrow, Debreu and other leading contributors to the Neo-Walrasian literature. Cf. Hahn (1973), p. 241.

increasing. In a similar vein, shopkeepers might at times (and possibly for long intervals) refuse to trade certain commodities because their present stocks were either exhausted or grossly in surplus. If such system malfunctions were common or, alternatively, if system malfunctions were normally uncommon but exogenous shocks were frequent and occasionally large, then the inability of shopkeepers to maintain effective control of inventories through price adjustments alone might cause some of them to stop operating altogether. This possibility conjures up sobering visions of an otherwise stable homeostatic economic system experiencing recurrent coordination failures because system communication channels are interrupted or become "noisy" when the system departs too far from its "equilibrium" motion[60]. The set of possible variations on this theme is effectively unbounded.

VI. Conclusion

Although the implications of a Neo-Marshallian view of economic phenomena are moderately radical in some respects they are thoroughly conservative in others. Some of the more conservative implications merit mention by way of conclusion, for they provide some assurance that the route of escape from the Keynesian Perplex suggested in this paper does not lead us down a tunnel into Bedlam.

First, the whole of established microtheory may be fitted neatly into Neo-Marshallian analysis by regarding the former as a schematic characterization of certain necessary conditions for stationary equilibrium. Of course, on this interpretation, it is fallacious to argue that standard theories of individual or market behavior can serve directly as a conceptual basis for models that describe the dynamics of disequilibrium motion; in particular, it would be wrong to regard established microtheory as a suitable foundation for macrotheory, for the central if not sole object of macrotheory is to enhance our understanding of short-run disequilibrium adjustment processes[61].

Second, the whole of Marshallian economics as well as that part of Keynesian thought that Leijonhufvud has labelled "The Economics of Keynes"[62] can be regarded as explicit special cases of Neo-Marshallian analysis. Viewed in this perspective, the author of the *General Theory* will not, I suspect, appear to deserve as much

---

[60] Cf. Leijonhufvud (1973), p. 32 ff., where possibilities of the kind referred to here are described as "corridor" phenomena.

[61] Leijonhufvud (1968).

[62] Cf. Leijonhufvud (1974).

credit for clear thinking as his distinguished mentor; but neither Keynes nor Marshall can be accused (as some have accused them) of constitutional ineptness as economic theorists. As is sufficiently indicated above, precise formal modelling of Neo-Marshallian systems is not a straightforward matter, even for persons of genius.

Third, and finally, Neo-Marshallian theory may be easily specialized to deal explicitly with monetary exchange. Perhaps the simplest way to accomplish this is to suppose that each shopkeeper restricts his dealings to just *two* commodities, one of them a commodity called "money" that is traded by *all* shopkeepers in the economy. The properties of such systems have been extensively explored by Peter Howitt in a series of papers[63] early drafts of which crucially influenced my own thinking about Neo-Marshallian models in general. Here it will suffice to say that the analytical implications of Howitt's work are essentially those of the non-monetary models that are the main concern of the present paper.

It appears that to obtain essentially new kinds of results we must recognize the existence of credit instruments (formal and informal loan contracts) as potential objects of trade. This procedure opens the door to a variety of complications — financial intermediation, endogenous expansion and contraction of means of payment, speculative purchase and sale of futures contracts — which cannot be fitted into Neo-Walrasian theory without doing violence either to logic or common sense, but which have a natural place in Neo-Marshallian theory (any class of contracts that can be traded at a profit is obviously an "object" of potential interest to profit-seeking middlemen). Clearly, it is just such complications that lie at the heart of Keynes' economics[64]. Just as clearly, that is the direction in which economic theory must go if we are ever to complete the Keynesian Revolution.

References

K. J. Arrow: "Samuelson Collected", Journal of Political Economy, October 1967, 75, pp. 730—737.

K. Arrow and F. H. Hahn: General Competitive Analysis, San Francisco, Holden-Day, 1972.

---

[63] Howitt (1973); also see Howitt (1974).

[64] This has always been a central theme in Hicks' writings, particularly since his "great awakening" in 1957. It has also figured prominently in the work of Paul Davidson and Hy Minsky [see, especially, Davidson (1972) and Minsky (1972)].

R. J. Barro and H. I. Grossman: "A General Disequilibrium Model of Income and Employment," American Economic Review, March, 1971, *61*, pp. 82—93.

G. S. Becker: "A Theory of Social Interactions", Journal of Political Economy, November/December, 1974, *82*, pp. 1063—1093.

J. Benassy: "Disequilibrium Exchange in Barter and Monetary Economies", Economic Inquiry, June, 1975, *13*, pp. 131—156.

K. Brunner and A. Meltzer: "The Uses of Money: Money in the Theory of an Exchange Economy," American Economic Review, December, 1971, *61*, pp. 784—805.

M. L. Burstein: Economic Theory: Equilibrium and Change, London, Wiley, 1968.

G. Chuchman: "A Model of the Evolution of Exchange Processes", University of Western Ontario, Money Workshop, November, 1974.

R. W. Clower: "The Keynesian Counterrevolution", The Theory of Interest Rates, Brechling and Hahn (eds.), London: Macmillan, 1965, *6*, pp. 103—125; reprinted in slightly revised form in Clower, Selected Readings in Monetary Theory, London: Penguin, 1969, pp. 270—297.

R. W. Clower: "A Reconsideration of the Microfoundations of Monetary Theory", Western Economic Journal, December 1967, *6*, pp. 1—9, Reprinted in Clower (1969), pp. 202—211.

R. W. Clower: Monetary Theory, Penguin Modern Economics Series of Selected Readings, London, 1969.

R. W. Clower and J. Due: Microeconomics, Homewood, Richard D. Irwin, 1972.

R. W. Clower and A. Leijonhufvud: "The Coordination of Economic Activities", American Economic Review, May, 1975.

P. J. Davidson: Money and the Real World, London, Macmillan, 1972.

P. J. Davidson: "Money and the Real World", Economic Journal, March, 1972, *82*, pp. 101—115.

G. Debreu: Theory of Value, Cowles Foundation Monograph No. 17, New York, 1959.

K. Y. Edgeworth: Papers Relating to Political Economy, 3 Vols., London: Macmillan, 1925.

M. J. Flannery and D. M. Jaffee: The Economic Implications of an Electronic Monetary Transfer System, Lexington, D. C. Heath, 1973.

D. K. Foley: "Economic Equilibrium with Costly Marketing", Journal of Economic Theory, 1970, *2*, pp. 276—291.

M. Friedman: Essays in Positive Economics, Chicago, University of Chicago Press, 1953.

H. I. Grossman: "Was Keynes a 'Keynesian'?", Journal of Economic Literature, March, 1972, *10*, pp. 26—30.

F. H. Hahn: "On Some Problems of Proving the Existence of an Equilibrium in a Monetary Economy", Hahn and Brechling (eds.), The Theory of Interest Rates, London, Macmillan, 1965, pp. 126—135; reprinted in Clower (1969), pp. 191—201.

F. H. Hahn: "Some Adjustment Problems", Econometrica, January, 1970, *38,* pp. 1—17.

F. H. Hahn: "Equilibrium with Transactions Costs", Econometrica, May, 1971, *39,* pp. 417—439.

F. H. Hahn: "On the Notion of Equilibrium in Economics", An Inaugural Lecture, Cambridge, Cambridge University Press, 1973.

F. H. Hahn: "Foundations of Monetary Theory", Essays on Modern Economics, M. Parkin (ed.), Longmans, London, 1973*, pp. 230—242.

J. R. Hicks: "Léon Walras", Econometrica, October, 1934, 2, pp. 338—348.

J. R. Hicks: "Mr. Keynes' Theory of Employment", Economic Journal, June, 1936, *46,* pp. 238—253.

J. R. Hicks: Value and Capital, Oxford, Clarendon Press, 1939 (second ed., 1946).

J. R. Hicks: "A Rehabilitation of 'Classical' Economies?", Economic Journal, June, 1957, *67,* pp. 278—289.

J. R. Hicks: "Critical Essays in Monetary Theory", Oxford, Clarendon Press, 1967.

J. R. Hicks: "Recollections and Documents", Economica, February, 1973, *40,* pp. 2—11.

J. R. Hicks: "The Mainsprings of Economic Growth", Nobel Memorial Lecture, The Nobel Foundation, 1973*.

J. R. Hicks: The Crisis in Keynesian Economics, Oxford, Clarendon Press, 1974.

A. G. Hines: On the Reappraisal of Keynesian Economics, London, Martin Robertson, 1971.

J. Hirshleifer: "Exchange Theory", Western Economic Journal (now Economic Inquiry), June, 1973, *10,* pp. 129—146.

P. W. Howitt: Studies in the Theory of Monetary Dynamics, Doctoral Dissertation, Northwestern University, 1973.

P. W. Howitt: "Walras and Monetary Theory", Western Economic Journal (Economic Inquiry), December 1973*, 11, pp. 487—499.

P. W. Howitt: "Stability and the Quantity Theory", Journal of Political Economy, January/February 1974, *82,* pp. 133—140.

P. W. Howitt and R. W. Clower: "The Optimal Timing of Transactions", Economics Department, University of Western Ontario Discussion Paper, May, 1974 (mimeo, 33 pp.).

W. Jaffé: Correspondence of Leon Walras and Related Papers, 3 vols., Amsterdam: N. Holland, 1965.

H. G. Johnson: "The General Theory after Twenty-five Years", American Economic Review, May, 1961, *51*.

H. G. Johnson: "The Keynesian Revolution and the Monetarist Counterrevolution", American Economic Review, May, 1971, *61*, pp. 1—14.

H. G. Johnson: "Major Issues in Monetary Economics", Oxford Economic Papers, July, 1974, *26*, pp. 212—225.

H. G. Johnson: "The Current and Prospective State of Economics", Australian Economic Papers, June, 1974*, pp. 1—27.

R. Jones: "The Origin and Development of Media of Exchange", forthcoming in Journal of Political Economy, 1975.

N. Kaldor: "The Irrelevance of Equilibrium Economics", Economic Journal, December, 1972, *82*, pp. 1237—1252.

R. B. Kershner and L. R. Wilcox: The Anatomy of Mathematics, New York: Ronald Press, 1950.

J. Kornai: Anti-Equilibrium, North Holland, Amsterdam, 1971.

J. M. Keynes: Collected Writings of John Maynard Keynes (abbreviated as CW), London, Macmillan, for the Royal Economic Society, 25 Vols., various dates.

J. M. Keynes: The General Theory of Employment, Interest and Money, New York, Harcourt, Brace and Co., 1936.

J. M. Keynes: "Poverty in Plenty: Is the Economic System Self-Adjusting", Collected Works, *13*, pp. 485—491.

M. Kurz and R. Wilson: "On the Structure of Trade", Economic Inquiry, December, 1974, *12*, pp. 493—516.

C. H. Lee: "Information Costs and Markets", Economic Inquiry, December, 1974, *12*, pp. 460—475.

A. Leijonhufvud: "Keynes and the Keynesians", American Economic Review, May, 1967, *57*, pp. 401—410.

A. Leijonhufvud: On Keynesian Economics and the Economies of Keynes, New York, Oxford University Press, 1968.

A. Leijonhufvud: Keynes and the Classics, IEA Occasional Paper No. 30, London, 1969.

A. Leinjonhufvud: "Life Among the Econ", Western Economic Journal, Sept., 1973*, *11*, pp. 327—337,

A. Leinjonhufvud: "Effective Demand Failures", Swedish Journal of Economics, 1973, *73*, pp. 27—48.

A. Leijonhufvud: "The Varieties of Price Theory: What Microfoundations for Macrotheory?", Department of Economics, UCLA, Discussion Paper No. 44, January, 1974, pp. 53.

A. Leijonhuvfud: Maximization and Marshall, Marshall Lectures, Michaelmas Term, 1974, Cambridge, forthcoming, Cambridge University Press, 1975.

W. W. Leontief: "Theoretical Assumptions and Nonobservable Facts", American Economic Review, March, 1971, *61*, pp. 1—7.

A. Marshall: Industry and Trade, London, Macmillan, 1919.

A. Marshall: Principles of Economics, 8th ed., London, Macmillan, 1920.

H. Minsky: "An Exposition of a Keynesian Theory of Investment", Mathematical Methods in Investment and Finance, Szego and Shell (eds.), Amsterdam, North Holland, 1972, pp. 207—233.

D. T. Mortensen: "Search Equilibrium in a Simple Multi-Market Economy", Center for Mathematical Studies in Economics and Management Science Discussion Paper No. 54, October, 1973 (mimeo, 48 pp.).

T. Negishi: "The Stability of a Competitive Economy", Econometrica, October, 1962, *30*, pp. 635—669.

P. K. Newman: Theory of Exchange, Englewood Cliffs, Prentice-Hall, 1965.

J. M. Ostroy: "The Informational Efficiency of Monetary Exchange", American Economic Review, Spetember, 1973, *63*, pp. 597—610.

J. M. Ostroy and R. M. Starr: "Money and the Decentralization of Exchange", Econometrica, November, 1974, *42*, pp. 1093—1113.

D. Patinkin: Money, Interest and Prices, Evanston, Row-Peterson, 1956; 2nd ed., New York: Harper-Row, 1965.

D. Patinkin: "The Collected Writings of John Maynard Keynes From the Tract to the General Theory", a review article forthcoming in the Economic Journal, 1975.

S. Reiter: "Market Price Formation", Abstract in Econometrica, April, 1959, *27*, pp. 313—314.

S. Reiter: "A Market Adjustment Mechanism", Institute for Quantitative Research, School of Industrial Management, Purdue University, mimeo (pp. 26), 1959.

J. Robinson: "The Second Crisis of Economic Theory", American Economic Review, May, 1974, *64*, pp. 1—10.

Joan Robinson: "What has Become of the Keynesian Revolution?", Challenge, January/February, 1974, pp. 6—11.

P. A. Samuelson: Foundations of Economic Analysis, Cambridge, Harvard University Press, 1947.

P. A. Samuelson: Collected Scientific Papers, Vol. 3, Merton (ed.), Cambridge: MIT Press, 1972.

J. Schumpeter: The Theory of Economic Development, Cambridge: Harvard University Press, 1949.

M. Shubik: "A Curmudgeon's Guide to Microeconomics", JEL, June, 1970, *8*, pp. 405—434.

E. H. C. Veendorp: "General Equilibrium Theory for a Barter Economy", Western Economic Journal (now Economic Inquiry), March, 1970, *8*, pp. 1—23.

D. A. Walker: "Leon Walras in Light of His Correspondence and Related Papers", Journal of Political Economy, July/August, 1970, *78*, pp. 685—701.

E. R. Weintraub: "Arrow and Hahn's General Competitive Analysis: A Perspective", Economic Inquiry, March, 1974, *12*, pp. 105—113.

J. Whitaker: "The Marshallian System in 1881: Distribution and Growth", Economic Journal, March, 1974, *84*, pp. 1—17.

D. Winch: Economies and Policy: A Historical Study, London, Hodder and Stoughton, 1969.

Address of author: Prof. Dr. Robert Clower, Department of Economics, University of California, Los Angeles, CA 90024, U. S. A.

Printed in Austria

[18]

The New Classical Economics, heralded a few years back as "the wave of the future in macroeconomics", now appears to be on its way out, leaving Keynesian economics in much the same state of disarray as the Monetarist counterrevolution placed in the early 1970's. New Classical Economics and Monetarism notwithstanding, few economists have ever seriously doubted the validity of Keynes's contention that "... the existing economic system is [not] , in any significant sense, self-adjusting" (JMK, XIII, p. 486). But equally few economists find themselves in agreement with Keynes because of anything in the *General Theory*; concensus obtains rather because of a shared conviction that, on the self-adjustment issue, Keynes's "vision" was vaguely right even when his analysis was clearly wrong.

But if light on the future direction of macroeconomic analysis is not to be found in the New Classical Economics, in Monetarism, or in conventional Keynesian economics, under what lamp post should we look? My purpose in this paper is to suggest an answer to this question. I start, as Keynes and most of his early interpreters started, by outlining a simplified aggregative model of classical theory which can plausibly be claimed to represent an essentially self-adjusting monetary economy. Later I ask (as so many economists since Keynes have asked): what characteristics of the classical theory might plausibly be altered to yield a model consilient with Keynes's "vision"? Once this rather special question has been answered, we may hope quickly to resolve the more general issue that is our main concern.

1. The Classical Tradition

No classical theory of short-run adjustment is to be found in the pre-Keynesian literature[1], probably because no classical writer thought it purposeful to attempt to reduce the complexities of real-time trading processes to analytical order. So my version of short-run classical theory is less a description of what any pre-Keynesian writer actually said than an account of what I think a Nineteenth Century "true believer" in the self-adjusting capabilities of the economic system might have said had he been trained in modern theory.

267

Taking our cue from John Hicks's influential 1937 paper on "Keynes and the Classics"[2], let us start by considering a fiat money economy with just four classes of non-money commodities: consumption goods (c), capital goods (k), labor (n) and loans (b). Suppose that the number of traders and the physical volume of trading in each commodity is sufficiently great that, even in the very short run, no seller or buyer either imagines himself or is, in fact, capable of significantly influencing the terms of trade by his own actions: more succinctly, *assume that any trader can buy or sell any desired quantity of any commodity on short notice at the "going" price.* For future reference, let us call this assumption the *Thick Market Hypothesis.* Then, whether we regard the typical trader as one of many transactors in an organized auction market or as a market-maker in his own right, we may suppose that short-run sale and purchase decisions are governed at every point in time by the prevailing (average) market prices, $p_c, p_k, p_n = w$, and $p_t = 1/r$.

Still following Hicks, let us further assume that the money wage rate, w, is given and that capital goods already in use are specialized to particular trades and have no second-hand market. Then we may set out our "classical" model as a system of three price-adjustment equations:

(1) $dp_c/dt = a_c \left[d_c(p_c, p_k, w, r, Y_n, M) - s_c(p_c/w) \right]$,

(2) $dp_k/dt = a_k \left[d_k(p_c, p_k, w, r, M) - s_k(p_k/w) \right]$,

(3) $dr/dt = a_b \left[x_b(p_c, p_k, w, r, M) \right]$,

where d, s and x stand for "demand", "supply" and "excess demand", M represents the quantity of money, and Y_n represents the realized money earnings of workers[3].

On the Thick Market Hypothesis, it is plausible to suppose that the motions of this system in the neighborhood of an equilibrium point are stable and heavily damped; hence, the average "observed" values of the dependent variables p_c, p_k, and r may be presumed to be given as reduced-form solutions of the excess demand equations. The qualitative properties of these solutions are standard.

Here it will suffice to remark that, assuming no money illusion, relative prices and the rate of interest - hence output and employment - will vary with changes in the quantity of money. Monetary neutrality holds only if we assume flexible money wage rates and add a wage-adjustment equation to the system[4].

This model captures the essential flavor of classical theory. Except as a "temporary abode of purchasing power", money has no significance as an asset because in normal circumstances it offers its holder no return and is no more "liquid" than any other commodity. Money plays a special role in the economy only because it enters into one side of every exchange transaction and so - through real balance effects - directly influences the absolute level of money prices. Individual economic activities are coordinated by "the price system". If changes in underlying parameters ("animal spirits", the "propensity to hoard", etc.) produce temporary inconsistencies in consumption, production or trading plans, these inconsistencies are quickly reconciled through movements in prices, any consequent changes in output and employment being incidental.

There are extreme cases, of course, in which the system could get into trouble. A sudden collapse in the marginal efficiency of capital, for example, might yield so low a price for capital goods that gross real investment would go to zero and remain there pending the elimination of excess capacity through gradual wear and tear. Similar consequences might ensue if trading in loans came to be dominated by speculative "bulls" and "bears" whose gambling proclivities pushed the real rate of interest to a level where new investment was chronically unprofitable. Notice, however, that in both these cases the underlying source of delayed adjustment is the absence of a market for second-hand capital goods. In effect, the assumption that existing capital goods can't be traded (as also the assumption that the money wage rate is given) is a violation of the Thick Market Hypothesis. Thus our discussion of extreme cases merely reinforces earlier indications that the classical conception of the economic system as naturally self-adjusting is intimately connected with the validity of the Thick Market Hypothesis.

II. Keynes's General Theory

Turning now to the *General Theory*, we have no need to invent a model; we can start with Keynes's summary of the analytical core of his argument, as set forth in Chapter 18 (pp. 247-9) of the *General Theory*. This summary has been formalized in various ways by later interpreters and critics; but John Hicks's 1937 "interpretation" sets out the nearest thing to a canonical representation of the Keynesian model, so let us settle for that (Modigliani's 1944 model has achieved much the same status, but is less general because it treats capital goods and consumption goods as identical rather than distinct commodities).

First we need some additional notation. Let Y denote total income, defined as the sum of income produced in the consumption goods industries, $Y_c = p_c s_c(p_c/w)$, and income produced in the investment goods industries, $Y_k = p_k s_k(p_k/w)$:

$$Y = Y_c + Y_k.$$

Similarly, let E_c and E_k denote total expenditure on consumption and investment goods: $E_c = p_c d_c(\cdot)$; $E_k = p_k d_k(\cdot)$.

Then, continuing as before to treat the money wage rate and the quantity of money as given parameters, we may express Hicks's schematic model of Keynes's "General Theory"[5] as

(4) $M = L(r, Y)$,

(5) $Y_k = E_k(r, Y)$,

(6) $Y_k = Y - E_c(r, Y)$.

This system of three equations may be presumed to determine solution values of Y, Y_k and r from which, taking account of earlier definitions and underlying production functions, we can work out corresponding solution values of employment and output. But in what sense can the system (4)-(6) be said to represent a "theory of output and employment" rather than a "theory of price"?

To answer this question, let us first rewrite the system to reveal the price variables that are suppressed in the present formulation. Making use of earlier definitions of Y, Y_k, E_k and E_c, and carrying out appropriate simplifications (specifically, the cancellation of price variables that appear on both sides of the last equations), we obtain

$$M = L(r, p_c/w, p_k/w),$$
$$s_k\{p_k/w\} \quad = d_k(r, p_c/w, p_k/w),$$
$$s_c\{p_c/w\} \quad = d_c(r, p_c/w, p_k/w).$$

This system, though formally equivalent to the system (4) - (6), is more naturally regarded as a "theory of price" than a "theory of output and employment". We may clinch the issue by expressing the model as a set of differential equations:

(1*) $dr/dt = b_r \left[M - L(r, p_c/w, p_k/w) \right]$,

(2*) $dp_c/dt = b_c \left[d_c(r, p_c/w, p_k/w) - s_c\{p_c/w\} \right]$,

(3*) $dp_k/dt = b_k \left[d_k(r, p_c/w, p_k/w) - s_k\{p_k/w\} \right]$.

This system differs from our earlier "classical" model in just two major respects. First, the excess demand for bonds is expressed in terms of "liquidity preference" rather than the demand and supply of "loanable funds". But this is merely a matter of form; for since money enters into one side of every transaction, we might also express the excess demands for consumption and investment goods in "liquidity preference" terms ("The reward for parting with liquidity is immediate gratification through consumption, or the expectation of a stream of future profit, or...")[6]. Second, the money variable is omitted from the excess demand functions in (2*) and (3*); but this merely reflects an implicit signification error in the underlying Hicks model. From a conceptual standpoint, therefore, the Keynesian system (1*)-(3*) is formally indistinguishable from our earlier classical model (1)-(3) and cannot plausibly be regarded as possessing behaviour properties that would permit us to reach any but "classical" conclusions[7].

Now, there can be no doubt that to accept the system (1*)-(3*) - and so the system (1)-(3) - as a model of Keynes's *General Theory* is equivalent to imputing to Keynes a faith in the efficacy of the price system that is utterly at variance with his actual beliefs. But neither can there be serious doubt that Hicks's simple model of the *General Theory* accurately reflects the substance - the letter if not the spirit - of Keynes's formal analysis. The crux of the matter is that Keynes in the *General Theory* not only failed to reject but positively embraced an essentially classical (more accurately, neo-classical) theory of short-run output determination, and thereby implicitly adopted the Thick Market Hypothesis as a basis for his own theory of aggregate supply.[8] Keynes's theory of aggregate demand, though outwardly novel because it makes the current level of total expenditure depend upon the prevailing level of output and employment, actually involves no significant departure from classical tradition. So the theoretical foundations of the *General Theory* are, albeit unintentionally, incompatible with the beliefs that led Keynes to write it.

III. Salvaging the General Theory

Evidently the central message of Keynes's *General Theory* can be salvaged only by discarding the conventional theory of short-run supply. But we cannot discard the conventional theory of short-run supply unless we also discard the conception of market organization on which it is based; for the conventional theory merely expressed how rational sellers would behave if their trading activities were confined to thick markets.

The *General Theory* contains no hint that Keynes was in any way dissatisfied with the conventional theory of supply; indeed, the conventional theory plays a central role in his claim that real wages generally move in the same direction as output over the trade cycle. It was not until 1939, in his response to criticisms of this claim by Dunlop and Tarshis,[9] that Keynes explicitly voiced doubts about the assumptions underlying his earlier analysis of aggregate supply and, more particularly, questioned the validity of what I have called the Thick

Market Hypothesis by linking producer discretion in short-period pricing policy with trading in thin rather than thick markets.[10]

A thick market, as noted earlier, is one in which traders can be presumed to know within narrow limits the price at which any desired quantity of a commodity can be bought or sold on short notice. A thin market is one in which the opposite presumption holds: trading volume is too slight to permit traders to gauge, even within broad limits, the price at which desired sales or purchases can be completed on short notice. The crucial difference is that, for thick markets, it makes sense to suppose that the short-run revenues of individual producers are determined by their output choices, while for thin markets the same supposition makes no sense at all. Let us explore the implications of the second case.

Consider a representative producer whose short-run average variable and average total costs are represented by the curves AVC an ATC in Fig. 1. By hypothesis, the producer has no useable information about his probable short-run sales at alternative asking prices, so there can be no question of choosing a combination of price and output that maximizes short-run profit. Over the long run, the producer can hope the influence sales by appropriate market maneuvres (advertising, temporary price cuts, etc.), but more immediately he is largely at the mercy of impersonal (and predetermined) market forces. Under these conditions, probably the simplest and most sensible strategy is for the producer to set his asking or list price at a reasonable level and hope for the best in the way of sales volume. What seems "reasonable" to the producer will depend, of course, on past sales experience, on present and prospective costs, and on present and prospective competition. Here, les us interpret "reasonable" to mean a price (p_o in Fig. 1) high enough to ensure that average total costs are covered for a range of sales levels significantly less than capacity output, $s*$.[11].

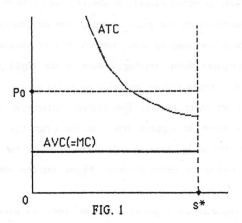

FIG. 1

Then since the "asking" or "list" price exceeds average variable (and marginal) cost for all outputs less than s*, the producer will be willing to produce and sell any less-than-capacity output at his posted price. But the amount that can actually be sold will depend upon customer demand at that price, which will depend on a host of conditions over which the producer has no short-run control. In these circumstances, it is plausible to argue that the producer will adjust output passively to match average sales at the posted price, holding buffer stocks of inventories to avoid frequent transient adjustments of output. Thus, on average, short-run output will move in the same direction as realized sales.

Taking account of the preceding argument, but referring now to an economy in which all produced goods are traded in thin markets, let us suppose that aggregative short-run output and interest-rate behavior may be characterized by the adjustment equations

(7) $dq_c/dt = h_c \, [d_c(\cdot) - q_c]$,

(8) $dq_k/dt = h_k [d_k(\cdot) - q_k]$,

(9) $dr/dt = h_b [x_b(\cdot)]$,

where q_i (i = c,k) represents current output as contrasted with "supply", and $(\cdot)=(p_c,p_k,w,r,Y,M)$ - the argument Y rather than Y_n appearing in $(\cdot)$ because, under our present assumptions, producers as well as workers may be "income constrained" in the short run.

The system (7)-(9) accurately portays what has come to be regarded as the distinctive feature of Keynesian economics: aggregate output is determined by aggregate sales and prices play no role in the short-run adjustment of income to changes in effective demand. This, of course, is the route to salvage of Keynesian economics that is taken in most textbooks, usually without notice to the reader that the underlying assumptions concerning short-period output variations are completely at odds with the conventional profit-maximization model of supply presented in later microeconomic sections of same text. It also corresponds to the extreme case of what Hicks has dubbed "fix-price theory"[12].

Apart from being a crude caricature of Keynes's analysis, the system (7)-(9) seriously misrepresents the role of prices in the short-run adjustment process. In situations involving significant unused capacity, producers can be expected to engage in competitive selling activities (temporary discounts, rebates, prize contests, etc.) in an effort to boost short-run sales, so average transaction price will tend to fall. Similarly, in situations involving little unused capacity, producers can be expected to compete for factors in ways that increase both variable and fixed costs, and some of these increases will be passed on in the form of higher asking prices. Arguing heuristically, we may suppose that both sorts of adjustment are adequately described by the aggregative equations

(10) $dp^*_c/dt = g_c d_c(\cdot) - s^*_c$,

(11) $dp^*_k/dt = g_k d_k(\cdot) - s^*_k$,

where p_i^* is an index of transaction prices and s_i^* is an index of production capacity[13]. Combining these relations with (7)-(9), we obtain a system of five adjustment equations to describe short-run movements in quantities, transaction prices, and the rate of interest.

The equation for dr/dt in this system calls for no special comment; we may view the loan market as "thick" and rapidly self-adjusting even in a Keynesian model. But the remaining four equations - two dealing with adjustments in output quantities and two dealing with movements in average transactions price - pose problems whose solutions are distinctly problematical.

To see this, suppose that the system starts in temporary equilibrium with capacity fully utilized and sales occurring only at posted list prices. Next, suppose that the equilibrium is disturbed by a decline in "animal spirits", "confidence", or what have you, causing investment expenditure to fall. Then investment goods output will quickly decline, because the speed of adjustment coefficients in equations (7) and (8) are, by hypothesis, large numbers. Prices will not decline noticeably in the short run because the adjustment coefficients in equations (10) and (11) are - again by hypothesis-relatively small. Both "workers" and "capitalists" are income constrained, because neither goods nor services are particularly "liquid" (though prices are "administered", and therefore known, quantities sold are unpredictable); so as investment output drops the demand for consumption goods will also decline, via the familiar multiplier process.

Now, initially at least, no counteracting forces will operate to stem the decline. Real balance effects will have no bite, because transaction prices will not fall noticeably; and though the money volume of transactions will decline, the potential effect of this on spending will be attenuated by rising uncertainty about future needs for cash to meet payrolls, etc. - hence a rise in the demand for precautionary balances. There will perhaps be some tendency for spare cash to go into loans; but this tendency will not be strong, because with sales falling and becoming more uncertain, producers will find it increasingly difficult to synchronize purchases with sales, and this will mean that average money balances will tend to increase even at lower volumes of monetary transactions (cf. Clower and Howitt, 1978, in Clower, 1984, pp. 168-70). Nor are matters likely to improve as the decline continues; for in thin markets trade credit (mainly in the form of bookkeeping entries) is likely to play a prominent, and perhaps dominant role as a short-run means of payment[14]. As sales decline and business confidence weakens, trade credit outstanding will shrink, possibly by substantial percentage amounts, even though currency and deposits subject to check are largely unchanged.

There is no need to carry the story further. Notice that nothing of substance in the above argument is changed if we relax the assumption of fixed wage rates and add a "thin" market for labour services to our model. In that more general case, as for the more restricted model (7)-(11), "observed" short-run behavior cannot be adequately characterized by static, reduced-form solutions of the adjustment equations. In effect, the normal state of the economy is one of Brownian motion; the system, even if asympotically stable, is so lightly damped that the probability of ever being in the neighborhood of equilibrium is close to zero.

Conclusion

No doubt more might be said about the reasons why the *General Theory* ultimately failed to convey Keynes's intended message, and about alternative ways in which Keynes's "vision" might be salvaged; but this is not the place to say it. Instead, let me conclude by drawing attention to some of the more immediate research implications of the preceding argument.

It seems to me that the key to further progress in macroeconomics lies in improved understanding of short-run price and quantity behavior in thin markets. For a variety of reasons, I doubt that conventional analytical methods will be of much use for this purpose. No doubt we may continue to presume that business firms - manufactures, service providers, wholesalers, retailers, banks and other financial institutions - seek to maximize present wealth; but this presumption will lead us nowhere unless we are able to specify relevant criterion functions and constraints, which does not presently appear to be feasible for firms that operate in thin markets. I say "not presently feasible" because I view the problem not as unsolvable but merely unsolved. My suspicision is that the problem cannot be satisfactorily resolved unless we take more seriously than heretofore has been our habit the role of transactions costs and related economies of scale as determinants of market organization and performance. And even in the best of cases, I doubt that any solution of the problem will yield neat models or precise conclusions. The analysis of business behavior in thin markets promises to be very messy by comparison with conventional thick-market analysis.

There is serious question also whether established comparative-statics techniques can be fruitfully used for short-run analysis. If, as seems to be the case, there is little probability that a thin-market economy will ever be found in the neighborhood of equilibrium, we must be prepared to work with explicitly dynamical models of market adjustment. Of course, if our underlying theories of business behavior are "messy" then our prospects for achieving professional concensus on the best way to model the stylized dynamical facts are rather bleak. All the same, I see no reason to be discouraged. The present situation of macroeconomics, like that of Ulysses as he set sail from Troy, is serious but not hopeless. We can, if we wish, continue to play innocuous intellectual games with macromodels that have no conceivable value for describing observable behavior. But surely our proper course is treat the description of reality as a challenge and get on the work of reconstructing microeconomics to deal meaningfully with the Economics of Thin Markets.

NOTES

(1) One finds numerous threads of such a theory, particularly in Hume, Thornton, Tooke and Mill (Cf. Hicks, 1967); but that is all.

(2) The full title is "Mr. Keynes and the Classics: A Suggested Interpretation".

(3) Y_n is included in d_c because, with the money wage rate given, the earnings of workers cannot be presumed to correspond to the money value of services offered for sale; i.e., the demand function for consumption goods is not independent of the current level of output. But this is just a Keynesian (or Marshallian) flourish; for since Y_n may be presumed to depend on prices via the demand for labor, it need not be included as an explicit argument in d_c.

(4) In the augmented system, equilibrium money prices and the money wage rate are directly proportional to the quantity of money, as implied by the "classical" quantity theory. This merely indicates the redundancy of the quantity theory in any model for which the classical invariance proposition holds; it does not validate the quantity theory - or the quantity equation - as a "behavior" relation. Hicks's 1937 version of classical theory is flawed in this respect.

(5) Hicks also has a model of Keynes's "special theory" in which the liquidity preference equation takes the form $M=L(r)$; but that will not concern us until later.

(6) Cf. Boulding, 1944, pp. 55-63.

(7) This is essentially the conclusion Hicks reached in his 1937 paper, though he studiously refrained from stating it explicitly either in that paper or in his 1957 *Economic Journal* review of Patinkin's *Money, Interest and Prices* (reprinted with minor revision as Chapter 8 of Hicks, 1967, pp. 143-154.

(8) Patinkin disputes this in various of his recent writings, but (to my mind) not at all convincingly. On this, see Patinkin, 1976, p. 93; Tarshis, 1978, pp. 60-63 (in Patinkin and Leith, 1978).

(9) Reprinted in *JMK*, Vol. VII, Appendix 3 (see especially pp. 406-408).

(10) Curiously, Keynes seems to have been more aware of the difficulties of the "theory of short-period supply" in the early 1930's than during the writing of the *General Theory*. In a letter to Hawtrey of Nov. 28, 1930, for example, responding to Hawtrey's criticisms of the *Treatise*, Keynes says: "I repeat that I am not dealing with the complete set of causes which determine volume of output. For this would have led me an endless long journey into the theory of short-period supply and a long way from monetary theory; - though I agree that it will probably be difficult in the future to prevent monetary theory and the theory of short-period supply from running together. If I were to write the book again, I should probably attempt to probe further into the difficulties of the latter; but I have already probed far enough to know what a complicated affair it is". (JMK, Vol. XIII, pp. 145-6).

(11) Cf. P.W.S. Andrews, "Competitive Prices, Normal Costs and Industrial Stability", in Andrews and Brunner, 1975, pp. 29-31. This is not the place to review recent work on so-called "customer markets"; suffice it to say that there is little dispute among economists about the "stylized facts" though there is (of course) much dispute about how they should be interpreted. For some recent comments on this topic, see A. Okun, 1981, Chapter 4 (esp. pp. 138 ff); E.S. Phelps, 1985, pp. 383-404; R.E. Hall and J.B. Taylor, 1986, pp. 389-94; R.J. Gordon, 1981, pp. 502-4.

(12) See Hicks, 1966, Chaps. 7-9; Hicks, 1982, pp. 231-5.

(13) This is no more than a rough schematic representation. The microeconomic theory of price adjustment in thin markets is still in its infancy. For discussion

of some of the difficulties that confront us in this area, see Bushaw and Clower (1957), Chapter 7, pp. 185-9; Phelps, *et. al.* 1970, pp. 309-337 (Phelps and Winter) and pp. 369-93 (Gordon and Hynes).

(14) This is a direct consequence of the desire of makers of thin markets to attract a clientele of "regular" customers in order to reduce sales uncertainty; trade credit as distinct from bank credit plays little role in thick markets precisely because there is no significant sales uncertainty in this case.

References

Andrews, P.W.S., and Brunner, E., *Studies in Pricing*, London: MacMillan, 1975.

Boulding, K., "A Liquidity Preference Theory of Market Prices", *Economica*, 11, (May, 1944), pp. 55-63.

Bushaw, D.W., and Clower, R.W., *Introduction to Mathematical Economics*, Homewood, Ill: Richard D. Irwin, 1957.

Clower, R.W., *Money and Markets*, ed. by D. Walker, Cambridge: Cambridge U. Press, 1984.

Gordon, R.J., "Output Fluctuations and Gradual Price Adjustment", *Journal of Economic Literature*, 19, June, 1981, pp. 493-530.

Hall, R., and Taylor, J., *Macroeconomics*, New York: Norton, 1986.

Hicks, J.R., "Mr. Keynes and the Classics: A Suggested Interpretation", *Econometrica*, 5, April, 1937, pp. 147-59.

Hicks, J.R., *Capital and Growth*, Oxford: Clarendon Press, 1966.

Hicks, J.R., *Critical Essays in Monetary Theory*, Oxford: Clarendon Press, 1967.

Hicks, J.R., *Money, Interest and Wages*, Oxford: Basil Blackwell, 1982.

Keynes, J.M., *Collected Works*, cited as *JMK*, London: MacMillan, published for the Royal Economic Society, various volumes and dates.

Modigliani, F., "Liquidity Preference and the Theory of Interest and Money",

Econometrica, 12, Jan, 1944, pp. 45-88.

Okun, A., *Prices and Quantities*, Washington: The Brookings Institution, 1981.

Patinkin, D., *Keynes's Monetary Thought*, Durham: Duke U. Press, 1976.

Phelps, E.S., *Political Economy*, New York: Norton, 1985.

Phelps, E.S., *Microeconomic Foundations of Employment and Inflation Theory*, New York: Norton, 1970.

Tarshis, L., "Keynes as Seen by his Students in the 1930s", in Patinkin and Leith, eds., *Keynes's Cambridge and the General Theory*, Toronto: U. of Toronto Press, 1978.

19

7   Keynes' *General Theory:* the Marshall connection

Robert W. Clower[1]

Some dozen years ago, in a paper entitled 'The Keynesian Perplex', I remarked in passing that Keynes' intention in writing the *General Theory* was 'to offer the world an analytically manageable aggregative version of the kind of general process analysis that Marshall himself might have formulated had he ever felt a need explicitly to model the working of the economic system as a whole'.[2] My object in that paper was to argue that Keynesian economics had been shunted onto the wrong track by the Neo-Walrasian resurgence, so I somehow never thought to ask: What kind of aggregative model *would* Marshall have constructed had he ever felt the need for one? It is another question whether such a counterfactual analysis is worth pursuing. Were contemporary macroeconomics in less of a muddle I might have some doubts; but as matters stand, some doctrine-history 'backtracking'[3] would seem to be in order.

1.   Preliminaries

It will be helpful to start with Marshall's earliest graphic account of short-period equilibrium of 'normal' demand and supply for a particular commodity.[4] Referring to a diagram like that shown in Figure 7.1, Marshall first describes the 'supply' curve S as showing, for 'any particular amount of a commodity [that] is to be brought to a certain market at a certain time . . . the price at which it can so be brought.' This price is called the *supply price* and may be denoted by p^s.[5] Similarly, the 'demand' curve D is described as showing, for any particular amount of a commodity that is 'to be sold in the market during [a] given time, [the] price at which it can be so sold.' This price is called the *demand price* and may be denoted by p^d.[6] As for the determination of market equilibrium, it seems best to let Marshall speak for himself (p. 132):[7]

> At a point at which the curves cut one another there will be equilibrium, that is the amount bought will be such that the price at which it can just be

133

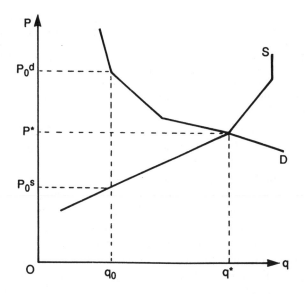

Figure 7.1.

brought into the market will be equal to the price at which that amount can be just got rid of . . . For let the amount supplied at any time be [q_0 in Figure 7.1] . . . If [p^s_0], the cost of supply, be less than [p^d_0], the price at which it can be sold, the trade will be a profitable one, production will be stimulated and [q] will move to the right. So if [p^s_0] be greater than [p^d_0], the trade will be an unprofitable one, production will be checked and [q] will move to the left.

A continuation of the same line of argument quickly establishes the familiar Marshallian 'stability' condition,[8] namely, that 'to the *left* of the point of intersection the supply curve lies *below* . . . the demand curve.' In contrast to the more common Walrasian stability criterion of modern textbooks, the Marshallian condition is independent of the absolute slopes of the S and D curves; as Marshall observes ('Essay on Value', Whitaker, I, p. 132), 'It has reference simply to the relative positions of the curves in the neighbourhood of the point of intersection.'

This account might seem to suggest that Marshall's short-period analysis – like that of Walras – was intended to model the working of a highly organized competitive auction market. In fact, Marshall seems to have had in mind a much more loosely organized, though still highly competitive market in which

the forces of demand and supply have free play; . . . there is no close combination among dealers on either side, but each acts for himself, and there is much free competition; that is, buyers generally compete freely with buyers, and sellers compete freely with sellers. But though everyone acts for himself, his knowledge of what others are doing is supposed to be generally sufficient to prevent him from taking a lower or paying a higher price than others are doing. This is assumed provisionally to be true both of finished goods and of their factors of production, of the hire of labor and of the hiring of capital. (*Principles*, 8th edn., p. 341)[9]

As Whitaker has observed (Whitaker I, p. 125): 'Marshall's conception of competition was from the first a qualified one akin to monopolistic competition.'

Starting from this conception of competition, it would have been but a short step for Marshall to develop an explicitly dynamic treatment of variations over time in the asking and sale prices of, and the quantities offered for sale and sold by individual producers within a particular market, proceeding along lines suggested by the phase-diagram method for handling a system of differential equations that he used in his 'Essay on International Trade' (*c.* 1873; cf. Whitaker, I, pp. 264–5; 11, p. 115). But Marshall lacked the intellectual audacity for such an undertaking. As he remarked in a related context (Whitaker, I, p. 162, fn. 4): 'the mathematical functions introduced into the original differential equation could not . . . be chosen so as to represent even approximately the economic forces that actually operate in the world. And by integrating them we should move further away from, instead of approaching nearer to the actual facts of life.'

So much for Marshall's short-period partial equilibrium analysis for a particular market. The preceding sketch does scant justice to the subtlety and wisdom of Marshall's thought. It was not without reason that, after Marshall's death in 1924, Keynes wrote of him: 'As a scientist he was, within his own field, the greatest in the world for a hundred years' (*JMK*, X, p. 173). It might be added that, as an analyst, Marshall had no peer in the art of 'recognizing hard problems and then hiding them in plain sight'[10].

2.   A Marshallian macro-model
It is a straightforward exercise to extend Marshall's short-period analysis of a particular market to the case of output as a whole, though we must deal with one or two complications along the way.

As in the preceding section, it is convenient to start with a supply and demand diagram (Figure 7.2). Suppose that short-period output for the economy as a whole – here assumed to be a meaningful notion – is initially at the level $q = q_o$ so that the demand price p^d_o, as given by the *ceteris paribus* demand curve $D(Z_o)$, is greater than the supply price p^s_o,

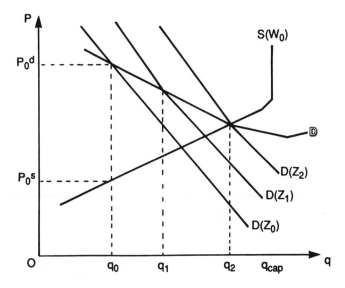

Figure 7.2.

as given by the *ceteris paribus* supply curve $S(w_o)$. If we assume that the current market price of output as a whole lies generally in the neighbourhood of the demand price,[11] then with aggregate output at q_o producers will have an incentive to hire additional factors in order to increase output. Here we run into our first complication.

Unless unemployed workers are available at the going wage rate, actual output cannot be increased except by bidding up the prevailing wage rate, in which case the supply curve will shift upward by an amount depending on the responsiveness of the wage rate to changes in output. To avoid this problem, let us assume provisionally that, at the wage rate w_o, unemployed workers are available for hire at all values of output less then q_{cap}. But then a second complication emerges. In general the demand price for output will depend on the prevailing level of 'aggregate producer outlay', $Z = p^s q$;[12] hence changes in output will produce shifts in the demand curve by amounts that will depend on the responsiveness of aggregate producer outlay to changes in output. This complication can be avoided by defining a *mutatis mutandis* demand curve D as illustrated in Figure 7.2, which shows demand price as a function of aggregate output, i.e. $p^d = D\{q, p^s(q,w_o){\cdot}q\}$, due allowance being made for the effect of changes in q on aggregate producer outlay and for the resultant effect of changes in aggregate producer outlay on demand price.[13]

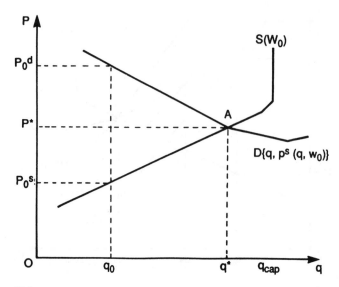

Figure 7.3.

Working now in terms of the *mutatis mutandis* demand curve D and the supply curve S, we obtain short-period equilibrium of aggregate output and price at the point A in Figure 7.3, where $q = q^*$, $p^s = p^d = p^*$, and aggregate expenditure, $E = p^d q = p^* q^* = E^*$ is equal to aggregate producer outlay, $Z = p^s q = p^* q^* = Z^*$ (i.e. where $Z-E = q(p^d - p^s) = 0$).[14] Applying the usual Marshallian stability condition, we may then describe the equilibrium as 'stable' if the supply curve S lies below the demand curve D to the left of the equilibrium point A.

This stability condition can be given a more interesting interpretation if we translate the relations shown in Figure 7.3 into a 'Marshallian Cross' diagram (Figure 7.4). Here, distances along the horizontal axis measure alternative levels of aggregate producer outlay, Z, as determined by the S curve in Figure 7.3 (i.e. distances along 0Y in Figure 7.4 correspond to areas such as $p^s_o q_o$ in Figure 7.3). Similarly, distances along the vertical axis in Figure 7.4 measure alternative levels of aggregate consumer outlay, E, as determined by the D curve in Figure 7.3 (i.e. distances along OE correspond to areas such as $p^d_o q_o$ in Figure 7.3). Then we may define the *aggregate spending function*, $E = f\{Z(q)\}$ parametrically in terms of the variable q, and define the equilibrium level of aggregate producer outlay, Z^*, by the requirement $E = Z$ (i.e., $q(p^d - p^s) = 0$), at which point the spending function must intersect the

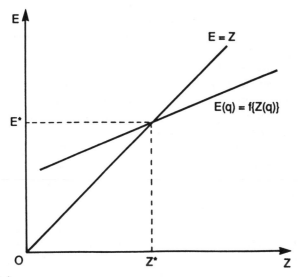

Figure 7.4.

45°-line. On this interpretation, the stability condition is that, in the neighbourhood of the intersection point, the slope of the spending function, which we shall call the *marginal propensity to spend*, must be less than one. But it can be shown that the marginal propensity to spend is less than, equal to, or greater than one according as the quantity elasticity of the demand curve D is less than, equal to, or greater than the quantity elasticity of the supply curve S.[15] Thus the Marshallian Cross 'stability'[16] condition, though it appears outwardly to depend only on the spending proclivities of consumers, depends also on the outlay proclivities of producers.[17]

The case where the marginal propensity to spend is equal to one is of particular interest in the light of post-Marshallian writings. In that case the D and S curves in Figure 7.3 – and therefore the E(q) and E=Z curves in Figure 7.4 – coincide throughout a range of values of q in the neighbourhood of the equilibrium point and we have what Marshall described as *neutral* equilibrium (see Whitaker, I, pp. 153–4). This corresponds to what Keynes (*JMK*, VII, pp. 25–6) later described as 'Say's Law'. Needless to say, this 'Law' forms no part of Marshall's thinking about either particular markets or product markets considered as a whole (cf. Marshall's remarks in a similar connection at p. 201 of Whitaker, II).

Let me conclude this section with a few remarks on some problems that arise if one attempts to generalize the Marshallian model of short-period output equilibrium to deal with broader questions of comparative statics or dynamics. Anyone who is familiar with Marshall's early writings, with his 1898 *Economic Journal* reply to criticisms by Hadley and Irving Fisher (reprinted in Guillebaud, II, pp. 62–75; see especially the long footnote on the theory of market interest rates at p. 74), with his testimony before select committees of Parliament (included in the Pigou volume of Marshall's *Official Papers*), and with early as well as late editions of the *Principles*, will have no difficulty recognizing that these materials provide an ample basis for constructing a 'closed' Marshallian macro-model closely analogous to that set out in Keynes' *General Theory*. In such a generalized model, the *mutatis mutandis* demand function D and the *ceteris paribus* supply function S would include as arguments variables representing such things as the quantity of (outside) money, the money rate of interest, the money wage rate, accumulated real wealth, etc., as well as a variety of shift parameters representing such things as consumer and business 'confidence', expectations of inflation, the state of technology, and so on. It would then be a simple matter to perform various comparative statics ('multiplier') exercises with the model. The question is whether such exercises, if performed at all, might best be carried out with the reduced form spending function that appears in the Marshallian Cross diagram, or with the aggregate demand and supply curves in terms of which the spending function is defined. Views may differ as to the proper answer to this question; but it seems to me that to work with the Marshallian Cross rather than the underlying aggregate demand and supply curves is to court a serious risk of misunderstanding and confusion.

As concerns dynamical extensions of the Marshallian macro-model, I would merely recall my earlier remarks concerning the complexity of the implicit micro-foundations of Marshall's analysis (see the penultimate paragraph of section 1, above). How one might best model a Marshallian macro-system would depend crucially on how one chose to model a competitive economy in which individual producers make their own markets, administer their own asking prices, and adapt their price and output policies in the light of prevailing excess demand conditions in their own 'particular' markets. If this is so, then clearly there is no short or easy path from Marshallian macro-models of short-period equilibrium to intectually satisfying macromodels of real-time dynamics.[18]

3. Was Keynes a Marshallian?

It is commonly argued that the major analytical contribution of the

General Theory lies in the 'theory of effective demand' set out in chapter 3 of Keynes' book.[19] Unfortunately, Keynes' argument in that chapter is occasionally ambiguous or confused, so to this day there is considerable doubt as to how his theory should be interpreted. In the pages that remain, I shall argue that only a Marshallian interpretation is consistent with the letter as well as the spirit of Keynes' argument. What this finding might portend for future research in macroeconomic theory will be the subject of a later paper.[20]

Let me proceed by first restating Keynes' central argument in terms of aggregate demand and supply functions in which output rather than employment is treated as the independent variable.[21] On this assumption, the Keynesian aggregate supply function shown as $Z(q)$ in Figure 7.5a indicates, for any given amount of output, 'the expectation of proceeds which will just make it worth the while of . . . entrepreneurs to produce [that output]' (*JMK*, VII, p. 24). Similarly, the Keynesian aggregate demand function shown as $E\{Z(q)\}$ in Figure 7.5a indicates, for any given amount of output, 'the proceeds which entrepreneurs expect to receive from [that output]' (*JMK*, VII, pp. 25).[22] With appropriate editorial insertions, Keynes' own statement of the theory of effective demand would then read as follows:

> [I]f for a given value of [q] the expected proceeds are greater than the aggregate supply price, i.e. if [E] is greater than Z, there will be an incentive to entrepreneurs to increase [output] and, if necessary, to raise costs by competing with one another for the factors of production, up to the value of [q] for which Z has become equal to [E]. Thus the volume of [output] is given by the point of intersection between the aggregate demand function and the aggregate supply function; for it is at this point that the entrepreneurs' expectation of profits will be maximized. The value of [E], where it is intersected by the aggregate supply function, will be called *the effective demand*. [This] is the substance of the General Theory of Employment, which it will be our object to expound [in] succeeding chapters.[23]

Keynes' argument can be easily translated into a form that makes it indistinguishable from the Marshallian model set out in section 2 above. We have only to interpret Keynes' 'aggregate supply price' as $Z = p^s(q) \cdot q$ and Keynes' 'aggregate demand price' as $E = p^d q = D\{q, Z\} \cdot q$. Then for any chosen value of q, say q_0, the corresponding supply price, p^s_0, is given by the *slope* of the secant OA in Figure 7.5a, while the corresponding demand price, p^d_0, is given by the slope of the secant OB. Equilibrium occurs when the level of output is such that the supply price and demand price secants coincide (so both secants pass through the intersection of Z with E in Figure 7.5a); only at this point are entrepreneurial profits maximized.[24]

But Keynes' theory of effective demand may also be assigned a

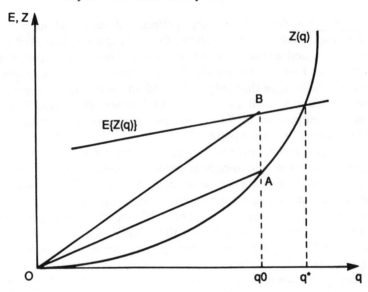

Figure 7.5a.

Walrasian interpretation. This is accomplished by defining 'aggregate supply' as $Z = p \cdot q^s(p)$ and defining 'aggregate demand' as $E = p \cdot q^d = p \cdot \mathbf{D}\{Z(p), p\}$, where p denotes 'market price' and **D** is the Walrasian counterpart of the Marshallian *mutatis mutandis* demand function D.[25] Then for any given value of p, say p_o, we can identify the corresponding profit-maximizing level of aggregate output, q_o, with the abscissa of the point of intersection of the aggregate supply curve, Z, with a secant through the origin of slope p_o (point A in Figure 7.5b). Aggregate quantity demanded at the same price can be identified as the abscissa of the point of intersection of the secant OB in Figure 7.5b with a horizontal line representing the value of aggregate expenditure corresponding to q_o, i.e. $E_o = p_o q_o$. On this interpretation, equilibrium occurs if and only if market price attains a value corresponding to the slope of the secant OC in Figure 7.5b so that $E - Z = p(q^d - q^s) = 0$.

We obtain yet another interpretation of Keynes' theory if we adopt a Hicksian 'fix-price' point of view. Specifically, define Z as qp^*, where p^* is some given value of the 'asking price' of producers, and define E as $p^* \mathbf{D}\{p^*, Z(p^*)\}$. These definitions yield a model in which entrepreneurs would like to produce and sell the profit-maximizing level of output $q(p^*)$, defined in Figure 7.5c by the abscissa of the intersection of Z with Z' (Z' is simply the product of output with marginal cost; thus

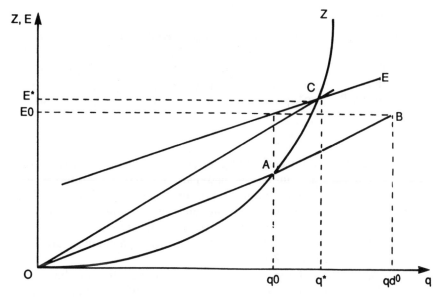

Figure 7.5b.

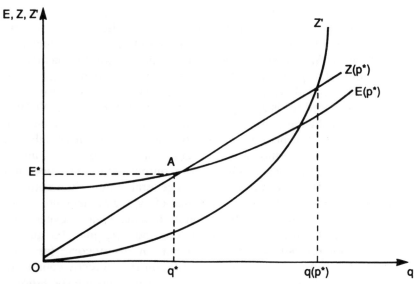

Figure 7.5c.

Table 7.1

Interpretation	Agg. Supply (Z)	Agg. Demand (E)	Equilibrium
Marshallian	$p^s(q) \cdot q$	$p^d(q) \cdot q$	$p^s(q) = p^d(q)$
Walrasian	$p \cdot q^s(p)$	$p \cdot q^d(p)$	$q^s(p) = q^d(p)$
Hicksian Fix-P	$p^* \cdot q$	$p^* \cdot q^d(p^*, q)$	$q = q^d(p^*, q)$

where Z and Z' intersect, asking price equals marginal cost). But short-period sales are limited by aggregate demand, so producers are assumed to aim not at an output that maximizes short-period profit but rather at an output that is saleable under prevailing conditions of aggregate demand. Thus equilibrium occurs in this model if and only if inventory accumulation (virtual or actual) is zero–defined in Figure 7.5c by the point A at which Z intersects E.

For convenient reference, the central characteristics of the three alternative interpretations of Keynes' 'theory of effective demand' are summarized in Table 7.1. The independent variable in the Marshallian case is q; $p^s(q)$ then corresponds to what would nowadays be called marginal (production plus marketing) cost, while $p^d(q)$ represents the highest (uniform) unit price that buyers would be willing to pay for any given (constantly maintained) flow of output q. The independent variable in the Walrasian case is p; $q^s(p)$ is then the profit-maximizing level of output at price p, while $q^d(p)$ is the utility-maximizing level of quantity demanded at p. Finally, in the Hicksian Fix-Price case, quantity produced (q) is again treated as the independent variable (just as in the Marshallian case) while quantity demanded is treated as a function of the fixed price p^* and of current output q (thus combining elements of the Walrasian and Marshallian cases). In this case, unlike the two preceding cases, equilibrium of output as a whole does not entail (expected) profit-maximization; in general, equilibrium output is simply determined by the prevailing state of aggregate demand.

Now, how do each of these interpretations square with Keynes' own statement of the theory of effective demand? As may be quickly confirmed by re-reading Keynes' account of his 'theory' (as cited earlier), the Hicksian Fix-Price interpretation runs directly counter to the letter and spirit of Keynes' argument; yet it is this interpretation – introduced tacitly into the literature through Samuelson's influential textbook presentation of the 'Keynesian Cross' – that has dominated classroom and editorial-page macroeconomics for the past forty years.

Whatever one's view might be about this interpretation as a rendition of Keynes' central message, therefore, there can be no doubt that this interpretation has been marvellously useful for teaching 'Keynesian' economics to bankers and undergraduates; the beauty of the interpretation is that it requires no previous knowledge of economics! It may well turn out that, in some yet-to-be-determined sense, the Hicksian Fix-Price interpretation of Keynes ultimately will be viewed as 'the only way to go' in macroeconomics; be that as it may, it would be grossly disingenuous to claim that this approach owes anything except its initial inspiration to Keynes. The 'theory' in *The General Theory* is decidedly not of the Hicksian fix-price variety.

The Walrasian interpretation fails to conform with Keynes' argument mainly because it presumes that output adjustments are driven by market-determined prices rather than by the competitive jostling of independent profit-seeking, market-making firms. Of course, this is of little consequence unless one is concerned with micro-foundations and related questions involving the dynamics of macroeconomic adjustment. It would surely be unfair to Keynes, however, to hitch his wagon of effective demand to the horse of neo-Walrasian general equilibrium analysis–though, admittedly, that is precisely what was done in early formalizations of the *General Theory* by Hicks, Harrod, Meade, Lange, Modigliani and Klein.

The Marshallian interpretation remains as the only one that faithfully mirrors both the letter and spirit of Keynes' argument. Ironically, it is also the only interpretation among those identified here that has been consistently overlooked or ignored in the post-Keynesian literature. It is not far-fetched to conjecture that the contemporary muddle in Keynesian macroeconomics is due in part to past professional neglect of the Marshall connection. Indeed, I have no doubt that just such a case could be made; but an affirmative argument to that effect must be left for another occasion.

Notes

1.   Hugh C. Lane Professor of Economic Theory, University of South Carolina. I owe much to Axel Leijonhufvud of UCLA for numerous conversations about the topics discussed in this chapter. I am grateful also to Daniel Friedman of UC, Santa Cruz, for supplying mathematical notes on the model that underlies the first two sections of the present chapter.
2.   Clower (1975, p. 187). For a similar view, see Ohlin (1981, p. 223).
3.   'Backtracking' is part of an oral tradition at UCLA. The term is defined in an unpublished essay by Axel Leijonhufvud on 'The Uses of the Past': 'when the workable vein [of an accepted research programme] runs out, [one] way to go is to backtrack. Back there, in the past, there were forks in the road and it is possible . . . that some roads were more passable than the one that looked most promising at the time' (Leijonhufvud, 1978, pp. 8–9).

Keynes' General Theory: *the Marshall connection   145*

4. I refer to his 'Essay on Value' (*c.* 1871), reprinted in Whitaker, 1975, vol.1, pp. 129–32. For the dating of Marshall's essay, see Whitaker's comments, ibid., p. 120.
5. Marshall's definition of (short period) supply price becomes increasingly detailed, though never entirely unambiguous, in later writings. His clearest statement is in the 8th edn of *Principles* (p. 373): 'The general drift of the term normal supply price is always the same whether the period to which it refers is short or long . . . In every case reference is made to a certain given rate of aggregate production . . . In every case the price is that the expectation of which is sufficient and only just sufficient to make it worth while for people to set themselves to produce that aggregate amount; in every case the cost of production is marginal; that is, it is the cost of production of those goods which are on the margin of not being produced at all, and which would not be produced if the price to be got for them were expected to be lower.'
6. Demand price is described in the 8th edn as the 'price at which each particular amount of [a] commodity can find purchasers in a day or week or year.' This concept is no doubt less slippery than the notion of supply price; but whereas Marshall was fairly clear about the factors upon which supply price does or might depend in various circumstances, he was never precise about the 'micro-foundations' of the demand price function.
7. The corresponding passage from the 8th edn of the *Principles* is longer and more explicit but conveys exactly the same message:

> When . . . the amount produced [in a unit of time] is such that the demand price is greater than the supply price, then sellers receive more than is sufficient to make it worth their while to bring goods to market to that amount; and there is at work an active force tending to increase the amount brought forward for sale. On the other hand, when the amount produced is such that the demand price is less than the supply price, sellers receive less than is sufficient to make it worth their while to bring goods to market on that scale; so that those who were just on the margin of doubt as to whether to go on producing are decided not to do so, and there is an active force at work tending to diminish the amount brought forward for sale. When the demand price is equal to the supply price, the amount produced has no tendency either to be increased or to be diminished; it is in equilibrium.

8. I put quotation marks around the word 'stability' because the stability at issue here is purely virtual. Marshall's analysis, like all exercises of its kind, is concerned with *tendencies* that are assumed to be operative in alternative initial situations; it does not refer to real-time adjustment processes (cf. Samuelson, 1947, p. 269ff.)
9. In the 1871 'Essay', Marshall remarks: 'We assume in our theoretical work that competition acts freely: but in so far as it does not the results obtained from the theory will require to be corrected . . . before they can be applied to any particular case.' He then goes on to discuss cases in which competition acts freely but prices *over very short periods* tend to be rigid. This remark might well provide the germ of an alternative treatment of what is now called the theory of monopolistic competition.
10. This is a paraphrase of a remark made originally by Joan Robinson.
11. This seems a sensible supposition in the present context; for if we start with Marshall's conception of competition, then 'impersonal market forces' drive individual asking prices towards equality at the highest price bid by any buyer (cf. Marshall, 1920, pp. 324–5).
12. Defined by Marshall in the 1st edn of the *Principles* (p. 420, fn. 2) as 'the aggregate outlay required for producing any given amount of a commodity'. The magnitude in question corresponds to what Keynes later called 'Aggregate Supply Price', so I follow Keynes' notation and denote it by Z.
13. The graphical derivation of the D curve is straightforward. It is the locus of intersections of alternative *ceteris paribus* demand curves, $D(Z_o)$, $D(Z_1)$, $D(Z_2)$,

146 Twentieth-century economic thought

etc., with perpendiculars erected from alternative values of aggregate output, q_0, q_1, q_2, etc., which enter into the determination of the corresponding values of aggregate producer outlays Z_0, Z_1, Z_2, etc. Cf. Parranello (1980, p. 72); Kregel, (1985, pp. 544–5).

14. Assuming that demand price is the same for all producers and that supply price may be identified with marginal cost, equilibrium for output as a whole can occur if and only if each producer is maximizing profit. Patinkin's contrary assertion (Patinkin, 1982, p. 127) is simply mistaken.

15. By definition:
$$dE/dZ = (dE/dq)/(dZ/dq) = [d(qp^d)/dq]/[d(qp^s)/dq]$$
$$= [1 + (q/p^d)(dp^d/dq)]/[1 + (q/p^s)(dp^s/dq)].$$
The elasticity result stated in the text then follows.

16. Again it should be emphasized that 'stability' here refers to virtual tendencies, not to real-time adjustment processes. Marshall's writings provide valuable materials for constructing models of real-time adjustment, but few of his actual models can be so construed.

17. Cf. Ambrosi (1981), p. 508.

18. For an apparently different view of this problem, see Patinkin, (1982), pp. 30–1.

19. Compare Patinkin (1982) pp. 8,9. 123; Tarshis (1979), pp. 361–2.

20. Some hint of my present thoughts on this subject may be gleaned from Clower (1988), pp. 85–6.

21. Keynes' failure to adopt the same procedure seems to have been related to his doubts about the theoretical meaningfulness of the concept of 'output as a whole' (cf. *JMK*, VII, p. 38). I don't question the validity of these doubts, but since the meaningfulness of the concept of 'employment as a whole' is equally suspect, I see no reason – other than considerations of analytical convenience – to prefer one concept to the other. For present purposes, aggregate output happens to be a more convenient variable than aggregate employment. For a similar view, see Tarshis (1979), p. 366.

22. Later on p. 25, Keynes changes his language and refers to 'the proceeds which entrepreneurs expect to receive' as 'expected proceeds', yet later (p. 29) as 'the amount which the community is expected to spend', and yet later (p.30) as 'the amount entrepreneurs can expect to get back'. A pedant might regard these different phrases as evidencing serious confusion of thought on Keynes' part, but I believe they reflect nothing more than a prose master's concern that his writing be moderately graceful as well as tolerably precise.

23. It is instructive to compare this paragraph from the *General Theory* with Marshall's analogous account of output equilibrium in a single market (see n. 7, above).

24. Cf. Tarshis (1979), pp. 366–8.

25. For a graphical derivation of **D**, see Kregel (1985), pp. 544–5.

References

Ambrosi, G. M. (1981), 'Keynes and the 45° cross', *Journal of Post-Keynesian Economics*, 3, Summer, pp. 503–9.

Clower, Robert W. (1975) 'Reflections on the Keynesian perplex', as reprinted in Donald Walker (ed.) (1984), *Money and Markets*, Cambridge: Cambridge University Press.

Clower, Robert W. (1987), 'Keynes and the classics revisited', in *Keynes and Public Policy After Fifty Years*, 2 vols, O. Hamouda and J. Smithin (eds), Upleaden: Edward Elgar, 1988, pp. 81–91.

Guillebaud, C. W. (1961), *Marshall's Principles of Economics*, 2 vols, New York: Macmillan.

Keynes, John Maynard (1930), *The General Theory of Employment Interest and Money*, *JMK*, Vol. VII.

Keynes, John Maynard (1933), *Essays in Biography*, *JMK*, Vol. X.

Kregel, Jan (1985), 'Sidney Weintraub's macrofoundations of microeconomics and the theory of distribution', *Journal of Post Keynesian Economics*, 7, Summer, pp. 540–58.

Leijonhufvud, Axel (1987), 'The uses of the past', paper prepared for the 14th Annual meeting of the History of Economics Society, Boston, 19 June–22 June 1987.

Marshall, Alfred (1920), *Principles of Economics*, 8th edn, London: Macmillan.

Myrdal, Gunnar (1972), *Against the Stream: Critical Essays in Economics*, New York: Pantheon.

Ohlin, Bertil (1981), 'Stockholm and Cambridge: Four papers on the monetary and employment theory of the 1930s', *History of Political Economy*, 13, Summer, pp. 189–238.

Patinkin, Don (1982), *Anticipations of the General Theory?* Chicago: University of Chicago Press.

Parrinello, Sergio (1980), 'The price level implicit in Keynes' effective demand'. *Journal of Post-Keynesian Economics*, 3, Autumn, pp. 63–78.

Pigou, A. C. (1926), *Official Papers of Alfred Marshall*, London: Macmillan.

Samuelson, Paul A. (1947), *Foundations of Economic Analysis*. Cambridge, Mass.: Harvard Univeristy Press.

Tarshis, Lorie (1979), 'The aggregate supply function in Keynes' *General Theory*', in *Essays in Honor of Tibor Scitovsky*, ed. M. J. Boskin, New York: Academic Press, pp. 361–92.

Walker, Donald A. (ed.) (1984), *Money and Markets: Essays by Robert W. Clower*. New York: Cambridge University Press.

Whitaker, J. K. (1975), *The Early Economic Writings of Alfred Marshall. 1867–1890*, 2 vols, New York: Free Press.

20

7 Keynes and the classics revisited
Robert W. Clower

'The thing can be done,' said the Butcher, 'I think,
  The thing can be done, I am sure.
The thing shall be done! Bring me paper and ink.
  The best there is time to procure.' (Lewis Carroll, *The Hunting of the Snark*)

Macroeconomics has been in a muddle longer than anyone now cares to remember. The muddle began with the *General Theory* when Keynes failed to identify 'a fatal flaw in that part of ... orthodox reasoning that deals with the theory of what determines the level of effective demand and the volume of aggregate employment' (*CW*, XIII, p. 486). It was exacerbated by the failure of Keynes's interpreters – Hicks, Hansen, Klein, Samuelson, Modigliani, Patinkin, Leijonhufvud, and others – to make sense of arguments that Keynes had bungled. The accompanying tumult of controversy produced a plethora of models and a babel of conclusions, all more or less plausible, none sufficiently compelling to command widespread acceptance – an enormous superstructure of macroeconomic knowledge in search of a unifying theory.

How best to bring this body of practical knowledge together within the framework of an intellectually satisfying theory, no doubt will remain an open question for a long time to come. My purpose here is merely to give focus to future work in this direction by taking a fresh look at the much-discussed issue of 'Keynes and the classics'. I start (as Keynes started) with a simplified aggregative model of classical theory which can plausibly be claimed to represent an essentially self-adjusting monetary economy, and I ask (as so many economists since Keynes have asked): what characteristics of the classical theory might plausibly be altered to yield a model consilient with Keynes's 'vision'? In answering this question, I think we shall find materials that are indeed helpful in suggesting fruitful directions for future macroecomic research.

The classical tradition
No classical theory of short-run adjustment is to be found in the pre-Keynesian literature,[1] probably because no classical writer thought it purposeful to attempt to reduce the complexities of real-time trading processes to analytical order. So my version of short-run classical theory is less a description of what any pre-Keynesian writer actually said than an

81

account of what I think a nineteenth-century 'true believer' in the self-adjusting capabilities of the economic system might have said had he been trained in modern theory.

Taking our cue from John Hicks's influential 1937 paper on 'Keynes and the Classics',[2] let us start by considering a fiat money economy with just four classes of non-money commodities: consumption goods (c), capital goods (k), labour (n) and loans (b). Suppose that the number of traders and the physical volume of trading in each commodity is sufficiently great that, even in the very short run, no seller or buyer either imagines himself or is in fact capable of significantly influencing the terms of trade by his own actions. More succinctly, *assume that any trader can buy or sell any desired quantity of any commodity on short notice at the "going" price.* For future reference, let us call this assumption the Thick Market hypothesis. Then, whether we regard the typical trader as one of many transactors in an organized auction market or as a market-maker in his own right, we may suppose that short-run sale and purchase decisions are governed at every point in time by the prevailing (average) market prices, p_c, p_k, $p_n = w$, and $p_b = 1/r$.

Still following Hicks, let us further assume that the money wage rate, w, is given and that capital goods already in use are specialized to particular trades and have no second-hand market. Then we may set out our 'classical' model as a system of three price-adjustment equations:

$$dp_c/dt = a_c \left[d_c(p_c, p_k, w, r, Y_n, M) - s_c(p_c/w) \right] \tag{1}$$
$$dp_k/dt = a_k \left[d_k(p_c, p_k, w, r, M) - s_k(p_k/w) \right] \tag{2}$$
$$dr/dt = a_b \left[x_b(p_c, p_k, w, r, M) \right] \tag{3}$$

where d, s and x stand for 'demand', 'supply' and 'excess demand', M represents the quantity of money and Y_n represents the realized money earnings of workers.[3]

On the Thick Market hypothesis, it is plausible to suppose that the motions of this system in the neighbourhood of an equilibrium point are stable and heavily damped; hence the average 'observed' values of the dependent variables p_c, p_k, and r may be presumed to be given as reduced-form solutions of the excess demand equations. The qualitative properties of these solutions are standard. Here it will suffice to remark that, assuming no money illusion, relative prices and the rate of interest – hence output and employment – will vary with changes in the quantity of money. Monetary neutrality holds only if we assume flexible money wage rates and add a wage-adjustment equation to the system.[4]

This model captures the essential flavour of classical theory. Except as a 'temporary abode of purchasing power', money has no significance as an asset because in normal circumstances it offers its holder no return and is no more 'liquid' than any other commodity. Money plays a special role in the economy only because it enters into one side of every exchange transaction and so – through real balance effects – directly influences the absolute level of money prices. Individual economic activities are coordinated by 'the price system'. If changes in underlying parameters ('animal spirits', the 'propensity to hoard', etc.) produce temporary inconsistencies in consumption, production or trading plans, these inconsistencies are quickly reconciled through movements in prices, any consequent changes in output and employment being incidental.

There are extreme cases of course in which the system could get into trouble. A sudden collapse in the marginal efficiency of capital, for example, might yield so low a price for capital goods that gross real investment would go to zero and remain there pending the elimination of excess capacity through gradual wear and tear. Similar consequences might ensue if trading in loans came to be dominated by speculative 'bulls' and 'bears' whose gambling proclivities pushed the real rate of interest to a level where new investment was chronically unprofitable. Notice, however, that in both these cases the underlying source of delayed adjustment is the absence of a market for second-hand capital goods. In effect, the assumption that existing capital goods can't be traded (as also the assumption that the money wage rate is given) is a violation of the Thick Market hypothesis. Thus our discussion of extreme cases merely reinforces earlier indications that the classical conception of the economic system as naturally self-adjusting is intimately connected with the validity of the Thick Market hypothesis.

Keynes's *General Theory*

Turning now to the *General Theory*, we have no need to invent a model; we can start with Keynes's summary of the analytical core of his argument, as set forth in chapter 18 (pp. 247–9) of the *General Theory*. This summary has been formalized in various ways by later interpreters and critics; but John Hicks's 1937 'interpretation' sets out the nearest thing to a canonical representation of the Keynesian model, so let us settle for that (Modigliani's 1944 model has achieved much the same status, but is less general because it treats capital goods and consumption goods as identical rather than distinct commodities.)

First, we need some additional notation. Let Y denote total income, defined as the sum of income produced in the consumption goods industries, $Y_c, = p_c s_c(p_c/w)$, and income produced in the investment goods industries, $Y_k = p_k s_k (p_k/w)$:

$$Y = Y_c + Y_k$$

302 *Economic Doctrine and Method*

Similarly, let E_c and E_k denote total expenditure on consumption and investment goods: $E_c = p_c d_c$ (.); $E_k = p_k d_k$ (.).

Then continuing as before to treat the money wage rate and the quantity of money as given parameters, we may express Hicks's schematic model of Keynes's *General Theory*[5] as:

$$M = L(r, Y) \tag{4}$$
$$Y_k = E_k(r, Y) \tag{5}$$
$$Y_k = Y - E_c(r, Y) \tag{6}$$

This system of three equations may be presumed to determine solution values of Y, Y_k and r from which – taking account of earlier definitions and underlying production functions – we can work out corresponding solution values of employment and output. But in what sense can the system in equations (4)–(6) be said to represent a 'theory of output and employment' rather than a 'theory of price'?

To answer this question, let us first rewrite the system to reveal the price variables that are suppressed in the present formulation. Making use of earlier definitions of Y, Y_k, E_k, and E_c, and carrying out appropriate simplifications (specifically the cancellation of price variables that appear on both sides of the last two equations), we obtain:

$$M = L(r, p_c/w, p_k/w)$$
$$s_k\{p_k/w\} = d_k(r, p_c/w, p_k/w)$$
$$s_c\{p_c/w\} = d_c(r, p_c/w, p_k/w)$$

This system, though formally equivalent to the system in (4)–(6), is more naturally regarded as a 'theory of price' than a 'theory of output and employment'. We may clinch the issue by expressing the model as a set of differential equations:

$$dr/dt = b_r[M - L(r, p_c/w, p_k/w)] \tag{1a}$$
$$dp_c/dt = b_c[d_c(r, p_c/w, p_k/w) - s_c\{p_c/w\}] \tag{2a}$$
$$dp_k/dt = b_k[d_k(r, p_c/w, p_k/w) - s_k\{p_k/w\}] \tag{3a}$$

This system differs from our earlier 'classical' model in just two major respects. First, the excess demand for bonds is expressed in terms of 'liquidity preference' rather than the demand and supply of 'loanable funds.' But this is merely a matter of form, for since money enters into one side of every transaction, we might also express the excess demands for consumption and investment goods in 'liquidity preference' terms ('The reward for parting with liquidity is immediate gratification through consumption, or the expectation of a stream of future profit, or...').[6] Secondly, the money variable is omitted from the excess demand functions in (2a) and (3a); but this merely reflects an implicit specification error in the underlying Hicks model. From a conceptual standpoint, therefore, the Keynesian system in (1a)–(3a) is formally indistinguishable from our earlier classical model in (1)–(3) and cannot plausibly be regarded as possessing behaviour properties that would permit us to reach any but 'classical' conclusions.[7]

Now there can be no doubt that to accept the system in (1a)–(3a) – and so the system in (1)–(3) – as a model of Keynes's *General Theory* is equivalent to imputing to Keynes a faith in the efficacy of the price system that is utterly at variance with his actual beliefs. But neither can there be serious doubt that Hicks's simple model of the *General Theory* accurately reflects the substance – the letter if not the spirit – of Keynes's formal analysis. The crux of the matter is that Keynes in the *General Theory* not only failed to reject, but positively embraced, an essentially classical (more accurately, neo-classical) theory of short-run output determination, and thereby implicitly adopted the Thick Market hypothesis as a basis for his own theory of aggregate supply.[8] Keynes's theory of aggregate demand, though outwardly novel because it makes the current level of total expenditure depend upon the prevailing level of output and employment, actually involves no significant departure from classical tradition. So the theoretical foundations of the *General Theory* are incompatible with the beliefs that led Keynes to write it albeit unintentionally.

Salvaging the *General Theory*
Evidently the central message of Keynes's *General Theory* can be salvaged only by discarding the conventional theory of short-run supply. But we cannot discard the conventional theory of short-run supply unless we also discard the conception of market organization on which it is based; for the conventional theory merely expresses how rational sellers would behave if their trading activities were confined to thick markets.

The *General Theory* contains no hint that Keynes was in any way dissatisfied with the conventional theory of supply; indeed the conventional theory plays a central role in his claim that real wages generally move in the same direction as output over the trade cycle. It was not until 1939, in his response to criticisms of this claim by Dunlop and Tarshis,[9] that Keynes explicitly voiced doubts about the assumptions underlying his earlier analysis of aggregate supply and, more particularly, questioned the validity of what I have called the Thick Market hypothesis by linking producer discretion in short-period pricing policy with trading in thin rather than thick markets.[10]

A thick market, as noted earlier, is one in which traders can be presumed to know within narrow limits the price at which any desired quantity of a commodity can be bought or sold on short notice. A thin market is one in

86   Keynes and public policy after fifty years

which the opposite presumption holds: trading volume is too slight to permit traders to gauge, even within broad limits, the price at which desired sales or purchases can be completed on short notice. The crucial difference is that for thick markets it makes sense to suppose that the short-run revenues of individual producers are determined by their output choices, while for thin markets the same supposition makes no sense at all. Let us explore the implications of the second case.

Consider a representative producer whose short-run average variable and average total costs are represented by the curves AVC and ATC in Figure 7.1.

By hypothesis, the producer has no usable information about his probable short-run sales at alternative asking prices, so there can be no question of choosing a combination of price and output that maximizes short-run profit. Over the longer run the producer can hope to influence sales by appropriate market manoeuvres (advertising, temporary price cuts, etc.), but more immediately he is largely at the mercy of impersonal (and predetermined) market forces. Under these conditions probably the simplest and most sensible strategy is for the producer to set his asking or list price at a reasonable level and hope for the best in the way of sales volume. What seems 'reasonable' to the producer will depend of course on past sales experience, on present and prospective costs and on present and prospective competition. Here, let us interpret 'reasonable' to mean a price (P_0 in Figure 7.1) high enough to ensure that average total costs are covered for a range of sales levels significantly less than capacity output, s^*.[11]

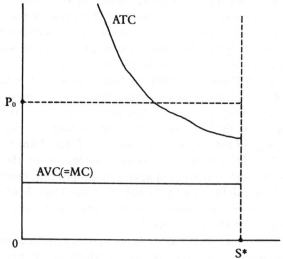

Figure 7.1

Then since the 'asking' or 'list' price exceeds average variable (and marginal) cost for all outputs less than s*, the producer will be *willing* to produce and sell any less-than-capacity output at his posted price. But the amount that can *actually* be sold will depend upon customer demand at that price, which will depend on a host of conditions over which the producer has no short-run control. In these circumstances it is plausible to argue that the producer will adjust output passively to match average sales at the posted price, holding buffer stocks of inventories to avoid frequent transient adjustments of output. Thus, on average, short-run output will move in the same direction as realized sales.

Taking account of the preceding argument, but referring now to an economy in which all produced goods are traded in thin markets, let us suppose that aggregative short-run output and interest rate behaviour may be characterized by the adjustment equations:

$$dq_c/dt = h_c[d_c(.) - q_c] \qquad (7)$$
$$dq_k/dt = h_k[d_k(.) - q_k] \qquad (8)$$
$$dr/dt = h_b[x_b(.)] \qquad (9)$$

where q_i $(i = c, k)$ represents current output as contrasted with 'supply' and $(.) = (p_c, p_k, w, r, Y, M)$ – argument Y rather than Y_n appearing in $(.)$ because, under our present assumptions, producers as well as workers may be 'income-constrained' in the short run.

The system in equations (7)–(9) accurately portrays what has come to be rgarded as the distinctive feature of Keynesian economics: aggregate output is determined by aggregate sales and prices play no role in the short-run adjustment of income to changes in effective demand. This of course is the route to salvage of Keynesian economics that is taken in most textbooks, usually without notice to the reader that the underlying assumptions concerning short-period output variations are completely at odds with the conventional profit maximization model of supply presented in later microeconomic sections of the same text. It also corresponds to the extreme case of what Hicks has dubbed 'fix-price theory'.[12]

Apart from being a crude caricature of Keynes's analysis, the system in equations (7)–(9) seriously misrepresents the role of prices in the short-run adjustment process. In situations involving significant unused capacity, producers can be expected to engage in competitive selling activities (temporary discounts, rebates, prize contests, etc.) in an effort to boost short-run sales, so average transaction prices will tend to fall. Similarly, in situations involving little unused capacity, producers can be expected to compete for factors in ways that increase both variable and fixed costs, and some of these increases will be passed on in the form of higher asking prices. Arguing heuristically, we may suppose that both sorts of adjustment are adequately described by the aggregative equations:

$$dp^*_c/dt = g_c[d_c(.) - s^*_c] \tag{10}$$
$$dp^*_k/dt = g_k[d_k(.) - s^*_k] \tag{11}$$

where p^*_i is an index of transaction prices and s^*_i is an index of production capacity.[13] Combining these relations with equations (7)–(9), we obtain a system of five adjustment equations to describe short-run movements in quantities, transaction prices and the rate of interest.

The equation for dr/dt in this system calls for no special comment; we may view the loan market as 'thick' and rapidly self-adjusting even in a Keynesian model. But the remaining four equations – two dealing with adjustments in output quantities, and two dealing with movements in average transactions prices – pose problems whose solutions are distinctly problematical.

To see this, suppose that the system starts in temporary equilibrium with capacity fully utilized and sales occurring only at posted list prices. Next suppose that the equilibrium is disturbed by a decline in 'animal spirits', 'confidence', or what have you, causing investment expenditure to fall. Then investment goods output will quickly decline, because the speed of adjustment coefficients in equations (7) and (8) are, by hypothesis, large numbers. Prices will not decline noticeably in the short run because the adjustment coefficients in equations (10) and (11) are – again by hypothesis – relatively small. Both 'workers' and 'capitalists' are income-constrained, because neither goods nor services are particularly 'liquid' (though prices are 'administered', and therefore known, quantities sold are unpredictable). So as investment output drops, the demand for consumption goods will also decline via the familiar multiplier process.

Now, initially at least, no counteracting forces will operate to stem the decline. Real balance effects will have no bite, because transaction prices will not fall noticeably, and though the money volume of transactions will decline, the potential effect of this on spending will be attenuated by rising uncertainty about future needs for cash to meet payrolls, etc. – hence a rise in the demand for precautionary balances. There will perhaps be some tendency for spare cash to go into loans; but this tendency will not be strong, because with sales falling and becoming more uncertain, producers will find it increasingly difficult to synchronize purchases with sales, and this will mean that average money balances will tend to increase even at lower volumes of monetary transactions (cf. Clower and Howitt, 1978, in Clower, 1984, pp. 168–70). Nor are matters likely to improve as the decline continues, for in thin markets trade credit (mainly in the form of bookkeeping entries) is likely to play a prominent, and perhaps dominant, role as a short-run means of payment.[14] As sales decline and business confidence weakens, trade credit outstanding will shrink, possibly by substantial percentage amounts, even though currency and deposits subject to check are largely unchanged.

There is no need to carry the story further. Notice that nothing of substance in the above argument is changed if we relax the assumption of fixed wage rates and add a 'thin' market for labour services to our model.

In that more general case, as for the more restricted model in equations (7)–(11), 'observed' short-run behaviour cannot be adequately characterized by static, reduced-form solutions of the adjustment equations. In effect, the normal state of the economy is one of Brownian motion; the system, even if asymptotically stable is so lightly damped that the probability of ever being in the neighbourhood of equilibrium is close to zero. This being so, we cannot expect to advance much further in studying Keynesian problems – problems associated with short-run adjustment processes – using the kind of analytical conventions and mathematical techniques that have served us so well during the past fifty years. What is needed if we are to make further progress in macroeconomics is a radical reconstruction of microeconomics along lines that are only dimly foreshadowed in the existing literature – a reconstruction that will deal seriously with the central unresolved theoretical issues of short-run competitive analysis – which is to say with the Economics of Thin Markets.

Conclusion
No doubt, more might be said about Keynes and the classics, about the reasons why the *General Theory* ultimately failed to convey Keynes's intended message and about alternative ways in which Keynes's essential 'vision' might be salvaged, but this is not the place to say it. Instead, let me offer a few concluding reflections on the rhetoric of the *General Theory*.

Keynes of course proceeded throughout the *General Theory* on the presumption that short-run behaviour could be adequately handled with static models, thereby adopting an analytical procedure that runs directly counter to some of his more distinctive claims, e.g. that there generally exists some 'involuntary' unemployment, that the economic system, if left to itself, tends to attain a state of full employment only by accident, if at all, etc. It is interesting to speculate whether the *General Theory* would have had a longer run, or indeed any run at all, had Keynes adopted an analytical procedure more in keeping with his implicit beliefs.

I have little doubt that Keynes made the right rhetorical decision a half-century ago; anything resembling an explicitly dynamical account of short-run behaviour in thin markets would surely have fallen to blind eyes and deaf ears in 1936. But I do not believe he made his decision consciously

90   *Keynes and public policy after fifty years*

or with a clear view to some of its consequences such as the subsequent albeit delayed rejection of the formal analysis of the *General Theory* by the great majority of professional economists. In retrospect, it seems clear that the essence of Keynes's message was not that labour markets, but that virtually *all* markets, are thin and fail to operate efficiently in a classical sense. But only now, with macroeconomics again in a state of disarray, is it conceivable that such a blanket denial of the Thick Market hypothesis might be accorded a sympathetic reception.

Notes

1. One finds numerous threads of such a theory, particularly in Hume, Thornton, Tooke and Mill (cf. Hicks, 1967), but that is all.
2. The full title is 'Mr Keynes and the classics: a suggested interpretation'.
3. Y_n is included in d_c because, with the money wage rate given, the earnings of workers cannot be presumed to correspond to the money value of services offered for sale, i.e. the demand function for consumption goods is not independent of the current level of output. But this is just a Keynesian (or Marshallian) flourish, for since Y_n may be presumed to depend on prices via the demand for labour, it need not be included as an explicit argument in d_c.
4. In the augmented system, equilibrium money prices and the money wage rate are directly proportional to the quantity of money, as implied by the 'classical' quantity theory. This merely indicates the redundancy of the quantity theory in any model for which the classical invariance proposition holds; it does not validate the quantity theory – or the quantity equation – as a 'behavioural' relation. Hicks's 1937 version of classical theory is flawed in this respect.
5. Hicks also has a model of Keynes's 'special theory' in which the liquidity preference equation takes the form $M = L(r)$, but that will not concern us until later.
6. Cf. Boulding (1944), pp. 55–63.
7. This is essentially the conclusion Hicks reached in his 1937 paper, though he studiously refrained from stating it explicitly either in that paper or in his 1957 *Economic Journal* review of Patinkin's *Money, Interest and Prices* (reprinted with minor revision as ch. 8 of Hicks (1967), pp. 143–54).
8. Patinkin disputes this in various of his recent writings, but (to my mind) not at all convincingly. On this, see Patinkin (1976), p. 93, and Tarshis (1978), pp. 60–3 (in Patinkin and Leith, 1978).
9. Reprinted in *CW*, VII, appendix 3 (see esp. pp. 406–8).
10. Curiously, Keynes seems to have been more aware of the difficulties of the 'theory of short-period supply' in the early 1930s than during the writing of the *General Theory*. In a letter to Hawtrey of 28 November, 1930, for example, responding to Hawtrey's criticisms of the *Treatise*, Keynes says: 'I repeat that I am not dealing with the complete set of causes which determine volume of output. For this would have led me an endless long journey into the theory of short-period supply and a long way from monetary theory; – though I agree that it will probably be difficult in the future to prevent monetary theory and the theory of short-period supply from running together. If I were to write the book again, I should probably attempt to probe further into the difficulties of the latter; but I have already probed far enough to know what a complicated affair it is' *CW*, XIII, pp. 145–6.
11. Cf. P.W.S. Andrews, 'Competitive prices, normal costs and industrial stability', in Andrews and Brunner (1975) pp. 29–31. This is not the place to review recent work on so-called 'customer markets'; suffice it to say that there is little dispute among economists about the 'stylized facts', though there is (of course) much dispute about how they should be interpreted. For some recent comments on this topic see A. Okun (1981),

ch. 4, esp. pp. 138 ff.; E.S. Phelps (1985), pp. 383–404; R.E. Hall and J.B. Taylor (1986), pp. 389–94; R.J. Gordon (1981), pp. 502–4.
12. See Hicks (1966), chs 7–9; Hicks (1982), pp. 231–5.
13. This is no more than a rough schematic representation. The microeconomic theory of price adjustment in thin markets is still in its infancy. For discussion of some of the difficulties that confront us in this area see Bushaw and Clower (1957), ch. 7, pp. 185–9; Phelps *et al.* (1970), pp. 309–37 (Phelps and Winter) and pp. 369–93 (Gordon and Hynes).
14. This is a direct consequence of the desire of makers of thin markets to attract a clientele of 'regular' customers in order to reduce sales uncertainty; trade credit as distinct from bank credit, plays little of a role in thick markets precisely because there is no significant sales uncertainty in this case.

References

Andrews, P. W. S. and Brunner, E. (1975) *Studies in Pricing*, London: Macmillan.
Boulding, K. (1944), 'A liquidity preference theory of market prices, '*Economica*, **11**, May, 55–63.
Bushaw, D. W. and Clower, R. W. (1957), *Introduction to Mathematical Economics*, Homewoood, Ill: Irwin.
Clower, R. W. (1984), *Money and Markets*, ed. D. Walker, Cambridge: Cambridge University Press.
Gordon, R.J. (1981), 'Output fluctuations and gradual price adjustment', *Journal of Economic Literature*, **19**, June, 493–530.
Hall, R. and Taylor, J. (1986), *Macroeconomics*, New York: Norton.
Hicks, J. R. (1937), 'Mr Keynes and the classics: a suggested interpretation', *Econometrica*, **5**, April, 147–59.
Hicks, J. R. (1966), *Capital and Growth*, Oxford: Clarendon Press.
Hicks, J. R. (1967), *Critical Essays in Monetary Theory*, Oxford: Clarendon Press.
Hicks, J. R. (1982), *Money, Interest and Wages*, Oxford: Blackwell.
Keynes, J.M. (var. dates), *Collected Works* (cited as JMK, London: Macmillan/Royal Economic Society.)
Modigliani, F. (1944), 'Liquidity preference and the theory of interest and money', *Econometrica*, **12**, January, 45–88.
Okun, A. (1981) *Prices and Quantities*, Washington, DC: Brookings Institution.
Patinkin, D. (1976), *Keynes's Monetary Thought*, Durham, NC: Duke University Press.
Phelps, E. S. (1985), *Political Economy*, New York: Norton.
Phelps, E.S. et. al. (1970), *Microeconomic Foundations of Employment and Inflation Theory*, New York: Norton.
Tarshis, L. (1978), 'Keynes as seen by his students in the 1930s', in D. Patinkin and J. Clark Leith (eds), *Keynes, Cambridge and the General Theory*, Toronto: University of Toronto Press.

[21]

GREEK ECONOMIC REVIEW, Vol. 12, Supplement, pp. 73-84

- KEYNES'S GENERAL THEORY: A CONTEMPORARY PERSPECTIVE

By Robert W. Clower*

INTRODUCTION

Time has not dealt kindly with the theoretical pretensions of Keynes's *General Theory of Employment, Interest and Money*. To be sure, few economists have ever seriously doubted the practical validity of Keynes's contention that '... the existing economic system is [not], in any significant sense, self-adjusting', (JMK, XIII, p. 486). But equally few economists find themselves in agreement with Keynes because of anything contained in the formal analysis of the *General Theory*; consensus obtains only because of a shared conviction that, on the self-adjustment question, Keynes's 'vision' was right even if his analysis was wrong. So all that remains of Keynes's greatest work after more than fifty years of exegesis and debate is a cluster of plausible conclusions. How best to bring these conclusions together within the framework of an intellectually satisfying theory remains an open question.

My purpose in this paper is not to answer this question but to give it sharper focus. I start (as Keynes started) with a simplified aggregative model of classical theory which can plausibly be claimed to represent an essentially self-adjusting monetary economy, and I ask (as so many economists since Keynes have asked) : what characteristics of the classical theory might plausibly be altered to yield a model consilient with Keynes's 'vision'? Once this preliminary question has been answered, I shall offer some tentative suggestions about directions in which future macroeconomic research should go if we are to have any hope of finally resolving the continuing crisis that has plagued Keynesian economics since its inception a half century ago.

I. THE CLASSICAL TRADITION

No classical theory of short-run adjustment is to be found in the pre-Keynesian literature,[1] probably because no classical writer thought it purposeful to attempt to reduce the complexities of real-time trading processes to

---

* I am grateful to David Littleboy for calling my attention to a misleading quotation of Keynes in the original draft of this paper.

1. One finds numerous threads of such a theory, particularly in Hume, Thornton, Tooke and Mill (Cf. Hicks, 1967); but that is all.

analytical order. So my version of short-run classical theory is less a description of what any pre-Keynesian writer actually said than an account of what I think a Nineteenth Century 'true believer' in the self-adjusting capabilities of the economic system might have said had he been trained in modern theory.

Taking our cue from John Hicks's influential 1937 paper on 'Keynes and the Classics',[2] let us start by considering a fiat money economy with just four classes of non-money commodities : consumption goods (c), capital goods (k), labor (n) and loans (b). Suppose that the number of traders and the physical volume of trading in each commodity is sufficiently great that, even in the very short run, no seller or buyer either imagines himself or is, in fact, capable of significantly influencing the terms of trade by his own actions : more succinctly, *assume that any trader can buy or sell any desired quantity of any commodity on short notice at the 'going' price.* For future reference, let us call this assumption the *Thick Market Hypothesis.* Then, whether we regard the typical trader as one of many transactors in an organized auction market or as a market-maker in his own right, we may suppose that short-run sale and purchase decisions are governed at every point in time by the prevailing (average) market prices, $p_c, p_k, p_n = w$ and $p_b = 1/r$.

Still following Hicks, let us further assume that the money wage rate, w is given and that capital goods already in use are specialized to particular trades and have no second-hand market. Then we may set out our 'classical' model as a system of three price-adjustment equations :

$$dp_c/dt = a_c[d_c(p_c, p_k, w, r, Y_n, M) - s_c(p_c/w)], \tag{1}$$

$$dp_k/dt = a_k[d_k(p_c, p_k, w, r, M) - s_k(p_k/w)], \tag{2}$$

$$dr/dt = a_b[x_b(p_c, p_k, w, r, M)], \tag{3}$$

where d, s and x stand for 'demand', 'supply' and 'excess demand', M represents the quantity of money, and Y_n represents the realized money earnings of workers.[3]

On the Thick Market Hypothesis, it is plausible to suppose that the motions of this system in the neighborhood of an equilibrium point are stable

---

2. The full title is 'Mr. Keynes and the Classics : A Suggested Interpretation'.

3. Y_n is included in d_c because, with the money wage rate given, the earning of workers cannot be presumed to correspond to the money value of services offered for sale; i.e., the demand function for consumption goods is not independent of the current level of output. But this is just a Keynesian (or Marshallian) flourish; for since Y_n may be presumed to depend on prices via the demand for labor, it need not be included as an explicit argument in d_c.

and heavily damped; hence, the average 'observed' values of the dependent variables p_c, p_k, and r may be presumed to be given as reduced-form solutions of the excess demand equations. The qualitative properties of these solutions are standard. Here it will suffice to remark that, assuming no money illusion, relative prices and the rate of interest — hence output and employment — will vary with changes in the quantity of money. Monetary neutrality holds only if we assume flexible money wage rates and add a wage-adjustment equation to the system.[4]

This model captures the essential flavor of classical theory. Except as a 'temporary abode of purchasing power', money has no significance as an asset because in normal circumstances it offers its holder no return and is no more 'liquid' than any other commodity. Money plays a special role in the economy only because it enters into one side of every exchange transaction and so — through real balance effects — directly influences the absolute level of money prices. Individual economic activities are coordinated by 'the price system'. If changes in underlying parameters ('animal spirits', the 'propensity to hoard', etc.) produce temporary inconsistencies in consumption, production or trading plans, these inconsistencies are quickly reconciled through movements in prices, any consequent changes in output and employment being incidental.

There are extreme cases, of course, in which the system could get into trouble. A sudden collapse in the marginal efficiency of capital, for example, might yield so low a price for capital goods that gross real investment would go to zero and remain there pending the elimination of excess capacity through gradual wear and tear. Similar consequences might ensue if trading in loans came to be dominated by speculative 'bulls' and 'bears' whose gambling proclivities pushed the real rate of interest to a level where new investment was chronically unprofitable. Notice, however, that in both these cases the underlying source of delayed adjustment is the absence of a market for second-hand capital goods. In effect, the assumption that existing capital goods can't be traded (as also the assumption that the money wage rate is given) is a violation of the Thick Market Hypothesis. Thus our discussion of extreme cases merely reinforces earlier indications that the classical conception of

---

4. In the augmented system, equilibrium money prices and the money wage rate are directly proportional to the quantity of money, as implied by the 'classical' quantity theory. This merely indicates the redundancy of the quantity theory in any model for which the classical invariance proposition holds; it does not validate the quantity theory — or the quantity equation — as a 'behavior' relation. Hicks's 1937 version of classical theory is flawed in this respect.

the economic system as naturally self-adjusting is intimately connected with the validity of the Thick Market Hypothesis.

II. KEYNES'S GENERAL THEORY

Turning now to the *General Theory*, we have no need to invent a model; we can start with Keynes's summary of the analytical core of his argument, as set forth in Chapter 18 (pp. 247-249) of the *General Theory*. This summary has been formalized in various ways by later interpreters and critics; but John Hicks's 1937 'interpretation' sets out the nearest thing to a canonical representation of the Keynesian model, so let us settle for that (Modigliani's 1944 model has achieved much the same status, but is less general because it treats capital goods and consumption goods as identical rather than distinct commodities).

First we need some additional notation. Let Y denote total income, defined as the sum of income produced in the consumption goods industries, $Y_c = p_c s_c(p_c/w)$, and income produced in the investment goods industries, $Y_k = p_k s_k(p_k/w)$:

$$Y = Y_c + Y_k .$$

Similarly, let E_c and E_k denote total expenditure on consumption and investment goods : $E_c = p_c d_c(\,.\,)$; $E_k = p_k d_k(\,.\,)$.

Then, continuing as before to treat the money wage rate and the quantity of money as given parameters, we may express Hicks's schematic model of Keynes's 'General Theory'[5] as

$$M = L(r, Y), \tag{4}$$

$$Y_k = E_k(r, Y), \tag{5}$$

$$Y_k = Y - E_c(r, Y). \tag{6}$$

This system of three equations may be presumed to determine solution values of Y, Y_k, and r from which, taking account of earlier definitions and underlying production functions, we can work out corresponding solution values of employment and output. But in what sense can the system (4)-(6) be said to represent a 'theory of output and employment' rather than a 'theory of price'?

To answer this question, let us first rewrite the system to reveal the price

5. Hicks also has a model of Keynes's 'special theory' in which the liquidity preference equation takes the form $M = L(r)$; but that will not concern us until later.

variables that are suppressed in the present formulation. Making use of earlier definitions of Y, Y_k, E_k, and E_c carrying out appropriate simplifications (specifically, the cancellation of price variables that appear on both sides of the last two equations), we obtain

$$M = L(r, p_c/w, p_k/w),$$

$$s_k\{p_k/w\} = d_k(r, p_c/w, p_k/w),$$

$$s_c\{p_c/w\} = d_c(r, p_c/w, p_k/w).$$

This system, though formally equivalent to the system (4)-(6),is more naturally regarded as a 'theory of price' than a 'theory of output and employment'. We may clinch the issue by expressing the model as a set of differential equations:

$$dr/dt = b_r[M - L(r, p_c/w, p_k/w)], \tag{1*}$$

$$dp_c/dt = b_c[d_c(r, p_c/w, p_k/w) - s_c(p_c/w)], \tag{2*}$$

$$dp_k/dt = b_k[d_k(r, p_c/w, p_k/w) - s_k(p_k/w)]. \tag{3*}$$

This system differs from our earlier 'classical' model in just two major respects. First, the excess demand for bonds is expressed in terms of 'liquidity preference' rather than the demand and supply of 'loanable funds'. But this is merely a matter of form; for since money enters into one side of every transaction, we might also express the excess demands for consumption and investment goods in 'liquidity preference' terms ('The reward for parting with liquidity is immediate gratification through consumption, or the expectation of a stream of future profit, or...').[6] Second, the money variable is omitted from the excess demand functions in (2*) and (3*); but this merely reflects an implicit specification error in the underlying Hicks model. From a conceptual standpoint, therefore, the Keynesian system (1*)-(3*) is formally indistinguishable from our earlier classical model (1)-(3) and cannot plausibly be regarded as possessing behavior properties that would permit us to reach any but 'classical' conclusions.[7]

Now, there can be no doubt that to accept the system (1*)-(3*) — and so

6. Cf. Boulding (1944), pp. 55-63.

7. This is essentially the conclusion Hicks reached in his 1937 paper, though he studiously refrained from stating it explicitly either in that paper or in his 1957 *Economic Journal* review of Patinkin's *Money, Interest and Prices* (reprinted with minor revision as Chapter 8 of Hicks, 1967, pp. 143-154).

the system (1)-(3) — as a model of Keynes's *General Theory* is equivalent to imputing to Keynes a faith in the efficacy of the price system that is utterly at variance with his actual beliefs. But neither can there be serious doubt that Hicks's simple model of the *General Theory* accurately reflects the substance — the letter if not the spirit — of Keynes's formal analysis. The crux of the matter is that Keynes in the *General Theory* not only failed to reject but positively embraced an essentially classical (more accurately, neoclassical) theory of short-run output determination, and thereby implicitly adopted the Thick Market Hypothesis as a basis for his own theory of aggregate supply.[8] Keynes's theory of aggregate demand, though outwardly novel because it makes the current level of total expenditure depend upon the prevailing level of output and employment, actually involves no significant departure from classical tradition. So the theoretical foundations of the *General Theory* are, albeit unintentionally, incompatible with the beliefs that led Keynes to write it.

III. SALVAGING THE GENERAL THEORY

Evidently the central message of Keynes's *General Theory* can be salvaged only by discarding the conventional theory of short-run supply. But we cannot discard the conventional theory of short-run supply unless we also discard the conception of market organization on which it is based; for the conventional theory merely expresses how rational sellers would behave if their trading activities were confined to thick markets.

The *General Theory* contains no hint that Keynes was in any way dissatisfied with the conventional theory of supply; indeed, the conventional theory plays a central role in his claim that real wages generally move in the same direction as output over the trade cycle. It was not until 1939, in his response to criticisms of this claim by Dunlop and Tarshis,[9] that Keynes explicitly voiced doubts about the assumptions underlying his earlier analysis of aggregate supply and, more particularly, questioned the validity of what I have called the Thick Market Hypothesis by linking producer discretion in short-period pricing policy with trading in thin rather than thick markets.[10]

8. Patinkin disputes this in various of his recent writings, but (to my mind) not at all convincingly. On this, see Patinkin, 1976, p. 93; Tarshis, 1978, pp. 60-63 (in Patinkin and Leitk, 1978).

9. Reprinted in JMK Vol. VII, Appendix 3 (see especially pp. 406-408).

10. Curiously, Keynes seems to have been more aware of the difficulties of the 'theory of short-period supply' in the early 1930's than during the writing of the *General Theory*. In a letter to Hawtrey of Nov. 28, 1930, for example, responding to Hawtrey's criticisms of the *Treatise* Keynes says : 'I repeat that I am not dealing with the complete set of causes

A thick market, as noted earlier, is one in which traders can be presumed to know within narrow limits the price at which any desired quantity of a commodity can be bought or sold on short notice. A thin market is one in which the opposite presumption holds : trading volume is too slight to permit traders to gauge, even within broad limits, the price at which desired sales or purchases can be completed on short notice. The crucial difference is that, for thick markets, it makes sense to suppose that the short-run revenues of individual producers are determined by their output choices, while for thin markets the same supposition makes no sense at all. Let us explore the implications of the second case.

Consider a representative producer whose short-run average variable and average total costs are represented by the curves AVC and ATC in Figure 1.

FIGURE 1

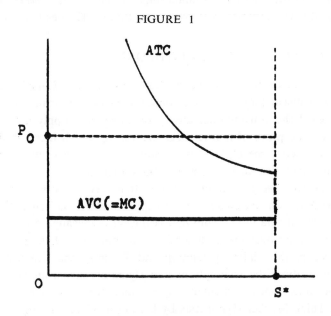

By hypothesis, the producer has no useable information about his probable short-run sales at alternative asking prices, so there can be no question of choosing a combination of price and output that maximizes short-run profit.

which determine volume of output. For this would have led me an endless long journey into the theory of short-period supply and a long way from monetary theory; — though I agree that it will probably be difficult in the future to prevent monetary theory and the theory of short-period supply from running together. If I were to write the book again, I should probably attempt to probe further into the difficulties on the latter; but I have already probed far enough to know what a complicated affair it is'. (JMK, Vol. 13, pp. 145-146.)

Over the longer run, the producer can hope to influence sales by appropriate market maneuvers (advertising, temporary price cuts, etc.), but more immediately he is largely at the mercy of impersonal (and predetermined) market forces. Under these conditions, probably the simplest and most sensible strategy is for the producer to set his asking or list price at a reasonable level and hope for the best in the way of sales volume. What seems 'reasonable' to the producer will depend, of course, on past sales experience, on present and prospective costs, and on present and prospective competition. Here, let us interpret 'reasonable' to mean a price (P_0 in Figure 1) high enough to ensure that average total costs are covered for a range of sales levels significantly less than capacity output, $s*$.[11]

Then since the 'asking' or 'list' price exceeds average variable (and marginal) cost for all outputs less than $s*$, the producer will be *willing* to produce and sell any less-than-capacity output at his posted price. But the amount that can *actually* be sold will depend upon customer demand at that price, which will depend on a host of conditions over which the producer has no short-run control. In these circumstances, it is plausible to argue that the producer will adjust output passively to match average sales at the posted price, holding buffer stocks of inventories to avoid frequent transient adjustments of output. Thus, on average, short-run output will move in the same direction as realized sales.

Taking account of the preceding argument, but referring now to an economy in which all produced goods are traded in thin markets, let us suppose that aggregate short-run output and interest-rate behavior may be characterized by the adjustment equations

$$dq_c/dt = h_c[d_c(\ .\ ) - q_c],$$ (7)

$$dq_k/dt = h_k[d_k(\ .\ ) - q_k],$$ (8)

$$dr/dt = h_b[x_b(\ .\ )],$$ (9)

where $q_i\ (i = c, k)$ represents current output as contrasted with 'supply', and $(\ .\ ) = (p_c, p_k, w, r, Y, M)$ — the argument Y rather than Y_n appearing in

11. Cf. Andrews, 'Competitive Prices, Normal Costs and Industrial Stability', in Andrews and Brunner (1975), pp. 29-31. This is not the place to review recent work on so-called 'customer markets'; suffice it to say that there is little dispute among economists about the 'stylized facts' though there is (of course) much dispute about how they should be interpreted. For some recent comments on this topic, see Okun (1981), Ch. 4 (esp. pp. 138 ff); Phelps (1985), pp. 383-404; Hall and Taylor (1986), pp. 389-394; Gordon (1981), pp. 502-504.

(.) because, under our present assumptions, producers as well as workers may be 'income constrained' in the short-run.

The system (7)-(9) accurately portrays what has come to be regarded as distinctive feature of Keynesian economics: aggregate output is determined by aggregate sales and prices play no role in the short-run adjustment of income to changes in effective demand. This, of course, is the route to salvage of Keynesian economics that is taken in most textbooks, usually without notice to the reader that the underlying assumptions concerning short-period output variations are completely at odds with the conventional profit-maximization model of supply presented in later microeconomic sections of the same text. It also corresponds to the extreme case of what Hicks has dubbed 'fix-price theory'.[12]

Apart from being a crude caricature of Keynes's analysis, the system (7)-(9) seriously misrepresents the role of prices in the short-run adjustment process. In situations involving significant unused capacity, producers can be expected to engage in competitive selling activities (temporary discounts, rebates, prize contests, etc.) in an effort to boost short-run sales, so average transaction prices will tend to fall. Similarly, in situations involving little unused capacity, producers can be expected to compete for factors in ways that increase both variable and fixed costs, and some of these increases will be passed on in the form of higher asking prices. Arguing heuristically, we may suppose that both sorts of adjustment are adequately described by the aggregative equations.

$$dp^*_c/dt = g_c(d_c(\ . \ ) - s^*_c),   \tag{10}$$

$$dp^*_k/dt = g_k(d_k(\ . \ ) - s^*_k),   \tag{11}$$

where p^*_i is an index of transaction prices and s^*_i is an index of production capacity.[13] Combining these relations with (7)-(9), we obtain a system of five adjustment equations to describe short-run movements in quantities, transaction prices, and the rate of interest.

The equation for dr/dt in this system calls for no special comment; we may view the loan market as 'thick' and rapidly self-adjusting even in a Keynesian model. But the remaining four equations — two dealing with adjust-

12. See Hicks (1966), Chaps. 7-9; Hicks (1982), pp. 231-235 and pp. 324-330.

13. This is no more than a rough schematic representation. The microeconomic theory of price adjustment in thin markets is still in its infancy. For discussion of some of the difficulties that confront us in this area, see Bushaw and Clower (1957), Ch. 7, pp. 185-189; Phelps, et al. (1970), pp. 309-337 (Phelps and Winter) and pp. 369-393 (Gordon and Hynes).

ments in output quantities and two dealing with movements in average trans-actions prices — pose problems whose solutions are distinctly problematical.

To see this, suppose that the system starts in temporary equilibrium with capacity fully utilized and sales occurring only at posted list prices. Next, suppose that the equilibrium is disturbed by a decline in 'animal spirits', 'confidence', or what have you, causing investment expenditure to fall. Then investment goods output will quickly decline, because the speed of adjustment coefficients in equations (7) and (8) are, by hypothesis, large numbers. Prices will not decline noticeably in the short run because the adjustment coefficients in equations (10) and (11) are — again by hypothesis — relatively small. Both 'workers' and 'capitalists' are income constrained, because neither goods nor services are particularly 'liquid' (though prices are 'ad-ministered', and therefore known, quantities sold are unpredictable); so as investment output drops the demand for consumption goods will also decline, via the familiar multiplier process.

Now, initially at least, no counteracting forces will operate to stem the decline. Real balance effects will have no bite, because transaction prices will not fall noticeably; and though the money volume of transactions will decline, the potential effect of this on spending will be attenuated by rising uncertainty about future needs for cash to meet payrolls, etc. — hence a rise in the demand for precautionary balances. There will perhaps be some tendency for spare cash to go into loans; but this tendency will not be strong, because with sales falling and becoming more uncertain, producers will find it increasingly diffi-cult to synchronize purchases with sales, and this will mean that average money balances will tend to increase even at lower volumes of monetary trans-actions (cf. Clower and Howitt (1978), Clower (1984), pp. 168-70). Nor are matters likely to improve as the decline continues; for in thin markets trade credit (mainly in the form of bookkeeping entries) is likely to play a prominent, and perhaps dominant role as a short-run means of payment.[14] As sales decline and business confidence weakens, trade credit outstanding will shrink, possibly by substantial percentage amounts, even though currency and de-posits subject to check are largely unchanged.

There is no need to carry the story further. Notice that nothing of sub-stance in the above argument is changed if we relax the assumption of fixed wage rates and add a 'thin' market for labor services to our model. In that

14. This is a direct consequence of the desire of makers of thin markets to attract a clientele of 'regular' customers in order to reduce sales uncertainty; trade credit as distinct from bank credit plays little role in thick markets precisely because there is no significant sales uncertainty in this case.

more general case, as for the more restricted model (7)-(11), 'observed' short-run behavior cannot be adequately characterized by static, reduced-form solutions of the adjustment equations. In effect, the normal state of the economy is one of Brownian motion; the system, even if asymptotically stable, is so lightly damped that the probability of ever being in the neighborhood of equilibrium is close to zero.

CONCLUSION

No doubt more might be said about the reasons why the *General Theory* ultimately failed to convey Keynes's intended message, and about alternative ways in which Keynes's 'vision' might be salvaged; but this is not the place to say it. Instead, let me conclude by drawing attention to some of the more immediate research implications of the preceding argument.

It seems to me that the key to further progress in macroeconomics lies in improved understanding of short-run price and quantity behavior in thin markets. For a variety of reasons, I doubt that conventional analytical methods will be of much use for this purpose. No doubt we may continue to presume that business firms — manufacturers, service providers, wholesalers, retailers, banks and other financial institutions — seek to maximize present wealth; but this presumption will lead us nowhere unless we are able to specify relevant criterion functions and constraints, which does not presently appear to be feasible for firms that operate in thin markets. I say 'not presently feasible' because I view the problem not as unsolvable but merely unsolved. My suspicion is that the problem cannot be satisfactorily resolved unless we take more seriously than here-to-fore has been our habit the role of transactions costs and related economies of scale as determinants of market organization and performance. And even in the best of cases, I doubt that any solution of the problem will yield neat models or precise conclusions. The analysis of business behavior in thin markets promises to be very messy by comparison with conventional thick-market analysis.

There is serious question also whether established comparative-statics techniques can be fruitfully used for short-run analysis. If, as seems to be the case, there is little probability that a thin-market economy will ever be found in the neighborhood of equilibrium, we must be prepared to work with explicitly dynamical models of market adjustment. Of course, if our underlying theories of business behavior are 'messy' then our prospects for achieving professional concensus on the best way to model the stylized dynamical facts are rather bleak. All the same, I see no reason to be discouraged. The present situation of macroeconomics, like that of Ulysses as he set sail from

Troy, is serious but not hopeless. We can, if we wish, continue to play innocuous intellectual games with macromodels that have no conceivable value for describing observable behavior. But surely our proper course is treat the description of reality as a challenge and get on the work of reconstructing microeconomics to deal meaningfully with The Economics of Thin Markets.

University of South Carolina, U.S.A.

REFERENCES

Andrews, P. W. S. and Brunner, E. (1975) *Studies in Pricing*, (London: Macmillan Press).

Boulding, K. (1944) 'A Liquidity Preference Theory of Market Prices', *Economica*, 11 : 55-63.

Bushaw, D. W. and Clower, R. W. (1957) *Introduction to Mathemetical Economics*, (Homewood, Ill. : Richard D. Irwin).

Clower, R. W. (1984) *Money and Markets*, in Walker, D. (ed.), (Cambridge: Cambridge University Press).

Gordon, R. J. (1981) 'Output Fluctuations and Gradual Price Adjustment', *Journal of Economic Literature*, 19 : 493-530.

Hall, R. and Taylor, J. (1986) *Macroeconomics*, (New York: Norton).

Hicks, J. R. (1937) 'Mr Keynes and the Classics : A Suggested Interpretation', *Econometrica*, 5 : 147-159.

—— (1966) *Capital and Growth*, (Oxford: Clarendon Press.).

—— (1967) *Critical Essays in Monetary Theory*, (Oxford: Clarendon Press).

—— (1982) *Money, Interest and Wages*, (Oxford: Basil Blackwell).

Keynes, J. M. *Collected Works*, cited as J M K (London: Macmillan Press), published for the Royal Economic Society, various volumes and dates.

Modigliani, F. (1944) 'Liquidity Preference and the Theory of Interest and Money', *Econometrica*, 12 : 45-88.

Okun, A. (1981) *Prices and Quantities*, (Washington: The Brookings Institution).

Patinkin, D. (1976) *Keynes's Monetary Thought*, (Durham: Duke University Press).

Phelps, E. S. (1985) *Political Economy*, (New York: Norton).

Phelps, E. S. et al. (1970) *Microeconomic Foundations of Employment and Inflation Theory*, (New York: Norton).

Tarshis, L. (1978) 'Keynes as Seen by his Students in the 1930s', in Patinkin and Leith, (eds.), *Keynes's Cambridge and the General Theory*, (Toronto: University of Toronto Press).

CHAPTER 10

Ohlin and the *General Theory*[1]

ROBERT W. CLOWER

> "'Tis a pitiful tale," said the Bellman, whose face
>   Had grown longer at every word:
> "But now that you've stated the whole of your case,
>   More debate would be simply absurd."
> Lewis Carroll, The Hunting of the Snark

In a 1972 volume of economic essays, Gunnar Myrdal describes the Keynesian Revolution as "mainly an Anglo-American occurrence. In Sweden, where we grew up in the tradition of Knut Wicksell, Keynes' works were read as interesting and important contributions along a familiar line of thought, but not in any sense as a revolutionary breakthrough" (Myrdal, 1972, pp. 4–5). This description applies with particular force to Bertil Ohlin, as indicated by the concluding paragraph of his 1937 "Notes on the Stockholm Theory of Savings and Investment":

> In his attempt to bring about a coordination of economic theory Keynes does not – at least from the Stockholm horizon – appear to have been radical or revolutionary enough. The equilibrium method instead of process analysis in which not more of the equilibrium idea is left than consideration of more or less stable positions, the insufficient distinction between "realisations" and "expectations," the retaining of physical marginal productivity, the disutility analysis of labour supply, in a way also the aggregate supply function, are all evidence of an exaggerated conservatism in *method* which has hampered his work.[2]

The inference is plain: Ohlin acknowledges the novelty of Keynes's application of equilibrium analysis to the theory of output as a whole, but he questions the probable scientific fruitfulness of such a conventional approach to unconventional problems.

If my interpretation of Ohlin is valid, what sense can one make of recent discussions of the question whether the Stockholm School and, more particularly, Bertil Ohlin can be credited with the simultaneous

245

"discovery" of the *General Theory?*[3] To be sure, no one before Keynes appears to have thought of applying equilibrium analysis to the demand and supply of output as a whole. A book that adopted such a perspective, particularly as a basis for interpreting the depression of the 1930s, surely would not have attracted so much professional attention had its author not already been an acknowledged economic genius (cf. Patinkin, 1982, p. 88). And there is no doubt that the *General Theory* produced a revolution in economics. But was there anything revolutionary in the analytical content of the *General Theory?*[4]

1   The Patinkin interpretation

How Keynes would have answered this question is indicated in Chapter 3 of the *General Theory* where, following a preliminary account of the determination of "effective demand" by aggregate supply and demand, Keynes remarks: "Since this is the substance of the General Theory of Employment, which it will be our object to expound, the succeeding chapters will be largely occupied with examining the various factors upon which these two functions depend" (JMK, VII, p. 25). In itself, of course, this passage settles nothing, since it leaves open the question whether Keynes's "central message"[5] lies in his theory of effective demand or in "succeeding chapters." Any doubts one might otherwise have had on this score, however, surely have been put to rest by Don Patinkin's analysis of this question (Patinkin, 1982, pp. 5–11), which definitively[6] rules out the "necessary originality"[7] of material found in succeeding chapters, thereby leaving Keynes's theory of effective demand as the sole contender for that title.

But here another issue arises, for as Patinkin himself acknowledges and emphasizes (1982, p. 9, fn. 7), what *he* means by "Keynes's" theory of effective demand "does not exactly accord with the presentation in Chapter 3 of the *General Theory.*" That is surely an understatement, for what Patinkin puts forward as an account of the "central message of the *General Theory*" is the familiar Keynesian cross analysis that has dominated textbook expositions of elementary macroeconomics since it appeared in the first (1948) edition of Paul Samuelson's *Economics.* Let me be clear on this point. I do not doubt the formal or economic validity of Patinkin's interpretation of the theory of effective demand; a coherent conceptual basis for Patinkin's interpretation is, in fact, adumbrated in Chapter XIII of Patinkin's *Money, Interest, and Prices* (pp. 214–21 of the 1956 edition, pp. 316–24 of the 1965 edition).[8] But that is not the issue; the issue is whether Patinkin's interpretation of Keynes's theory of effective demand, like his identification of Keynes's "central message," can be regarded as definitive? As matters presently stand, the answer is problematic.

So we come to the point of this discussion: If Patinkin's interpretation of Keynes is accepted, the Swedes cannot validly claim to have anticipated the distinctive analytical contribution of the *General Theory*, for they surely did not anticipate Samuelson's Keynesian cross analysis; but if Patinkin's interpretation is rejected, then the central issue in the controversy about the relation between Keynes's *General Theory* and the earlier writings of Ohlin and the Stockholm School remains to be resolved.

My purpose in this paper is to bring the controversy to a head. Specifically, I shall suggest an interpretation of the theory of effective demand that is both more general than Patinkin's and more consistent with the conceptual framework of Keynes's *General Theory*, and I shall show that – on this more general view – Patinkin's unfavorable assessment of the claims of the Stockholm School has no force. Indeed, I shall argue for a stronger result: Patinkin to the contrary notwithstanding, there is merit in Ohlin's contention that "the Keynesian reasoning about underemployment equilibrium is . . . chiefly a simplified demonstration of some of the results of the sequence analysis in Stockholm"[9] (Ohlin, 1981b, p. 222).

2   An alternative interpretation[10]

My point of departure is a provocative remark that appears in Ohlin's posthumously published essay on "Pre-War Keynesian and Stockholm Theories of Employment" (Ohlin, 1981b, p. 223): "Keynes' theory of effective demand is based on [Marshallian] supply and demand curves [that refer to] aggregate income and output in the whole country."[11] Evidently, Ohlin is suggesting that Keynes's supposedly novel apparatus of aggregate demand and supply, as presented in Chapter 3 of the *General Theory*, is actually a disguised version of Marshall's short-period theory of demand and supply.

Following this lead, let us consider the supply and demand diagram in Figure 1 where, in keeping with Marshall's practice, we assume that the *D* and *S* curves[12] relate demand and supply prices to "the aggregate volume of production" rather than quantities demanded and supplied to "market price" (cf. Marshall, 1920, pp. 342 ff.). Suppose initially that the short-period "output of the economy as a whole" – here presumed to be a meaningful concept – is at the level q_0 so that the demand price p_0^d as given by the demand curve $D(Z_0)$ is greater than the supply price p_0^s as given by the supply curve $S(w_0)$. If we assume that the current

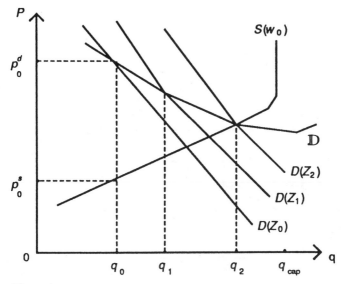

Figure 1.

market price lies generally in the neighborhood of the demand price,[13] then on standard Marshallian reasoning, producers will have an incentive to increase output and employment.

Here we run into a complication: Unless unemployed workers are available at the going wage rate, producers can increase output only by bidding up the prevailing money wage rate, in which case the supply curve will shift. To avoid this problem, let us assume that, at the existing money wage rate, w_0, unemployed workers are available at all values of output less than q_{cap} so that the aggregate level of output and employment may be presumed to depend solely upon the hiring decisions of business firms. A second complication then arises: Unless the demand curve is independent of "aggregate producer outlay" (defined as $Z = p^s q$),[14] changes in output will produce shifts in the demand curve, the amount of such shifts depending on the responsiveness of aggregate producer outlay to changes in output and on the responsiveness of demand to changes in aggregate producer outlay. This problem can be handled, at least in principle, by defining a *mutatis mutandis* demand curve (illustrated by curve D in Figure 1) that shows demand price as a function of aggregate output, due allowance being made for the effect of changes in output on aggregate producer outlay and for the resultant effect of changes in aggregate outlay on the *ceteris paribus* demand curves $D(Z_i)$.[15]

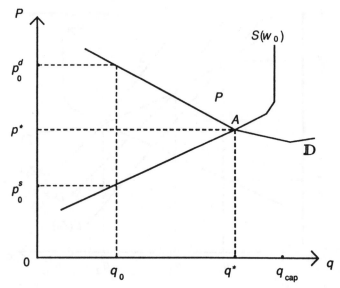

Figure 2.

Working now with the demand curve **D** and the supply curve *S*, we identify short-period equilibrium of aggregate output and price with the point A in Figure 2, where $q = q^*$, $p^s = p^d = p^*$, and aggregate expenditure, $E = p^d q = p^* q^* = E^*$, is equal to aggregate producer outlay, $Z = p^s q = p^* q^* = Z^*$ [i.e., $q(p^d - p^s) = 0$]. Applying the usual Marshallian "stability" condition, we may then describe the equilibrium as "stable" if the demand curve **D** lies above the supply curve *S* to the left of the equilibrium point *A*.[16]

The meaning of this stability condition for the theory of output as a whole may be brought out more clearly by translating the relations shown in Figure 2 into a "Marshallian Cross" diagram as shown in Figure 3. Here, distances along the horizontal axis measure alternative (notional) levels of aggregate producer outlay, *Z*, as determined by the *S* curve in Figure 2 (i.e., distances along *OZ* in Figure 3 correspond to *areas* such as $Z_0 = p_0^s q_0$ in Figure 2). Similarly, distances along the vertical axis in Figure 3 measure alternative (notional) levels of aggregate consumer outlay, *E*, as defined by the **D** curve in Figure 2 (i.e., distances along *OE* in Figure 3 correspond to *areas* such as $E_0 = p_0^d q_0$ in Figure 2). Treating the output variable as a parameter, we first define the *aggregate spending function* by writing $E(q) = f(Z(q))$. The equilibrium level of aggregate producer outlay, Z^*, is then defined by the requirement $E = Z$ [i.e., $q(p^d - p^s) = 0$], at which level the aggregate spending func-

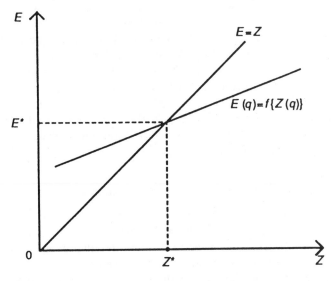

Figure 3.

tion must intersect the 45° line. On this interpretation, the Marshallian
stability condition is that, in the neighborhood of the intersection point,
the slope of the spending function, which we may call the *marginal propensity to spend*, must be less than one. Thus, through straightforward
development of an analysis that is now more than a century old,[17] we
have "discovered" the "fundamental psychological law" (JMK VII, p.
96) that Keynes, pursuing an independent route, took perhaps two years
to find![18]

If the marginal propensity to spend is equal to one, then the D and S
curves in Figure 2 – hence the aggregate spending function and the 45°
line in Figure 3 – coincide in the neighborhood of the equilibrium point
and we have what Marshall called "neutral" equilibrium (see Whitaker,
1975, p. 153). This corresponds, of course, to what Keynes later defined
as "Say's Law" (JMK, VII, pp. 25–6). Needless to say, this "Law"
formed no part of the thinking of Marshall or any other "orthodox"
economist. Keynes's confusion on this matter is just one aspect of a
more general confusion about the foundations of his theory of effective
demand to which Patinkin has drawn attention (Patinkin, 1982, Chapter 5, particularly pp. 149–53). These same confusions are, of course,
strong evidence of the "subjective originality" of Keynes's version of the
theory.

The present line of argument might be extended in several directions, but to carry it further would serve no useful purpose here. Already it will be evident that our Marshallian "theory of effective demand" is what Keynes himself probably would have arrived at[19] had he been less concerned to "raise a dust" (JMK, XIII, p. 548). Considered in this context, there is nothing "revolutionary" about Keynes's theory as such; it is just the "classical" equilibrium economics of Marshall, Walras, Pigou, and Wicksell, applied to the determination of the general price level and aggregate output and employment on the assumption that there exist unemployed resources (the last condition being rationalized by supposing that wages and prices are rigid or sticky).[20]

3   Alternative theories of short-period supply

I turn now to the task of showing that Patinkin's version of the theory of effective demand inaccurately characterizes Keynes's analysis. This task might be approached directly through detailed exegesis of textual evidence, but the heart of my argument can be reached more effectively by another route. Specifically, I shall begin by sketching two alternative models of short-period competitive output and price determination. Though the two models have a common source in the writings of Alfred Marshall, and though the models differ conceptually only in that one deals with trading in "thick" markets while the other deals with trading in "thin" markets, we shall discover that their behavioral implications are unambiguously distinguishable. It will then be a simple matter to show that one model is substantially equivalent to the theory of short-period supply that underlies Keynes's analysis in the *General Theory*, while the other is substantially equivalent to the different conception of short-period supply that underlies Patinkin's version of Keynes's theory of effective demand.

Taking our cue from Marshall, let us imagine a money economy in which the typical market is one where traders are so numerous and the physical volume of trading so large and continuous that, even in the very short run, no seller or buyer either imagines himself or is, in fact, capable of significantly influencing the terms of trade by his own actions. More succinctly, assume that every trader can buy or sell any desired quantity of any traded commodity on short notice at the "going" price (for future reference, let us call this assumption the *thick market hypothesis*).[21] Suppose, further, that the typical producer independently chooses both his asking price and his output. On the thick market hypothesis, we may assume that the producer feels free to choose his current output without regard to his present level of sales, for he can be presumed to know that "undesired" inventory holdings produced by unanticipated differences between output and sales can quickly be eliminated by moderate adjustments in asking price. Assuming that the producer seeks to maximize profits, therefore, it is plausible to define short-period equilibrium output by the requirement that marginal cost equal current asking price, and to define short-period equilibrium asking price by the requirement that inventories be at some desired level (possibly zero).

There is little point in carrying this sketch further. Except that the model makes individual producers responsible for setting asking prices, it is simply an alternative (Marshallian) version of the familiar textbook theory of short-period demand and supply. Though asking prices are "administered," the "going" price is governed by impersonal market forces that tend always to drive individual asking prices toward equality; so short-period market equilibrium is defined by the usual requirement that the "going" price equate aggregate quantity demanded with aggregate quantity supplied (the latter magnitude being defined, of course, as the sum of the profit-maximizing outputs of individual producers).[22]

The simplicity and analytical tautness of the thick market model depends crucially on the fact that, because of high volume and continuous trading, individual producers can reliably predict the qualitative effect of changes in asking price on individual sales. In these circumstances, rational behavior implies that individual producers treat asking prices as short-period instruments of inventory control. Thin markets are different. Here, by hypothesis, trading volume per unit of time is too slight and too erratic to permit individual producers to gauge even the qualitative effect of changes in asking price on short-period sales (call this the *thin market hypothesis*). Thus, asking prices are neither efficient nor reliable short-period instruments of inventory control. Just what kind of behavior would be "rational" in these circumstances is problematic,[23] but to vary asking price in response to short-run variations in sales plainly would be "irrational."[24]

There is a vast literature on thin markets,[25] for in every actual economy such markets account for the bulk of all trade in retailing, food processing, wholesaling, manufacturing, transportation, and service; so we have a surfeit of "seat-of-the-pants" knowledge about the way these markets work in practice. The stylized fact that stands out from all others is that short-period output in such markets is demand-determined. Another well-confirmed fact is that asking prices are governed more by past and prospective costs and by actual and potential competition than by short-run demand conditions. Let us suppose, then, that rational behavior in thin markets requires the typical producer to: (1) set short-period asking price at a level that ensures average total costs will be cov-

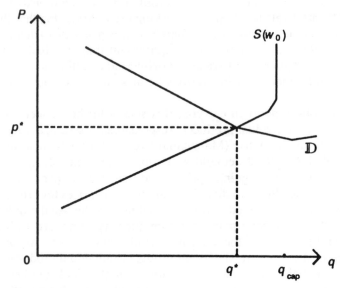

Figure 4.

ered for a range of sales significantly less than capacity output; (2) adjust
output passively within the period to match the average volume of sales;
(3) hold buffer stocks of inventories to avoid frequent transient adjustments in output. In situations of significant unused capacity, producers
can be expected to engage in competitive selling activities (temporary
discounts, rebates, prize contests, etc.) in an effort to boost short-period
sales, so average transaction prices will tend to fall. Similarly, in situations involving little unused capacity, producers can be expected to
compete for factors in ways that increase both variable and fixed costs,
and some of these increases will be passed on in the form of higher asking prices. By and large, however, we may suppose that in thin markets
an individual producer's short-period asking and transaction prices are
inflexible and that short-period output is determined by short-period
sales (subject, of course, to the proviso that marginal cost be no greater
than price).

So much for the microeconomics of thick and thin markets. Proceeding once more on the assumption that aggregate output, aggregate sales,
and so on are heuristically meaningful concepts, we may illustrate the
macroeconomic implications of the two models by considering the corresponding aggregate demand and supply diagrams as shown in Figures
4 and 5. On the *thick market hypothesis* the relevant relations are those
shown in Figure 4, which are, of course, replicas of those shown earlier

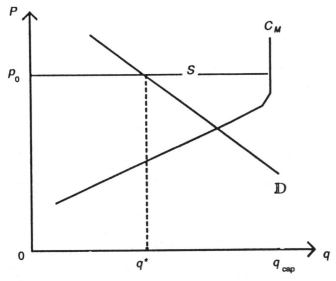

Figure 5.

in Figure 2. On the *thin market hypothesis*, however, the relevant relations are those shown in Figure 5. Here the short-period aggregate supply curve, S, appears as a horizontal line segment, situated at the (given) aggregate asking price p_0 and terminating at the "capacity" level of output q_{cap}. In keeping with earlier discussion, S in Figure 5 is assumed to lie everywhere above the aggregate marginal cost curve C_M (C_M is, of course, a replica of the S curve shown in Figure 4). Because the form of the *mutatis mutandis* demand curve depends in part on the form of the aggregate supply curve, the *mutatis mutandis* demand curve D in Figure 5 also differs from its analogue in Figure 4.

Obviously the short-period comparative statics of these two macromodels differ in just one important respect: In a world of thick markets, shifts in aggregate demand produce equilibrating shifts in both output and price; but in a world of thin markets, shifts in aggregate demand produce equilibrating shifts in output alone.

No serious argument is required to establish that the thin-market hypothesis underlies Patinkin's interpretation of Keynes's theory of effective demand; Patinkin himself effectively affirms this in his 1978 assessment of Ohlin's 1933 essay on monetary theory (Patinkin, 1978; see also Patinkin, 1982, especially pp. 52–6).[26] Indeed, Patinkin's implicit rejection of the thick market hypothesis was a recurrent target of wrath for Ohlin in his posthumously published reply to Patinkin

(Ohlin, 1981b, pp. 206–12, especially the comment on p. 211: "[Keynes] left to Patinkin the role to regard it as a *deathly sin* to give a more complicated picture than his own exceedingly simplified one.").

There remains the question whether the thick market hypothesis underlies Keynes's *General Theory*. On that issue, Patinkin has the dubious distinction of being perhaps the only Keynes scholar who seems to have any serious doubts. He expressed these doubts most forcefully in his 1982 "Critique of Keynes' Theory of Effective Demand," where he concludes:

> [T]he obscurity with which the aggregate supply curve is presented in the *General Theory* is a sign not of profundity, but of obscurity: not, as some would have us believe, of a deep underlying analytical framework in which everything falls into place, but of the same confusions and imprecisions which manifested themselves in the 1933 drafts of the book and which continued to live on in Keynes' mind furtively, below the surface, through the final version as well.

The truth of these observations may be granted. Keynes undoubtedly was confused in his handling of aggregative concepts that were new to him and, in his mind at least, not directly derivable from conventional theory because (as he put it): "the community's output of goods and services is a non-homogeneous complex which cannot be measured, strictly speaking, except in certain special cases. . . ." But does this mean that Keynes also repudiated Marshall's theory of short-period competitive supply? That is the crux of the matter, for as our earlier argument makes clear (see especially the concluding paragraph of section 2), acceptance of the conventional theory of short-period supply is logically equivalent to acceptance of the thick market macromodel.

Did Keynes in the *General Theory* mean to repudiate the conventional profit-maximization theory of short-period competitive supply? Surely, had Keynes intended anything so radical, we should find better evidence of it in the *General Theory* than the indirect indications of "obscurity and confusion" on which Patinkin relies. But to clinch the matter, let me cite three pieces of evidence that, when considered together, seem to me to remove "all reasonable doubt."

In Chapter 3 of the last 1933 draft table of contents of the *General Theory*, Keynes writes:

> The process which decides the volume of employment is as follows. Each firm calculates the prospective selling price of its output and its variable cost in respect of output on various possible scales of production. Its variable cost per unit is not, as a rule, constant for all volumes of output but increases as output increases. Output is then pushed to

the point at which the prospective selling price no longer exceeds the marginal variable cost. In this way the volume of output, and hence the volume of employment, is determined. (JMK, XXIX, p. 98)

In mid-1935, some months before the *General Theory* was finally published, we find further evidence of Keynes's commitment to standard analysis in a letter from Keynes to R. F. Kahn:

> I have been making rather extensive changes in the early chapters of my book, to a considerable extent consequential on a simple and obvious, but beautiful and important (I think) precise definition of what is meant by effective demand: –
> Let W be the marginal price cost of production when output is O.
> Let P be the expected selling price of this output.
> Then OP is effective demand.
> The fundamental assumption of the classical theory, "supply creates its own demand," is that OW = OP *whatever* the level of O, so that effective demand is incapable of setting a limit to employment. . . . On *my* theory OW [is not equal to] OP for *all* values of O and entrepreneurs have to choose a value of O for which it *is* equal; – *otherwise the equality of price and marginal prime cost is infringed.* This is the real starting point of everything. (JMK XIII, pp. 422–3; my italics in the penultimate sentence)

Finally, we have evidence from Keynes's 1937 personal correspondence with Ohlin over publication of Ohlin's "Notes." In the third instalment of the "Notes," Ohlin put forward a criticism of Keynes's *General Theory* based explicitly on dissatisfaction with the conventional theory of short-period competitive supply or, as Ohlin calls it, "the old reasoning." At one point he even chides Keynes for apparently having "never discussed imperfect competition with Mrs Robinson."[27] Keynes's response (JMK, XIV, p. 190) was blunt: "I have not been able to make out here what you are driving at. The reference to imperfect competition is very perplexing. I cannot see how on earth it comes in." There is an obvious irony here: Patinkin's assessment of Ohlin implicitly rests on his attribution to Keynes of a conception of the theory of short-period supply for which Ohlin expressed support and Keynes expressed disdain![28]

4   The anticipation issue once more

As intimated earlier, I side with Ohlin in feeling that Keynes's theory of effective demand contained nothing essentially new; that Keynes's analysis, though subjectively original, was ". . . chiefly a simplified demonstration of some of the results of the sequence analysis in Stockholm."

In light of my subsequent elaboration of the Mashallian foundations of Keynes's theory, this conclusion may well appear disingenuous, for what I am effectively arguing is that neither Keynes nor the Swedish economists of the 1930s discovered anything essentially new: *The analytical substance of Keynes's* General Theory *and of the "Stockholm Theory" is already contained in earlier work by Marshall and Wicksell.*

Patinkin reaches a different conclusion – or so I conjecture – because he starts from the presumption that "a book on economic theory which ... revolutionize[d] the way the world thinks about economic problems" (JMK, XIII, p. 492) must have contained at least one great analytical "discovery." I believe this presumption reflects an erroneous standard for evaluating scientific achievement. What most impresses me about the work of so-called "great scientists" is not the originality of their analytical ideas but the catalytic quality of their conceptual perspectives. It is this aspect of scientific thought that leads us unhesitatingly to put Copernicus, Galileo, Newton, Darwin, Einstein and a handful of other seminal thinkers in a class by themselves. It is for similar reasons that, in economics, only a few people such as Smith, Ricardo, Marshall, Wicksell,. and Keynes are universally thought to merit the encomium "great."

Two further observations are in order before I conclude. First, I find it hard to imagine that anyone could read Ohlin's "Notes on the Stockholm Theory" carefully and doubt that Ohlin understood Keynes's *General Theory* perhaps better than its author. Ohlin's detailed critical remarks – about the consumption function, the multiplier, the liquidity preference theory of the rate of interest, the relation between movements in output and real wage rates, user cost, the definition of savings and investment, the aggregate supply function, and a host of other contentious topics – were generally "right on target," as subsequent professional discussion has revealed. Such acuteness, such prescience, is hardly likely to be found except in a critic who independently has already "discovered" the essential ideas of the theory under review. Second, I should like to draw attention to a passage in Ohlin's 1933 essay on monetary theory where he effectively enunciates what I would call "the Marshall-Keynes condition" for the stability of macroeconomic equilibrium:

> Neo-Wicksellian theory habitually expresses as follows the conditions for an interruption of [a] price decline. Since investment is too low relative to saving, either more must be invested or less saved. But such reasoning is conclusive only if income is thought of as given and independent of what is happening within the period. In that case, the alternatives laid down simply imply ˜an increase of either investment demand or consumption demand. But if income is falling, aggregate

demand and prices may fall. *A correct formulation would quite simply be that the price fall will tend to be ending whenever aggregate demand is growing relative to supply.* (Ohlin, 1978, p. 379)

V   Conclusion

The Stockholm School is alive and well, but the new one seems to draw its inspiration more from Samuelson than from Wicksell. The "old" Stockholm School is gone, but the spirit that moved it still flourishes in Sweden and elsewhere: the urge to maintain close links between economic theory and its applications. Who can say that the theoretical insights of Ohlin and other Swedish economists of the 1930s will not bear fruit in the decade of the 1990s? Who, more particularly, can say that the future of Keynesian economics does not lie in the direction suggested by Ohlin in the passage of his "Notes" quoted at the outset of this paper: "process analysis in which not more of the equilibrium idea is left than consideration of more or less stable positions"?[29] My own conjecture is that the last and most significant chapter in the Ohlin-Keynes story has yet to be written.

Notes

1 I have received valuable comments from participants at the Stockholm School conference.

2 These remarks are from the posthumously published third instalment of Ohlin's "Notes" (Ohlin, 1981a, p. 249), but similar – indeed, much more sharply worded – critical observations are a prominent feature of the two installments published in the 1937 volume of the *Economic Journal* (Ohlin, 1937).

3 See Patinkin (1982, Chapter 2) for discussion and references.

4 Cf. T. S. Kuhn's comment on Copernicus: "The significance of the *De Revolutionibus* lies . . . less in what it says itself than in what it caused others to say. The book gave rise to a revolution that it had scarcely enunciated. It is a revolution-making rather than a revolutionary text" (Kuhn, 1957, p. 135).

5 This is Patinkin's term. For a characteristically erudite discussion of its meaning, see Patinkin (1982, Chapter 4).

6 The word "definitively" is perhaps a bit strong; after all, Marx reached his labor theory of value by a similar elimination process.

7 *Pace* Gunnar Myrdal, who is perhaps best known among modern-day economists as the Nobel Laureate who described Keynes's *Treatise* as "unnecessarily original."

8 I say "adumbrated" because the argument presented there is so clear an example of "seat-of-the-pants" analysis. As Patinkin remarks in a final footnote (fn. 9, both editions): "There is . . . a basic analytical problem here

whose full solution is still not clear to me. [. . .] It may be that, as Mr. [Nissan] Liviatan has suggested, *a complete answer to this question depends on the development of a theory of the firm operating under conditions of uncertainty with respect to the size of its market*" (italics mine).

9   Cf. Myrdal, 1982 (as cited in Jonung, 1987, fn. 7): "we in the Stockholm School were not only far ahead of Keynes and his colleagues in breaking away from the conventional view on monetary and stabilization policy but our approach was superior to that of Keynes in a number of respects."

10   This section draws freely from a paper on "Keynes's *General Theory:* The Marshall Connection" that I presented at the June 1978 meetings of the History of Economics Society in Boston.

11   This is not a continuous quotation, but it accurately expresses the sense of Ohlin's remark. For a similar view of Keynes's theory, see my "The Keynesian Perplex" (Clower, 1975, as reprinted in Walker, ed., 1984, 189–90).

12   For convenience in working with my computer, I have shown the "curves" in Figure 1, and also in later graphs, as linear or piecewise-linear relations. needless to say, this aspect of the geometry of the diagrams plays no essential role in the subsequent theoretical argument.

13   This is eminently plausible in the context of Marshall's thinking, for to Marshall the typical market was one in which ". . . the forces of demand and supply have free play; . . . there is no close combination among dealers on either side, but each acts for himself, and there is much free competition; that is, buyers generally compete freely with buyers, and sellers compete freely with sellers. But though everyone acts for himself, his knowledge of what others are doing is supposed to be generally sufficient to prevent him from taking a lower or paying a higher price than others are doing. This is assumed provisionally to be true both of finished goods and of their factors of production, of the hire of labor and of the hiring of capital" (Marshall, 1920, p. 341).

14   Marshall described the same notion on page 420 (fn. 2) of the first edition of his *Principles* but omits it from later editions. The magnitude in question corresponds precisely to what Keynes later called "Aggregate Supply Price," so I follow Keynes and denote it by the letter Z.

15   The derivation of the *mutatis mutandis* demand curve is straightforward: It is the locus of intersections of alternative *ceteris paribus* demand curves, $D(Z_0)$, $D(Z_1)$, $D(Z_2)$, and so on, with perpendiculars erected from alternative values of aggregate output, q_0, q_1, q_2, and so on, that enter into the determination of corresponding values of aggregate producer outlay Z_0, Z_1, Z_2, and so on. Cf. Parinello (1980, p. 72) and Kregel (1985, pp. 544–5).

16   I put quotation marks here because the "stability" in question is purely virtual. Marshall's analysis, like all exercises of its kind, is concerned with *tendencies* that are assumed to be operative in alternative initial situations, not with real-time adjustment processes (cf. Samuelson, 1947, pp. 273 ff.).

17   Marshall's ideas, in virtually modern form, are set out in work that Marshall completed before 1875 (on this, see Whitaker, 1975, Vol. 1, pp. 37 ff.).

18   This time estimate is based on the careful analysis of Patinkin in Chapter 2

of Patinkin and Leith (1977), and on a fascinating paper by Ingo Berens entitled "From the 'Banana Parable' to the Principle of Effective Demand" that was presented at the annual conference of the History of Economics Society in Boston, June 1987.

19 Just such a development was suggested in the "manifesto" that Joan and Austin Robinson and Richard Kahn sent to Keynes in May 1932 (JMK, XXIX, pp. 43 ff.) and was later urged upon him by Joan Robinson as a "method more general than yours" (JMK, XXIX, p. 47). In his reply, Keynes treated the issue as a "question of which is the best of two alternative exegetical methods. Here I am open to conviction [but] I lack at present sufficient evidence to the contrary to induce me to scrap all my present half-forged weapons" (JMK, XIII, p. 378).

20 Axel Leijonhufvud has disputed the "rigid-wage-rate" interpretation of Keynes in various publications over the past twenty years (see especially Leijonhufvud, 1969, section IV, and his comments as reported in the volume on Cambridge University Keynes Centenary celebration of July, 1983 (Worswick and Trevithick, 1983). Whether he would still dispute it, given the Marshall connection established here, I do not know.

21 Notice that, on this definition of thick markets, all non-purely competitive models in which demand *as seen by the individual seller* is assumed acurately to reflect demand *as it actually is* would be classified as "thick" (this includes all "large group" models of monopolistic competition as well as the conventional theory of monopoly). The now-standard textbook distinction between "price takers" and "price searchers" is clearly misleading: If an individual seller "knows" his demand curve, he has no need to "search" for the price at which alternative levels of output can be sold.

22 The model incidentally provides a simple answer to Arrow's query about who determines competitive price if there is no "auctioneer" (Arrow, 1959, pp. 42–3, 1986, p. 387). The mere posing of that query should have suggested the inappropriateness of the Walrasian model for considering such issues.

23 Cf. the similar remark by Patinkin (note 8) that precedes his summary of Liviatan's prescient suggestion about the need for a "theory of the firm operating under conditions of uncertainty with respect to the size of its market."

24 Cf. JMK, VII, p. 407; Arrow, 1986, p. 386.

25 An account of some particularly instructive items in this literature is given in Okun (1981, pp. 178 – 81). (Okun's "customer market" is, of course, a particular instance of my "thin market.")

26 In this same connection it is also pertinent to recall Patinkin's earlier analysis of "Keynesian" unemployment in Chapter 13 of his *Money, Interest, and Prices* (see note 8).

27 Ohlin might have conveyed his true meaning more effectively had he expressed wonder that Keynes apparently had never read Chamberlin's book on *monopolistic* competition which, unlike Joan Robinson's *imperfect* competition, contains numerous insightful remarks about the economics of thin markets (cf. note 20).

28 As is well known, Keynes changes his mind later in response to criticism by

Dunlop and Tarshis that mirrored precisely the criticisms advanced earlier by Ohlin (see section v of Keynes's response to Dunlop and Tarshis, reprinted as Appendix 3 of JMK, VII).

29 Compare the argument in the penultimate section of my "Keynes's *General Theory:* A Contemporary Perspective" (forthcoming in a volume of the Oxford Money Study Group containing papers from the September 1986 conference in honor of Sir John Hicks's contributions to monetary economics).

References

Arrow, K. J. (1959), "Toward a Theory of Price Adjustment," in Moses Abramovitz and others, *The Allocation of Economic Resources: Essays in Honor Of Bernard Haley,* Stanford Studies in History, Economics, and Political Science, 12. Stanford: Stanford University Press.

— (1986), "Rationality of Self and Others in an Economic System," *Journal of Business,* 59 (No. 4, Pt. 2), 385–98.

Berens, Ingo (1987), "From the 'Banana Parable' to the Principle of Effective Demand: On the Origin, Development and Structure of Keynes' Thought," paper presented at the Fourteenth Annual meeting of the History of Economics Society, Boston, June 19–22.

Clower, Robert W. (1975), "Reflections on the Keynesian Perplex," as reprinted in Walker, *Money and Markets,* Cambridge, England: Cambridge University Press, 1984.

— (1987a), "Keynes's General Theory: The Marshall Connection," draft of paper presented at the History of Economics Society meeting in Boston, June 1987.

— (1987b), "Keynes's *General Theory:* A Contemporary Perspective," forthcoming.

Jonung, Lars (1987), "The Stockholm School After 50 Years," paper presented at the June meeting of the History of Economics Society, Boston.

Keynes, John Maynard (1930), *A Treatise on Money,* as reprinted in Keynes, *Collected Writings* (cited as JMK), Vols. V and VI.

— (1936), *The General Theory of Employment, Interest and Money,* JMK, Vol. VII.

Kregel, Jan (1985), "Sidney Weintraub's Macrofoundations of Microeconomics and the Theory of Distribution," *Journal of Post-Keynesian Economics,* 7 (Summer), 540–58.

Kuhn, Thomas S. (1957), *The Copernican Revolution.* New York: Vintage Books.

Leijonhufvud, Axel (1969), "Keynes and the Classics," published by The Institute of Economics Affairs, Westminster, July.

Marshall, Alfred (1920), *Principles of Economics,* 8th ed. London: Macmillan.

Myrdal, Gunnar (1972), *Against the Stream: Critical Essays in Economics.* New York: Pantheon.

Ohlin, Bertil (1937), "Some Notes on the Stockholm Theory of Saving and Investment," *Economic Journal,* 47 (March), 53–69; 47 (June), 221–40.

(1978), "On the Formulation of Monetary Theory," 1933 essay translated by Hans Brems and William Yohe, *History of Political Economy,* 10 (Fall), 353–88.

(1981a), "Some Notes on the Stockholm Theory of Saving and Investment, (1937)," Appendix III, *History of Political Economy,* 13 (Summer), 239–55.

(1981b), "Stockholm and Cambridge: Four Papers on the Monetary and Employment Theory of the 1930s," *History of Political Economy,* 13 (Summer), 189–238.

Okun, Arthur (1981), *Prices and Quantities,* Oxford: Basil Blackwell.

Parrinello, Sergio (1980), "The Price Level Implicit in Keynes' Effective Demand," *Journal of Post-Keynesian Economics,* 3 (Fall), 63–78.

Patinkin, Don (1956, 1965), *Money, Interest and Prices,* 1st ed., Evanston: Row Peterson, 1956; 2nd ed., New York: Harper & Row, 1965.

(1978), "Some Observations on Ohlin's 1933 Article," *History of Political Economy,* (Fall), 413–18.

(1982), *Anticipations of the General Theory?* Chicago: University of Chicago Press.

Patinkin, Don, and Clark Leith, eds. (1977), *Keynes, Cambridge and the General Theory.* Toronto: University of Toronto Press.

Samuelson, Paul A. (1974), *Foundations of Economic Analysis.* Cambridge, Mass.: Harvard University Press.

Walker, Donald A., ed. (1984), *Money and Markets: Essays by Robert W. Clower.* New York: Cambridge University Press.

Whitaker, J. K. (1975). *The Early Economic Writings of Alfred Marshall, 1867–1890.* New York: Free Press.

Worswick, David, and James Trevithick, eds. (1983), *Keynes and the Modern World,* Proceedings of the Keynes Centenary Conference, King's College, Cambridge. Cambridge, England: Cambridge University Press.

PART IV

MISCELLANEOUS NOTES
AND REVIEWS

[23]

MAINSPRINGS OF AFRICAN ECONOMIC PROGRESS

I. Introduction

I am grateful to Professor Shepperson, Convener of the Committee of the Centre of African Studies at the University of Edinburgh, and to Professor Carter, Director of the Program of African Studies at Northwestern University, for this opportunity to commemorate the work of a much-admired colleague.   My last talk with Professor Herskovits was not entirely happy, for I was just recovering from 18 months of research in one of the gloomier regions of West Africa and my views about the prospects for African economic development* were much too pessimistic to suit his naturally sanguine temperament.   Since then I have visited other areas of Africa, have read and pondered much additional literature, and have, I think, shed any lingering biasses that might have influenced my earlier judgement.   Were I to discuss African economic prospects with Professor Herskovits today, however, I fear that the conversation would be even more awkward than before; for my pessimism has deepened as my knowledge of African and other underdeveloped areas has grown.

A full account of the reasons for my pessimism – or, as some might say, my cynicism – would require more space than is available here.   In common with all but a few hopeless idealists, I doubt the capacity of any backward society rapidly to carry through major cultural and economic transformations of the kind that would be required to take advantage of modern machine technology and applied science.   As Dalton has observed: **

> The problem of inducing successful development of primitive countries has economic, technological, social and cultural dimensions..... But social organization and cultural practices constitute intangible rules and ingrained values which are not directly amenable to deliberate change by policy measures... The real task is not to force change but to induce it in a manner which will be meaningful to the members of the societies it affects.

* See Clower, Dalton, *et. al., Growth Without Development: An Economic Survey of Liberia* (Evanston, Ill.; Northwestern University Press, 1966), Chapter 1.

**Dalton, George, "The Development of Subsistence and Peasant Economies in Africa," *International Social Science Journal,* Vol. XVI, No. 3, 1964, pp. 1–12.

2

Since the time scale relevant to "inducing" meaningful social change must be marked off in generations rather than years or decades, a fairly comprehensive "pessimists handbook" might be written without ever venturing outside the limits suggested by Dalton's theme.   It is not from this point of view, however, that I wish to approach my subject.   In common with most other students of African economic development Dalton focusses primary attention on factors that account for prevailing *differences* in per capita real income between advanced and under-developed countries rather than factors that *impede progress* —on distances travelled along the road to affluence, as it were, rather than rates of advance.   Granted that no society can move rapidly from a low to a high level on the international income scale, it does not follow that societies that currently occupy relatively low income levels must also be advancing along the income scale at relatively slow rates.   As I see it, the central problem confronting the student of economic development is not to explain prevailing differences in income levels between rich countries and poor, but rather to account for the apparent inability of poor countries to eliminate existing differences with the passage of time.

This is not an unfamiliar issue.   There is much discussion in the development literature of the political and social dangers inherent in a situation where more than two-thirds of the world's people are chronically poor.   What is commonly overlooked is that most people in already developed countries such as the United States and the United Kingdom also are chronically poor relative to richer members of the same societies. The force of this remark may be brought home by glancing at the U.S., U.K. and World distributions of income shown in Figure 1.*   Data for earlier years indicate that the U.S. and U.K. distributions have been relatively stable since at least 1900, and a similar remark undoubtedly applies to the world at large.   Accordingly, I am inclined to argue – in opposition to suggestions made by most previous writers – that international differences in income level are not a consequence of historical accidents that soon can be remedied by legislative or other purposive programs of social engineering, but rather are a result of deep-seated cultural forces that are common to all societies, advanced as well as backward – forces of such power that we may confidently predict continued "poverty" for at least two-thirds of the world's people and countries as long as the human race survives.

So much by way of introduction.   My purpose in the discussion that follows is to elucidate the factors that seem to me to account for the chronic poverty of the great bulk of human beings, including specifically the mass of people who happen to be Africans.   To be perfectly

* I have to thank Priscila Jimenez and Warren Prunella for performing the laborious statistical calculations underlying the world Lorenz distribution of income.

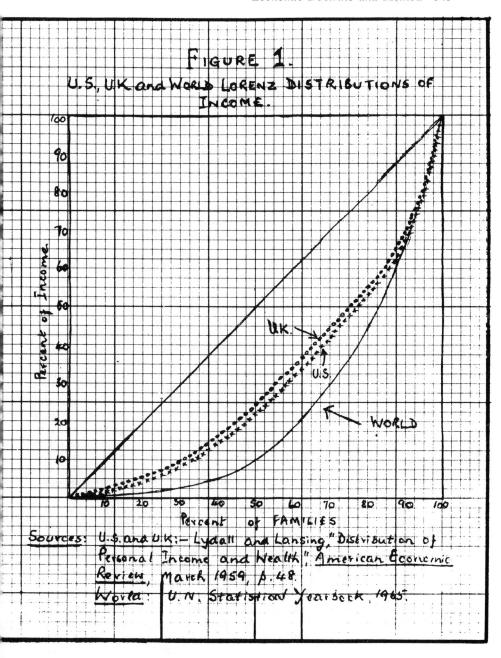

FIGURE 1.

U.S, UK and WORLD LORENZ DISTRIBUTIONS OF INCOME.

Sources: U.S. and UK:- Lydall and Lansing, "Distribution of Personal Income and Wealth", *American Economic Review*, March 1959, p.48.
World: U.N. Statistical Yearbook, 1965.

candid, most of what I have to say is conjectural, and designed to persuade, rather than factual and capable of demonstration. The difficulty is that economists are no more knowledgeable than other social scientists about the precise character of the forces that have generated sustained growth in per capita income among what are presently conceived to be the economically advanced countries of the world. Lacking an intellectually and empirically satisfactory explanation of development processes, they have more often than not taken refuge with brother anthropologists and sociologists in jargonized descriptions of historical experience. Given an appropriate mixture of "social tension," "entrepreneurial ingenuity," "backward and forward linkage," "cultural adaptability," "mutually reinforcing cultural and technological stresses," and a "minimum critical increase in per capita resources," an economy – so it is argued – will sooner or later develop sufficient impetus to achieve a "take-off into sustained growth." It is a major undertaking merely to explicate this terminology. To demand that the explication should tell us something we did not already know about the mainsprings of economic growth would perhaps be asking too much. However that may be, the demand certainly has not been met.

The account of development processes that I shall put forward is, in its present form, little more than a rearrangement of existing ideas. This rearrangement has the virtue, however, of opening up several new lines of inquiry some of which may prove to be empirically fruitful as well as academically interesting. Briefly, my central thesis is that every society, whether rich or poor, has available to it the material and technical requisites for rapid economic progress. The problem for most societies is not to obtain resources or invent technology but rather to take advantage of existing development opportunities. The true mainsprings of economic progress consist in every case of human attitudes towards the holding and maintenance of income-producing wealth. Unfortunately, the great bulk of individuals, hence virtually all societies, although objectively able are constitutionally unwilling to hold more than a few months' income in the form of productive wealth; i.e., virtually every society tends to consume the whole of its output as rapidly as it is produced. In these circumstances, the miracle is not that so many societies are poor but rather that any societies are rich. The explanation lies – or so I shall argue – in the fact that initial accumulations of income-producing wealth by isolated groups of individuals indirectly create conditions that are favorable to the coalescence in particular areas of ever larger groups of accumulation-minded individuals. Which is to say that social institutions favorable to the accumulation of wealth are more accurately regarded as a consequence than a cause of economic progress. I turn now to the task of defending this thesis and exploring its implications.

5

II. The Anatomy of Growth

It is convenient to proceed by outlining an idealized description of the technical and institutional framework of economic growth — a description that is sufficiently devoid of empirical content to apply to any society. To this end, let us imagine a world with just two kinds of commodities: "goods" such as food, clothing, automobiles, roads, raw materials, and buildings that can be *either* consumed to meet immediate human needs and desires *or* used to facilitate future production; "labor," skilled, unskilled, administrative, and managerial that is available for organizing and carrying on production, distribution, and exchange activities. To assign unambiguous measures to quantities of these two "commodities," we must in strict logic suppose that the proportional composition of each is fixed; i.e., that each consists of a certain number of "baskets" all of which contain precisely the same individual items. Whether or not this condition is exactly satisfied, however, we may think of the annual (per capita) output of goods of any society as a function of its accumulated stock of unconsumed goods, its current labor force, and its present technology. This relation may be represented graphically by a curve such as YY' in Figure 2, which I shall refer to henceforth as the *income locus*. The intercept of the income locus with the vertical axis represents the annual per capita flow of output that can be achieved by labor alone, without the assistance of previously produced capital goods. The curve slopes upward from left to right indicating that larger per capita rates of (net) output (Y) are obtainable the greater the quantity of accumulated wealth (W) available for current use as productive capital. The slope of the income locus at any point thus represents the marginal rate of return on wealth — the real rate of interest, as it were, on previously accumulated capital.

The form and position of the income locus will depend on the technology of the society, the term "technology" being interpreted in the broadest possible sense to include the skill and energy of the labor force, the intelligence and ingenuity of managers, and the flexibility of social and legal arrangements, as well as the state of engineering knowledge in a narrow sense. The income locus in effect summarizes an endless list of *environmental obstacles* to economic progress, obstacles that can and might be altered gradually with the passage of time, but only by measures that fundamentally alter existing technical and institutional arrangements.

Granted that every society confronts an income locus, economic well-being can be increased in the short run only by abstaining from current consumption, thereby increasing the quantity of productive wealth

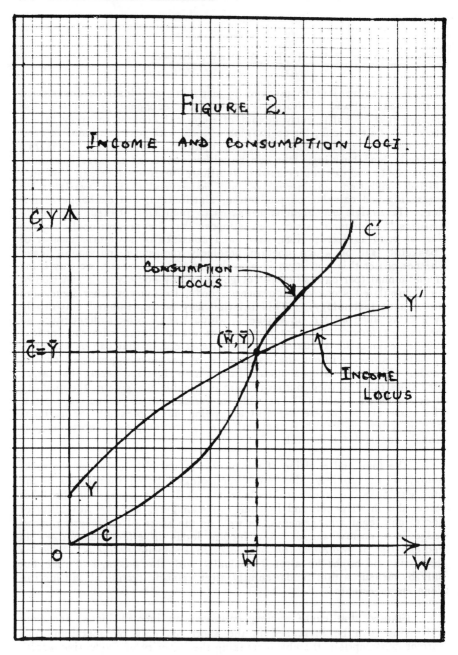

FIGURE 2.

INCOME AND CONSUMPTION LOCI.

available to facilitate future production.   Here we have to deal with *volitional obstacles* to economic growth, though in practice the distinction between environmental and volitional forces is likely to be one of degree rather than kind;   for many of the social constraints that affect the form and position of the income locus will also influence individual attitudes towards the accumulation of wealth.   For purposes of analysis, however, it is useful to think of a society as exhibiting a certain propensity to consume current wealth, a propensity that is largely independent of its current resources, technology, and level of output.   We may express this fact formally by supposing that there exists a functional relation between current (per capita) consumption and current (per capita) wealth as illustrated by the *consumption locus* CC' in Figure 2.

The consumption locus may be described in more operational terms by saying that it indicates for each alternative level of per capita wealth what the level of per capita income must be in order for the society to be willing to maintain its existing stock of capital intact.   According to this conception, a "thrifty" society, whether rich or poor, is characterized by a relatively flat consumption locus − a relatively low *marginal propensity to consume wealth*.   Correspondingly, a "spendthrifty" society is characterized by a relatively steep consumption locus, indicating that small increases in current wealth tend to generate proportionally much larger increases in per capita rates of consumption.

The point of intersection of the income locus with the consumption locus $(\overline{W}, \overline{Y})$ in Figure 2 defines a stationary state − a level of wealth such that per capita income is just equal to per capita consumption, hence a situation in which existing wealth is neither rising nor falling over time.   Provided that the slope of the consumption locus (representing the marginal propensity to consume wealth) is everywhere greater than the slope of the income locus (representing the marginal rate of return on wealth) it is apparent that the economy will tend over time to approach such a stationary state, regardless of the initial level of its accumulated wealth.   For if wealth is initially below the stationary level, income will exceed consumption, saving will be positive, and wealth will therefore increase over time.   But as wealth increases, consumption will rise more rapidly than income;   hence saving will gradually converge to zero (i.e., wealth will eventually cease to grow).   A similar analysis applies to the contrary situation in which the initial level of wealth is such that consumption exceeds income.   In this case, wealth will decrease with the passage of time.   Provided that the slope of the consumption locus is greater than the slope of the income locus, however, consumption will fall more rapidly than income as wealth is depleted;

hence a point will eventually be reached at which dissaving is zero (i.e., wealth will cease to decline).

As indicated by the alternative possibilities illustrated in Figure 3, capital accumulation *may* be a permanent phenomenon even with given income and consumption loci.   This will be true if the slope of the consumption locus is less than the slope of the income locus in the neighborhood of a stationary level of wealth, as illustrated in Figures 3b and 3c.   Except as theoretical curiosities, however, these possibilities are of little interest.   Factual studies of household spending and saving indicate that the behavior of the vast majority of households *even in advanced societies* conforms with the pattern illustrated in Figure 3a.   That is to say, most families tend over time to consume virtually the whole of their income.   Saving thus appears as a transitory rather than a permanent phenomenon, a consequence of autonomous changes in realized income (or in household preferences) rather than a result of purposive efforts to save and accumulate wealth.

In every society, to be sure, there exist some individuals, misers and others, who tend to save and accumulate wealth regardless of their income level.   By and large, however, household saving and dissaving appears to represent nothing more than a lagged adjustment of consumption to changes in income.   When income rises, consumption also tends to rise, but not so rapidly as income.   When income is increasing, therefore, saving will tend to be positive and the wealth of the household will tend to increase over time.   Conversely, when income falls, consumption will also tend to fall but not so rapidly as income.   When income is declining, therefore, saving will tend to be negative and the wealth of a household will tend to decrease over time.   Accordingly, if we wish to account for the rapid growth of productive capital that has characterized advanced societies during the past century or two, we must look not to misers and other lovers of wealth, but rather to impersonal economic forces of invention and innovation that have acted continuously to produce autonomous increases in real per capita income.

The assertion that the forces generating income growth are impersonal is subject to certain qualifications.   Invention and innovation would be of little practical consequence were it not for the existence in some societies of a substantial number of entrepreneurs – individuals whose marginal propensity to consume wealth is so weak that relatively small increases in income induce them to add relatively large increments to previously accumulated wealth.   Such individuals are important not because of the direct impact of their activities on current levels of production – though this may be considerable in some cases.   Their significance lies mainly in the fact that improvements in technology typically

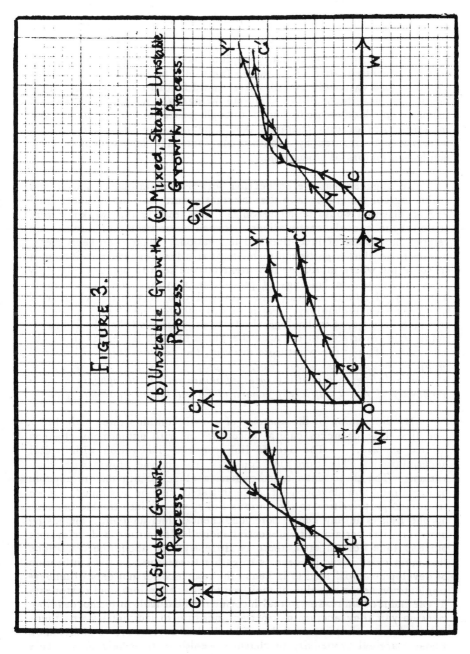

Figure 3.

(a) Stable Growth Process.

(b) Unstable Growth Process.

(c) Mixed, Stable–Unstable Growth Process.

are embodied in newly produced capital goods.   If increases in real income generated little or no saving (as would be the case if consumption loci are extremely steep), there would be little scope for the introduction of new technology.   Human beings are no doubt capable of improved productive performance through education and training, but improvements of this character would be of little importance if they were not accompanied by simultaneous increases in the efficiency of non-human factors of production.

To suggest that the connection between capital accumulation and technological progress is either straightforward or clearly understood and documented would be misleading.   The truth is that we know very little about causal interrelations between entrepreneurial saving and related processes of invention and innovation.   What does seem clear, however, is that significant technological advances are possible only in societies where increases in current income tend to produce relatively large increases in holdings of productive wealth.   One can imagine a society of misers in which the accumulation of wealth has little if any impact on technology;   but it is difficult to conceive of a society in which significant technological advances occur even though all households tend invariably to consume the whole of such increases in wealth as occur.   To put the point more directly, *the existence of a substantial group of households whose marginal propensities to consume wealth are low relative to prevailing rates of return on wealth appears to be a necessary if not a sufficient condition for sustained economic growth.*

My discussion of the anatomy of growth contains three main links. The first link connects capital accumulation with autonomous changes in real income.   The second link connects innovation with capital accumulation.   The third link connects real income growth with innovation.   The three links together form a closed chain that is capable of explaining how development, once initiated, may be sustained.   If we try to assign priorities to the various links, we run into trouble because no one link is in any sense more fundamental than another.   Supposing however, that certain entrepreneurial individuals initiate a development process in a certain area, there is little mystery about the conditions that must exist if the process is to gather momentum.   The initiation of development will tend to increase the real incomes not only of innovating entrepreneurs but also of their employees, suppliers, and customers. These induced increases in real income will bear fruit in further development only if they accrue in important measure to individuals who themselves have entrepreneurial leanings — that is to say, to individuals whose marginal propensity to consume wealth is relatively low.   This

11

is likely to be true only if the initial development process serves to attract to the area in which it occurs a substantial number of people who are dedicated to improving not only their income but their wealth position.

We know historically that such attractive forces have operated; the effects are discernable in the high degree of geographical concentration of industry and wealth that characterizes advanced economies. A common-sense explanation of this phenomenon is provided by noting that it is typically easier to obtain the initial wherewithal to establish one's own enterprise in an already developed and developing area (where real incomes are relatively high and rising) than to perform the same feat in a backward and underdeveloped area (where real incomes are relatively low and stagnant). In effect, the superior income prospects associated with developed areas serve to strengthen the first link in the development chain – the link connecting capital accumulation with real income growth. The concentration of development activities in particular areas then follows as a matter of course.

III.   Implications for African Economic Progress

The central contention of the preceding argument is that the rate of economic progress of any society, advanced or backward, is a function not only of its resources and technology, but also – and perhaps more important – of its willingness to abstain from consuming increases in productive wealth, the latter factor being a crucial determinant of the rate at which potential improvements in technology are actually introduced. I know of no way to test this contention directly. Data on wealth-holding habits are scarce and difficult to interpret even for economically advanced societies. Such data are simply not obtainable for any underdeveloped area. In these circumstances, it would be presumptuous to claim very much for my analysis; my argument puts the problem of economic development in a new and possibly accurate perspective and is worth serious consideration on these grounds.

Perhaps the greatest puzzle of development economics is the inability of presently underdeveloped countries effectively to exploit known techniques for increasing output from existing resources. Unlike advanced countries whose further economic progress depends in an essential way on the discovery of new techniques, the underdeveloped countries have only to apply existing knowledge to achieve vast increases in agricultural and manufacturing output. Granted that no underdeveloped country can hope to do as well as an already developed country even if it somehow managed to introduce all *feasible* technical improvements, the fact remains that no underdeveloped country has so far exploited even a minor fraction of such possibilities, despite substantial technical and material assistance from the developed nations of the world. If my analysis of growth processes is valid, the puzzle is solved by supposing—in conformity with such evidence as is available — that virtually all households in underdeveloped countries tend to consume rather than hold increments in wealth. This would account for the poor showing of technical assistance programs. To be effective, such programs must not only raise output from existing resources but also be accompanied by sustained increases in holdings of productive wealth. But the latter condition cannot be satisfied in a society where households tend to consume virtually the whole of any increment in wealth produced by rises in income — unless households are not left to themselves but instead are forced by government action to save and accumulate as productive wealth a significant portion of increases in output.

Another problem that has bemused development economists is the failure of indigenous entrepreneurial talent to emerge and successfully exploit development opportunities that expatriate firms would gladly seize upon if they were permitted to do so. The usual explanation of this phenomenon runs in terms of the inexperience, lack of education, scarcity of funds, or administrative shortcomings of indigenous businessmen. It seems never to have been noted — except by Karl Marx — that the one essential characteristic of the successful entrepreneur is a passion to accumulate income-producing wealth. Vast numbers of people in advanced countries have the education, know-how, organizing talent, etc., to function brilliantly as managers of large enterprises. But few such persons have sufficient itch for wealth to undertake the short-run sacrifices of consumption that are necessary to establish and develop their own businesses. Academics and other professional men are classic examples; possessing the talent but lacking the will to accumulate and hold wealth, most of them will be found in the ranks of the moderately comfortable, few of them in the ranks of the rich. Entrepreneurs are known as managers of assets; professors are more noted for managing debts. The lack among underdeveloped countries of talented people is no doubt regrettable, but I very much doubt if this has anything to do with the lack of entrepreneurs.

I remarked earlier that the distribution of income within any advanced society is similar to the distribution of income among countries.

13

The sad truth is that most individuals in every society are far more effective at dissipating than acquiring or maintaining income-earning assets. We often hear of "self-made" men, by which we ordinarily mean men of considerable means. In a very real sense, however, men of little means are also self-made, for a few individuals — and fewer societies — are compelled by nature or external circumstances to be as poor as they are. Economic development, for nations as for individuals, seems to me to be far more a matter of temperament than of resource endowments or technical skills.

If this is correct, the underdeveloped countries of Africa — in common with underdeveloped nations elsewhere — have little hope of improving their lot through external assistance, material or otherwise. Development grants and loans can never be anything but minuscule in relation to resources that are available domestically, and cannot in any case be expected to yield new fruit in fields where additional seed might have been but has not been sown since time out of mind. Neither can anything useful be expected to result from indigenous efforts to improve communications for cities, educate citizens, eliminate disease, and generally enhance the economic and social environment. Where increased consumption is the primary goal of the great bulk of people, economic development is simply not attainable by means that merely increase income. What is required are programs that aim at increased abstinence — programs that diminish the marginal propensity to consume wealth. Successful efforts in this direction can be expected to increase income through induced effects on capital formation and, more importantly, to set the stage for rapid and sustained improvements in technology. The difficulty is that we have no clear idea how to promote abstinence, no firm notions about the design of programs to accomplish this objective.

One possibility, suggested by the Russian experience, is for the government of underdeveloped countries directly to undertake — through various tax and regulatory devices — to save and invest productively resources that would be dissipated in current consumption if left at the disposal of individuals. Such procedures are easier to describe than execute and are unlikely anyhow to meet with popular approval. Judging from recent events in Ghana, Guinea, Uganda, Nigeria and elsewhere, however, this path to development — or something very similar — may be very common in years to come. Another possibility, suggested by the experience of Japan, is for the governments of underdeveloped countries to adopt legislation and provide subsidies to attract foreign investment on a large scale. Militating against this possibility is the

14

irrational but very real fear of foreign domination that people of under-developed countries have come to feel as a result of past colonial experiences.

Speaking as a pessimist, I must confess that I do not expect to see any presently underdeveloped country in Africa make significant economic progress within my lifetime or within that of my children or grandchildren. In this age of worldwide communication and rapid travel, economically adventurous souls tend to gravitate to already developed countries, and to already developed areas within developed countries, leaving behind them a few able people with a talent for local politics and vast numbers of hewers of wood and drawers of water.

Printed by the University of Edinburgh
for the Centre of African Studies,
Edinburgh, 1968.

[24]

THE PRESENT STATE OF INTERNATIONAL LIQUIDITY THEORY

By ROBERT CLOWER, *Northwestern University and University of Essex*
and RICHARD LIPSEY, *University of Essex*

"Half-baked theory is not of much value in practice, though it may be half-way towards final perfection."—J. M. KEYNES.

International liquidity, like marital bliss, is a term that everyone uses but few understand. To avoid devoting most of our paper to insoluble semantic questions (which would in any case only reveal that we were in the majority), we shall restrict our review to that portion of the literature that is specifically concerned with the adequacy of international financial reserves.

I. *Reserve Needs: General Considerations*

Official holdings of foreign reserves derive from attempts by national authorities to maintain fixed rates of exchange between domestic and foreign currencies. In a world where all currencies were backed 100 percent by a single commodity such as gold, or where all exchange rates were freely flexible, every national currency could be used to discharge trading debts in any country. Where rates of exchange are fixed by government fiat, however, or where fiduciary issues are pegged in relation to other currencies or to gold, different currencies are substitutable as media of exchange only as long as each is freely obtainable at prevailing rates in all countries. The latter condition can be satisfied continuously only if national authorities assume major responsibility for the purchase, sale, and holding of foreign currencies and simultaneously pursue policies of economic control that enable them to maintain reserves at levels that permit all demands to be met.

A person who insisted on eating meals while standing on his head clearly would have problems. If he sought our help, we should probably suggest that he adopt a more convenient posture. Many economists are inclined to offer similar advice to central bankers and other perplexed managers of international reserves. If governments insist on maintaining their present stance in international financial affairs, however, the necessity of reserves must be granted and the question arises, "By what criteria, if any, may a country arrive at a reasoned judgment about the adequacy of its existing reserves?"

Professor Machlup has suggested, not altogether facetiously, that judgments about adequacy are at best quixotic: ". . . the 'need' for

reserves is determined by the ambitions of . . . monetary authorities."[1]
There is no doubt much to be said for this view; but before concluding
that problems of reserve adequacy are more appropriately discussed by
psychiatrists than economists, we must see if any of the reasons for
holding reserves is amenable to rational assessment.

Under a system of flexible rates, individuals engaged in foreign trade
would hold foreign currency for much the same transactions, precautionary, and speculative purposes as they would hold domestic currency. None of the basic needs for foreign reserves would disappear
under a system of fixed exchange rates. Centralization of private
precautionary and speculative balances might involve some reduction
in total reserve requirements. But government officials tend to think
more in terms of shibboleths and conventions than in terms of social
costs and benefits, so rather than permit temporary variations in
reserves to be evened out by appropriate rate variations around established levels, official managers are likely to hold extra reserves sufficient
to meet temporary drains head on. In a system of pegged rates, however, additional reserves typically would be held to ward off potential
attacks by foreign and domestic speculators.[2] Indeed, to avoid recurrent speculative crises arising out of short-run movements in reserves,
official balances held for "war-chest" purposes alone might well be
maintained at a level several times as large as aggregate holdings under
an otherwise identical system with flexible rates. Professor Machlup's
theory of monetary reserves should perhaps be modified, then, to
assert that needs are determined by the nightmares as well as by the
ambitions of central bankers.

It should be clear from the foregoing discussion that the adequacy of
reserves to meet some contingencies cannot be assessed in terms of
reasoned criteria. However that may be, it is surely important to distinguish conceptually between reserves that are needed to facilitate trade
and reserves that authorities desire for other reasons. For purposes of
discussion, it is convenient to distinguish four main reasons for holding
official reserves. The first and most obvious reason is to accommodate
systematic and random fluctuations in current account receipts and
payments. The second reason is to allow for temporary nonspeculative

---

[1] Fritz Machlup, "The Need for Monetary Reserves," *Princeton Reprints in International
Finance*, No. 5 (Oct., 1966), p. 27. The cited passage provides only a partial statement of a
more general doctrine known as "the Mrs. Machlup's Wardrobe Theory of Monetary Reserves."

[2] The role of gold in international trade merits brief comment in this connection. In a world
of flexible prices and exchange rates, gold would occupy no special place as an international
means of payment. A similar observation applies to a system of fixed exchange rates, provided
that no country pegs its currency to gold. If a country is so ill-advised as to introduce (or
maintain) such a peg, however, the effect is to create an extraneous "international money"
and an equally extraneous "exchange rate." Speculators may then use the first as a weapon
to attack the target provided by the second. Hence there arises not only a need for reserves
but for reserves of gold. As if standing on one's head to eat were not enough, one hand is now
tied as well.

variations in capital account items. The third reason is to buy time when a country finds itself in fundamental disequilibrium—time to determine whether or not such a situation exists, time to decide by how much prevailing exchange rates should be altered, time to devise domestic policies that will maximize the effectiveness of the proposed changes. The fourth and final reason is to enable a country to weather speculative storms.

Judgments about the adequacy of reserves held for the first two reasons clearly fall within the ambit of economic analysis. However, only a very minor fraction of the literature is specifically concerned with these requirements, and most of that fraction is basically exploratory. Judgments about the adequacy of reserves held to buy time belong partly within the province of economics, partly within that of politics and social psychology. The great bulk of the literature on international reserves is concerned directly or indirectly with such judgments.[3] Since most of these contributions barely rise above the level of social conversation, we shall have little to say about them in what follows.

The adequacy of reserves held to meet speculative crises has so far not proven amenable to rational assessment. We suspect that this will always prove to be the case since speculative crises are never wholly rational affairs themselves. If this is correct, we shall never be able to arrive at operationally meaningful measures of overall reserve adequacy. Speculative behavior as a routine aspect of merchandise and other nonspeculative trading activities is, of course, a legitimate object of inquiry in connection with the first two reasons for holding reserves. Speculative crises are in the nature of electrical fires, however: protection lies not in better insulation but in new wiring.

II. *Measures of Reserve Adequacy*

It is important to distinguish between qualitative and quantitative concepts of reserve adequacy. Qualitative concepts—measured by ratios of reserves to imports, exports, net overall trade balance, or the variance of reserves—are not without interest for descriptive and comparative purposes but are of no direct use for analytical, predictive, or policy purposes. Quantitative concepts—measured by estimates of the probability that any given quantity of reserves will suffice to meet reserve needs during a given time interval—are apparently necessary if we are to pursue the problem of reserve adequacy beyond the stage of statistical anecdote.

To arrive at empirically meaningful measures of quantitative adequacy is a regrettably difficult task. As is true of any econometric

---

[3] For a representative sample, see Herbert G. Grubel, *World Monetary Reform* (Stanford Univ. Press, 1964).

analysis, we must begin by formulating an explicit statistical model to represent the processes that are assumed to generate relevant time series data. If this step is to constitute anything more than a theoretical exercise, the model next must be estimated and shown to yield results that accord satisfactorily with historical experience. The derivation of appropriate measures of reserve adequacy, either by direct calculation or by indirect simulation techniques, can then be carried out to some purpose.

When we specify a model we have to isolate the reasons being studied for holding reserves. The main reason analyzed so far, and the one to which we shall confine ourselves in this section, concerns transaction balances used to accommodate systematic and random fluctuations in current account receipts and payments. The following is a typical set of isolating assumptions: (1) a small country, (2) trading at fixed import prices and a fixed exchange rate, (3) no autonomous capital movements, (4) fundamental equilibrium rules so that the equilibrium rate is unchanging through time and is equal to the official rate, (5) receipts and payments are subject to disturbances[4] such that reserves vary over time. A critical assumption must then be made over (5): either the disturbances are random in time or they are in some way serially correlated.[5]

Having specified a model, it is necessary to ask precise questions of it. One approach is to ask what is the probability under stated conditions (including an initial level of reserves $R_{\bullet}$) that reserves will fall below some stated level $L(L \geq 0)$ at some time between the present and some finite future date T. This approach fits naturally into the theory of random walks. Specifically, we have to calculate the probability that a particle, starting at a level $R_{\bullet}$ and moving in a series of discrete steps (each equal to the expected value of a one-period gain or loss[6]) will fall below a line with ordinate L at any time on or before date T.[7]

---

[4] It is important to observe that balance -of-payments figures measure transactions and not payments (cf. Leland B. Yeager, *International Monetary Relations*, Harper and Row, 1966, Chap. 3, esp. pp. 36–37). Thus fluctuations in the current account balance will greatly overstate fluctuations in net current account payments whenever traders indulge in stabilizing behavior (e.g., by postponing repatriation of funds from abroad and accelerating payment to foreign points whenever they think the current rate is too high). Data on official reserves are free of this particular defect since they reflect payments rather than transactions; but they have other faults since they show the net effect of autonomous capital transactions as well as and inseparably from that of current account transactions.

[5] It is worth noting that the argument that export and import transactions are subject to thousands of independent causal forces (see, e.g., Kenen and Yudin, as cited below, p. 244, n) would not establish serial independence and a normal distribution for payments and receipts even if it did establish it for transactions. The actual purchase and sale of currency does not have to be synchronized with transactions; hence, both purchases and sales may be significantly affected by an important common cause: the relation between the current rate of exchange and the expected future rate.

[6] The more accurate formulation is for the magnitude of each step to be determined by a random drawing from a normal distribution. For long walks, the expected value of the one period change can be used, giving a substantial simplification of the analysis. For short walks,

The second approach is to determine some optimal level of reserves and then to compare actual with optimal levels. As we shall see, this poses more difficult problems than merely calculating the probability of reserves falling to some crisis level.

Needless to say, practice as reflected in contributions to the literature conforms imperfectly with these precepts. Economic theory furnishes few tools for explicit treatment of disequilibrium processes of the kind that characterize trading in a system of inflexible exchange rates. In the present state of economic science, one must either rely on *ad hoc* theoretical models or (what comes to much the same thing, only more obviously) choose an equation with convenient statistical properties and attempt to rationalize the choice after it has been fitted to data.

Early empirical work was based mainly on ratio comparisons, the implicit theory being that the need for reserves was related to some level such as that of imports or exports. These measures have been reviewed critically by Machlup.[8] In order to go beyond purely qualitative measures it is essential to realize that the job reserves have to do is related to variability rather than the level of receipts and payments. Caves[9] seems to be the first person to have stated this publicly. A transitional step in the same direction is taken by Weir M. Brown,[10] who hints at Caves's point but who is still so wedded to the ratio approach that he tries to judge reserve adequacy by comparing, internationally and intertemporally, ratios of a country's reserves in any one year to the "net overall balance" in that year.[11]

A closer approach to an acceptable quantitative measure is provided by Heller.[12] He calculates the optimum reserves for a country by relating the cost of a unit of reserves (measured by the long-term rate of interest)

---

however, the two formulations can give substantially different results. For example, in the expected value approach there is a zero chance of running out of reserves until the elapse of a number of periods equal to initial reserves divided by the expected value of a one period change. In empirical applications, it is necessary to estimate this expected value and the usual procedure (which is to measure average gains and average losses over recent periods) obviously may involve large sampling errors.

[7] We do not set an upper bound and ask the probability of passing through it before reaching the lower bound (which would turn the problem into a gambler's ruin problem), because although the authorities can be driven out of the game (reserves fall below L) they can never drive out traders by a favorable run of reserve increases. It is also necessary to make T finite, not only because the authorities probably have a finite time horizon, but also because the probability that the particle will reach any finite bound approaches unity as T approaches infinity.

[8] *Op. cit.*, pp. 4–25.

[9] Caves, "International Liquidity: A Home Repair Manual," *Rev. of Econ. and Statis.*, May, 1964.

[10] Weir M. Brown, "The External Liquidity of an Advanced Country," *Princeton Studies in International Finance*, No. 17.

[11] Brown's analysis produces some curious arguments; e.g., the reasoning (p. 10) on the treatment of positive as well as negative balances, and some zany results; e.g., the U.K. series from 1953-63 which runs 84.5, 24.2, 7.6, 27.8, 6.4, 9.1, 2382.5, 405.5, 12.7, 10.7. The conclusion to be drawn is not that U.K. reserve adequacy varied wildly from year to year, but that ratios of current reserves to current balances tell us nothing about the adequacy of current reserves.

[12] H. R. Heller, "Optimal International Reserves," *Econ. J.*, June, 1966, pp. 296–311.

to the expected value of the gain obtainable from the reserves (measured by the loss of national income that would occur if external balance had to be obtained by expenditure damping policies multiplied by the probability of the occurrence of a fluctuation large enough to require the use of the ith unit of reserves). Heller begins by assuming that changes in reserves are not serially correlated, and then calculates the probability that a country will run out of reserves in a single unbroken series of losses, each one equal to the average (trend-removed) change in reserves that the country has actually experienced.[13] He next compares actual reserves with his calculation of each country's optimal reserves to obtain ratios that—assuming the theory on which they are based is valid—have some quantitative significance.

In formulating the problem as one of determining optimal reserves rather than merely calculating the probability of running out of reserves, Heller raises the important question of how to evaluate the advantages of holding reserves that provide a given level of security. Heller's particular approach makes it rational, however, to hold reserves that have a very small probability of being used. For example, if the opportunity cost of reserves is 5 percent and if the marginal propensity to import (m) is 0.1, then the alternative to financing $1.00 of imports through reserves is to lower national income by $10.00 and it would pay to hold reserves which had only one chance in 200 of being used in the current year.[14]

The approach is suggestive, but its implementation poses problems. Because the only alternative to holding reserves that Heller considers is an expenditure-damping policy to cut imports,[15] the potential value of reserves held is a multiple ($1/m$) of reserves. As a practical matter, countries faced with deficits—particularly those with small m's—will surely consider other alternatives. Selective controls will have a much smaller cost, as will covering current account deficits by raising short-term interest rates to induce temporary capital inflows. If a temporary deficit can be covered by raising the short-term interest rate from 5 to 6 percent, for example, the cost of not holding reserves is simply the extra 1 percent that must be paid on funds borrowed to cover the deficit.[16] This would make the cost of not having $1.00 in reserves $0.06

[13] The probability of running out of reserves is thus $(.5)^{b/c}$, where c is total reserves and b is the average gain or loss in reserves.

[14] Heller calculates only the probability of running out of reserves in a single unbroken sequence of unfavorable steps. What we really need to know in his formulation is the probability of using the marginal dollar this year.

[15] He does mention alternatives briefly on p. 309, but his analytical treatment relies exclusively on the expenditure-damping policy.

[16] If foreigners already hold short-term debt in the deficit country, there will be an additional interest cost on any debt that is refinanced during the period of higher interest rates. Since the rise in interest rates needed to attract a marginal dollar of foreign capital would be minute, the amount of foreign loans being refinanced in the period would have to be vast before the cost of attracting the dollar by this means would exceed the cost of cutting imports by fiscal measures.

rather than $10.00, which would reduce Heller's calculation of the optimum level of reserves by a factor of over 100. This alters ratios of actual reserves to optimal reserves from the range 0.5–2.0 in advanced countries to 5.0–200.0. Of course, our example is crude; but the point is made that the calculation of optimal reserves is extremely sensitive to the set of policy alternatives considered.

It should be remarked, in passing, that if world reserves were "adequate" in Heller's sense and were serving the purpose of financing temporary deficits, some countries would have "too much" reserves and some "too little." We must beware, therefore, of the common conclusion that reserves are wrongly distributed. A not-yet-attempted disequilibrium formulation would be required adequately to handle the problem.

Many variants of the random fluctuations model are possible. Peter B. Clark,[17] for example, sets up a system in which random variations in reserves are partially offset by changes in income, some fraction λ of any discrepancy between actual and desired reserves being eliminated in each period by conscious policy. The protection afforded by a given level of reserves is then calculated as a function of two parameters, the variance of the payments distribution, and the policy parameter λ. Not surprisingly, it can then be shown that the level of protection varies inversely with the variance of payments and directly with the size of λ. The smaller is the policy reaction, the greater is the chance that reserves will be eliminated by an unfavorable run of chance disturbances.

Both Heller and Clark build on the basic assumption that changes in reserves are serially independent. Since we know that trade is subject to seasonal and cyclical patterns, the validity of the independence assumption is questionable.[18] Indeed, Kenen and Yudin have shown that much of the data drawn from a large sample of countries is adequately described by the first-order Markov process:

(1) $$\Delta R_t = \lambda \Delta R_{t-1} + \gamma.$$

Starting from this foundation, Archibald and Richmond (in an as yet unpublished paper) have analyzed the security provided by given levels of reserves.[19] Because the random walk problem with serially correlated outcomes has not yet been solved analytically, the authors are forced to fall back on Monte Carlo experiments. They produce many detailed

[17] "Optimum International Reserves and the Speed of Adjustment" (unpublished paper based on M.I.T. doctoral dissertation).

[18] See Peter B. Kenen and Elinor B. Yudin, "The Demand for International Reserves," *Rev. of Econ. and Statis.*, Aug., 1965, pp. 242–50; William Poole, "Speculative Prices as Random Walks," *Southern Econ. J.* Apr., 1967, pp. 468–78.

[19] G. C. Archibald and J. Richmond, "The Theory of Foreign Exchange Reserves: A Probabilistic Approach" (University of Essex, mimeographed discussion paper). We owe our own view of the formalization of the problems in this section largely to the Archibald-Richmond paper.

and interesting quantitative results. Perhaps the most obvious but also the most important from our point of view is that a given level of reserves provides substantially less security when the parameter λ is greater than zero than when reserves are not serially correlated.

This formulation of the problem also makes it possible to handle rationally the question, "Do we need larger reserves as the volume of trade increases?" The usual analysis of this question draws almost exclusively on casual empirical observation to arrive at a resounding answer of "Yes." The question is simply, "Does the distribution of estimated disturbances show a pattern of homoscedasticity or of heteroscedasticity when plotted against the volume of trade?" The answer to this question is by no means clear. Until further evidence is available, therefore, we should view with skepticism the common belief that the level of reserves should expand more or less in line with increases in the volume of trade.

All of this work is interesting and represents a distinct advance on earlier ratio calculations, but how much further it can or should be carried is debatable. There is a clear danger that this aspect of the reserve adequacy problem, because it is amenable to rational formulation, will attract a great deal of effort at the end of which we may delude ourselves into believing that we know something about reserve adequacy in general. However that may be, it appears that two theoretical points, although well known, need to be made as a caution to other workers in the field. The first is that alternative theoretical specifications of the payments process may give very different results for the probability of running out of a given level of reserves yet generate data that give a reasonable statistical fit to equation (1). Unless the difficult task of testing for the empirical balance of evidence between alternative specifications has been carried out with extreme care, we can have little confidence either in the hypothesis that the Markov process is the correct specification or in calculations of reserve adequacy based on the assumption that it is.[20] The second point is that it is impossible to learn anything from such simple equations as (1) about the probability of running out of reserves in a system the underlying structure of which is changing over time, even if the equation produces a fairly high R^2 when fitted to the data. Since low levels of reserves invariably produce speculative movements and strong counter measures on the part of the central authorities, a model of random or systematic fluctuations in current account payments will invariably be a misspecification at just

[20] Assume as an alternative that the underlying structure is sinusoidal. Then if we take observations on Δr fairly close together, they will lie along a narrow loop to which equation (1) will provide a reasonable statistical fit; but the estimated value of the parameter α will depend on the essentially arbitrary choice of the number of observations per cycle—approaching unity as the number of observations increases.

those times when there is a serious chance of running out of reserves, and it will be completely misleading if it is used to predict the probability that a struggle between central authorities and speculators will end in victory for either side.

III. *Unsettled and Insoluble Questions*

As far as we know, all existing quantitative measures of reserve adequacy have been derived on the assumption that reserves are held to meet random and systematic drains associated with varying flows of current account payments and receipts. As indicated in the preceding section, numerous theoretical and statistical difficulties remain to be overcome before we can place much confidence in our ability to assert what reserves are adequate to satisfy even these relatively predictable requirements. The situation becomes much worse if we also take account of nonspeculative and temporary capital transfers and of fundamental disequilibria.

The main difficulty in handling temporary capital movements is that we have virtually no foundation in theory or fact for arriving at estimates of their probable magnitude in alternative circumstances. Short-term capital movements are probably responsive to changes in the international structure of short-term interest rates, but are almost certainly influenced by a host of other and less obvious factors as well. Ask any government how long, for purely domestic reasons, they might want to maintain short-term rates out of line with the international structure, and the extent of our ignorance would surely become obvious. The answer would almost certainly be, "We don't have any idea." And our reply would have to be, "Then we don't have any idea how large your reserves for this purpose should be."

The most serious difficulties of all arise when we turn our attention to the third and fourth reasons for holding reserves. Here we join forces with most other writers on international liquidity and indulge in social conversation. The crux of the problem is that the main justification for holding any but working balances of international reserves is to allow the government time to mobilize its defenses before speculators have occasion to launch an effective attack. It might be possible to arrive at an informed estimate of the time required for effective government action in alternative circumstances; military commanders carry out similar if simpler exercises every day of the week. But even with this information, how could we possibly gauge with any accuracy the conditions in which speculators might decide to attack in force? For the sake of argument, suppose that a country has a perfectly clear idea of the reserves that it needs for normal trading purposes and manages to assemble such reserves together with a substantial margin as a hedge against the possible emergence of a situation of fundamental disequilibrium. Suppose further that a fundamental disequilibrium actually occurs, but that its existence is not recognized until reserves have fallen to a level where speculators (assumed to be as informed as economists and government officials) are reasonably certain that quiet discussions are taking place in official circles concerning possible changes in domestic economic policy and/or prevailing exchange rates. Regardless of the size of official reserves, what follows will be understandable only as a semipsychological battle of nerves, wit and bluff. Forecasting turning points in the trade cycle is as child's play in comparison with predicting speculative crises—but we have not done well with the former problem either.

The moral is gloomy but plain. We cannot really hope to judge the overall adequacy of reserves in the present situation in which destablizing speculation is encouraged. If we are ever to be in a position to make such judgments, the system itself will have to be changed by working out techniques that will permit governments to demoralize speculators at any desired point in time.[21] Otherwise, no measure of reserve adequacy can have any operational significance, for speculative reserves will always have to be held. A distinctly preferable alternative might be permanently to demoralize central bankers by devising a workable system of flexible rates and simultaneously eliminating gold as a reserve currency. The world might then go about its proper business of providing for the adequacy of more important things than international liquidity and related national status symbols.

[21] It would be difficult to overestimate the ingenuity of economists as a group in devising workable solutions to practical problems and equally difficult to underestimate their ability to sell such solutions to the public. As Yeager has so aptly observed (*op. cit.*, p. 297): "When some economists recommend policies they really expect to work best while others recommend compromises based on their amateur assessments of political acceptability, they create a spurious impression of disagreement among themselves and undermine the authority of their technical knowledge. Unsatisfactory and misinterpreted experience with some compromise system far from gradually educating people . . . is likely to make [desirable changes] even more politically impossible than they are now."

[25]

THE THESIS OF ADMINISTERED PRICES

In an influential report published in 1935, Gardiner C. Means puts forward a case for revision. He notes first that the prices of most commodities are determined in practice not by impersonal forces of demand and supply, as reflected in the bids and offers of traders in organized markets, but rather by the personal administrative actions of the sellers (or buyers) of particular products. Then, Means argues that the area of "price discretion" in many industries is large and that the prevalence of administered prices, especially in the corporate sector, adversely influences the overall performance of the economic system [308, 310, 311].

Means does not provide precise criteria for distinguishing between "administered" and "market" prices. Nor does he explain the rationale of discretionary pricing, or provide reasons why administered prices should be less responsive than market prices to changes in demand. These are serious omissions. Economists do not need Means to tell them that individual producers, wholesalers, retailers, and employers set all but a handful of commodity prices (more accurately, "asked" or "bid" prices), for this has been common knowledge for at least two centuries. The only relevant issue that remains is whether or not the ubiquitousness of administered prices fundamentally alters the normal working of "impersonal forces of supply and demand." Means's argument sheds no significant light on this question.

EVIDENCE ABOUT ADMINISTERED PRICES

Means's "administered price thesis," however, deserves to be taken seriously. Stigler and Kindahl do take it seriously in the most ambitious attempt to resolve some of the issues that Means poses [426]. They show that BLS price data generally reflect "quoted" or "list" prices, rather than prices at which actual trades take place. They show also that actual transaction prices for a large group of industrial products are significantly more flexible than reported BLS prices for the same products. Even their data indicate, however, that industrial prices tend to respond sluggishly to changes in demand. Other studies, proceeding along similar lines, bear out this finding. Hence, it is settled that transaction prices respond relatively slowly to changing economic conditions in administered price industries [269, 375].

"STICKY" PRICES AS SHOCK ABSORBERS

This stipulation, however, fails to resolve the central issue, for sellers (or buyers) in virtually all industries are price administrators. Restaurant owners, barbers, corporate and noncorporate department and grocery store managers, automobile dealers, refrigerator manufacturers, ice cream vendors, and university employment officers all set "asked" or "bid" prices at their own discretion, at levels that seem to them suitable for maximizing the net wealth of their enterprises over a long period of time. This observation holds for noncorporate and "competitive" business firms, as well as for corporate and "noncompetitive" business firms. Thus, administered pricing is in no way connected with corporate forms of business organization or with monopolistic or oligopolistic restrictions on output or entry per se.

The economic significance of administrative pricing, if any, is that it contributes to price rigidity [269]. Thus the question one must answer is not: "Does administrative pricing contribute to price rigidity?" I presume that it does, if only for the sake of argument. Rather, the question to answer is: "Do rigidities associated with administrative pricing, as compared with some other feasible, alternative method of pricing, adversely affect the allocation of resources and the stability of markets?"

It is not immediately obvious that "sticky" prices necessarily are a "bad thing." Just as shock absorbers contribute to the stability of an automobile driven over rough roads, so may price rigidities contribute to the stability of an economy often exposed to natural and man-made disturbances. Real economies, like real automobiles, do not always travel along smooth roads. If economic conditions are "rough," institutions will evolve that ensure sufficient absorption of shocks to allow the economy to survive. In analogous circumstances, an automobile without shock absorbers would simply fall apart. In considering the implications of administrative price rigidities, therefore, one should ask whether business people "rig" prices to promote their own interests, or whether they permit buyers and sellers to overcome problems of resource allocation inherent in an imperfect and uncertain world.

THE NECESSITY OF ADMINISTERED PRICES

By considering first commodities whose prices are "market"—determined—commodities such as basic agricultural products, government and corporate securities, gold, silver, and foreign exchange—one can gain some idea of why most prices are administered. Goods whose prices are seldom administered are homogeneous or easily standardized, and they are traded in considerable volume by many buyers and sellers. Neither buyers nor sellers have any reason to prefer doing business with particular persons on the other side of the market, and purchasers need not inspect goods before taking delivery. Hence, a seller who tries to sell above the going price finds few if any buyers, and a buyer who tries to purchase below the going price is ignored by potential sellers. Even in markets of this kind, individual dealers set prices, not machines or ghostly forces of "supply and demand." But, the "area of price discretion" in such markets is small or nonexistent.

Matters are quite different, of course, for the great bulk of all commodities traded in the modern world. Steel is a basic industrial raw material, but it comes in endless shapes, sizes, and varieties, many of which must be produced almost to order to meet the specifications of particular customers. Grocery products come in countless brands, qualities, and kinds of containers; one cannot effectively trade such goods except in conveniently located retail markets that carry stocks for immediate delivery. Restaurant meals might be priced by bids and offers communicated to brokers in a single national market, but no superior chef would find it either necessary or profitable to observe the prices in his or her establishment.

Central markets, more generally, do not and could not exist for commodities that are not standardized (branded goods, personal services), that require inspection before purchase or delivery (furniture, automobiles), that are purchased frequently in small lots (groceries, cigarettes, gasoline), or that are produced to order (tailored suits, machine tools, residential dwellings). In all such cases, the volume of trade of any *specific* commodity is extremely small compared with the total volume of trade in any *general* category. A central market for "automobiles" might make sense if automobiles come in just one variety; but, how would such a market accommodate the great number of makes and models that actually exist? Obviously the only viable form of market organization in this case and in similar cases is one that assigns primary responsibility for the pricing of specific products to particular sellers or buyers. This is a market characterized by administered prices.

THE BENEFITS OF "STICKY" PRICES

Prices in such a market should be relatively rigid—first, because it is costly for sellers (or buyers) to change posted prices. Catalogs must be reprinted, menus altered, and sales people and customers alerted, for example. For this reason of cost alone, administered prices generally are unresponsive to small or erratic changes in demand. Advertising and special sales and discounts take the place of price changes to lure customers if demand becomes slack; inventories are allowed to run down if demand becomes strong.

The second reason why prices in such a market should be relatively rigid is that sellers (or buyers) who set administered prices have no way of knowing in advance what sales (or purchases) at these prices will be. Past experience is their only guide, and this guide is often treacherous. Hence, prices often will be changed not in response to movements in demand (which are difficult to interpret) but, rather, in response to changes in costs. This kind of pricing can lead, of course, to serious and expensive errors, as well as to price movements that, to an external observer, appear misguided, if not perverse. Prices, for example, can go up as demand goes down. This kind of pricing can also lead to sticky prices, for where mistakes are inevitable, it is natural for price administrators to proceed cautiously, taking no action at all until they have compelling reasons to do so.

Armen Alchian suggests a third and undoubtedly crucial reason for the inflexibility of administered prices [8]. Alchian's contention is that sellers keep prices constant to reduce search costs to buyers. If sellers were continuously to adjust prices in response to every fluctuation in sales, buyers would be induced to search for relatively favorable prices before buying any products. This search would be a clear waste of time and effort if the prices actually paid after the search were much the same as would be paid by always purchasing from single sellers at constant prices. Variable prices would be particularly bothersome for industrial buyers; they would have great difficulty predicting their own production costs to be able to negotiate effectively with potential customers. Thus, by maintaining relatively rigid prices, sellers perform a highly useful economic service for their customers. Even though they might set better terms (resulting in costly search), they provide a ready market in which the customers can purchase goods on predictable terms that are, on the average, favorable.

Alchian illustrates his theory by noting that restaurant owners do not raise prices when the number of customers rises above normal or post lower prices outside their doors when customers inside are few. Prices could be adjusted hourly so that a restaurant always operates at or near full capacity. This practice would stabilize output, but potential customers would then have an incentive to shop around among competing restaurants before buying a meal, and this would be costly and inconvenient. Most customers are willing, and some are actually anxious, to pay slightly higher fixed prices (which are required when capacity often is excessive) to eliminate the need for search. Hence, rigid prices, idle capacity, and fluctuating output occur not because restaurant owners insist on this arrangement but, rather, because most customers prefer it.

SUMMARY

This brief explanation of administered prices by no means exhausts the subject. Nor does the analysis of this chapter decisively refute the belief that administered prices contribute to the misallocation of resources and encourage economic instability. The argument shows, nevertheless, that criticisms of administered prices rest on shaky facts and on inadequate analysis.

ADDITIONAL READINGS: 10, 188, 204, 431, 438.

26

19

MONEY AND MARKETS

Professor Walker has kindly invited me to write an afterword so that (to paraphrase his suggestions) I might have an opportunity both to reflect on my earlier work and to express some thoughts about contemporary trends in monetary economics. To be candid (as one feels bound to be in the privacy of an afterword), I did not find the first suggestion appealing. I recall Joan Robinson once saying (in reference to her book on imperfect competition), "I'm so glad I wrote it, because that way I didn't have to read it." I thought her remark amusing at the time; now I know she meant it. The second suggestion was more tempting. I should have recalled my mother saying, "Don't go looking for arguments." I ignored her then; I now think it wasn't bad advice. But all this is by the way. What follows may not be quite what Walker demanded, nor quite what I set out to supply, but I trust that in most respects it is responsive to the invitation that called it forth.

I. DOUBTS ABOUT ORTHODOXY

My "doubts about orthodoxy," as Walker describes them, occurred long before I knew any economics. What others may see as an intellectual development, I know to be a personality trait. My first serious reading in economics was Keynes's *General Theory*, which I found fascinating not because I understood much of it (though I thought I understood all of it at the time), but rather because of Keynes's irreverent yet graceful style. So I wrote an undergraduate thesis in which I mimicked Keynes and slashed away at contemporary writers who struck me as defenders of orthodox theory. When shortly thereafter I studied under John Hicks at Oxford and learned what orthodox theory was actually about, I took a mental vow to moderate my tone in later writings. I also cast about for more promising targets to attack, but by then Keynesian economics had developed its own orthodoxy, so I did not have far to look. I don't deny that my writings display a certain intellectual coherence, nor that a logical progression links my later with my earlier work; how else should it be for one to whom economics is more a way of life than a way to make a living? But it would be disingenuous to deny that much of my work is some-

259

what iconoclastic. Considering the areas in which I have tended to concentrate—monetary theory and macroeconomics—some of this is surely justified. For the rest, I gladly admit to an ingrained distrust of "authority."

Professor Walker infers from my published writings that the early 1960s were a crucial period in my intellectual development. His inference is surely correct, but behind each of my papers from that period lies a personal story that perhaps is also worth telling. In professional publications as in marriages, things are not always as they seem on the surface.

The "Keynes and the Classics" essay (Chapter 1) is a revised version of a much longer paper on Keynesian microdynamics that made use of various mechanical price and quantity adjustment rules that I thought were plausible but for which I could provide little economic motivation. The paper yielded some results that were sharply at variance with conventional multimarket stability analysis, so I was delighted with it. But my delight was short-lived, for the paper was expeditiously rejected by the *Journal of Political Economy* as "intriguing but unpersuasive." Then as now I could see no special virtue in the excess-demand adjustment rules of established theory. I knew too much about economic organization to imagine that the prices of more than a handful of commodities were determined on a day-to-day basis by impersonal market forces, but I could not construct a coherent account of the logistics of trade that would support my use of nonconventional adjustment rules. So I put such questions on my mental back burner, and sent an appropriately expurgated version of the essay to the *Quarterly Journal of Economics*. The published paper barely hints at the perplexing problems that were the centerpiece of the original analysis. Even less does it reveal my frustration at being unable to resolve them.

The question of price and quantity adjustment rules is mentioned obliquely but then sidestepped once more in my note on classical monetary theory (Chapter 2). On the surface, this essay does little more than clarify the then- (and perhaps still-) prevalent confusion between "temporary" and "full" equilibrium supply and demand functions. It was designed also to clear up some other loose ends in Patinkin's work (thus it is closely related to my 1960 paper with Burstein, reproduced here as Chapter 11). I like the paper as a whole, partly because it is craftily (*sic!*) executed, but mainly because it reveals so clearly the intellectual emptiness of quantity theory accounts of short-run adjustment processes. The paper may strike some as a regression toward orthodoxy, but the careful reader will rightly view the interpretative passages in the middle of the paper as mildly sarcastic reminders of the utter silence of established theory on price and quantity adjustment issues about which it ought to make at least some noises.

Judging from the literature it has spawned, my most influential single work is "The Keynesian Counter-Revolution" (Chapter 3). There is a certain irony in this, because it was probably the easiest of all my papers to write. But justice will be served. Many of my "followers" have since gone off in directions different from mine, so I'm more a bugler for the rear echelons than the leader of an army (I shall say more of this later).

The "Counter-Revolution" paper has a curious history, some of which is worth recounting. It owes its existence to a letter I received in January 1962 inviting me (very belatedly) to present a paper on "The Role of Money in General Equilibrium Theory" at an International Economic Association conference to be held in France during April of the same year. The invitation reached me in Liberia, where I was then laboring with some other economists to alter prevailing conceptions of that country as "the white man's grave"; so, to put it mildly, I was ecstatic—even though the deadline for finished drafts was just three weeks away. I put aside all other work and settled down to write, but nothing wrote; my hand was willing, but my head refused to work. The reason was simple: I could think of nothing to say about money and general equilibrium that had not already been said, most of it by Patinkin (and Patinkin was to be my discussant!). After a week of agonizing, I considered withdrawing from the conference—for all of ten seconds. Instead, recalling an exchange between Hicks and Patinkin in the *Economic Journal* some five years earlier to which I thought I had something to add, I switched my topic to "Keynes and General Equilibrium Theory." An hour later I had an introduction. A day later I had another title: the one the paper now bears. Ten days later, slightly dazed, I put a finished draft in the mail; the paper seemed almost to have written itself.

Two days before the conference convened, I met Frank Hahn in London and we exchanged papers. With uncharacteristic modesty (perhaps he was merely being jocular) he told me that his contribution—on some problems of proving the existence of equilibrium in a money economy—was "a trivial thing, of no importance." I expressed sympathy, and told him that my contribution, by contrast, was "a major breakthrough." When we met the next morning, I told him I had read his paper and that it was indeed of no importance, to which he replied: "That's all right, neither is yours." Of course his paper was brilliant—and mine grew on him with the passage of time.

I shall postpone comment on the argument of the "Counter-Revolution" paper and reactions to it, except for one extended remark. The paper does not take issue with the price adjustment rules of established theory, nor with the presumption that all prices (including wage rates) are freely flexible. So in no obvious respect does it anticipate later work with fix-price models. The novelty of the paper lies in its demonstration that the "notional" excess demands of established theory may not be operative in disequilibrium. It is another question whether effective demands of the kind defined in the paper can usefully be regarded as operative in the same circumstances. I claimed nothing of the kind in the paper, nor do I support such a claim now. On the contrary, my view is that the entire issue is moot, because the adjustment rules of established theory cannot plausibly be regarded as useful ingredients for a fruitful theory of disequilibrium economics.

"Monetary History and Positive Economics" (Chapter 4) was more fun to read than to write. When I was invited to review Milton Friedman and Anna Schwartz's *A Monetary History of the United States, 1867–1960* for the *Journal of Economic History,* I accepted with alacrity, partly because I was flattered, but mainly because it gave me a much-desired opportunity to take some shots at the non-Keynesian "opposition." (I wasn't quite sure to what other camp I belonged, but I was sure it wasn't Friedman's!) I then knew Friedman only slightly, and Anna Schwartz not at all, and though I had a grudging admiration for Friedman's book on the consumption function, the rest of his writings left me angry or unmoved. All in all, therefore, I was disposed to give Friedman and his coauthor a hard time before I had even seen a copy of their book. Nor did my attitude change after my first or second pass through the volume; on the contrary, I had by then compiled a list of "targets for attack" that was nearly fifty pages long. But knowing Friedman's reputation as a debater, I decided to go once more through the entire book, this time very carefully, to search for passages that might cause my otherwise deadly shots to ricochet back at me. When I was done, I had nearly fifty pages of crossed-out "targets" and a completely ungrudging admiration for the book and both its authors.

The published review was a surprise to my friends. In all candor, it was even more of a surprise to me. In part, of course, my about-face was simply a quiet tribute to the scholarship of Friedman and Schwartz. More important, it marked my personal emancipation from more than fifteen years of intellectually debilitating ideological bias against the Chicago school. Chicago is one of the few centers of economic study where the existence of organized arrangements for coordinating economic activities—"markets" in common parlance—has always been regarded as a problem to be investigated rather than, as at most other schools, an independent presupposition of economic analysis. Thus it is in keeping with the Chicago tradition to inquire into the self-organizing capabilities of a private enterprise economy, which seems to me precisely the direction that one must take if one hopes successfully to question the price-adjustment rules of neo-Walrasian theory. Before my encounter with Friedman and Schwartz, my mind was resistant to this line of research; after the encounter, it was at least open to persuasion.

I don't think my "emancipation" had any immediate effect upon my thinking, though the strong methodological motif of the review might suggest otherwise. My views on method were not then, nor are they now, at all doctrinaire. In describing myself as a neo-Walrasian (see the Editor's Introduction), I meant mainly to contrast my outlook with that of the inductivist, black-box, curve-fitting school of theorists to which Friedman was popularly supposed to belong. Probably I should also have dissociated myself from the empty-box brand of neo-Walrasianism that had already drawn my fire in the "Counter-Revolution," but the English version of that essay was still in process, and I saw no point in raising an issue that was not germane to my immediate task. So I chose instead to distance myself indirectly by paying the methodology of positive economics rather more than its due.

II. TOWARD GENERAL PROCESS ANALYSIS

The papers in Parts II and III document my transition from conventional theory to general process analysis: from thinking of markets as vaguely synonymous with "impersonal forces of demand and supply" to thinking of them concretely as specialized trading institutions, organized and operated by economic agents for the purpose of coordinating, for a profit, the economic activities of other agents. The content and thrust of the various papers is masterfully characterized by Walker in his Introduction. I shall continue to confine my reflections, therefore, to matters that lie behind or beyond the published papers.

Economics is less obviously a young man's game than mathematics, but I doubt that many economists have had a really new idea after the age of thirty-five. I must confess that, one way or another, everything I've done in the second half of my life reminds me (at least retrospectively) of something I did or thought about earlier. This is especially true of my papers on money, which are full of rearranged ideas, some drawn from earlier published work on unrelated subjects, others from ruminations that earlier came to nothing. Some of what is original in them is a matter more of emphasis and perspective than of fundamental insight. Indeed, what struck me most when rereading these papers was not their content (though I confess I enjoyed some of it) but their style, which reflects a strategy of argument that underlies all of my work.

I have always thought that the essential art of economics, as of any other science (or of literary fiction, for that matter) is to tell a good story in a persuasive way. No doubt this leaves a good many things (some might think too many) to individual taste; for what is deemed "good" depends on one's perception of what is important, interesting, and likely to interest or amuse others, and what is deemed persuasive depends as much on prevailing fashions in argument as on established canons of logic. Still, most of us would agree that to be "good" a story must deal with recognizable subject matter. That is why so much of economics is essentially topical, and also why so-called seminal contributions typically contain as much motivating material as formal analysis. Even more strongly, most of us would agree that to be persuasive a story must be conceptually coherent; in other words, the actors in the story and the actions they are assumed to perform must make sense, both taken in isolation and when considered as a whole. That is why we frown on ad hoc argument, and also why, despite sometimes serious flaws in logic, the works of great economists never seem to lose their savor.

To me, as perhaps to most economists, conceptual coherence is ultimately a matter of intuition: Given some initial thought experiment that serves to motivate a model, the question is not just whether the model describes salient aspects of the experiment in a logically satisfactory way, but also whether the model does so without implying other consequences that seem intuitively at odds with the same underlying thought experiment. To put the matter another way: *The model is not the message; the message is always more than the model.*

The central role that the principle of conceptual coherence plays in my work is perhaps brought out most clearly by the story that goes with my "Reconsideration of the Microfoundations of Monetary Theory" (Chapter 5). This paper has had a surprisingly favorable reception, considering its limited scope and accomplishments. I have the impression, however, that most readers have seen it as the beginning of a series of papers on money rather than a continuation of my earlier work on Keynesian economics. In fact, I can't think offhand of any writer who has linked the formal model in the "Reconsideration" with the dual-decision model of the "Counter-Revolution"; yet, in truth, the two models are simply alternative formalizations of a single thought experiment. Indeed, the dichotomized budget constraint model of the "Reconsideration" not only portrays the thought experiment of the "Counter-Revolution" more accurately in a logical sense than does the dual-decision setup, it also expresses a point of view that is more appealing to common sense. Let me explain.

The thought experiment that underlies the dual-decision model is set out at the beginning of Section VI of the "Counter-Revolution" paper (Chapter 3). There I contemplate an individual who, for some reason, finds that his realized money income will not support his desired money expenditures. I then argue that such an individual must sooner or later consider ways to economize, since he cannot convert mere offers to work into effective (money) purchasing power. I might have left it at that, or I might have argued that a person who is unable to sell as much as desired today would, if rational, treat that fact as relevant information in forming a reasonable expectation of his earnings tomorrow, an expectation that, in turn, would affect his expenditure plans for tomorrow. This last thought experiment, correctly modeled, would have introduced realized money income into individual excess-demand functions as a loose proxy for expected future earnings, thereby resolving my immediate problem (which was to cast doubt on the universal relevance of conventionally defined demand functions). But I was after something more, something that at one stroke not only would put realized earnings into the demand functions, but also would establish a clean separation in the choice constraints between current plans to buy and current plans to sell. How to do this was not obvious, at least not to me. Though suggested by my reading of Keynes, the formal model finally adopted was literally an act of desperation, and it could be improved, both descriptively and analytically. Its main deficiency is that to some degree it conveys a false impression of what I meant to say (and, if I remember correctly, of what I thought I was saying). But that was perhaps just as well; a model that more accurately portrayed my underlying thought experiment might well have been less effective for making my central point.

I can't recall being aware of a hiatus in the "Counter-Revolution" argument until some years later when, during a year of research leave, I tried to introduce the dual-decision hypothesis into an otherwise conventional model of price dynamics. It quickly became apparent that, taken literally, the constraints of the dual-decision model were "too tight"; they made sense only if one viewed expenditures and earnings as averages over an interval of time rather than as instantaneous rates of flow. Furthermore, the model implied the direct dependence of effective demands not just on prices but also on quantities exchanged of each and every commodity. To say anything about the dynamics of effective demand, one would thus have to add to the usual price-adjustment equations an extra and highly complex array of rationing rules that would specify just which agents transacted precisely what quantities of each commodity in every conceivable state of the economic system. It seemed a bit excessive to impose this new burden on an already overworked "invisible hand." In any case, unlike the technically more gifted economists who later trod much the same path, I was unable to formalize any but trivial rationing schemes. So, defeated by this line of inquiry, I gave up and went back to rethink the problem.

In the mid-1960s, the monetarist movement was just gathering steam, so "money" was a central topic of conversation and controversy. I was involved in these discussions, along with everyone else, but I soon became impatient with what I heard and read—and said—because neither I nor anyone else seemed to have any idea how one might distinguish analytically between money and other commodities, much less how one might construct a formal model in which just one commodity (or a few) could be shown to play a role similar to that assigned to money in every text on money and banking. Somehow these concerns entered into my rethinking of the dual-decision hypothesis (or perhaps it was the other way around!). In any event, the result was the dichotomized budget constraint model of the "Reconsideration." Realized income did not appear explicitly in the new demand functions, but it did appear with a lag via the money stock variable, which implied that a sustained excess of expenditure over income would produce an eventual reduction in planned expenditures. So the new model not only accurately conveyed the message contained in my original thought experiment, it also linked disequilibrium analysis with monetary theory in a conceptually coherent and intellectually satisfying way.

As for the dual-decision hypothesis, I gave it up, for the reasons indicated, long before the "Reconsideration" appeared (and also before the "Counter-Revolution" was published). Imagine my astonishment when a virtually distinct branch of economic theory began to develop from the dual-decision hypothesis and from the surprisingly similar (but, to my mind, even less coherent) Patinkin model of constrained supply. I refer, of course, to the fix-price models of Barro and Grossman, Dreze, Negishi, Grandmont, Benassy, Malinvaud, Varian, and other writers. Although I am an acknowledged "grandfather" of all these "babies," I disowned them at the 1980 Aix-en-Provence World Conference of the Econometric Society as "monsters" begotten by a father (the dual-decision process) whose paternity I admitted but whose character I deplored. I then gave my blessing to other babies— a motley lot, except for their distinctively Marshallian grins—describing them as well-formed offspring of a fraternal twin of the father whose babies I had just disowned. The audience was puzzled by my remarks, and I can't say I blame them. What was obvious to me was not only not obvious but not even true for most of my listeners. The fix-price literature had by then developed its own impetus and analytical uses, quite apart from the source (or sources) that originally inspired it. So, while I do not myself regard this line of inquiry as particularly promising, neither would I now defend my earlier condemnation of it.

As mentioned earlier, the "Reconsideration" was originally conceived as an extension of the "Counter-Revolution" paper. In the writing, however, other matters intruded—so much so, indeed, that the original conception dropped out of sight. What was left was a model of household choice in a money economy that raised more questions than it answered. Specifically, the model implied that the choice alternatives confronting households were more restrictive in a money than in a barter economy, which meant that monetary exchange is less efficient than barter exchange, contrary to both common sense and two hundred years of conventional wisdom. Something obviously was wrong, but what? Not the model: If trading activity were costless, as was tacitly assumed in the model, then no agent would voluntarily accede to any restriction on direct pairwise trades; hence, monetary exchange as defined by the model would simply not occur. Thus I was driven by the logic of the model (more accurately, by the principle of conceptual coherence) to inquire into an area that I had hitherto ignored: the logistics and costs of individual trading in a world without organized markets.

The results of my inquiries are reported sequentially—in ever greater detail and with increasing precision—in the papers reprinted here as Chapters 6–10 and 13. Since they represent stages in the development of a new outlook on the analysis of the economy, and since they were each written in response to outside demands rather than as independent research papers, it is hardly surprising that the ideas put forward in them appear somewhat unfinished. Eventually, however, those ideas coalesced into a well-focused research program: general process analysis, the main outlines of which are set forth in "Reflections on the Keynesian Perplex" (Chapter 14) and further elaborated in other papers in Part IV of this volume.

III. CONTEMPORARY PERSPECTIVES

One does not have to be a compulsive reader of the professional journals to recognize that monetary theory has been a relatively inactive field since the middle to late 1970s. Activity in the more topical field of monetary economics has meanwhile quickened and intensified, reflecting prevailing pressures to "say something relevant" about current problems of unemployment and inflation. This is an unfortunate state of affairs. Monetary theory turned quiescent just as its accomplishments had set the stage for constructive rethinking of conventional theories of market behavior, so no such rethinking has occurred. On the contrary, monetary economics has continued to develop in its customary fashion as a seat-of-the-pants discipline that stumbles blindly from one real-world problem to the next without drawing from or adding to the accumulated stock of fundamental economic knowledge.

Why have modern developments in monetary theory been so generally overlooked or ignored in the recent literature on monetary economics and macroeconomics? The explanation lies, I suspect, in the fact that these developments occurred in the context of a long-standing intellectual problem the significance of which was generally regarded as problematical at best. Specifically, the problem was to account for the use of intrinsically worthless objects as common media of exchange. The solution preferred by modern research (see Chapter 17) runs in terms of transactions costs and the physical characteristics of commodities, complications that are ignored in conventional theory. The validity of this solution appears to have been generally acknowledged by specialists in monetary theory; what previously had been the central problem of traditional monetary theory thus became a non-issue for all practical purposes. For most economists, however, including the authors of leading modern texts in money and banking, this solution meant little or nothing. The problem it resolved was a source of concern only to fastidious theorists who felt uneasy about putting money into models where it didn't seem to fit. A more important question, first posed clearly by Keynes in the *General Theory*, was whether conventional wisdom about the self-adjusting capabilities of the economic system could survive the construction of an intellectually satisfying theory of monetary exchange. When monetary theory returned an apparently affirmative answer to this question, at least in a limited class of models for which an immediate answer was possible, most economists simply left matters there. No longer uncomfortable about putting money into their models, they returned to "business as usual" and devoted themselves to more pressing problems: unemployment, inflation, supply shocks, stagflation, *et hoc genus omne.*

Now, the real significance of modern work in monetary theory extends well beyond any single specialty. The hallmark of conventional models of value and monetary theory is that rules of price and quantity adjustment that govern market interactions are routinely devised and just as routinely imposed without explicit (if, indeed, any) reference to their consistency with the more fundamental notions of self-interest that are assumed to determine the production and consumption decisions of individuals. By contrast, modern research in monetary theory indicates that, to account for the very existence of monetary exchange, we must presume that the organization of trading arrangements—and hence, the specification of price and quantity adjustment rules governing market interactions—is undertaken by agents within the economic system, and so is responsive to the same forces of greed and competition as operate in other spheres of economic activity.

The implications of this inconvenient finding can, of course, be overlooked or ignored without fear of logical contradiction, but conceptual coherence and hopes for an empirically fruitful reconstruction of established theory are at stake. To ignore those implications consciously is, I suggest, to acknowledge that one cares less about the subject matter of economics than about intellectual games. So, to be charitable, I presume that the "business as usual" school is presently operating in a state of unfortunate ignorance rather than studied neglect.

However that may be, the consequences are serious. The economics profession is currently divided as never before on theoretical fundamentals as well as on policy issues. There is no way that these divergences of opinion can be brought to a head, much less resolved, unless attention is somehow focused on the general problem of the self-organizing and self-adjusting capabilities of a decentralized production and exchange economy. These issues cannot be addressed within the framework of conventional equilibrium theory or variants of it because that theory either presumes that the economy requires no organization (the coordination of economic activities is costless) or that its organization is established by an external agent (the neo-

Walrasian auctioneer) whose costs, if any, do not count. Given either of these hypotheses, conventional theory allows us to address the self-adjustment question, but to what purpose is then unclear. The performance characteristics of "toy" models that command neither widespread professional nor popular respect are, I suggest, neither here nor there; to work with such models at all is simply to evade the central problem.

Consider, for example, the kinds of models used by those who are generally considered (and consider themselves) to be Keynesians—James Tobin being perhaps the most notable member of this group. The standard construction here is one or another kind of IS–LM construction. Some are very simple, some are very elaborate, but all are at bottom variants of the temporary general equilibrium model set out in Hicks's *Value and Capital*. In the nature of the case, these constructions have no immediate empirical implications. They can be made to produce such implications only if they are padded out with various ad hoc restrictions suggested by casual empirical observation or econometric research: Phillips curves, Okun's law, adaptive expectations, mark-up pricing, implicit labor contracts, and so on. Inevitably, few of these devices survive the march of time. Invented to explain one set of facts, they are sooner or later contradicted by some new turn of events. But the basic models survive, because they are impervious to empirical or theoretical criticism. They are not so much wrong as fraudulent, because they promise what they cannot deliver, namely, rational understanding of major forces governing movements in aggregate income, employment, and prices.

The case of the monetarist branch of the "business as usual" school is no better. Like the Keynesians, the monetarists base themselves squarely on general equilibrium analysis, but upon a much vaguer version than anything to be found in the modern literature. Like the Keynesians, who assume without serious argument that the economic system generally doesn't work, the monetarists presume for equally poor reasons that the economic system always works almost perfectly. The monetarists have but one solid string in their bow. They argue, correctly, that in a money economy with determinate prices there must be some monetary magnitude that, if appropriately fixed, will ultimately put a slow anchor on upward movements in the general price level. But the monetarists then compromise the usefulness of this string by encrusting it with a large collection of contentious empirical hypotheses that are dredged up from the historical record. Their policy shots are correspondingly inaccurate and unreliable. Moreover, though the monetarists originally gained notoriety as opponents of the Keynesians, the passage of time has brought the two camps ever closer together. They are united by a common belief in ad hoc methods and a common unwillingness to reexamine the analytical preconceptions from which their arguments proceed. From the monetarists as from the Keynesians, therefore, we can expect to see much more of what we have already seen, and nothing that significantly advances our understanding of the world in which we live.

The currently most prominent branch of the "business as usual" school is the new classical economics of Lucas, Sargent, Wallace, and Barro. In some respects, the new classical economics is more accurately regarded as a throwback to pre-Keynesian modes of analysis than as a modernist extension of monetarism; its uncompromising reliance on conventional market-clearance presumptions and on the rational expectations hypothesis (the stochastic equivalent of perfect foresight) is almost quaintly anachronistic. Its analytical procedures, however, are anything but antiquated; indeed, observing the new classical economists in action, encumbered as they are by self-imposed methodological constraints, one is reminded of nothing so much as a world-class hurdler performing his specialty with both legs tied together. It is an awesome sight, but very unreal.

To be fair to the new classical economists one must recognize the narrow focus of their research. It is directed almost exclusively at devising a parsimonious theoretical explanation of business fluctuations. The explanations start with conventional market-clearing assumptions, which can be justified as logical implications of individual maximizing behavior in a world where transactions are costless. The Muthian hypothesis of rational expectations has obvious merit in this same context; indeed, for this case it might be regarded as a straightforward implication of what I have earlier called the principle of conceptual coherence. As numerous critics of rational expectations models have shown, one can imagine worlds in which rational expectations are anything but reasonable. In those cases, the rational expectations hypothesis looks more like a technical gimmick than a model-building principle. That is nevertheless not an effective criticism of the hypothesis as it is actually used by the new classical economists. A more pertinent criticism, it seems to me, is that to account for observed business fluctuations the new classical economists must somehow introduce autoregressive exogenous shocks into their equilibrium models. This is accomplished by supposing that the monetary authorities are irresponsible, and that monetary disturbances are propagated asymmetrically, and with occasional lags, through the rest of the economic system. Of course, this explanation is simply a *deus ex machina*. One cannot introduce these kinds of complications into an otherwise pristine new classical economic model without doing violence to the principle of conceptual coherence. The major objection to the new classical economics is much more straightforward; namely, that it equates theoretical progress with improved econometric performance of theoretical models rather than with enhanced understanding of the way in which decentralized economic systems work.

This brings me back to my starting point. I have argued that the approaches of the Keynesians, monetarists, and new classical economists to monetary theory and macroeconomics will get us exactly nowhere because each is founded, one way or another, on the conventional but empirically fallacious assumption that the coordination of economic activities is costless. Now, I do not deny that rational analysis of unreal worlds can yield results that are of immense practical importance; the examples of Newtonian physics and classical hydrodynamics are obvious cases in point. Nevertheless, for some purposes, such as the fruitful study of particle physics and supersonic flight, models based on radically different assumptions are essential. Similarly, while no one would wish to dispute either the intellectual or the practical merit of established value theory, neither can one doubt that for some purposes, such as the fruitful analysis of ongoing processes of monetary exchange, models of a very different kind may be required. My contention is that they are.

27

COMMENT

'On the Behavioral and Rational Foundations of Economic Dynamics' by Herbert A. Simon

Robert W. CLOWER

Professor Simon has given us a very nice paper: interesting, thoughtful, and thought-provoking. Though, chronologically speaking, I am myself a post-Keynesian, I share Simon's sense of deja vu in relation to certain modern development in economic theory. But I don't think this reflects a 'ferris wheel' type of cycle in economic theory; it seems to me that the cycle is more in the nature of a 'circular staircase'. True, we return again and again to the same scenes, but our perspective changes, generally for the better, the higher we mount. That is surely true in the case of Behaviorism, which also comes in cycles and so is likely to provoke occasional attacks of deja vu in anyone who knows something of the history of our discipline. But Simon's version of Behaviorism is much richer in content and deeper in motivation than anything that comes before, so its attraction is not diminished (at least for me) by the fact that something like it has been around for a long time.

I have little but good things to say about Simon's paper as a whole. I share his view — and also in large measure accept his reasons for holding it — that the time has come for empirical work in economics to take the direction of micro-level investigation of actual decision-making processes, along the lines suggested by Behaviorism. But I think one can reach the same conclusion by other routes, including some that involve less shedding of conventional ideas than Simon would seem to favor. As Simon remarks in a related context (pp. 25–26 of his paper), support for his central thesis has come from surprising sources, such as Robert Lucas. I would mention another, namely Frank Hahn, who in his 1968 Presidential Address to the Econometric Society (*Econometrica*, January 1970, p. 1) remarked 'To discuss and analyze how the economy works it may be necessary to go and look'. With support from 'friends' such as Lucas and Hahn, Simon can perhaps use a few enemies.

That is the lead-in for my few critical comments. I will return later to the role of friend though, as already suggested, the distinction between friend and foe may not amount to a difference in the present context.

Simon starts by describing classical and neo-classical theory as based on two tautologies, namely, Say's Law and the Quantity Theory of Money, and a postulate of rationality. I have no quarrel with the third of these items, especially when 'rationality' is interpreted as broadly as Simon later describes it (pp. 37 ff.). But Simon's version of Say's Law is Keynesian rather than classical or neo-classical. So stated it is not tautologous but false; correctly stated, it becomes the (definitional) tautology usually described as the 'national income accounting identity'. The classical version of Say's Law (here I rely mainly on the writings of Say and John Stuart Mill) merely denies the possibility of a 'general glut', and that on two behavioral (not definitional) grounds: (i) the non-satiability of individual wants, and (ii) individual selfishness [i.e., goods are supplied to others only on the assumption that a quid pro quo will be forthcoming in return; cf. Leijonhufvud (1982, ch. 5)].

As from the Quantity Theory of Money, it is neither a premise of classical theory nor a theorem. It *is* a theory of some modern (Patinkinesque) versions of general equilibrium analysis, but not a definitional tautology even there. The version described by Simon is, indeed, a definitional tautology, but that version plays no significant role in either classical or neo-classical theory.

I don't want to make more of these two 'lapses of attention' than they deserve. I mention them only because their inclusion in an early section of Simon's paper caused me serious puzzlement and temporarily distracted my attention from his central — and clearly valid — opening theme (p. 22) namely, that the rationality postulates of classical and neo-classical theory do not per se provide any basis for reasoned economic analysis of disequilibrium adjustment processes. I would go further. The rationality and other postulates of conventional theory — here I commit a solecism by using the term 'conventional' to include the work of Debreu and Arrow in the 1950s and early 1960s — do not provide a basis for recognition, much less reasoned analysis, of what in common parlance are referred to as markets, money, firms, or inventories.

The empirical vacuousness of conventional theory — though admirably catalogued by Simon in his later discussions of long-term dynamics, the business cycle, inventory cycles, price expectations, and unemployment — is, I suggest, far more complete than Simon's discussion would lead one to believe. Most of the action is provided not by the logical muscle of the theory — which is truly minuscule — but rather by its verbal (at what Simon refers to as its 'auxiliary assumptions', cf. pp. 33 and 37).

But can the research program of modern Behaviorism supply what is needed to fill this void? I frankly doubt it. Even with the best will in the world, and even given the full cooperation of the actual 'agents' whose behavior is to be scrutinized and catalogued, it seems to me that Behaviorism unsupported by a formal theory similar in structure, albeit richer in content than the one we now possess, is unlikely to produce anything more than a pile of uncoordinated facts. I agree with Simon that we need more facts; but which ones, and to what purpose? Obviously Simon has some considered views on just this matter (cf. his discussion of inventory cycles, bounded rationality, and unemployment), but these views are tossed out to us in bits and pieces, not served up in an orderly arrangement as would be the case if they were connected with an underlying theoretical menu.

At this point I begin to feel a bit like Mark Antony must have felt at Caesar's funeral: I seem to have come here not to praise Simon but to bury him! Altogether, I fear that I have too much emphasized a few negative aspects of a paper about which my feelings are almost entirely positive. I would particularly mention Simon's demolition of the rational expectations approach as a method of model construction; Simon obviously regards rational expectations as a theoretical gimmick rather than a general principle, and so do I. In effect, my criticism of Simon is simply that he seems to me to misconceive the essential nature of our problems with conventional theory. Our problem is not that we have taken conventional theory too seriously, but rather that we have not taken it seriously enough. We have paid too much attention to what it clearly does not say. Some of the most forceful criticisms of conventional theory have been advanced by those who are presumed to be its most ardent adherents — such writers as Arrow, Hahn, Debreu, etc. These and other writers have effectively recognized that the weakness of conventional theory lies mainly in its lack of essential empirical content (it does not deal with 'frictions' and other 'complications' that are clearly relevant to all real world economies). Thus, contrary to Simon, who suggests that conventional theory be abandoned, more sympathetic critics would argue that what is required is not a change in approach but merely an improvement in execution. I count myself with the sympathetic critics.

[28]

An editor's apology[1]

When I retired from UCLA in 1986 to accept a newly established research and teaching chair in Economic Theory at The University of South Carolina, I had recently concluded 12 consecutive years as managing editor of a professional journal, seven years with *Economic Inquiry* (1973–80), followed by five years with *The American Economic Review* (1981–85). It was an instructive – and sobering – dozen years, in ways too numerous to mention or even count, some of them surprising. Here I will talk about just a few things that are germane to the present volume.

My seven years with *Economic Inquiry* (originally *The Western Economic Journal*, ably managed and edited from its inception until 1973 by Alice Vandermeulen) I recall as wholly pleasurable. I handled only about 300 manuscripts a year, published about 50, and dealt mostly with authors who were, as Ben Franklin once described older women with young lovers, 'so grateful'. I also arranged to publish or republish several minor or buried classics: Leijonhufvud's *Life Among the Econ* (1973), Jack Hirshleifer's *Exchange Theory: The Missing Chapter* (1973), Peter Howitt's *Walras and Monetary Theory* (1973), Haavelmo's (Norwegian) paper on 'What Can Static Equilibrium Models Tell Us?' (1980), and John Hicks (first written in English and published in German – now re-translated back into English by Barry Schecter) *Equilibrium and the Trade Cycle* (1980).

In sharp contrast with my seven years with *Economic Inquiry*, I recall the lustrum with the *American Economic Review* as consistently unsatisfying and, in the final two years, consistently depressing. I handled nearly a thousand manuscripts each year, published about a hundred, and dealt mostly with authors who had what Harry Johnson (my subjective model of the ideal journal editor) called 'delusions of adequacy' – meaning technically competent professional hacks with a driving itch for professional advancement but no emotional commitment to creative work in economics or any other empirical science. I was forced to acknowledge that I belonged in a different kind of work when a former friend whose paper I had summarily rejected later responded to my request for a referee report by writing: 'I do not wish to referee any papers for the *AER* while you are editor. However, should you learn the date in advance, I would be pleased to be present at your hanging.'

It is possible that my recollection of the two editorial episodes was different simply because I passed from my 40s into my mid-50s just as I joined the *AER*; in any event, I do now distinctly recall how uncharitably I felt toward 'old fogeys' of

---

[1]The title of this note was suggested by G.H. Hardy's 1940 *A Mathematician's Apology* (Cambridge University Press, reprinted with foreword by C.P. Snow, 1967, 1969 and 1973).

50 when I was in my callow 30s. But I believe there was more to my problem with the *AER* than mere advancing age or senility.

For one thing, the 1980s were economically vastly different from the 1970s. I joined the *AER* at the end of a decade of rapid inflation (the GNP Deflator doubled and the CPI more than doubled between 1972 and 1981) during which real academic incomes fell sharply – by an average of something like 40 per cent as I recall – and, having reasonably normal appetites for food and shelter, many economists were impelled to turn from intellectual pursuits to more lucrative consulting opportunities; it was not a time for prolonged cultivation of 'the instinct of idle curiosity'.

For another thing, the profession changed markedly between the 1970s and the 1980s; starting in the late 1960s and continuing through the 1970s, new PhDs tended increasingly to be skilled in mathematics and econometrics and (one was often tempted to surmise) wilfully imbecile about economic history, the history of economic thought, and of factual subject matter generally.

Finally, and I now suspect most importantly, in 1980 I had a different attitude than in 1973 towards prospects for significant progress in professional understanding of real-life economic systems (in that respect, if in no other, I was still an unreconstructed and unapologetic Keynesian). In the late 1960s and early 1970s, important advances towards formal conceptualization of monetary exchange technologies had been suggested by the work of Harry Johnson, John Hicks, Armen Alchian, Douglas North, Brunner and Meltzer, Jurg Niehans, Robert Jones, Peter Howitt, Joe Ostroy, Ross Starr, Arrow and Hahn, E. Veendorp, and Axel Leijonhufvud. I and numerous other economists (among others, Barro and Grossman, Stan Fischer, Allen Drazen, Franklyn Fisher, Ned Phelps, and Dan Friedman) believed that what it was then (pre-Lucas) still respectable to call *disequilibrium economics* promised shortly to bring forth major advances in monetary theory and macroeconomics. Ten years later, I maintained lingering hopes along the same lines, but these hopes soon expired in the spate of uninspired submissions that flooded my *AER* editorial office. In the early 1980s, younger members of the economics profession seemed suddenly to have become victims of a modern variant of the intellectual virus Schumpeter called 'The Ricardian Vice', known more popularly these days as 'the rational expectations revolution', whose effect has been to move economic thinking back not to Neoclassicism or even to Classicism, but to something more nearly resembling the metaphysical imbecilities of the late Middle Ages.

So why do I call this note 'An Apology'? Mainly, I suppose, because now that my *AER* depression has lifted and I am almost ten years older and correspondingly wiser, I feel intellectually more vigorous and creative than I can recall ever having felt before; so I am tempted – and don't intend to resist the urge – to assert a position on the present state and prospects of our discipline. I call my note an apology because what I have to say in these final remarks will (I sincerely hope) offend many readers.

There has been much talk recently about the increasingly scientific character of modern economics, by which is meant its increasing use of sophisticated statistics and mathematics. In his 1982 presidential address to The Econometric Society,

Gerard Debreu tried to inject a little common sense into the more outlandish claims of those who see economics as being in very nearly the same class of science as physical chemistry and molecular biology; but I don't imagine that his remarks did much to dampen the ardor of the more passionate devotees of the cult of 'Science **Is** Rigor' (**Is** Rigor, **Is** Rigor,...).

I believe that contemporary economic theory provides not a correlation of sense experience with coherent conceptual entities, but a thoroughly sham portrait of real economic life. Along with this portrait goes a research agenda that focuses on solutions to academic exercises rather than solutions to real problems. I strongly affirm my belief in 'science for its own sake' but I hasten to add that science in that sense can be, and in much recent work in economics, seems to me to have been, overdone. In modern mathematical economics, in particular, economists seem to have become conditioned to regard precise answers to purely academic puzzles as 'meaningful' and 'interesting' regardless of their mindlessness for any conceivable practical purpose.

If our discipline consisted in principle as well as practice only in the writing and teaching of fantasy fiction, all of this would hardly merit comment, but on common belief and according to some leading practitioners – although clearly not to admirers of so-called 'eclectic economics' (cf Mankiw, 1992, *Macroeconomics*, p. 11), who seem committed only to systematic absence of belief in anything definite – economics is supposed to be an *empirical* science. If that is granted, then economic theory, one might presume, should be directed to resolving subject matter problems rather than purely intellectual puzzles.

To proceed as we seem for well over half a century to have been proceeding is, in effect, to confuse means with ends: our discipline has become directed not towards subject matter applications but towards problems posed by our choice of analytical technique. Thus, we find numerous recent journal articles that are concerned with extending or amending a 'seminal' article or book that first appeared almost as recently as the work that claims to derive from it, and we observe that much of the space in more technical professional journals is devoted primarily to cleaning up logical details of the Arrow-Debreu model, and (in journals that cater to game theory and other technique-driven 'research' work) to showing how we might extricate ourselves from puzzles created by our own terminology.

No discipline can forego rigor without becoming impotent, but neither can any *empirical science* thrive on rigor alone. By and large, the worth of an empirical science is measured better by the robustness of its applications than the elegance of its theorems. By this standard, as P.W.S. Andrews once suggested, economics is not a serious science; indeed (paraphrasing Veblen), economics might justly be said to bear much the same relation to serious science as astrology bears to astrophysics. If we cannot make economics into something more significant than a branch of formal mathematics that uses a peculiar terminology, then why should we expect anyone but another economist – least of all and most affirmatively **not** our students – to take us or our work seriously?

The Obscurantist Approach to Economics: Shackle on Keynes. A review of G. L. S. Shackle, *Keynesian Kaleidics*. Chicago: Aldine Publishing Co., 1974. Pp. vi + 92.

Neo-Walrasian equilibrium theory has come in for some hard knocks in recent years. Touted initially as a general technique for studying interrelations among markets—a technique that would simultaneously clarify classical value theory and definitively establish what was "right" and what was "wrong" with Keynes—it now stands exposed as just another of those "pretty, polite techniques" on which Keynes poured so much scorn in his 1937 *Quarterly Journal of Economics* "review" of the *General Theory*. Aficionados of general competitive analysis might justly respond by raising an eyebrow and remarking, "What competent student of technique could ever have thought otherwise?" The fact remains that many supposedly competent contributors to the Neo-Walrasian literature (the present reviewer included) *did* for many years believe that the relation between Neo-Walrasian theory and economics was somewhat closer than that between bullfighting and agriculture. Whether or not they were competent, their belief appears not to have been well-founded!

To assert that Neo-Walrasian analysis is not the Holy Grail of economic theory is not the same thing, of course, as to deny *either* that the theory has significantly advanced practical as well as logical understanding of economic phenomena *or* that market economies of actual record are amenable to formal representation

in terms of models that portray such economies as "naturally self-adjusting." The only relevant moral to be drawn from recently revealed shortcomings of established microeconomic theory is expressed in the old adage: If at first (or second, or third . . .) you don't succeed, try, try again. The acknowledged failures and frustrations of post-Keynesian economics testify not to the weakness of established theory but to its strength; unambiguous ignorance is more favorable to scientific progress than unsuspected confusion.

Shackle's *Keynesian Kaleidics* conveys a very different message. According to Shackle, the central and most valuable of Keynes' contributions to economics is not a *message* (or set of messages) but rather a *point of view*, namely (Shackle, page 42):

. . . the view that the expectations, which together with the drive of needs or ambitions make up the 'springs of action', are at all times so insubstantially founded upon data and so mutably suggested by the stream of 'news', that is, of counter-expected or totally unthought-of events, that they can undergo complete transformation in an hour or even a moment, as the patterns in the kaleidoscope dissolve at a touch; the view that men are conscious of their essential and irremediable state of un-knowledge and that they usually suppress this awareness in the interest of avoiding a paralysis of action; but that from time to time they succumb to its abiding mockery and menace, and withdraw from the field.

Shackle sees this point of view as the essential basis not only for Keynes' conviction that existing economic systems are not naturally self-adjusting, but also for much of Keynes' formal analysis. Accordingly, he criticizes Keynes for failing to hew to a single method of analysis in his laborious grappling with disequilibrium adjustment processes in the *Treatise* and *General Theory*. His central contention is that Keynes should have retained the implicitly dynamic method that underlies the pure theory of the *Treatise* in order to drive home in later work the fundamentally *expectational* character of all states of economic "equilibrium." The vacuousness of later attempts to squeeze Keynes' ideas into the "perfect knowledge, perfect foresight" framework of Neo-Walrasian theory would then have been clear from the outset and we should have been spared forty years of fruitless wandering in the intellectual wilderness of Arrow-Debreuland.

Personally, I have no sympathy with this point of view. Not only do I look with greater favor than Shackle on the accomplishments of Neo-Walrasian theory; I also question his interpretation of the genesis and development of Keynes' ideas and his tacit acceptance—claiming Keynes as a fellow spirit—of the view that economics is inherently so imprecise a subject (Shackle, pp. 73-74) as to preclude even the possibility that any but relatively uninteresting economic events should ever be accurately simulated by formal models that satisfy standards of rigor and precision comparable to those that prevail in the "hard sciences" and in contemporary general competitive analysis.

A review obviously is not the place to elaborate upon these themes, but a few remarks on each of them is very much in order.

First, as concerns the accomplishments of Neo-Walrasian theory, I would observe that the set of possible interpretations of a formal model generally is vastly larger than—and in considerable measure independent of—the conceptual experiments in terms of which standard expositions of the theory are couched. Shackle's unreservedly negative assessment of general competitive analysis seems to me to re-

flect nothing more than a mistaken conception of the relation between theory and practice. *All* theories are false—but some are false in more interesting ways than others. At the very least, Neo-Walrasian theory serves as a solid intellectual benchmark whose "falsehoods"—like those of Newtonian mechanics in post-Einsteinian physics—must be roughly reproducible as possible special cases of *any* proffered alternative.

Second, concerning Shackle's interpretation of Keynes, I would grant it no more—and no less—validity than any one of countless other interpretations that might be adduced from "reading between the lines" of Keynes' various published works, while ignoring much if not most of what Keynes *actually* wrote. Shackle's attempt (Chapter 2) to rescue Keynes' "fundamental equations" from the oblivion to which most other scholars would consign them seems to me to say more for his piety than for his scholarship. Isn't it just possible that, on this particular subject, Keynes managed quite literally to make an ass of himself? And if that could have happened once, could it not have happened twice, thrice, ...? Surely it is enough that Keynes' ideas, whether right, wrong, muddled or just plain silly, provoked an incredibly fruitful revival of interest in scientific economics at a time when the subject showed unmistakable signs of intellectual malaise. What more needs to be said? Do we add to Keynes' stature by casting him in the role of inspired prophet and infallible law-giver, thereby denying him credit for the many interesting mistakes that he made as a scientist?

Finally, what is one to make of Shackle's implicit acceptance (pages 82-83) of poetry and metaphysics as part of the warp and woof of economic analysis? No doubt these things have something to do with scientific creativity in general, but as Shackle convincingly demonstrates by his own example (see especially his utterly vacuous description of "money", pp. 2-3), when intuitive imagery and a fascination for words are permitted to intrude too easily into logical discourse, the result is pure confusion.

As the tone of the preceding remarks no doubt has indicated, I have found much in Shackle's book to provoke me. Its central aim, it seems to me, is to make a case for obscurantism—to deny that economic science can or ought to be more than a species of glorified poetry. Of course, he may be right; as Science with a capital S, economics has not so far covered itself with glory. But I have hopes for better things, and so, I think, had Keynes. Still, this is a book that deserves to be read—though not so much for what it actually says about the economics of Keynes as for what it suggests about the possible methodological presuppositions of some who profess themselves to be Keynesians.

Robert W. Clower
University of California, Los Angeles

[30]

Journal of Economic Literature
Vol. XXII (September 1984), pp. 1115–1164

Book Reviews

000 General Economics; Theory; History; Systems

020 GENERAL ECONOMIC THEORY

Keynesian economics: The search for first principles. By ALAN CODDINGTON. Boston, London and Sydney: Allen & Unwin, 1983. Pp. xiv, 129. $18.50. ISBN 0–04–330334–X.

JEL 83–0588

In this posthumous book, Alan Coddington characterizes Keynesian economics not in terms of the work of any particular school but rather as ". . . theories and models of economic functioning . . . in which there is some scope for adopting a utilitarian perspective on public finance" (p. 2). He thereby skirts some of the more contentious doctrinal and exegetical issues that have dominated earlier contributions to the Keynesian debate. Still open for discussion, however, are the most contentious issues of all: Is the economic system essentially self-organizing and self-adjusting? If so, does the economy work well enough most of the time to be treated with benign neglect, or does it generally perform so poorly as to require constant nudging or kicking from the authorities? Supposing the economy requires a nudge or a kick, do sufficiently reliable policy levers exist to ensure that desired objectives can be attained? So, despite his narrowed perspective, Coddington is left with more than enough material for several books. That he is able to say something useful and instructive not just on these but on a host of related issues in a relatively slim volume is high testimony to his scholarship, didactic skill, and intellectual engagement—and a sober reminder of what the profession has lost by his untimely death.

Coddington is at his best when discussing alternative economic cosmologies and related semantic issues. Thus in his chapter on "The Keynesian Dichotomy," he neatly disposes of the still common view of Keynes versus the Classics as a conflict between mutually exclusive theoretical alternatives, not by the usual (evasive) route of the neoclassical synthesis ("It all depends on the elasticities of the IS and LM curves"), but rather by pointing out that the two "theories" differ mainly in the *order* in which they take up the analysis of real as contrasted with monetary phenomena. Thus, what Patinkin and others would regard as an integration of value and monetary theory, Coddington sees as a suppression of value theory in order to focus attention temporarily on short-run interactions between monetary and real phenomena. The conventional view has generated little but heat; Coddington's view generates a bit of light.

Similarly, in his chapter on "Demand Deficiency," Coddington cuts through the analytic and conceptual confusions associated with the notion of involuntary unemployment by arguing persuasively that the concept becomes useful only at such time as we are able clearly to distinguish "involuntary" from other and presumably "non-involuntary" types of unemployment, which hardly seems possible until we know enough about the performance capabilities of the economic system in general and of labor markets in particular to assign some part of observed unemployment to the residual category described by Keynes. But suppose it were possible. Then presumably our understanding of how to manage the economic system would enable us to eliminate the "involuntary" component of unemployment. So Coddington concludes: ". . . as the purpose of the [concept] is to help us, from a state in which that understanding is lacking, to move towards its attainment, it evidently becomes usable at exactly the same point at which it becomes unnecessary. It becomes usable at just that point at which we know what it is supposed to help us find out; but not before" (p. 46).

In similar fashion, and just as persuasively,

Coddington disposes in his chapter on "Deficient Foresight" of the quaint post-Keynesian notion of Shackle, Davidson and others that "true uncertainty" is at the heart of the Keynesian revolution. Were that so, Coddington argues, we should be left with no theory at all; all behavior would appear to be equally capricious and unintelligible, and there would be nothing left but for the whole profession to shut up shop.

Coddington is less satisfying, because less perspicacious, when he deals with specific modeling approaches and related doctrinal issues. Here, I refer to the last two of the six substantive chapters in his book, one a reprint of his 1979 *JEL* paper on "Hicks's Contribution," the other a reprint of his 1976 *JEL* paper on "The Search for First Principles." In the first of these essays, Coddington argues as if the whole stream of Hicks' writings, from the early 1930s to the present time, were the product of a single, unchanging intellect. Single the intellect undoubtedly was, but unchanging it most certainly was not. Coddington also displays a remarkable ignorance (or disregard?) of earlier discussions of Hicks' role in the propagation of Keynesian ideas. The essay on "First Principles" is better, perhaps because it deals more with issues of method and approach (where Coddington is always strong) and less with issues of substantive analysis. But it is also unsatisfying; for while it neatly pigeonholes a variety of approaches to Keynesian economics into three cute categories—Fundamentalist, Hydraulic, and Reconstituted Reductionist—it sheds no useful light on the search for First Principles, not even an indication of where we might find a lamp post to lean on while we look about.

Because it refers so much to analysis but deals mainly with methodology, Coddington's book is difficult to evaluate in any but personal terms. Taken as a whole, I liked it. It is elegantly written, often witty, never dull. Moreover, it provokes constant thought, even though it is not constantly thoughtful. My only true regret after reading the volume is that I shall not have the pleasure of reading another by the same delightful author.

ROBERT W. CLOWER
*University of California,
Los Angeles*

REFERENCES

CODDINGTON, ALAN. "Keynesian Economics: The Search for First Principles," *J. Econ. Lit.*, Dec. 1976, *14*(4), pp. 1258–73.

———. "Hicks's Contribution to Keynesian Economics," *J. Econ. Lit.*, Sept. 1979, *17*(3), pp. 970–88.

Book reviews

Franklin M. Fisher, Disequilibrium Foundations of Equilibrium Economics
(Cambridge University Press, Cambridge, 1983), pp. xii + 236, $34.50.

Fisher argues that the study of disequilibrium should be a major concern
of economists, partly for its own sake, but mainly to provide firm foundations for what economists have always done best: equilibrium analysis. The
bulk of his book is directed accordingly to establishing conditions under
which '...the rational behavior of individual agents drives an economy to
equilibrium' (pp. 9–10).

To maintain generality, Fisher works with Hahn Process models in which
trading activity is treated as a 'do-it-yourself' affair: there is no Walrasian
'auctioneer', or, indeed, any other explicit coordinator of economic activities.
As is well known, this procedure poses logistical problems for which no
satisfactory solution has yet been found: how can individual traders hope to
exhaust potential gains from trade if they have to discover for themselves
what, where, when, with whom and on what terms various commodities can
be traded?

One way to resolve these logistical problems is to work with models that
involve set-up costs of acquiring information and of negotiating and executing trades, thereby providing grounds to argue that rational self-interest will
lead some agents in the economy to undertake for profit the task of

coordinating trades among other agents. Such models are attractive because they capture obviously important aspects of reality; but they also have important drawbacks because they do not lend themselves to rigorous analysis. Fisher nowhere displays more than a passing interest in models of this kind. Elevating rigor over relevance and form over substance, he fills the place of the absent Walrasian auctioneer with mathematical assumptions that are equally devoid of economic sense but serve just as effectively to guarantee that trading in unorganized markets is 'orderly'. Thus Fisher evades rather than resolves the problems that are mainly responsible for modern discontents with disequilibrium analysis. Of what scientific value is a general proof of stability for an economy whose operating characteristics cannot be described constructively? What light can such a proof shed on possible sources of instability in any actual economy? More generally, what can Fisher's line of argument add to what is already known on the basis of earlier formal analyses of disequilibrium and stability? Surely no mathematical economist needs to be instructed at this late date in 'methods and techniques' of dynamic analysis; but what other purpose is served by elaborate study of models that differ from conventional 'tatonnement' models mainly in being more complicated?

Though Fisher's book is disappointing as a positive contribution to disequilibrium analysis, it is not without interest from other points of view. Fisher's historical account of disequilibrium analysis and value theory (Chapter 1) and of methods and problems of traditional stability theory (Chapters 2 and 3) are excellent and should be of considerable value to students who want a quick introduction to this literature. Fisher's attempt to add constructively to disequilibrium analysis (Chapters 4–9) will not impress, and because of its discursiveness may even bore specialists in theory; but it may prove instructive to some in showing how little in the way of worthwhile results can be extracted by even the most brilliant and ingenious of analysts from disequilibrium models that remain essentially Walrasian in structure.

In his final chapter, Fisher (p. 217) remarks: 'I can only offer the model of the present book as a starting point, a framework within which it may be possible to begin to analyze [disequilibrium] questions.' For various reasons, only some of which are alluded to above, this reviewer must demur. Fisher's work is not the start of a new wave in disequilibrium analysis nor even a force to make old waves move faster. It is more aptly and accurately characterized as an extended excursion down a blind alley. If we are ever to make significant progress in disequilibrium economics, we shall have to look to other avenues of analysis and probably to other guides than Fisher.

Robert W. Clower
University of California
Los Angeles, CA

*The origins of the Keynesian revolution: The
development of Keynes' theory of employment
and output.* By ROBERT W. DIMAND. Stanford, CA: Stanford University Press, 1988.
Pp. vii, 213. $32.50. ISBN 0–8047–1525–4.

JEL 89–0374

Dimand's book has much the same aim as
Don Patinkin's classic study of *Keynes' Monetary Thought* (1976): to reexamine the development of Keynes' ideas, from the *Tract on Monetary Reform* and the *Treatise on Money* to the
General Theory and beyond, in the light of
Keynes' *Collected Writings* and other docu-
mentary evidence that has become available to
scholars only during the last two decades.
Where the two books overlap (and the overlap
is substantial), Dimand's analysis is less inten-
sive than Patinkin's; but within its chosen limits, Dimand's coverage is thorough, his scholarship impressive, and the story he tells highly
readable. On these grounds alone, Dimand's
book must be counted a useful addition to the
literature.

Chapter 1 sets the tone and general direction

of later chapters with a concise account of Keynes' many-splendored contributions to economic theory during his unregenerate years as an acknowledged adherent to Marshallian economics, to Cambridge monetary theory, and to the classical belief in a self-adjusting economic system. Chapter 2 summarizes the central ideas of Keynes' *Treatise*. Here Dimand follows earlier interpreters—notably Axel Leijonhufvud (1966, pp. 20–26), Sir John Hicks (1967, ch. 11) and Patinkin (1976, ch. 2)—in emphasizing similarities rather than differences between the *Treatise* and the *General Theory*. Dimand's presentation is detailed in some directions but curiously sketchy in others, so his argument may seem opaque to readers not already thoroughly familiar with the notation and terminology of the *Treatise*. Such readers will find Hicks' masterful "A Note on the *Treatise*" (1967, ch. 11) helpful if not essential supplementary reading.

Chapter 3 breaks new ground with a detailed account of the reception of the *Treatise* as reflected in contemporary reviews. This is good reading and leaves one in no doubt that the *Treatise* was greeted by most economists in the early 1930s as an original and provocative contribution to monetary theory and central banking policy. But, as noted by Dimand, the review published by Keynes' colleague A. C. Pigou (1931) damned the *Treatise* with faint praise. One wonders why? Was it perhaps for reasons similar to those that later led Pigou to write an even more damning review of the *General Theory*? Dimand provides no clue. On this as on numerous other incidental issues, he displays little sympathy for the possible intellectual curiosity—or perversity—of potential readers.

Chapters 4 and 5 trace Keynes' road from the *Treatise* to the *General Theory*. The first of these chapters concentrates on the transition from price to output adjustment which—thanks to prodding first from Hawtrey and Hobson and later from R. F. Kahn and other members of the Cambridge "circus"—led Keynes' to his theory of effective demand. The second focuses on the development of Keynes' "monetary theory of production" up to the first clear statement of all of the central ideas of the *General Theory* in Keynes' lectures of 1933.

Dimand's sixth and final chapter deals in part with the *General Theory* in its final form, but consists mainly of a recapitulation of leading themes discussed in earlier chapters. The chapter as a whole suggests that Dimand's fascination with Keynes goes deeper than mere admiration for Keynes' scholarly contributions would seem to warrant. This is borne out by the curiously flat and uncritical assessment of Keynes' ideas with which Dimand concludes his book.

Like other books that attempt to shed new light on ideas and issues about which most of the giants of our profession had already had their say, this one is not easy to assess. Dimand's argument shows him to be a competent if not particularly insightful theorist. The book sheds little fresh light on the origins and development of Keynes' thought. Neither does it take serious issue with earlier interpretations by Don Patinkin, Donald Moggridge, and other leading authorities in this area of doctrinal history. But it does explore some byways along Keynes' road to the *General Theory* that earlier writers overlooked or chose to ignore; and taken as a whole it seems to me to offer a clearer picture of the continuity of Keynes' thought from 1913 to his death in 1946 than perhaps any earlier book has done.

One could wish that Dimand had been able to make more of the mountain of material he has examined. The ghost of Marshall runs like a red thread through the whole of Keynes' theoretical writings; but Dimand leaves that connection unexplored. The validity of the theoretical rationale for Keynes post-*Treatise* "vision" of a non-self-adjusting economic system, which the *General Theory* was supposed to make clear, has never been established; at this date, indeed, its validity seems not so much problematical as improbable. Though Dimand often mentions, he nowhere seriously addresses this issue. But these comments are more in the nature of quibbles than criticisms; to have dealt adequately with such issues, Dimand would have to have written a much longer book.

Few economists these days regard doctrinal history and exegesis—even when it concerns Keynes and post-Keynesian macroeconomics— as choice material for an intellectual feast. But those who do—particularly those who have already consumed and digested Vols. XIII, XIV and XXIX of the *Collected Writings*—will enjoy Dimand's reexamination. And even those who

generally do not like this sort of thing could
do worse than sample Dimand's offering; a taste
may whet their appetite for more.

ROBERT W. CLOWER
University of South Carolina

REFERENCES

HICKS, SIR JOHN. *Critical essays in monetary theory.*
Oxford: Clarendon Press, 1967.

LEIJONHUFVUD, AXEL. *On Keynesian economics and
the economics of Keynes.* NY: Oxford U. Press,
1968.

PATINKIN, DON. *Keynes' monetary thought.* Durham,
NC: Duke U. Press, 1967.

PIGOU, A. C. "Mr. Keynes on Money," *Nation and
Athenaeum,* Jan. 24, 1931.

Value and Capital: Fifty Years Later.
Edited by Lionel W. McKenzie and Stefano Zamagni. New York: New York University Press, 1991. *Pp. xxxvi, 490. $95.00.*

In his 1940 *OJE* review of the first edition of John Hicks's *Value and Capital*, Abba Lerner (then at Columbia University) remarked:

> To say that Professor Hicks' "Value and Capital" is the most important publication for economic theory since the appearance of Mr. Keynes' "General Theory of Employment Interest and Money" does not quite do it justice. For not only do some of the important "Keynesian" results, reached independently and earlier by Professor Hicks, appear in their final form in this volume, but the elegance and precision with which fundamental notions are presented and the astonishingly simple way in which the intricate argument unfolds itself make it certain that the book will remain a classic for students to read and re-read long after Mr. Keynes' book has been rendered obsolete. . . .

Other reviewers, most notably Oskar Morgenstern in the 1941 *JPE*, were less kind (cf. the comment in the first paragraph of the editorial introduction to the present volume, p. xviii); but subsequent events show that Lerner's assessment was prescient. Indeed, as perusal of any modern economics text or treatise will reveal, no writer of this century has done more than John Hicks to shape contemporary modes of teaching and writing. So it is fitting that, nearly fifty years after publication of Hicks's great classic—the book that painlessly introduced English-speaking economists to the theretofore largely ignored general equilibrium writings of the Lausanne School—two former students of Hicks should organize a conference to celebrate its Fiftieth Anniversary.

The volume under review, a major product of that conference, consists of fifteen commissioned papers and eleven related comments, together with a short postscript by Hicks (who, at nearly 85 years of age, attended the conference and (so the editors inform us) sat through and commented on most of the presentations). The volume is thus a testimonial, or seems to have been so intended, to the "flowering of economic theory" (xvii) that followed post-World War II publication [1946] of the second edition of *Value and Capital*. On close inspection, however, one finds it difficult to regard the contributions in this volume as "testimonials" to ideas set forth in *Value and Capital*.

When Hicks originally wrote *Value and Capital*, it was still possible seriously to view general equilibrium theory as broadly descriptive of actual market economies. Indeed, Hicks originally conceived himself to be writing a book that would provide "a technique for studying the interrelations of markets." Not until some thirty years later (in lectures first delivered at the London School of Economics, later published in revised form as *Critical Essays in Monetary Theory*, 1967) did Hicks explicitly acknowledge [pp. 6 ff.] that the costless coordination presumptions underlying the Walrasian and related conceptual schemes precluded logical recognition of separate markets or of intermediaries of any other kind except the *deus ex machina* now usually referred to as the "auctioneer" (or, by analogy with Maxwell's famous thermodynamical "being", Walras' "demon") and so ruled out *economic* analysis of the logistics of exchange in ongoing systems. That message apparently had still to reach the organizers and contributors to this volume, for here one finds no evidence of critical understanding of any of the conceptual shortcomings of *Value and Capital* much less of related flaws in such subsequent offshoots as the Arrow-Debreu-Mckenzie, Patinkin, and Grandmont models.

The individual papers in the volume are concisely and accurately summarized in the editors "Introduction" [pp. xviii–xxix], which I strongly recommend to readers who are (understandably) averse to immersion in the main waters of the book. But neither in the introduction, nor elsewhere, is any attempt made to assign *Value and Capital* a place in the history of economic thought, to assess its influence on post-1950 writings, or to suggest where the general equilibrium tradition to which *Value and Capital* belongs may now be heading. So the book as a whole is a great disappointment. In a volume intended to celebrate the fiftieth anniversary of a classic book, and, more particularly, a book whose still living author was on hand to share the occasion, one would expect to find at least one paper that did Hicks the honor of treating his work as worthy of the kind of hard-hitting criticism that he himself often directed at it during the last forty years of his life.

The volume contains no such paper. Even the concluding, and outwardly critical papers on "Intertemporal General Equilibrium," one by Radner, the other by Duffie, are curiously stale and uninstructive. From these samples, and from similar evidence provided by other papers in the volume, one might suggest that what the editors in the Preface describe as a "flowering" of economic theory could more accurately be characterized as a "going to seed." But the plain truth is that the present volume cannot be regarded as a source of reliable evidence on this or any other deep issue of contemporary economics. So I do not recommend the book, or any of the individual papers in it, as desirable reading for students or professionals. At a price of $95.00, one may even question whether the book deserves shelf space in libraries other than those that make a virtue of "possessing everything."

Robert W. Clower
University of South Carolina

[34]

The Joan Robinson Legacy.
Edited by Ingrid H. Rima. Armonk, N.Y.: M. E. Sharpe, Inc., 1991. *Pp. 300. $42.50.*

This volume starts with a lovely portrait (the frontispage) of Joan Robinson (circa 1970, I should guess) that perfectly captures her warmth, thoughtfulness, intelligence and beauty during the latter part of the period when I met her most frequently and knew her best. Ms. Rima has here assembled a mixed collection of essays (mostly by persons who would style themselves "Post Keynesian") on various aspects of Joan Robinson's many contributions to economic doctrine and method, Joan's own writing was so limpid that mere commentators, whatever their literary and intellectual talents, have an impossible act to follow. Joan Robinson may not always have been everyones' cup of tea, but at one time or another she was every reader's glass of champagne.

Like many Cambridge students in the 1920s, and like Alfred Marshall (cf. Keynes, *Essays in Biography*, Collected Work Vol. X, p. 146), Joan Robinson ". . . belonged to the tribe of sages and pastors [and so] was endowed with a double nature. . . ." But—again like Marshall—"As a preacher and pastor . . . [she] was not particularly superior to other similar natures." And while one could not be in Joan's presence for more than a few minutes without recognizing her incredible keenness of intellect and quick logic, neither can one read her books and collected works and imagine that anyone of Keynes's stature would say of her, as Keynes did say of Marshall, ". . . as a scientist [she] was, within [her] own field, the greatest in the world for a hundred years." Despite her sharp intelligence, Joan had no discernable feel for what Polya calls "shaded inference"—the essential quality of mind that separates the great empirical scientist from the great logician or mathematician. Though Joan often spoke and wrote sensibly about scientific methodology (one of the more notable instances being her remark that "in a subject where there is no agreed procedure for knocking out error, doctrine has long life.") she seemed to view economic theories either as nearly white —so Marx and Keynes were seen not as wrong but merely sometimes confused or misguided —or (especially anything she associated with Walras or classical theory) as perfectly black. Her collected works may entertain future historians of economic science, but they will not add much to what future generations will regard as "accumulated economic knowledge."

With few exceptions, the essays in this volume are "in the spirit" if not in the literary style of Joan Robinson: long on preaching, assertion, and exhortation, short on content. But the exceptions merit mention. The introductory essay by Ingrid Rima is clear, thoughtful, well crafted, and provides an excellent overview of the bulk of the remaining essays; it is well worth reading. Then there is the brilliant essay [Chap. 5] by Meyer Burstein on "History versus Equilibrium" which seems to me good enough to compensate any reader for the entire price of the book. Burstein somehow manages to punch through the mindless rhetoric that surrounds most nonconventinal discussions of "historical time" and at the same time gives Joan ample credit for consistently stressing (if not always with complete lucidity) the strictly virtual character of all so-called Walrasian models (I say "so-called" because Joan never seemed to recognize that contemporary general equilibrium theory owes virtually nothing to Leon Walras and owes everything to J. R. Hicks's bowdlerized version of Walras's *Elements* as set forth in *Value and Capital*.)

403

Phyllis Deane's "Biographical Memoir" [Chap. 2] also merits special mention for its clarity and its scholarly focus, though I do not share Deane's assessment of Joan's scientific accomplishments. I heartily agree, however, with Deane's observation [p. 19] that ". . . few of the many young professionals who had come to sit at [Joan's] feet . . . failed to respond to a mind that refused to be confined by conventional techniques of economic analysis." Still I cannot help reflecting that those who "refuse to be confined" might first make a serious effort to learn enough about conventional analysis to make informed judgments about what deserves to be ignored and what deserves to be kept.

Before concluding, I must draw attention to the superb twenty-five page bibliography of the writings of Joan Robinson by Maria Marcuzzo of Universita degli Studi di Modena, Italy; it is a labor of dedicated scholarship that will be much appreciated by those who seek inspiration or enlightenment from Joan's extensive contributions to the economic literature of this century. As for the fourteen or so other essays that I have not so far mentioned, to discuss them further might give me a certain personal satisfaction but would otherwise serve no useful purpose. Suffice it to say that all of them are longer on piety towards Joan than on material that would interest other economists, and that most of them are blessedly free of invective about "bastard" Keynesianism (Joan's favorite epithet for the "illegitimate" brand of Keynesian economics that she associated (rightly or wrongly) with the post-1936 and pre-1960 writings of Hansen, Hicks, Klein, Samuelson, and other (probably most) American "Keynesians."

Finally, I must mention the penultimate essay in the volume [Chap. 18] entitled "Why Not a Nobel Laureate?" by Marjorie Turner, whose 1989 book on *Joan Robinson and The Americans* has been receiving deserved praise from reviewers. Even if one believed that recipients of the Nobel Prize in Economics had an honor conferred on them rather than the other way around (conferring honor on a committee that would otherwise have hardly any credibility), to write about the nonaward of the prize to any particular person strikes me as puerile. For reasons alluded to earlier, Joan probably stood a better chance for the prize in Literature or Peace than in Economics, but despite that and despite the generally disappointing quality of the essays in this volume, surely we must all be thankful that such a great lady as Joan Robinson graced our profession through the middle half of the Twentieth Century. The Joan Robinson Legacy may be hard to describe and surely is not reflected in this book, but who can doubt that such a legacy exists?

Robert W. Clower
University of South Carolina

PART V

APPENDIX

Appendix

Writings (published or forthcoming) of Robert W. Clower, 1949–1994

Books

In progress
Monetary Economies (with Peter W. Howitt), expected completion, 1996.

Published
Intermediate Microeconomics (with Phil Graves and Robert Sexton), Harcourt, Brace and Jovanovich, San Diego, 1988.
Money and Markets: Selected essays of R. W. Clower, Cambridge University Press, 1984 (edited and with an introduction by Donald A. Walker; afterword by R.W. Clower). Paperback edition, 1986.
Microeconomics (with J.F. Due), Richard D. Irwin Inc., 1972 (Spanish Translation, *Biblioteca Technos de Ciencias Economicas*, Madrid, 1978).
Monetary Theory (editor), Penguin Books Ltd, London, 1969 (Italian Translation, *La Teoria Monetaria* (ed. Franco Angeli), Milan, 1972).
Growth Without Development, An Economic Survey of Liberia (with G. Dalton, A. Walters and M. Harwitz), Northwestern University Press, Evanston, Ill., 1966.
Puerto Rico Shipping and the U.S. Maritime Laws, (with John Harris), Transportation Center, Northwestern University, 1965.
Intermediate Economic Analysis (with J.F. Due), Richard D. Irwin Inc., Homewood, Ill., 4th edn, 1961; 5th edn, 1966.
Introduction to Mathematical Economics (with D.W. Bushaw), Richard D. Irwin Inc., Homewood, Ill., 1957.

Papers 1992–93; in press and/or forthcoming, 1995
'Foundations of Economics', with Peter W. Howitt, Conference paper, Paris, October 1992.
'Money, Markets and Coase', with Peter W. Howitt, Conference paper, Paris, October 1992.
'Towards a Reconstruction of Economic Theory', Address delivered to Canadian Economic Association, Ottawa, 5 June 1993.
'Foundations of Monetary and Financial Theory', *Greek Economic Review*, June 1994.
'Taking Markets Seriously: Groundwork for a Macrofoundation', with Peter W. Howitt, paper delivered at Eastern Economic Association, Boston, 18 March 1994.
'Effective Demand Revisited': *Part I*, 'The Principle of Effective Demand: Chapter 3 of *The General Theory* (Revised)'; *Part II*, 'The Principle of Effective Demand: Chapter 3 of *The General Theory Revisited*'. Parts I and II (56 pages incl. diagrams)

forthcoming as Chapter 3 of second edition of *The General Theory* (eds G.C. Harcourt and Peter Riach), Routledge.

'On Truth in Teaching Macroeconomics', Conference paper, Montevideo, Uruguay, September 1993.

'The Last Classical Economist', Conference paper, Northwestern University, September 1993.

Published articles

'Economics as an Inductive Science', *Southern Economic Journal*, **60**(4), April 1994, pp. 805–14.

'The Fingers of the Invisible Hand', *Brock University Review*, **3**(1), April 1994, pp. 3–13.

'Incorporating Inventories into Supply and Demand Analysis', with P. Graves, D. Lee and R. Sexton, *Atlantic Economic Journal*, **20**(4), December 1992, pp. 41–5.

'Keynes's *General Theory*: A Contemporary Perspective', *Greek Economic Review*, **12**, Supp, Autumn 1990, pp. 73–84.

'Ohlin and the *General Theory*', in *The Stockholm School of Economics Revisited* (ed. Lars Jonung), 1991, New York, Cambridge University Press, pp. 245–62.

'Keynes' *General Theory*: The Marshall Connection', in *Perspectives in the History of Economic Thought, Vol. II* (ed. Donald Walker), 1989, Edward Elgar Publishing, Aldershot, pp. 133–47.

'How Economists Think', *Business and Economic Review*, University of South Carolina Division of Research, **36**(1), Oct.–Dec. 1989, pp. 9–17.

'Keynes and the Classics Revisited', in *Keynes and Public Policy After Fifty Years, Vol. I, Economics and Policy*, (eds Omar F. Hamouda and John N. Smithin), Edward Elgar Publishing, Aldershot, 1988, pp. 81–91.

'The Ideas of Economists', in *The Consequences of Economic Rhetoric*, (eds Klamer, McCloskey and Solow), Cambridge University Press, Cambridge, 1988, pp. 85–99.

'New Directions for Keynesian Economics', *Siena University Economic Review*, Spring 1987, pp. 1–17.

'Trade Specialists and Money in an Ongoing Exchange Economy' (with Daniel Friedman), in *The Dynamics of Market Economies* (eds Richard Day and Gunnar Eliasson), Elsevier Science Publishers B.V., New York, 1986, pp. 115–29.

'Monetary Theory and Macroeconomics: A Perspective', *Keizai Shushi*, **54**(3) (Nihon University), 1985.

'The Genesis and Control of Inflation', in *The Stability of Contemporary Economic Systems* (eds Oldrich Kyn and Wolfram Schrettl), Vandenhoek and Ruprecht, Germany, 1979.

'The Transactions Theory of the Demand for Money: A Reconsideration' (with Peter W. Howitt), *Journal of Political Economy*, June 1978, pp. 449–66.

'The Anatomy of Monetary Theory', *American Economic Review*, (Proc.), **67**, May 1977, pp. 206–12.

'A Reconsideration of the Theory of Inflation', in *Resource Allocation and Economic Policy* (eds M. Allingham and M.L. Burstein), Macmillan, London, 1976, pp. 14–25.

'Reflections on the Keynesian Perplex', *Zeitschrift für Nationalökonomie*, **35**, 1975, pp. 1–24.

'The Coordination of Economic Activities: A Keynesian Perspective', *American Economic Review*, (Proc.), **65**, May 1975, pp. 182–8.

'Reflections on Science and Economics', *Intermountain Economic Review*, Spring, 1974, pp. 1–12.

'Say's Principle: What It Means and Doesn't Mean' (with Axel Leijonhufvud), *Intermountain Economic Review*, Fall, 1973, pp. 1–16.

'Snarks, Quarks, and Other Fictions: The Role of Formal Theory in Economic History', *Business Enterprise and Economic Change* (eds L.P. Cain and P.J. Uselding), Kent State University Press, 1973, pp. 3–14.

'The Ideas of Economists', *Monash Lecture, 1972*, Monash University, Clayton, Victoria, 1973, 23 pp.

'Theoretical Foundations of Monetary Policy', *Monetary Theory and Monetary Policy in the 1970s*, (eds Clayton *et al.*), Oxford Press, London, 1971, pp. 15–28.

'Is There an Optimal Money Supply?' *Journal of Finance*, **XXV**(2), May 1970, pp. 425–33 (reprinted in *Frontiers of Quantitative Economics*, ed. M. Intriligator), N. Holland (1970).

'What Traditional Monetary Theory Really Wasn't', *Canadian Journal of Economics*, **II**, May, 1969, pp. 199–202.

'Conditions for African Economic Progress', Melville J. Herskovitz Memorial Lecture, University of Edinburgh, Centre for African Studies, 1968 (14 pp.).

'Income, Wealth, and the Theory of Consumption', (with M.B. Johnson), *Essays in Honour of Sir John Hicks*, Edinburgh University Press, 1968, pp. 45–96 (reprinted in Surrey, *Macroeconomic Themes*, OUP, 1976, pp. 101–15).

'Stock-Flow Analysis', *International Encyclopedia of the Social Sciences*, 1968, pp. 273–7.

'The Present State of International Liquidity Theory', (with R.G. Lipsey), *American Economic Review*, May, 1968, pp. 586–95.

'A Reconsideration of the Microfoundations of Monetary Theory', *Western Economic Journal*, December, 1967, pp. 1–8.

'Effective Control Through Coherent Dcentralization with Preemptive Goals', *Econometrica* (with A. Charnes and K. Kortanek), April, 1967, pp. 294–320.

'The Keynesian Counterrevolution: A Theoretical Appraisal', *The Theory of Interest Rates* (eds Hahn and Brechling), The MacMillan Co., London, 1965, pp. 103–25.

'Monetary History and Positive Economics', (review articles), *Journal of Economic History*, September, 1964, pp. 364–80.

'Permanent Income and Transitory Balances: Hahn's Paradox', *Oxford Economic Papers*, July 1963, pp. 177–90.

'Classical Monetary Theory Revisited', *Economica*, May, 1963, pp. 165–70.

'Die Keynesianische Gegenrevolution: eine theoretische Kritick', *Schweizerische Zeitschrift*, **1**, 1963, pp. 8–31 (English version published in 1965 – see above.)

'Statistics and Development Policy in Decisions' (with A. Walters and G. Dalton), *Development Research Review*, July, 1962, pp. 65–74.

'Mathematics and Economics: The Contemporary Prospect', *Quarterly Review of Economics and Business*, May, 1961, pp. 37–45.

'On the Invariance of the Demand for Cash and Other Assets' (with M.L. Burstein), *Review of Economic Studies*, October, 1960, pp. 32–6.

'Keynes and the Classics: A Dynamical Perspective', *Quarterly Journal of Economics*, May, 1960, pp. 318–23.

'Some Theory of an Ignorant Monopolist', *Economic Journal*, December, 1959, pp. 705–16.

'Competition, Monopoly, and the Theory of Price', *Pakistan Economic Journal*, September, 1955, pp. 219–26.

'Price Determination in a Stock-Flow Economy' (with D.W. Bushaw), *Econometrica*, July, 1954, pp. 328–43.

'Productivity, Thrift and the Rate of Interest', *Economic Journal*, March, 1954, pp. 107–15.

'An Investigation into the Dynamics of Investment', *American Economic Review*, March, 1954, pp. 64–81.

'Professor Duesenberry and Traditional Theory', *Review of Economic Studies*, XX, 1952–53, pp. 165–78.

Notes and comments

'The State of Economics: Serious but not Hopeless?', in *The Spread of Economic Ideas*, (eds D. Colander and A.W. Coats), Cambridge University Press, Cambridge, 1989, pp. 23–9.

'The Dismal State of Economic Science: An Editor's Lament', *Asian Economist*, 17 May, 1985, pp. 16–23.

'On the Behavioral and Rational Foundations of Economic Dynamics' comment on a paper by Herbert Simon, in *The Dynamics of Market Economies* (eds Richard H. Day and Gunnar Eliasson), 1986, Elsevier Science Publishers B.V., pp. 42–4.

'Money and Markets', Afterword, in *Money and Markets* (ed. Donald Walker), 1984, Cambridge University Press, pp. 259–72.

'Shared-Monopoly Theories', *Southwestern University Law Review*, 12(2), 1981, pp. 271–3.

'The Role of Economic Analysis in Antitrust Litigation', *Southwestern University Law Review*, 12(2), 1981, pp. 355–8.

'The Administered Price Thesis: An Appraisal', in *The Attack on Corporate America* (ed. M.B. Johnson), 1978, McGraw-Hill, pp. 174–7.

'The Economic Constitution and the New Deal: Discussion', in *Regulatory Change in an Atmosphere of Crises* (ed. G.M. Walton), Academic Press, New York, 1979, pp. 27–9.

'Marshall on Deposit Multipliers', *Economic Inquiry*, 13, June, 1975, p. 252.

'Foundations of Money Illusion in a Neoclassical Micro-Monetary Model: Comment', (with J.G. Riley), *American Economic Review*, 66, March, 1976, pp. 184–5.

'Comment: The Optimal Growth Rate of Money', *Journal of Political Economy*, 76(4), Part II, July/August, 1968, pp. 876–80.

'Causal Systems and Stability', *Econometrica*, 33(3) (July, 1965), pp. 241–2.

'Oligopoly Theory: A Dynamical Approach', *Proceedings of the Western Economic Association*, 1959, pp. 16–19.

'Business Investment and the Theory of Price', *Proceedings of the Western Economic Association*, 1953, pp. 22–4.

'Stock and Flow Quantities', *Economica*, August, 1959, pp. 251–2.

'The Analogy Between Ordinary and Relative Preference Analysis', *Review of Economics and Statistics*, November, 1953, pp. 353–4.

'Mr. Graaff's Producer–Consumption Theory: A Restatement and Correction', *Review of Economic Studies*, **XX**, 1952–53, pp. 84–5.

Book Reviews

'The Joan Robinson Legacy', Ingrid H. Rima, *Southern Economic Journal*, **60**(2) (October, 1993), pp. 508–9.

'Value and Capital: Fifty Years Later', (eds. L. McKenzie and S. Zamagni), *Southern Economic Journal*, **58**(4) (April, 1992), pp. 1127–8.

'The Origins of the Keynesian Revolution', Robert W. Dimand, *Journal of Economic Literature*, **27**, (Dec. 1989), pp. 1679–81.

'A Nation in Debt', R.H. Fink and Jack C. High. *USC Business and Economic Review*, **34**(7), April–June 1988, pp. 34–5.

'Disequilibrium Foundations of Equilibrium Economics', by Franklin M. Fisher. *Journal of Economic and Business Organization*, **7**(2) (June, 1986), pp. 222–3.

'Keynesian Economics: The Search for First Principles', by Alan Coddington. *Journal of Economic Literature*, **22**, (Sept. 1984), pp. 1115–16.

'The Obscurantist Approach to Economics: Shackle on Keynes', *Eastern Economic Journal*, **2**, January 1975, pp. 99–101.

'Money and Markets: A Monetarist View', by Beryl W. Sprinkel, *Economica*, August 1972, **XXXIX**(155), p. 340.

'The Theory of Imperfect Competition: A Radical Reconstruction', by Donald Dewey, *Journal of Economic Literature*, December 1970, pp. 1212–13.

'Critical Essays in Monetary Theory', by Sir John Hicks, *Journal of Political Economy*, May, 1970.

'Forecasting and Recognizing Business Cycle Turning Points', by R. Fels and R. Hinshaw, *Annals of the American Academy of Political and Social Science*, January, 1969, pp. 207–8.

'Foundations of Money and Banking', by Pesek and Saving, *Economica*, **XXXVI**(141) (February 1969), pp. 84–8.

'Measuring Benefits of Government Investments', edited by Robert Dorfman, *Annals of the American Academy of Political and Social Science*, November, 1965, p. 178.

'Macroeconomics and Programming', by K.K. Kurihara, *American Economic Review*, September, 1965, p. 889.

'Asset Prices in Economic Analysis', by Samuel B. Chase, Jr., *Annals of the American Academy of Political and Social Science*, 1964.

'Exercises in Economic Analysis' by Joan Robinson, *American Economic Review*, 1961, pp. 701–2.

'The Theory of Capital', (eds F.A. Lutz and D.C. Hague), New York: St Martins Press, *Southern Economic Journal*, July, 1962, pp. 54–5.

'Economic Development of Libya, International Banks for Reconstruction and Development', *Journal of Political Economy*, October 1961, p. 521.

'Problems and Practices of Development Banks', by S. Boskey, *Journal of Political Economy*, June, 1961, p. 313.

'Introduction to Mathematical Analysis', by Daus and Whyburn, *Econometrica*, October, 1959, pp. 715–16.

Miscellaneous

McGraw-Hill Encyclopedia of Economics, 2nd edn, 1994, Articles on 'Economics', 'Factors of Production', 'Money Illusion', 'Scarcity'.

'The Problem of Second Best and the Efficient Pricing of Electricity', with M. Bruce Johnson, EPRI Special Report, May 1981, EPRI, Palo Alto.

'Foreword' to *The Political Economy of Policy Making* (eds Dooley, Kaufman and Lombra) Sage Publications, Beverly Hills, 1979.

'Foreword' to Sir John Hicks' *The Crisis in Keynesian Economics*, Basic Books, Inc., New York, 1974.

'A Study of Elementary Learning and Response Mechanisms in Dynamical Monopoly Models', *Office of Naval Research, Research Memorandum No. 12*, Northwestern University Technological Institute, December 1958.

'Inductive Inference and Business Behavior', abstract of paper delivered at 1959 meetings of Econometric Society, *Econometrica*, July, 1960, pp. 685–6.

'On the Microdynamics of Price Formation in n-Seller Markets', abstract of paper delivered at 1958 meetings in Econometric Society, *Econometrica*, April 1959, pp. 312–13.

'Some Views on University Education in Pakistan', *Al-Iqtisad*, Hailey College of Commerce, Lahore, Pakistan, June, 1955, pp. 1–6.

'The Future of Banking in Pakistan', *Al-Iqtisad*, March, 1956, pp. 5–10.

Letter to London Daily Times on devaluation of pound sterling, 23 Sept. 1949.

Name index

Economists of the Twentieth Century

Monetarism and Macroeconomic Policy
Thomas Mayer

Studies in Fiscal Federalism
Wallace E. Oates

The World Economy in Perspective
Essays in International Trade and European Integration
Herbert Giersch

Towards a New Economics
Critical Essays on Ecology, Distribution and Other Themes
Kenneth E. Boulding

Studies in Positive and Normative Economics
Martin J. Bailey

The Collected Essays of Richard E. Quandt (2 volumes)
Richard E. Quandt

International Trade Theory and Policy
Selected Essays of W. Max Corden
W. Max Corden

Organization and Technology in Capitalist Development
William Lazonick

Studies in Human Capital
Collected Essays of Jacob Mincer, Volume 1
Jacob Mincer

Studies in Labor Supply
Collected Essays of Jacob Mincer, Volume 2
Jacob Mincer

Macroeconomics and Economic Policy
The Selected Essays of Assar Lindbeck, Volume I
Assar Lindbeck

The Welfare State
The Selected Essays of Assar Lindbeck, Volume II
Assar Lindbeck

Classical Economics, Public Expenditure and Growth
Walter Eltis

Money, Interest Rates and Inflation
Frederic S. Mishkin

The Public Choice Approach to Politics
Dennis C. Mueller

The Liberal Economic Order
Volume I Essays on International Economics
Volume II Money, Cycles and Related Themes
Gottfried Haberler
Edited by Anthony Y.C. Koo

Economic Growth and Business Cycles
Prices and the Process of Cyclical Development
Paolo Sylos Labini

International Adjustment, Money and Trade
Theory and Measurement for Economic Policy, Volume I
Herbert G. Grubel

International Capital and Service Flows
Theory and Measurement for Economic Policy, Volume II
Herbert G. Grubel

Unintended Effects of Government Policies
Theory and Measurement for Economic Policy, Volume III
Herbert G. Grubel

The Economics of Competitive Enterprise
Selected Essays of P.W.S. Andrews
Edited by Frederic S. Lee and Peter E. Earl

The Repressed Economy
Causes, Consequences, Reform
Deepak Lal

Economic Theory and Market Socialism
Selected Essays of Oskar Lange
Edited by Tadeusz Kowalik

Trade, Development and Political Economy
Selected Essays of Ronald Findlay
Ronald Findlay

General Equilibrium Theory
The Collected Essays of Takashi Negishi, Volume I
Takashi Negishi

The History of Economics
The Collected Essays of Takashi Negishi, Volume II
Takashi Negishi

Studies in Econometric Theory
The Collected Essays of Takeshi Amemiya
Takeshi Amemiya

Exchange Rates and the Monetary System
Selected Essays of Peter B. Kenen
Peter B. Kenen

Econometric Methods and Applications (2 volumes)
G.S. Maddala

National Accounting and Economic Theory
The Collected Papers of Dan Usher, Volume I
Dan Usher

Welfare Economics and Public Finance
The Collected Papers of Dan Usher, Volume II
Dan Usher

Economic Theory and Capitalist Society
The Selected Essays of Shigeto Tsuru, Volume I
Shigeto Tsuru

Methodology, Money and the Firm
The Collected Essays of D.P. O'Brien (2 volumes)
D.P. O'Brien

Economic Theory and Financial Policy
The Selected Essays of Jacques J. Polak (2 volumes)
Jacques J. Polak

Sturdy Econometrics
Edward E. Leamer

The Emergence of Economic Ideas
Essays in the History of Economics
Nathan Rosenberg

Productivity Change, Public Goods and Transaction Costs
Essays at the Boundaries of Microeconomics
Yoram Barzel

Reflections on Economic Development
The Selected Essays of Michael P. Todaro
Michael P. Todaro

The Economic Development of Modern Japan
The Selected Essays of Shigeto Tsuru, Volume II
Shigeto Tsuru

Money, Credit and Policy
Allan H. Meltzer

Macroeconomics and Monetary Theory
The Selected Essays of Meghnad Desai, Volume I
Meghnad Desai

Poverty, Famine and Economic Development
The Selected Essays of Meghnad Desai, Volume II
Meghnad Desai

Explaining the Economic Performance of Nations
Essays in Time and Space
Angus Maddison

Economic Doctrine and Method
Selected Papers of R.W. Clower
Robert W. Clower

Economic Theory and Reality
Selected Essays on their Disparity and Reconciliation
Tibor Scitovsky

Doing Economic Research
Essays on the Applied Methodology of Economics
Thomas Mayer

Institutions and Development Strategies
The Selected Essays of Irma Adelman, Volume I
Irma Adelman

Dynamics and Income Distribution
The Selected Essays of Irma Adelman, Volume II
Irma Adelman

The Economics of Growth and Development
Selected Essays of A.P. Thirlwall
A.P. Thirlwall

Theoretical and Applied Econometrics
The Selected Papers of Phoebus J. Dhrymes
Phoebus J. Dhrymes

Innovation, Technology and the Economy
The Selected Essays of Edwin Mansfield (2 volumes)
Edwin Mansfield

Capitalism, Socialism and Post-Keynesianism
Selected Essays of G.C. Harcourt
G.C. Harcourt